Social and Personality Development

Infancy through Adolescence

William Damon is the editor of

Social and Personality Development
Essays on the Growth of the Child

Social and Personality Development

Infancy through Adolescence

William Damon

CLARK UNIVERSITY

W • W • NORTON & COMPANY • New York • London

ISBN 0-393-01742-7 {CLOTH}
ISBN 0-393-95248-7 {PAPER}

Library of Congress Cataloging in Publication Data
Damon, William, 1944–
    Social and personality development.
    Includes bibliographical references and indexes.
    1. Child development.   2. Infant psychology.
3. Child psychology.   4. Adolescent psychology.
5. Socialization.   6. Individuation.   I. Title.
HQ767.9.D35   1983   305.2'3   83-3952

Cover illustration: *Boys in a Pasture* by Winslow Homer. c. 1874. Courtesy, Museum of Fine Arts, Boston. Charles Henry Hayden Fund.

Acknowledgments and copyrights appear on pages 374–76, which constitute a continuation of the copyright page.

W. W. Norton & Company, Inc., 500 Fifth Avenue, New York, N.Y. 10110
W. W. Norton & Company Ltd., 37 Great Russell Street, London WC1B 3NU

1 2 3 4 5 6 7 8 9 0

To Helen and Maria Damon

Contents

Preface

FOR several years, I have taught social and personality development to both undergraduate and graduate students. In presenting to students the research and literature in this area, I have found it necessary to integrate readings in ways not available in current textbooks. This is because the few existing textbooks on social and personality development are organized into chapters that cover topics like attachment or aggression. But the child is not divided, like topical chapters, into distinct processes of attachment or aggression. In the child, such processes always operate and change in *relation* to one another and not in isolation. Understanding social and personality development means understanding how such processes influence one another, and how they arise from and contribute to the child's entire developmental history. For this reason, I have organized this book around two principles. The first principle is a descriptive one: I have chosen to follow the development of the child chronologically, from infancy through adolescence. The second principle is more theoretical and based on the notion that social and personality development fulfills two complementary life functions, socialization and individuation. Accordingly, the book begins with the newborn and follows the child's socialization and individuation through the first two decades of life. Topics that usually stand as chapter headings for textbooks in this area are related to one another within this chronological framework.

Goals and Implications of a Chronological Account

By now, we know that there are developmental relations that can be traced from the earliest signs of infant sociability through the child's later, more intricate interactions with intimate friends and society-at-large. I have organized this book chronologically in order to demonstrate how the social skills and achievements of the mature individual have their roots in early childhood and infant social interactions. The book begins with as positive as possible a picture of infant sociability and infant individuality. This provides us with a foundation for seeing how childhood and adolescent social development build upon processes that are very much present (though in primitive form) when the baby is first born.

The chronological approach, therefore, is more than an attempt merely to describe various aspects of children's social behavior. It is an attempt to explicate the developmental relations between social behavior at different periods in life. This is why this book does not have individual chapters on "moral development," "attachment," or "parental styles of child rearing," even though all of these topics are discussed at length within this book. Rather than being discussed within themselves, these topics are presented in the context of the social relations and interactions that characterize a particular age period. For example, the attachment between an infant and his or her caregiver is presented as one critical mode of social interaction and communication. It is explained as one manifestation of the infant's sociability, and it is analyzed according to its contribution to the infant's potential for further social relationships. This presentation enables us to see how infant attachment paves the way for parental and peer relations in childhood, for adolescent intimacy and autonomy, and for many other subsequent social-developmental achievements. If we were to consider attachment as a self-contained "research topic" to be segregated within its own chapter, we would likely neglect the relation between attachment and the rest of the infant's rich social life, as well as between attachment and the social relations that children establish later in development.

As we identify the developmental relations between early social interaction and later developmental achievements, we will be led as a consequence to go beyond mere descriptive accounts of children's social behavior. Our awareness of developmental relations will force us to consider the future significance of social interactions at any time of life. This means that children's social behavior will become interesting to us for more than one reason. First, of course, we are interested in characterizing the nature of social behavior at different periods in development, as are all traditional accounts of social development. This is an interest in the social interactions occurring during infancy, childhood, and adolescence, in themselves, for the purpose of charting the general course of social development through the first twenty years. But since we are also interested in the future significance of the social interactions that we are characterizing, we will adopt an additional perspective on children's social interactions. We must look at social interactions as an integral part of the growth process and examine how they function in contributing to this process. In doing so, we will not only describe how children interact with their social world at different ages, but we will also show how these very interactions play a role in the developmental changes that lead to new forms of social interactions at later ages.

For example, we are certainly interested in attachment between an infant and his caregiver as a profoundly important phenomenon in its own right. But beyond describing attachment and its place in the infant-caregiver relation, we should also set ourselves another task. We should discover how the caregiver-child interactions that constitute the attachment relation prepare the child for further, and different, types of social interactions with a variety of others later in life. In order to do so, we must analyze attachment interactions in terms of their developmental effects on the infant. That is, we must examine the ways in which engaging in close, emotional interactions with a caregiver enables an infant to extend his or her social life into new and more challenging areas. We will show how the attachment experience prepares the infant for taking new risks, acquiring new social competence, and establishing new social relations. In short, we will consider attachment not only as a phenomenon that is central to an infant's social life, but also as a process that contributes to development of the infant's social abilities and social experience.

Infancy through Adolescence as a Time Frame for This Book

It is not difficult to explain why this account of social development begins with infancy. First, there is ever-increasing evidence that the infant is a highly social creature, even at birth. Second, the infant's remarkable sociability no doubt is linked to his or her potential for social and personal growth later in life. Third, social interactions at early ages influence social-personality achievements at later ages. For these reasons, we begin this account in the infant years.

But social development is a lifelong process, or at least we hope it is. Most of us expect to continue developing socially right up through old age. We might concede that our physical powers diminish after adolescence. We might even grant an eventual decline in our intellectual acuity. But we would hope that our social understanding, our ability to relate to others, and our sense of self change in a positive way all through life. This is because we generally believe that the social experiences of adulthood impart a wisdom and a competence unavailable to the adolescent. Why, then, end a book on social development with adolescence?

One reason is that, in the period from infancy through adolescence, there are many age-related patterns of growth that apply quite generally across individuals. This is less true during the adult years. As Paul Baltes, Hayne Reese, and Lewis Lipsett have written, "intcrindividual variability apparently increases with increasing age, particularly in adulthood and aging. Consequently, the organizational power of chronological age per se decreases as life-span development unfolds."[1] Since this book will examine normal developmental trends in socialization and individuation, the best period to examine is that between infancy and the end of adolescence.

Another reason for framing this account from infancy through adolescence has to do with the course of social and personality development between these two age periods. In adolescence, many of the strands and themes of social development born in the infant years are woven together for the first time into an integrated system. There is even a new integration of social development's two complementary functions, socialization and the construction of personal identity. This integration takes place as one's social relations and moral character interpenetrate with one's sense of self in a number of profound ways never before possible. In providing a chronicle of this process, this book does in fact tell a story that has a beginning and an end. Its end does not coincide with the final chapter of human life, or even of human social development. But it is an end that has a certain logic and a certain sense of closure. In short, the saga of social development from infancy to adolescence makes a good story, and this book was written for the purpose of telling it.

Plan of the Book

This book provides a chronological account of social and personality development during infancy, childhood, and adolescence. There are sections on each of these three main life phases. Each section is organized according to the complementary functions of social development—the socializing function and the individuating function. That is, within each section, there is a chapter on the development of social relations and a chapter on the development of self-identity (except that, for the childhood section, there are two chapters covering social relations during this age period, because of the extensive literature that is available on this topic). In this manner, the book traces the individual's integration into and differentiation from the social network through approximately the first two decades of life.

The social-relational chapters of this book (Chapters 2, 4, 5, and 7) focus on the individual's manner of connecting with others throughout the course of development. The main issues considered in these chapters are (1) the types of interactions and relationships the individual establishes with others at different ages, and (2) how these interactions and relationships become transformed through psychological changes within the individual and social changes in the individual's environment. In the context of these social-relational issues, we take up the following specific topics: attachment, peer relations, parental child-rearing practices, moral development, social cognition, children's play, sociocultural influences, friendship patterns in childhood and adolescence, the

[1] Baltes, Reese, & Lipsett, 1980, p. 74.

school, other socializing institutions, and teen-age sexuality. The literature that we review for the purpose of discussing these social-relational topics is rich with empirical studies of infants, children, and adolescents in their home, play, and school environments.

The individuation chapters of this book (Chapters 3, 6, and 8) focus on the psychological separation of the individual from others in the social world. The main issues here are (1) the manner in which the individual establishes a sense of self at different ages, and (2) how this sense of self eventually forms the basis of the individual's unique personal identity. The following topics are discussed in the context of these individuation issues: self-knowledge at different age periods, individual differences in temperament, gender differences, personality differences, psychosocial development, the identity crisis, and the process of identity consolidation. For the purpose of examining these topics, we rely on case studies and individual life histories. In each of the individuation chapters in this book, the processes of self-identity formation are illustrated by an in-depth analysis of at least one such individual life.

Acknowledgments

In writing this book, my intellectual debts are scattered throughout the pages of the text, and they are too many to acknowledge here. But a number of persons have directly contributed valuable advice and support to my writing efforts. John Broughton of Columbia University and James Youniss of Catholic University and Boys Town Center for the Study of Youth Development saw parts of the manuscript at an early phase and offered me insightful and formative guidance. John Masters of Vanderbilt University, Carolyn Shantz of Wayne State University, and Alan Sroufe of the University of Minnesota provided extensive feedback on a later version, and their comments led to important improvements. My colleague at Clark University, Roger Bibace, also generously gave me his astute critique of large sections of the book.

My reviews of the self-concept literature were originally done in collaboration with Daniel Hart of Clark University, as part of my own research on self-understanding in childhood and adolescence. Dan's thoughtful efforts are reflected throughout my own summaries and interpretations of this literature. I am also grateful to Karen Pakula of Clark University for her contributions to the self-development analyses, and to Wendy Praisner for her dedicated secretarial work. I especially wish to thank Bobbi Karman for her exceptionally intelligent work on every phase of this manuscript, as well as for her good-natured patience and sympathetic support. I have also been fortunate to have at Norton a wise editor, Don Fusting, and a talented copy editor, Sandy Lifland.

Although my own research is not a prominent part of this book as a whole, it has helped me formulate my approach to the field of social and personality development, as well as to gain some special understanding of certain social-developmental processes. I am grateful to the funding agencies that have made my past and present research in this area possible. In particular, I wish to thank Barbara Finberg of the Carnegie Corporation of New York and H. Thomas James of the Spencer Foundation for their generous support of my studies in social and self development.

Worcester, Mass.   *W.D.*

Social and Personality Development

Infancy through Adolescence

Chapter 1

Introduction

SOCIAL development is a life process built upon a paradox. The paradox is that at the same time we are *both* social and individual beings, connected with others in a multitude of ways, as well as ultimately alone in the world. This dual condition of connectedness and separateness begins at the moment of birth and remains with us all through life. The phrase *social and personality development* describes a two-fronted life movement within this paradoxical state of affairs. In the course of development, we become better able both to establish connections with others and to realize our own distinctness from others. In short, we become more social while at the same time becoming more individual and unique.

Paradoxes, of course, are only seeming contradictions, not real ones. The strange mix of sociability and individuality that develops in the course of human life can be seen as two complementary developmental functions, rather than as contradictory life directions. These are, respectively, the *social* and the *personality* functions of social development. Although these two functions seem to pull us in opposite ways, in actuality the two functions go hand in hand, each contributing to growth and to the individual's successful social adaptation.

The Two Functions of Social Development

The first of social development's complementary functions usually is called *socialization*. The socialization function includes all of one's tendencies to establish and maintain relations with others, to become an accepted member of society-at-large, to regulate one's behavior according to society's codes and standards, and generally to get along well with other people. We may consider this to be the *integrating* function of social development, since it ensures the integration of the individual into society as a respected participant.

As a child grows, she experiences many different kinds of incentives toward socialization and integration into society. The baby needs close physical and emotional contact with her mother, and must respond actively in ways that encourage such contact. The toddler is subject to direct disapproval until she becomes toilet trained. By middle childhood, children must learn to act cooperatively and fairly if they are to enjoy the companionship of friends. By the time of adolescence, the standards of society-at-large must be understood and respected. If an adolescent does not obey the law, there will be legal repercussions; if the adolescent does not do well in school or at work, her future career prospects may suffer. In these and many other ways, children experience the multiple needs and demands of socialization throughout their development.

The second function of social development is the formation of the individual's personal identity. This function, often called *individuation*, includes the development of one's sense of self and the forging of a special place for oneself within the social order. It entails understanding one's idiosyncratic personal characteristics and reconciling these characteristics with the requirements of interpersonal relations, as well as of occupational, sex, and family roles. We may consider this to be the *differentiating* function of social development. The formation of a personal identity requires distinguishing oneself from others, determining one's own unique direction in life, and finding within the social network a position uniquely tailored to one's own particular nature, needs, and aspirations.

As with socialization, the demands of individuation and differentiation begin early and continue throughout life. Babies struggle to recognize themselves as separate persons, distinct from their caregivers. Toddlers learn to say "no" as an assertion of their autonomy (such assertions are so common that during this period, children are considered to be in "the terrible twos"). By middle childhood, children in school and at play are busy discovering the particular talents and interests that may set them apart from their peers. The young adolescent's need to establish independence from home and family is well known. Moreover, late adolescence is a primary proving ground for one's personal sense of identity. One's personal identity, once constructed, is continually evaluated and reassessed throughout development.

Both functions of social development are absolutely essential for a person's adaptation to life. Through the integrating function, a person maintains satisfying and productive relations with others and with society-at-large. Continued failures here can lead to interpersonal conflicts, social isolation, or even to social deviance and delinquency. In addition, poor social relations during development can leave a person impoverished in cognitive skills and emotional responsiveness. Through the differentiating function, a person acquires a coherent identity and a feeling of control over her own destiny. Failure here can lead to a sense of confusion, paralysis, and despair.

Further, these two essential functions are deeply interconnected in the course of a person's development, often relying upon each other's achievements. Thousands of years ago, Aristotle wrote, "All friendly feelings towards others come from the friendly feelings that a person has for himself." Conversely, a shaky sense of self can impair one's social interactions, and a maladaptive history of social relations can bear unfortunate consequences for one's personal identity.

Together, these two functions penetrate into every area of life. Intellectual activity, for example, is frequently affected by one's social and personal adaptation. Both social and personal chaos can easily disrupt one's intellectual processes, just as confused thinking can disturb one's efforts to make sense out of problematic social and personal issues. There are, of course, unusual cases in which intellectual and social competence seem to become divorced from one another. One such example is the stereotype of the brilliant scholar who has great insights but who cannot manage the simplest of personal affairs. But for most individuals, their social and personality growth is closely reflected in their intellectual achievements.

Although social and personality development penetrates into every sphere of human life, including the intellectual, the scientific study of social and personality development is not a field without boundaries. Cognitive and perceptual processes, with the exception of those directly bearing upon the apprehension of persons, are generally excluded. So are nondeveloping aspects of social and personal behavior. The domain of social and personality development as a field of inquiry, and as the province of this book, centers on developmental changes in (1) an individual's social behavior, including the individual's interpersonal relations and the individual's capacity for social interaction and relationship, and (2) an individual's personal identity. The former pertains to the socializing function of social and personality development, the latter to the individuating function.

Relations between Socialization and Individuation

In some ways, socialization and individuation are quite distinct processes, even at times operating in opposition to one another. Establishing one's individuality very often requires a different sort of activity than that required for "socialized" behavior in the traditional use of the term. Defining one's distinctness from others and staking out one's unique social position sometimes place one in an antagonistic relation to others. Conversely, being "socially acceptable" sometimes means forgoing personal wishes and habits in deference to the expectations of others.

Psychoanalytic writing has always emphasized this distinction between the individual and society. This was the subject of Sigmund Freud's treatise, *Civilization and Its Discontents*.[1] Freud argued that to become civilized (his word for socialized) means renouncing some of one's most basic drives, in particular those of sex and aggression. But these drives do not simply go away once they are renounced: they remain as a source of conflict and discontent for the individual who has accommodated to civilized life. It is as if, in a far less extreme way, we are all seething Mr. Hydes contained within mild-mannered Dr. Jekylls, always in danger of bursting through our civilized veneers. Normally this universal conflict can be contained and even productively channeled without too great a toll on the individual's happiness. In less fortunate cases, it may lead to psychopathology or social deviance. But in all cases, according to classic Freudian analyses, it typifies the universal and constant tension between a person's individualistic and social needs. Freud may or may not be correct in his belief that "antisocial" drives like aggression are an intrinsic part of human nature. But the dichotomy that he described between individual and social tendencies, along with the conflict that the dichotomy sometimes produces, cannot be denied.

Yet there is a sense in which there are profound connections between socialization and individuation. Developmentally, the two often go hand in hand for important psychological reasons: as one learns more about others, one learns more about the self, and vice versa. This is because interactions between self and others simultaneously provide one with feedback about both the nature of the other and about the nature of the self. Such feedback includes information about relations with other people, about other people's view of the self, and about characteristics of persons that are shared by both self and other. In the course of conducting social relations with others, one learns simultaneously about how to get along with others, about what others are like, and about what the self is like. In this sense, socialization and individuation are really opposite sides of the same coin: they are the yin and yang of social development.

At the turn of the century, James Mark Baldwin introduced this two-directional notion of social development to the field of psychology.[2] Baldwin wrote that children come to know themselves only as a consequence of social interactions with many others:

> The growing child is able to think of self in varying terms as varying social situations impress themselves upon him.... The development of the child's personality could not go on at all without the constant modification of his sense of himself by suggestions from others. So he himself, at every stage, is really in part someone else, even in his own thought of himself.[3]

[1] Freud, 1930.
[2] Baldwin, 1902.

[3] Ibid., p. 23.

Just as the self is constructed through feedback received from others, Baldwin wrote, knowledge of others is constructed through feedback in the opposite direction: from the self projected outward. Thus, a young child who discovers that she gets angry when she is treated unfairly will assume that others also react this way to unfairness. An adolescent who learns that he can feel jealous of a rival becomes aware that people have a capacity for jealousy. In this manner, the child's sense of self and other grow simultaneously, inextricably woven together in the course of development. As both the self and other become clearly known, the child's thoughts of self are "filled up by thoughts of others" and the child's thoughts of others are "mainly filled up by thoughts of (the) self. . .but for certain minor distinctions in the filling."[4]

Baldwin's theory perhaps goes too far in emphasizing the similarity between the processes by which the self and the other are known. In many respects, as we shall see, the construction of the self poses unique cognitive and affective problems not encountered by the child in other aspects of his social development. To claim that realizing one's individuality is identical in every way to learning about others and one's relations with others is clearly overstating the case. Individuality may in fact lead one into antisocial directions. Moreover, there are certainly more than "minor distinctions" between one's attitude toward the self and one's attitude toward others throughout the course of development. But despite its overstatement, Baldwin's argument has made social scientists aware of a fundamental connection between individual and social development, a connection based on the bidirectional process of understanding self and other. In later chapters of this book, we shall see how Baldwin's analysis of this connection prepares the ground for contemporary work on children's social-cognitive development, particularly with regard to moral judgment, role taking, and the understanding of social experience in all its forms.

In short, socialization and individuation are to a certain extent distinct from one another, and there is always the possibility that actions which will further one may not be in the service of the other, or may even stand in opposition to the other. But in the normal course of development, they go hand in hand, supporting each other's growth. There is a creative tension between the two, a dialectical interplay between the needs of the individual to maintain relations with others and the needs of the individual to construct a separate self. The individual can only construct the self in the context of relations with others, but at the same time, the individual must step beyond the confines of those relations and forge a unique destiny. We shall see this dialectical process at work as early as infancy, when the child uses the mother as a secure base from which to explore the world, and in the course of this exploration, discovers the ways to separate and establish independence from the mother. Good social relations create an atmosphere in which a healthy exploration of self can flourish.

---

[4] Ibid., p. 18.

Socialization and the Active Child

As part of their integration into society, children are required to adopt certain behavioral standards. These standards vary somewhat from society to society, but generally they are the key regulators that guide the child toward prosocial and away from antisocial behavior. Adults spend a good deal of time and effort attempting to transmit such standards to their children, and they often feel directly responsible for the extent to which their children have understood and adopted the message.

In exerting their socializing influences, adults have many possible techniques at their command. They can tutor or lecture their children on the proper ways to behave, they can administer rewards for desired behavior and punishment for undesired behavior, and they can arrange their children's lives in order to expose them to certain experiences and restrict them from others. Adults, by their own behavior, can also set an example for their children to imitate. Through their many agents, such as the schools, the churches, the media, adults also control the information that is available to children. Perhaps most importantly, in their parenting roles, adults protect and nurture their children, and they maintain intensely emotional bonds with them. These bonds themselves may act as a powerful incentive for children to heed the directives of adults.

Yet, with all this, children do not always turn out exactly as the adults in their lives may wish. Sometimes they resist adult guidance, sometimes they fail to comprehend it, sometimes they simply may not be able to live up to standards that they do accept. Even in the normal cases of children who are destined to become well-adjusted citizens of their societies, conformity to adult standards is neither instantaneous nor uniform. By any measure, socialization takes years, and children of a new generation never exactly replicate their elders' social behavior. Despite the many tools of adult influence over children, transmission of standards and values from one generation to the next is a slow and uncertain process.

The main reason that children do not quickly become simple reflections of their elders is that children are not passive recipients of social input. A child's behavior cannot be explained by the sum total of social experience that the child has received, however detailed or complex a history we provide. Rather, children themselves are active agents in creating the social experiences that influence their development. They participate in determining the nature of their social relations, bringing their own dispositions and characteristics to any interaction in which they engage. They also process adult attempts at social influence in their own way. Whether a child comprehends or agrees with an adult directive is very much up to the child, as any parent instinctively knows. In addition, children can choose the persons that they will be influenced by; and often, they will choose peers rather than adults, or an idealized figure distant in time and place from their immediate families. Many a parent has been frustrated and bewildered by a child who adopts the mannerisms (and perhaps even some of the values) of a popular music star the child has never met.

The puzzle of socialization is how an active child comes to adopt behavioral standards consistent with the values embedded in the child's culture. Clearly, adults cannot directly transmit these standards to the child as if they were simply innoculating the child against disease. Nor do children passively copy what they see. Rather, socialization is a complex process of interaction between the child and others in the child's social network. This interaction has bidirectional effects, changing both the child and those with whom the child interacts. That this interaction occurs is now admitted by virtually all socialization theorists. The exact nature of this interaction, however, is the subject of much debate and controversy.

Biology, Culture, and Interaction

There is an old and a new form of the debate about the interaction between the child and others. The old form hinged on the opposition between "nature" and "nurture," or between "biology" and "culture." The key issue, as framed in this manner, is the extent to which particular behavior patterns can be explained by the child's inherent attributes, as opposed to the child's social experience. Is a tendency toward aggressiveness inherited or inculcated? Is communicative competence preprogrammed in the human species, or is it learned? How much of a particular child's talent is due to the child's genetic structure and how much is it due to a favorable upbringing? Are orderly developmental changes instigated by a natural "ground plan" evolved through the ages, or are they triggered by changes in the child's social environment as the child grows older? These and other nature-nurture questions have been traditional subjects for debate since the dawn of social science, and they show few signs of either being resolved or of losing their interest for social scientists.

A more recent, and more productive, form of this debate assumes that the child's biology and culture inevitably interact, but it questions the nature of this interaction. The focus of the debate, therefore, is neither on *whether* nature or nurture plays a role, nor on *how much* of a role either plays. Both are assumed always to work together in shaping every form of human behavior. The focus of the debate is now on *how* the two interact with one another to direct the child's behavior and development.

A theoretical model that reflects this approach is presented in Figure 1-1. This model assumes that biological and environmental determinants interact with one another to influence human development. The model then specifies three different types of specific influences, *each* of which includes both biological and environmental factors. Normative age-graded influences are those that come about as the child grows older. Examples of these are puberty, graduation from school, and so on. Normative history-graded influences are those that affect a particular cohort of youth. A war or a great depression that causes a generation of youth to interrupt its schooling would both be examples of such

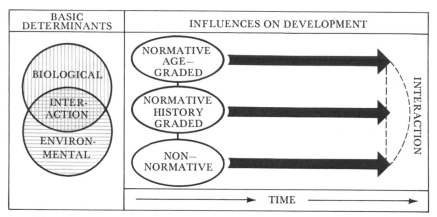

Figure 1-1. Three Major Influence Systems on Life-Span Development. Normative age-graded, normative history-graded, and non-normative life events all influence human development. These influence systems interact and differ in their combinatorial profile for different individuals and for different behaviors.

Source: P. Baltes, W. Reese, & L. Lipsett, Life-span developmental psychology. *Annual Review of Psychology*, 1980, *31*, 75. Reprinted with permission.

historical influences. Non-normative influences are life events that affect particular individuals. Disease, school success, parental divorce might all be examples of such events.

Even though this approach does not question the basic "socializing" interaction between society and the child, it still leaves many questions to be investigated. Questions that are specifically directed at uncovering the nature of this interaction include: Do the forms of interaction change with age, and if so how? What are the consequences to the child's development of the various types of interaction? Do certain combinations of child disposition and social experience lead in directions that are better for the child's development than do others? What are the consequences of different parental child-rearing styles upon various types of children (such as boys versus girls, temperamentally easy versus difficult children, and so on)? What are the mechanisms through which adults, peers, and others in society influence children? How do children of varying ages and constitutional characteristics receive and act upon such influence? How does the child integrate all the multiple biological and cultural influences upon her development into a coherent personality and sense of self?

Answers to these questions have been offered by every socialization and personality theorist, but these answers often differ greatly from one another. Some theorists believe that biological endowment and early experience combine to shape a young child's personality in ways that remain stable throughout much of life. Other theorists believe that, as the child grows, biological and cultural influences on personality are increasingly mediated through the child's own cognitive (or "social-cognitive") processes, and therefore that persons always retain the potential to alter the course of their own development. As for the social influence processes responsible for the child's acquisition of behavioral standards, there is much debate about their exact nature. There is even dispute concerning whether one or many processes are implicated. Some believe that all cultural norms are learned in essentially the same manner, whereas others believe that certain kinds of behavioral standards are acquired in special ways. Finally, other theorists have offered innumerable modifications and variations on all of the above positions. This book will by no means resolve these issues for once and for all. But it will present the competing positions on major issues. It will also take some stands about which positions are best supported by evidence to date, and about which positions seem most theoretically plausible in light of our best knowledge about human development.

In sum, persons are not simply products of society, but rather they are active participants in their own socialization. All aspects of social behavior and development result from an interaction between the person's own characteristics and the person's social experience. Exactly how these interact as the child grows from infancy through adolescence is a primary focus of this book.

Social Relations as Context for Children's Behavior

Just as individuals are not simply products of society, neither are they entirely isolated within their own separate worlds. Persons are deeply embedded within social relations at all times in their lives. A person's significant social relationships may or may not be present in time or place: often, persons may be most attuned to the memories of prior relations or the anticipation of future ones. But in some form or other, an individual's social relations always provide a context for the individual's behavior and development (even though, as suggested in the previous section, they do not *determine* the individual's actions). This is as true at the beginning of life as at any other period: as we shall see in Chapter 2, even the newborn baby acts within a complex of social relations.

A child's social relations, of course, constantly change as the child grows older. An infant's intense attachment relations with caregivers soon are supplemented by extended family relations, peer relations, and ultimately by more distant relations with society-at-large. By adolescence, the individual's interpersonal life includes a diversity of social relations that differ greatly in purpose, quality, closeness, and emotional tone. As the child's social network changes in this manner, he develops new social behaviors and new social competence. The child also adopts a new perspective on many of his relations and takes on new, less "childlike" roles. In part, such development is spurred by the child's changing social network and the challenge that more "grown-up" social relations present. In part, however, the child's increasing social competence itself motivates the child to broaden his social network and seek new types of relations. This is why children's social development is totally intertwined with their changing social relations.

Because of the overriding importance of children's social relations for their behavior and development, this book will discuss children's social activity in the context of their social relations. In so doing, we shall draw upon Robert Hinde's theoretical analysis of interpersonal interaction and relationships. Hinde has written that social acts often take place within interactions, and interactions within relationships. In order to assess the interpersonal significance of an interaction, it is important to establish the social-relational context of that interaction. If the interaction is part of a continuing social relation, we must determine the nature and purpose of that relation. How does the interaction function within that relation? Does it help maintain that relation, does it initiate a new relation, does it terminate an old one? This is not to say that *all* social actions and interactions are part of ongoing social relations. Many actions and interactions, particularly in childhood, are isolated episodes in and of themselves. But where interactions do contribute to identifiable social relations, they should be understood in light of these relations, since to a large degree the relation determines the character and meaning of the interaction.

The connection between continuing social relations and their constituent interactions has been proposed by Hinde as a starting point for the study of interpersonal behavior and its development.[5] Hinde writes that "A relationship involves a series of interactions *in time.*"[6] Interactions are specific sequences of behavioral events, such as two children fighting or playing. When one child does something and another child responds, an interaction has occurred. As such, interactions in themselves need not have permanence or meaning beyond their immediate consequences. But social relations endure over time and are comprised of a pattern of interactions that has a broader significance to the relation's participants. This significance, of course, varies from relation to relation and is determined largely by the purposes and goals of the specific relation.

Social relations, therefore, go beyond simple social interactions in at least two ways: (1) Relations are comprised of many interactions, rather than isolated or solitary interactions; and (2) in addition to consisting of many interactions, relations are based upon a common meaning or purpose shared by the persons participating in the relation. As Hinde has written: "In studying relationships, it is proper assumption that each interaction affects the course of the relationship, if only by confirming the status quo."[7] This is an assumption that we shall adopt in this book.

The Self and Self-Knowledge

The individuation aspect of social and personality development centers on the person's establishment of a unique personal identity. The individual's own

[5] Hinde, 1976.
[6] Ibid., p. 4.

[7] Ibid.

awareness of her unique identity is called the individual's "sense of self," or the individual's *self-knowledge*. We may define self-knowledge as everything that one knows about one's own experience in the world as an individual, about one's unique position and status in the social order, about one's personal characteristics, and about one's identity over time (past, present, future), and place. This is a formidable amount of knowledge, and from a developmental point of view the intriguing question is: how do individuals know themselves at different periods in the life cycle?

In analyzing the elements of a person's self-knowledge, psychologists traditionally have distinguished two major aspects of the self. These have been variously called the *self-as-subject* versus the *self-as-object*; the *self-as-knower* versus the *self-as-known*; or more simply, the *I* versus the *me*. Just before the turn of the century, William James pioneered the use of this distinction in his psychological analysis of self-knowledge:

> Whatever I may be thinking of, I am always at the same time more or less aware of *myself*, of my *personal existence*. At the same time it is I who am aware; so that the total self of me, partly known and partly knower, partly object and partly subject, must have two aspects discriminated in it, of which for shortness we may call one the *Me* and the other the *I*.[8]

The Self-as-Known: The Me

For James, the *me* consisted of everything that can be known about the self. This includes characteristics of a person's *material* self (one's physical body, clothes, possessions), a person's *social* self (one's social identity, behavior, reputation), and a person's *spiritual* or *psychological* self (one's capacities for knowing, manner of thinking, and remembered states of consciousness). Together these categories constitute the major components in a person's self-definition. They are what a person can say about himself if asked, "Who are you and what are you like?"

To some extent, the characteristics of the *me* are determined by a person's physical constitution. A male is not likely to define himself as a girl, nor is a tall man likely to describe himself as short. But physical inheritance is only one part of the self-definition, and even this is susceptible to interpretation. What seems tall to one person may seem short to another; and the very importance of height as an element in a person's sense of self can vary from one individual to the next. Other people's attitude toward oneself greatly influences the importance of any physical attribute in one's self-concept. It is for this reason that George Herbert Mead, following in James's footsteps, wrote:

> The self has a character which is different from that of the physiological organism proper. The self is something which has a development; it is not initially there, at

[8] James, 1961, p. 43.

birth, but arises in the process of social experience and activity, that is, develops in a given individual as a result of his relations to that process as a whole and to other individuals within that process.. . . The self, as that which can be an object to itself, is essentially a social structure, and it arises in social experience.[9]

It is particularly easy to see this point in the aspect of the *me* self that James called the *social me*. Certainly one's notion about how one fits into the social scheme of things is influenced by the reactions of others to the self and by the types of relations that one forms with others. These, in turn, influence one's self-esteem and one's sense of worth. Society, of course, is pluralistic, being made up of many individuals with whom one establishes many different types of relations. For this reason, one may develop many distinct aspects of the self, each of which is brought out through interactions with particular types of people. This is the familiar phenomenon of acting differently with different people and of consequently having "many sides" to one's personality. In a famous statement, James wrote that "a man has as many social selves as there are individuals who recognize him and carry an image of him in their mind."[10]

George Bernard Shaw, in an autobiographical statement, described his own construction of self in the following manner: "Therefore, I had to become an actor, and create for myself a fantastic personality fit and apt for dealing with men, and adaptable to the various parts I had to play as an author, journalist, orator, politician, committee man, man of the world, and so forth."[11] Although Shaw believed that he was reporting the specifics of his own self-development, he was really describing more broadly the process by which all persons create for themselves a multifaceted personality in order to deal with the diverse demands of social life.

It may sound from all this that a person's sense of self is (1) determined by what others think of the person, and (2) fractionated into a multiplicity of different personalities that come and go from moment to moment as a person's social environment changes. This is true to some extent, but it is too strong a statement. Although a person's self-knowledge is socially influenced, nevertheless self-knowledge is not totally dependent, at least from moment to moment, upon the views and opinions of others. Although self-knowledge is diverse and multifaceted, there is also coherence and stability in a person's identity over time and context. In short, people construct and organize their own self-knowledge, even though this is always done within a context of multiple social influences. How can we explain the paradox of multiple social influences and diversity, along with a self-organized and coherent sense of self? This is where the *I*, or the self-as-subject, comes in.

The Self-as-Knower: The I

It is the *I* aspect of self, in James's theory, that organizes and determines

[9] Mead, 1934, p. 135.
[10] James, 1961, p. 46.
[11] Erikson, 1980, p. 117.

the quality of a person's experience from moment to moment. It appropriates all aspects of the known world, including the *me*, in constructing the meaning of events, past and present. This is the "ego" or the "subject" that cognitively organizes the world and determines its significance to the individual. Through knowledge of the fact of its distinctness from others, the self-as-knower establishes its own individuality, using the characteristics of the self-as-known (the *me*) to fill in the details of this individuality. Through knowledge of its own sameness over time, the self-as-knower establishes its own sense of personal continuity, again using characteristics of the *me* to provide itself with evidence of this sameness. Both of these are accomplishments whose difficulty should not be underestimated. They are the primary aspects of self-development in the early years.

The *I* aspect of self, therefore, regulates the various inputs to one's self-definition, the social as well as the physical. As George Herbert Mead pointed out, the *I* enables a person to be free from relying absolutely on others' views for one's sense of self. In the final analysis, the individual alone takes the initiative and determines the final nature of his own self-knowledge. Whereas the *me* is chained to the collective attitude of a person's community, the *I* is free to change or reject this attitude. The *I*, in Mead's words, is the "answer which the individual makes to the attitude which others take towards him when he is assuming an attitude towards them."[12] The *I* response can never be wholly determined by forces outside the self. For this reason, a person's self-knowledge can never be entirely predictable, despite the debt that the *me* aspect of self owes to the physical constitution and to social influence. In self theory, the *I* is the psychological equivalent of free will. It is also that component of self that, in the last analysis, assures one of an unimpeachable individuality, a uniqueness of experience, and a distinctness from other people.

In each of this book's sections on infancy, childhood, and adolescence, we shall trace the development of self-knowledge and the connections of self-knowledge to personal identity. We shall examine both the *I* and the *me*, drawing on James's theoretical framework.

Age-related Changes in Social Development

During childhood and adolescence, growing older brings many predictable changes in children's physical, cognitive, social, and personal characteristics. These changes generally lead to improvements in children's functioning. As children grow, they become physically stronger and more adept, cognitively more informed and able, socially more astute, and so on. Age-related changes during childhood and adolescence can be easily recognized by specialist and nonspecialist alike. The pediatrician Benjamin Spock has commented that age during childhood is such a powerful factor that two same-age children with

[12] Mead, 1934, p. 177.

widely different personalities will seem more alike in many respects than will two different-age children with similar personalities.[13]

This book focuses on the period from infancy through adolescence, when predictable age-related changes abound. Thus, this book will describe many sequences of age-related "levels" or "stages" in social and personality development. Some of these will be levels of specific behavior, such as parent-child attachment or peer social play. Others will be sequences of broader psychological processes, such as the formation of personal identity. Some of these age-related sequences will derive from what has been called a "strong" model of development, whereas others will derive from a so-called "weak" model.[14] "Strong" developmental models posit the following assumptions: Developmental change will occur in a sequence of stages. These stages are qualitatively rather than quantitatively distinct from one another—that is, each new stage represents a new kind of behavior, rather than a simple increase in a behavior or an ability—and the stages describe whole systems of behavior, rather than discrete acts. The sequence of the stages are irreversible, except in cases of pathology or other abnormal functioning, with the sequential order directed toward some definable end point of development. Both the sequential order and the end point are universal, describing the development of persons in all social and cultural contexts.

Social scientists vary greatly in the extent to which they use "strong" developmental models to describe age-related changes in behavior. The cognitive theory of Jean Piaget, the personality theory of Erik Erikson, and the moral judgment theory of Lawrence Kohlberg, all rely on strong developmental assumptions. On the other hand, many researchers wish to describe phases of children's growth without implying that these phases are necessarily irreversible, holistic, qualitatively distinct, or universal. A researcher may accept some of these stage characteristics but not others in order to describe the changes that the researcher has observed. In such cases, the researcher is said to employ a "weak" model of development.

Aside from the large-scale systems of Erikson and Kohlberg, most of the age-related sequences in this book derive from weak rather than strong models, since they each reject at least some of the traditional assumptions about developmental stages. This does not mean that these researchers have "weak" theories. In many cases, investigators using "weak" developmental models have been able to explain developmental trends with greater precision than have investigators using the most traditional "strong" models. Investigators using "weak" developmental models believe that some age-related changes do not conform to all of the assumptions of a strong developmental model, and consequently, they use a modified notion of stages or levels in order to capture the behavioral sequence that they have observed.

The primary purpose of this book is to convey the broad sweep of progress in children's social and personality development during the first two decades of

[13] Spock, 1982.   [14] Reese & Overton, 1970.

life. To understand this progress in all of its forms, we need to examine all the important changes that socialization and individuation bring about. Some of these changes may be best described by strong developmental models, others by weak ones. Some changes, such as the construction of a personal identity, encompass entire systems of thought and emotion. Other changes, such as becoming toilet trained or learning to get along better with one's friends, hinge upon the acquisition of particular skills and conceptions. Social and personality development is made up of many such advances, large and small; throughout this book, we shall refer to several theoretical models in order to cover the range of these progressive changes.

Chapter 2

Infant Social Relations

Sociability of the Newborn

INFANTS are born with a natural tendency toward sociability. This tendency consists first and foremost of a ready responsiveness to social stimulation. Within a family environment that is itself sensitive to the infant's needs, this initial responsiveness quickly flowers into a full-fledged capacity for participation in social interactions and relationships. Further, the newborn does even more than respond passively to the overtures of others. Through his own primitive behavioral repertoire, the infant has crude yet effective means of initiating social contact. For example, the newborn can suck, can grasp, and can cry when distressed. These and other inborn behaviors serve as unintended social signals for responsive adults anxious to give the infant care and attention.

Until surprisingly recently, the infant's natural sociability went unrecognized by social scientists. This is no doubt because it is deceptively easy to notice the shortcomings in a newborn's social skills. Born without conventional speech, an infant comes into this world unable to understand or participate in the vast majority of human communications.[1] Born without the ability to crawl or walk independently, the infant begins life with severely limited means of initiating contact with other persons. Little wonder that until recently, most writers on child development characterized the newborn as a virtual social isolate—mute, unknowing, indisposed to interact meaningfully with human society.[2] Moreover, statements like "Socially and emotionally he begins with an alternation between self-contained indifference when he is satisfied and grief-stricken but undirected rage when he is not"[3] still abound in the developmental literature.

What has caused developmental psychologists to recognize that the newborn is a social person rather than an isolate? Two revolutions in the field of developmental psychology have brought about this new point of view. Both a conceptual and a technological revolution have generated a greater respect for the social responsiveness with which infants begin life.

Conceptual Revolution: Infant as Active Partner

The conceptual revolution began with a recognition of the infant's active role in his own survival. Although newborns cannot care for themselves or protect themselves in any effective manner, they can and do perform actions that ensure their care and protection. These actions may seem rudimentary to us as adults; but for centuries they have enabled infants to enjoy the ministrations of society. The Scottish philosopher, John MacMurray, has presented the infant's case in this way:

> The baby must be fitted by nature at birth to the conditions into which he is born; for otherwise he could not survive. He is, in fact, "adapted," to speak paradoxically, to being unadapted, "adapted" to a complete dependence upon an adult human being. He is made to be cared for. He is born into a love relationship which is inherently personal. Not merely his personal development, but his very survival depends upon the maintaining of this relation. . . .
>
> The baby's "adaptation" to his "environment" consists in his capacity to express his feelings of comfort or discomfort; of satisfaction and dissatisfaction with his condition. Discomfort he expresses by crying; comfort by gurgling and chuckling, and very soon by smiling and crowing. The infant's cry is a call for help to the mother, an intimation that he needs to be cared for. . . .
>
> The conclusion is not that the infant is still an animal which will become rational through some curious organic process of development. It is that he cannot, even theoretically, live an isolated existence; that he is not an independent individual. He lives a common life as one term in a personal relation. . . . From all this it follows that a baby is not an animal organism, but a person.[4]

This conception, that the baby is a social person right from the start of life, has radical implications for the way that we think about infant behavior and

---

[1] Appropriately, the Latin root of infant means "not talking."

[2] Skinner, 1938; Bijou and Baer, 1961; Klein and Riveria, 1964; Lizd, 1968; Mahler, 1977.

[3] Stone & Church, 1957.

[4] MacMurray, 1961.

development. It means looking for the communicative value in the infant's earliest expressions of feeling; it means viewing the infant as an active partner in the caregiver-child relation; and, more broadly, it means recognizing the bidirectional effect of an infant and the social world upon each other, rather than assuming only that the social world has certain effects upon the infant. These conceptual implications, as we shall soon see, have been substantiated by recent empirical research into infant social behavior.

Technology and the Study of the Infant

The technological revolution restoring personhood to infants has resulted from the recent use of sophisticated film and videotape techniques in developmental research. With such techniques, it is possible to observe minute and momentary patterns of behavior that normally might escape the observer's eye. Behavior can be played back, slowed down, even stopped in freeze frames for careful analysis. This contemporary, microanalytic observational technique has proven especially valuable in helping scientists witness aspects of infant social interaction that have hitherto gone unnoticed. By directly comparing, frame by frame, visual recordings of an infant's behavior during one moment with recordings during subsequent moments, it becomes possible to discover sequences of behavior between infant and other that are not detectable at life's normal speed.

Using such techniques, researchers have been able to find evidence that, as early as the first day of life, newborn babies regulate their behavior to synchronize with the patterns of human speech.[5] Hours of newborn behavior were recorded on film and on videotape, and those awake moments during which the newborns were exposed to adult speech were observed and analyzed. These behaviors were minute indeed: for example, slight bodily movements such as the rotation of a hip, the lifting of a finger, the raising of an eyebrow. By connecting such transient body movements with the rhythmic sounds of normal speech, the investigators determined that their newborn subjects were indeed actively responding to spoken language. This does not mean, of course, that the infants in any way comprehended the meaning of the words. Rather, they were simply participating, at the outset of life, in a rudimentary social interaction. The interaction did not include the actual communication of information in the manner of shared speech, but it did demonstrate some initial social awareness on the part of the newborn infant:

> For example, as the adult emits the *kk* of "come," which lasts for .07 seconds, the infant's head moves slightly, the left elbow extends slightly, the right shoulder rotates upward, the left shoulder rotates outward slightly, the right hip rotates outward fast, the left hip extends slightly, and the big toe of the left foot adducts.[6]

Newborn infants were observed to sustain synchronized responses of this sort for as long as 125-word sequences of speech. Further, recorded Chinese

[5] Condon & Sandor, 1974.   [6] Ibid., p. 100.

speech was as good at engaging infants in such synchronized body movements as was English speech, even though all the babies in the study were American-born. Nonsense speech, however, did not work; nor did other environmental sounds. It seems that newborns at birth are particularly responsive to the regular patterns of meaningful speech. In their own way, they recognize the difference between a genuine social signal and random noises or vocalizations. They do not, however, confine their responsiveness to the language of a particular culture, but rather seem ready to be members of a quite general human community.

The more closely and systematically scientists observe infant behavior, the more apparent the social significance of seemingly random and "infantile" activity becomes. The infant's engagement with the mother has a smooth and rhythmic character that distinguishes it from the infant's engagement with nonsocial objects like toys or food. Eye contact between mother and child is maintained and broken at regular intervals, and the infant's build-up and disengagement of attention in the mother are slow and gradual. Facial expressions like smiling or grimaces develop in response to the activity of others. At only a few weeks of age, babies can be seen to "take turns" with the mother in expressing vocal sounds and bodily gestures.[7] The same infants' interactions with the nonsocial world do not show signs of this well-regulated turn-taking.

The pediatrician T. Berry Brazelton has observed early sequenced interactions between newborns and their mothers and has called these interactions "the origins of reciprocity."[8] Directly upon birth, the newborn is capable of several socially significant types of behavior. Among these are: (1) turning toward the sound of a human voice and actively searching for the source of the voice; (2) attending to the pitch of a female voice over another tonal pitch; (3) selectively stopping activity like sucking only when confronted with human voice sounds; (4) visually following a complete picture of a human face but not following scramble pictures; and (5) preferring milk smells above sugar-water smells and responding particularly to human milk over cow's milk. By observing infants as young as two weeks of age, Brazelton and his co-workers have confirmed the special nature of social interactions, even at the beginning of life. Initial social interactions, they maintain, are smooth, rhythmic, and cyclic, unlike the infant's choppier and more abrupt interactions with toys and other objects.

> We found that, as early as we could film it, we saw completely different kinds of behavior and attention with a mother and with an attractive object.
> With an attractive object, as it was brought into "reach"—the infant's attention and face became "hooked," his extremities and even his fingers and toes pointed out towards it, and he attended with a rapt, fixed expression on his face. When he was satiated, his attention broke off abruptly and he averted his eyes or turned his whole head and body away for a brief period before he came back for a further period of "hooked" attention. . .
> With his mother, his attention and motor behavior were entirely different: his

---

[7] Stern, 1977.   [8] Brazelton, 1976.

eyes, his face, his mouth, his extremities all became smooth and cyclic. As he attended, he moved out slightly toward the object with his head, his mouth, his eyes, and even with his legs, arms, fingers and toes. But, almost immediately, the approach behavior was followed by smooth, cyclic withdrawal behavior, as if he expected his mother (or father) to come out to him... The parent cycled too, playing a kind of swan's mating dance, as he or she moved in to pass on information or behavior when the infant was looking, and withdrew slightly to let up in intensity when the infant withdrew.[9]

It is certainly impressive that so soon after birth, infants are able to participate in such reciprocal social interactions. Nevertheless, we must be careful not to give the newborn too much initial credit. In any well-regulated social interaction between two persons, both partners must contribute. Until recently, the contribution of the newborn to parent-child interactions was by and large overlooked. But now that we are more aware of this contribution, we must not make the mistake of placing the source of parent-child interactions primarily in the infant's behavior. This would be no better than the previous, opposite mistake of thinking that it is the parent alone who initiates and maintains these interactions.

Contribution of Infant

What, then, is the contribution of the newborn to social interactions? In addition to the cries and other affective expressions that draw the parent close, the newborn's contribution is in her selective and appropriately timed responsiveness to social interactions above all other kinds of stimulation. ("Appropriately timed" refers to the synchronous, rhythmic, and cyclic quality of infant responsiveness that recent research has documented.) This special responsiveness certainly must facilitate the parent's attempts to stimulate or comfort a newborn child. To say that, beyond this, the newborn is responsible for *intentionally* creating the "reciprocity" that Brazelton and others have observed in parent-newborn interactions would be going too far.

This, then, is one critical qualification that must be added to any celebration of the infant's early social skills: there is no evidence whatsoever that either newborns or very young infants perform their social acts with any direct *intention* to interact. By intention is meant a sense of purpose; a conscious awareness that, in the case of social behavior, the goal is to establish or maintain contact with another. Evidence of such intention would be repeated, specific attempts to gain and hold the other's attention, stopping only when this goal is satisfactorily reached.[10] Although young infants' behavior can have the

---

[9] Brazelton, Koslowski, & Main, 1974, p. 34.

[10] As Jerome Bruner has defined it: "Intention, viewed behaviorally, has several measurable features; anticipation of the outcome of the act, selection among appropriate means for achievement of an end state, sustained behavior during development of means, a stop order defined by an end state, and finally some sort of substitution rule whereby alternative means can be deployed for correction of deviation or to fit idiosyncratic conditions." (Bruner, 1973, p. 1.)

effect of eliciting social responses from others, we have no evidence that infants consciously intend their behavior to have such effects.

The other qualification that must be added concerns the nature of the *reciprocity* between young infants and the adults with whom they interact (particularly mothers). Reciprocity means exchange, or give-and-take. But it does not always mean giving the same thing that one is taking, as when one exchanges one hug for another hug. This would be called *direct reciprocity*, which is only one type of reciprocal action. Reciprocity does not even necessarily mean an *equal* exchange, as when one gives up a dollar bill in order to receive four quarters. This would be called *compensatory reciprocity*, which also is not the only kind of reciprocity that is possible between persons. There are, in fact, many kinds of reciprocal action that do not consist of identical or equal exchanges, but rather that consist of a giving and taking of qualitatively different things. These types of reciprocal acts are called *complementary* and *asynchronous*, because the two partners make different contributions. This is precisely the nature of the infant's social exchanges with his parents.

Daniel Stern has used the phrase "turn-taking" to denote the reciprocity inherent in such rudimentary "conversations" as the exchange of gestures and sounds between parent and infant.[11] But he points out that it is the parent who has the ability precisely to coordinate her behavior with the sequences of a newborn's activity. A mother, for example, can interject her words and gestures into the pauses in her child's babbling and bodily movements. Therefore, by her sensitivity to the rhythms and cycles in her newborn's social responding, the mother in large part creates the turn-taking that is present in the earliest parent-child interactions. This initial reciprocity in parent-child interaction is largely created by the parent's carefully coordinated responding to the baby's social cues. According to Stern, only when the infant is several months old is he able to initiate his own intentionally reciprocal responses. If this analysis is correct, we may give the newborn credit for facilitating parent-child interactions through the newborn's behavioral readiness and openness to such interactions; but the turn-taking nature of such interactions (at least during the first weeks of life) comes largely from the parent's carefully interjected responses. The nature of parent-infant reciprocity, therefore, is one of complementary exchange. Both partners make essential contributions, but these contributions are neither identical nor equal. The parent bears the greater responsibility because of the adult's far clearer social awareness.

A clear illustration of the distinct and complementary roles played by parent and child in conducting reciprocal interactions has been provided by the observations of Colwyn Trevarthen.[12] By carefully analyzing filmed interactions between two-month-old infants and their mothers, Trevarthen was able to observe how parent and child both play their own parts in the establishment of coordinated social exchanges. In a typical sequence:

---

[11] Stern, 1977. [12] Trevarthen, 1974, 1977.

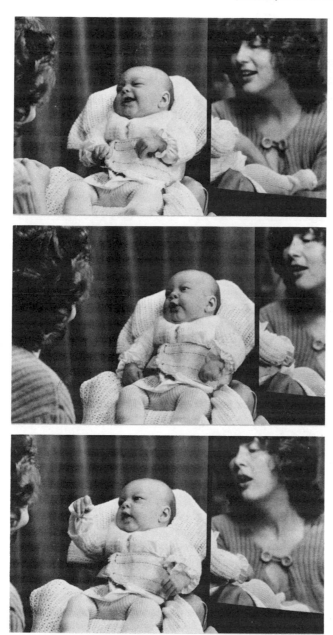

Figure 2-1. The Earliest Form of Interpersonal Expression. A girl, six weeks old, smiles at her mother's face, then responds to gentle baby talk with cooing vocalization and a conspicuous hand movement. In the third picture, the mother is imitating the preceding vocalization of her baby.

Source: D. R. Olson (Ed.), *The Social Foundations of Language and Thought.* New York: W.W. Norton, 1980, p. 319. Reprinted with permission.

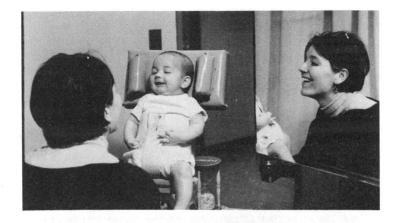

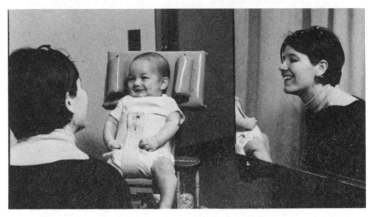

Figure 2-2. Imitation of Baby by Mother. A mother of a two-month-old boy responds to the child's social initiations by imitating the child's facial expression.

> . . .a mother may adopt postures and expressions to closely mirror what her baby does. The intense mutuality or harmony of the behavior comes initially from the infant responding to the mother's friendly behavior in kind. The development is principally due to the mother accepting the expressions of the infant as models for her expression, or, rather, as indicative of an emotion which she may both share with her infant and express in like manner.[13]

The mother therefore structures the communication by responding meaningfully to the infant's initial cue, perhaps by imitating it. This establishes a common ground between her and her child. The infant in turn responds by bodily and vocal signals that are appropriately timed to match or complement the rhythms of the mother's communicative activity. The mother then purposefully continues the "dialogue," and so on. In this manner, the parent and the

[13] Trevarthen, 1977, p. 118.

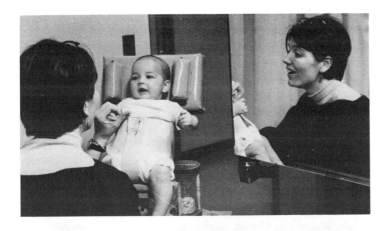

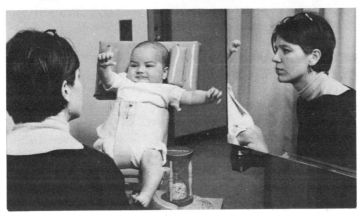

Source: H. R. Schaffer (Ed.), *Studies in Mother-Infant Interaction*. New York: Academic Press, 1977, pp. 244–45. Reprinted with permission.

child together manage to coordinate their activity, achieving a *mutual regulation* of expression, gesture, imitation, response, and vocalization. The parent, of course, does so with a far clearer sense of purpose and a greater sophistication than does the newborn (see Figures 2-1 and 2-2).

In all of this, it is important to realize that "many of the gestures which young infants emit have the status of communication gestures only to the extent that the mother imputes that status to them."[14] For this reason, the full social significance of infant behavior is realized only in the context of the infant's interaction with another person, particularly his caregiver. Although babies actively participate in social interactions, as noted above, they do not do so in a fully intentional manner, as does the older child or the adult. For this reason, we must remain cautious not to attribute too great a range of behavioral capabilities to the infant himself, apart from the interacting parent. This would

[14] Newson, 1974.

be an easy mistake to make, particularly in light of the exquisite parent-child social interactions described above.

The Infant's Openness to Social Influence

Some of the researchers who have conducted the recent ground-breaking studies in this area have argued that we now have evidence that infants inherit genetic endowments that enable them to act in socially sophisticated ways at birth, and that such endowments lead directly to specific social skills like language.[15] This type of explanation is concordant with Noam Chomsky's notion that humans inherit a specific *language acquisition device* that makes possible the speedy and successful learning of language during childhood.[16] It also accords with the recent "sociobiology" vogue, which claims that even the most sophisticated of human social behaviors are somehow genetically preprogrammed in the species. But none of the infant studies to date provides evidence nearly powerful enough to confirm such ambitious claims. To convincingly link up newborn behavior with later achievements such as language acquisition, a number of infants must be closely observed from birth until they learn to speak. Children's early behavior can then be connected with the later skill, for example, by comparing the relative ease and speed of the later acquisition with how well each child performed the earlier behavior. Children with early (and supposedly genetic) deficits would be expected to have the most trouble later on. And for a truly convincing demonstration, the deficits would have to be shown to be specific to the behavior that is believed to be the basis of the later achievement. In the present case, this would mean showing that children who at birth do not synchronize their movements or engage reciprocally with adults, but who are normal in every other way, would be the ones with later linguistic and interpersonal difficulties. But there is no evidence for this.

Failing such evidence, let us look at a more conservative interpretation of infants' social responsiveness. Certainly the findings demonstrate that infants are social from the start of life, that they are ready to engage immediately (though not fully intentionally) in coordinated social interchanges with adults. They are, in fact, active participants in the social relations that will sustain and protect them through the first years of life. Although this does not mean that specific social competencies are necessarily written into the newborn's inherited constitution, it does mean that the baby is psychologically disposed toward social exchange at birth. Whether this initial disposition is due to genetic factors or to prenatal experience (such as the child hearing her mother talk while in the womb) cannot be determined. But, regardless of its source, this initial sociability has dramatic developmental implications for the child.

Because they are psychologically attuned to social exchange when they are born, children from the start of life are to some extent always open to social

---

[15] Condon & Sander, 1974; Bower, 1977.   [16] Chomsky, 1975.

influence, which is important to their psychological growth. If the infant at the start of life were totally closed to social influence, we would be forced to attribute all initial psychological development simply to biological maturation. Nothing more would be needed, given food and shelter, than time for the newborn organism physically to grow up a bit. Although this "maturational" explanation of development always may be entertained as a possibility, most scientists have concluded that psychological growth requires an inextricable combination of biological maturation *and* social learning.[17] This "interactional" explanation is the most reasonable position because it can account for the human species' continual adaptation to a changing world. If this interaction between biological maturation and learning is generally true in human development, why not at birth as well?

Now that we recognize the rudimentary sociability with which the newborn begins life, our explanations of initial psychological development in the infant can become richer and more plausible. We now can include in these explanations the notion that even at birth, infants are able to benefit developmentally from their social interactions. This conclusion follows from our knowledge that, however primitively, infants at all ages actively engage themselves in social interactions. We could *not* come to such a conclusion if we accepted the once-common notion that the infant begins life as a social isolate, confined to totally egocentric thinking and behavior, that is, thinking and behaving without regard to others. Therefore, although we soon shall note many indications of *relative egocentrism* in children, we should never conclude that this is all there is to the child's point of view. Rather, it will greatly enrich our understanding of lifelong social-developmental processes to acknowledge from the start that, to some small but crucial degree, the child is socially oriented.

Attachment to the Caregiver

When one looks at an infant, what does one see? Certainly if one chooses to look during one of the infant's many sleeping moments, one will see an individual little body, distinct and complete within itself. Even during the infant's waking activity, any visual inspection will confirm that the infant is physically whole and separate from the rest of his environment. But a focus upon the infant's waking *behavior*, rather than merely on the infant's physical constitution, will reveal an entirely different picture.

When an infant cries, very often there is someone there to do something about it. When an infant clings, very often it is to another person, rather than to an object. When an infant looks and smiles, very often it is toward someone's face. Indeed, much of what a young infant does during waking hours is not done in a state of total physical separateness at all. Often, someone is holding

[17] Vygotsky, 1962; Piaget, 1966.

the infant when he cries, clings, looks, and even eats. Further, and remarkably enough, this "other someone" is usually the same person—a person whom we shall call the infant's "caregiver."[18] In short, one cannot observe an infant's waking behavior for very long without noticing the actions and reactions of the infant's caregiver. It is also not possible fully to describe the bulk of an infant's behavior without placing it in the context of the caregiver's coordinated activity.

Recognizing this, many writers on child behavior refuse to consider infants as independent entities in any sense, writing, for example, "The infant and the maternal care together form a unit" and ". . .if you set out to describe a baby, you will find you are describing a baby and someone. A baby cannot exist alone, but is essentially part of a relationship."[19] To them, the only language that has seemed appropriate for describing caregiver and child is the word "system," implying that the unit of scientific analysis must be the *interaction* of the two partners, rather than either considered separately.[20] This attempt of child developmentalists to accommodate their writings to the unity of caregiver-child behavior is a conscious acknowledgment of the almost incredible psychological bond between the two. That we, as adults, often take this bond for granted only attests to how common this bond is, but it does not make it any less remarkable. Aside from its widespread existence,[21] the bond is long-lived and intensely affective.

Bonding and Attachment

Bonding and *attachment* are two concepts that scientists have used to explain how the caregiver-child bond is maintained.[22] These concepts have contributed greatly to our understanding of children's social development, but these terms are only metaphors. By what is the child attached to the caregiver? The umbilical cord is snipped moments after delivery. There are no chains, ropes, or other physical ties. If there is "bonding," it is entirely without the help of glue. What then, keeps the two components of the caregiver-child "unit" together?

How do we explain the intense caregiver-child relation? The terms "bonding" and "attachment" themselves reflect two such explanations. *Bond-*

---

[18] For most infants, now and since the beginning of human history, the primary caregiver is the mother. Consequently, many writings on infant social relations refer to "mothering" or the "mother-child relation" as the ground in which the seeds of attachment are sown. But a large minority of children in the world do not have their mother as their primary caregiver. It is an open question—and one that we shall take up in this chapter—whether there are substantial differences between mother-child and other types of caregiver-child re-

lations. Without prejudging this issue, we shall begin with a general consideration of *caregiver*-child relations, of which the mother-child relation is only one (though by far the most frequent) example.

[19] Winnicott, 1960, 1974.

[20] Bowlby, 1969; Fafouti-Milenkovic & Uzgiris, 1979.

[21] Ainsworth, 1967.

[22] Bowlby, 1969; Klaus & Kennell, 1976; Sroufe & Waters, 1977; Ainsworth, Blehar, Waters, & Wall, 1978.

ing has been used in the psychological literature to refer to a rapid, biologically based process that occurs in mothers shortly after birth, during an hypothesized "maternal sensitive period."[23] It is an immediate but long-lasting emotional response triggered off naturally in mothers by contact with their newborn. *Attachment*, on the other hand, refers to a relation between caregiver and infant that takes most of the infant's first year to develop.[24] It, too, is considered to be long-lasting (perhaps for years), but it is changing in nature. That is, behaviors that constitute the attachment relation are transformed as the infant grows and as the caregiver-child relation develops.

Evidence for the biologically based "bonding" process has been mixed.[25] One particularly careful study found virtually no signs of a biologically based bonding process arising out of mothers' initial contacts with their infants.[26] The evidence for the gradually developing relation known as attachment, on the other hand, has been anything but ephemeral. In fact, the robustness of the attachment phenomenon has spawned one of the richest research traditions in contemporary social science. For this reason, we shall focus our following discussion more on the developing attachment relation than on the more speculative notion of bonding.

The attachment between caregiver and child is best understood by examining how the two interact with each other. It is perhaps too easy for us to attribute the creation of the attachment to the caregiver alone. A popular notion, for example, is that it is the mother's love, or her sense of responsibility, that establishes a close relation between mother and child. The mother's contribution certainly is critical; but the infant, too, plays an active part, as we might expect from the discussion at the beginning of this chapter.

The Infant's Means of Contacting the Caregiver

Not too long ago, observers of infant behavior saw much of the infant's activity as random, unconnected expressions of behavior and affect. What, after all, could crying have to do with smiling or looking? The writings of British psychiatrist John Bowlby have changed that view, even though Bowlby's theory itself is still largely controversial within the field of developmental psychology. Bowlby found a way to connect seven of the most common behaviors of infants: crying, cooing, babbling, smiling, clinging, nonnutritional sucking, and following. He believes that the common thread uniting these diverse behaviors is their role in bringing the infant into close contact with the caregiver: "From an early phase of development, each sort [of behavior] has proximity to mother as its predictable outcome."[27] The first three of these behaviors may be called *signaling* behavior, since their effect is to bring the mother closer to the child. The last four may be called *approach* behavior, since their effect is to bring the child closer to the mother.

[23] Klaus & Kennell, 1976.
[24] Ainsworth, 1973.
[25] DeChateau & Wilberg, 1977;

Carlsson et al., 1979.
[26] Svejda, Campos, & Emde, 1980.
[27] Bowlby, 1969, Vol. 1.

In grouping together these seven basic infant behaviors, Bowlby asserts their "functional equivalance." That is, Bowlby claims that whatever else the differences may be between these behaviors, they are similar in at least one respect: they all serve the purpose of maintaining proximity between caregiver and child. Further, Bowlby assumes that, for the infant, seeking proximity to the caregiver is essential for survival. This was especially true at earlier times in human history, when the caregiver was responsible for protecting the infant from predators. But it is even true today, since the infant is still dependent upon the caregiver for food, shelter, and many types of protection. Therefore, crying, cooing, babbling, smiling, clinging, sucking, and following are all means through which infants have assured their own survival since the beginning of human time.

As in our previous discussion of parent-child interaction, we must once again be careful not to give the newborn too much credit. Bowlby does not mean that the infant *intentionally* acts for his own survival by crying, babbling, and so on; nor that the infant even realizes that he is signaling the caregiver by such means. Only with subsequent development will the infant acquire the cognitive ability intentionally to act *in order to* achieve a specifically desired end. For rudimentary behaviors like crying and babbling to have survival value for the newborn, an attentive caregiver is needed. It is the *interaction* between the child's behavior and the caregiver's responding that protects the child, and not either in itself. This is why, once again, we must be careful to consider parent and newborn together, as an interacting system, if we are to understand the meaning of either's behavior.

Bowlby has pointed out something that was long overlooked: that the seemingly random behaviors of the newborn (crying, cooing, babbling) serve a necessary survival function when these behaviors are viewed in the context of the newborn's relation to her parent. This means that the newborn takes an active part in her own protection, but not that she is aware of this part, nor that her behavior would have any survival value apart from a concerned caregiver.

Bowlby names this functionally equivalent cluster of infant activity *attachment behavior*, using the word attachment as a metaphor for the proximity between caregiver and child that the cluster of behaviors helps establish. Psychologists before Bowlby, of course, had observed the infant's tendency to seek contact with the caregiver.[28] But many of these psychologists had assumed that this tendency was derived from some more basic drive such as hunger. One operating hypothesis was that the infant came to desire the caregiver's presence only after discovering that the caregiver was the source of many pleasurable and need-satisfying experiences.[29] Bowlby, on the other hand, was convinced of the absolute primacy of attachment behaviors in and of themselves. The infant's goal of maintaining proximity to the caregiver, Bowlby wrote, is basic to the biological constitutions of all infants throughout the human species, and does not have to be learned through any particular set of experiences. Humans

[28] Buhler, 1933; Maccoby & Masters, 1970.   [29] Freud, 1920.

are "biologically biased," in Bowlby's phrase, toward attachment. This means that the general goal of seeking proximity to a caregiver and certain behavioral means of doing so have become part of our genetic endowment because of their evolutionary survival value.

Bowlby was careful to distinguish his biological hypothesis from the traditional notion of instinct. He did not want to indicate that all attachment behaviors are themselves instinctive in the sense that they represent inherited, fixed patterns of action that inflexibly manifest themselves whenever the infant is in the presence of the caregiver. Rather, Bowlby emphasized that it is the goal that is built in, as well as some initial ways of implementing this goal. With development, the infant becomes more aware of the goal, and his proximity-seeking behavior becomes more purposive and intentional. Also, further ways of seeking proximity develop, and the infant soon is able to select quite flexibly from all of his ways of achieving closeness with his caregiver. This flexibility that comes with development is important, because the caregiver-child interaction is constantly changing along with the individual situations of both caregiver and child. Clinging may be the most appropriate means of attachment in one instance, smiling in another, crying in yet another. The infant must continually moderate his behavior to the specifics of the situation in order to maintain proximity to the caregiver.

Bowlby likened this flexible manner of operating to a *control system*, a machine that can use alternative means to seek a wired-in goal. A control system works by making one attempt, receiving feedback from the results of that attempt, and on the basis of this information making a new and sometimes different type of attempt. The nature of the new attempt is dependent on the original goal (built into the machine) as well as on the input that the machine receives concerning the success of its first attempt.

A good deal of evidence can be marshaled in support of Bowlby's biological explanation for infant attachment behavior. Some of this evidence comes from ethological studies of animal social life. For example, observations of birds have demonstrated that in many species, a baby bird's attachment to its mother (called *imprinting* by ethologists) is not a learned need or an acquired behavioral response, but rather emerges in an instinctual, spontaneous manner that is similar throughout the bird's entire species.[30] Studies with rhesus monkeys have shown that, in this species, many prototypical attachment behaviors are unlearned. Infant monkeys raised apart from their mothers still show strong tendencies to cling to surrogate objects, as well as to nonnutritively suck parts of their own bodies.[31] Further, infant monkeys who were well-cared for in every way but deprived of proximity to other monkeys suffer disastrous consequences. These include high mortality rates from increased susceptibility to infection, extreme manifestations of fear and withdrawal, and an inability to establish social and sexual relations with peers later in life. We must always be cautious in drawing implications for human development from studies of other

---

[30] Hess, 1970; Lorenz, 1970.   [31] Harlow, 1959; Harlow & Harlow, 1962.

animals, but this type of evidence does suggest that in many species there are autonomous systems of behavior similar in function to human attachment that do not owe their existence to more basic needs, drives, or activity. It also supports the plausibility of Bowlby's notion that a goal like proximity seeking can organize much of an infant's early activity and that infants may well have several types of behavior which can serve this goal.

Attachment and Infant's Emotions

Some contemporary developmental psychologists have amplified Bowlby's control system model of attachment by adding the infant's affective feelings as an essential part. Bowlby recognized the existence of infant emotions that accompany attachment behaviors, but he treated these emotions simply as a part of the process by which the infant selects the appropriate means of seeking proximity to the caregiver. L. Alan Sroufe and Everett Waters, on the other hand, have argued that emotion plays a more central role in the infant's general attempts to seek proximity with the caregiver.[32] They conclude that *felt security*, rather than proximity by itself, is the main goal of the system of behaviors that Bowlby grouped together in his attachment concept. In this way, Sroufe and Waters link infant behaviors like crying, clinging, smiling, and following to the infant's desire for emotional security. Although they do not dispute the proximity goal as the early biological, or survival, function of attachment, they emphasize the later goal of felt security as the ultimate goal *for the infant.* This significantly different emphasis in explaining attachment does account more easily than Bowlby's model for certain often-observed patterns of infant behavior. For example, infants who are separated and reunited with the caregiver become increasingly upset at a new separation.[33] This can only be explained if the infant's emotional state is seen as the primary referent for the infant's attachment efforts. A control system of the type hypothesized by Bowlby would impartially greet the new separation as information to be incorporated into another round of proximity seeking, without experiencing greater-than-usual emotional upset.

The Sroufe and Waters critique has accepted the main body of Bowlby's theory, but it has added a new emphasis. Other critiques have been less sympathetic to the very notion of attachment as a means of organizing such diverse behaviors as crying, smiling, and cooing.[34] Some consider the infant-caregiver relation to have much the same qualities as any other social interaction during infancy and refuse to accept the idea that there is an overriding proximity-seeking goal or unique affective bonds that draw the two together with special force on occasion after occasion.[35] Many of these arguments have been made in the light of experimental evidence that we shall consider in the following section. For now, let us conclude this section with a tentative ac-

[32] Sroufe & Waters, 1977.
[33] Ainsworth, Blehar, Waters, & Wall, 1978.
[34] Gewirtz, 1972a, 1972b; Weinraub,

Brooks, & Lewis, 1977.
[35] Cairns, 1972; Rosenthal, 1973.

knowledgment of the aspects of infant social behavior that Bowlby's theory has pointed out. It now seems indisputable that infants are born with several ways of establishing contact with the caretaker, and that they frequently use these ways to bring themselves and the caretaker into closer proximity with each other. It is an intriguing possibility that the goal of proximity seeking as well as some rudimentary means of fulfilling this goal are built into the human species (as well as into many other species). Some experience of affect, too, seems to be associated with the proximity-seeking goal and may well provide a goal in itself, called "felt security."

Developmental Phases of Attachment

Up to this point, our discussion has focused upon what the young infant, even at birth or soon thereafter, is able to do socially. Indeed, the infant is actively able to contribute to social interactions, albeit in a rudimentary way (through crying, gazing, responding positively, and so on). Before long, however, these contributions become increasingly less rudimentary. This is the phenomenon of social-developmental change.

Attachment itself does not emerge full-blown in the newborn's relations with his caregiver, but rather develops gradually throughout the first months and years of the infant's life. Bowlby has described four phases in the development of attachment to the caregiver, and Mary Ainsworth has amplified and refined Bowlby's descriptions.[36] The summaries below are condensations of Bowlby and Ainsworth's phases in the development of caregiver-child attachment.

Phase 1: *Preattachment* (from birth through the first eight to twelve weeks). The baby responds with particular vividness to other people but cannot yet discriminate one person from another. The baby can direct his vision to others and can grasp and reach out toward others. At birth, the baby can "promote contact" with others by crying and soon thereafter can do so by babbling and smiling.

Phase 2: *Attachment-in-the-making* (from the end of phase 1 until seven months to a year). The intensity of the baby's social responses to other people increases, with signs of friendliness and delight directed particularly toward familiar persons. In addition, the infant is able to distinguish his primary caregiver from all others and expends special effort in promoting proximity with this one person.

Phase 3: *Clear-cut attachment* (from the end of phase 2 until the second or third year of life). The infant develops locomotion (crawling, walking), which greatly enhances the infant's ability to seek proximity to the caregiver, as well as to explore the physical environment in general. The infant begins using the caregiver as a "base" from which to explore

[36] Bowlby, 1969, Vol. 1; Ainsworth, Blehar, Waters, & Wall, 1978.

the world, returning to the caregiver whenever a need for security is felt, then departing again for further explorations. The infant may greet the impending departure of the caregiver with protest, clinging, or expressions of alarm.

Phase 4: *Goal-corrected partnership* (from the end of phase 3 onward). The child begins to understand the caregiver's goals, feelings, and point of view, adjusting his own behavior accordingly. A more complex, richly communicative caregiver-child relation becomes possible.

From these descriptions, it can be seen that attachments form gradually over the first years of life and require a number of related developmental (particularly cognitive) acquisitions on the part of the child. For example, for movement into phase 2, the child must be capable of discriminating between people. For movement into phase 3, the child must be capable of anticipating the whereabouts of the other in relation to the self. For movement into phase 4, the child must be capable of mentally representing the point of view of the other, an activity that some have called *role taking*[37] (which we shall take up in Chapter 4). In presenting these phases, John Bowlby and later Mary Ainsworth referred to the developmental theory of the late Swiss psychologist, Jean Piaget, to account for the related aspects of cognitive growth that parallel these phases of attachment. The changes-with-age that Piaget described in infant intellectual abilities come at approximately the same time as one would expect them to come from analyzing the intellectual requirements of Bowlby and Ainsworth's four attachment phases.

In particular, two milestones in Piaget's theory of infant intellectual growth are critical in understanding the development of caregiver-infant relations in the first year. The first of these notions is *object permanence*, which in the social realm translates to *person permanence*. Piaget showed that in the first months of life, infants are not surprised when objects suddenly disappear, and they do not bother to search for them. It is as if the infant had no reason to believe that objects existed once they are removed from their view. That is, the objects have no permanence over time and space. Studies in infant social cognition have shown that young infants are also unaware that persons have permanence.[38] There is some dispute as to which type of permanence—object or person—infants acquire first, but most child psychologists agree that both types are generally lacking for at least the first six months.[39] Clearly, stable relations with another person (such as the caregiver) cannot be established until the infant realizes that the person can be counted on not to suddenly and entirely disappear from the infant's life. For this cognitive reason alone, we would not expect clear-cut attachment (phase 3) to appear during the first six months of an infant's life.

The second critical notion from Piaget's theory of cognitive development

---

[37] Mead, 1934; Flavell et al., 1968.
[38] Piaget, 1954; Jackson, Campos, & Fisher, 1975.

[39] Decarie, 1965; Bell, S.M., 1970; Jackson, Campos, & Fisher, 1975.

is *intentionality*, discussed briefly above. According to Piaget, infants are not capable of fully intentional behavior (that is, the conscious pursuit of specified goals) until the second half of their first year. This, too, corresponds with phase 3 attachment. By then, the infant can anticipate the caregiver's departure with purposeful protests. Prior to this, the infant can only pursue the general goal of proximity through behavior (Bowlby's seven "signals") that neither anticipates nor intends the specific, direct result of the caregiver's return (even though the young infant is indeed comforted by renewed contact with the caregiver). There is ample controversy as to exactly when infants become capable of fully intentional behavior, but most studies have placed this achievement somewhere in the middle of the first year.[40]

Separation Protest, Wariness of Strangers, and the Strange Situation

As the infant becomes clearly attached to a caregiver, sometime at the beginning of phase 3, a striking pattern of infant-caregiver interaction emerges. Upon the impending departure of the caregiver, the infant often fusses, cries, screams, stamps, and clings to the caregiver, expressing what is called *separation protest*.[41] The child is not easily comforted by another person but rather demands the caregiver's return. Bowlby, borrowing a phrase originally introduced by Sigmund Freud, has suggested that such protest is one sign of *separation anxiety*, a general syndrome of infant distress resulting from the caregiver's absence.[42] Observers of infant behavior have reported that separation anxiety becomes evident at about seven months, peaks in intensity at about a year, then declines a bit, peaks again between a year and a half and two years, and then gradually tapers off as the child grows older.[43]

Appearing at about the same time as separation anxiety, and equally striking, is another pattern of infant distress called "stranger anxiety." Stranger anxiety is really a kind of wariness that is demonstrated by the infant's turning away and sometimes crying when an unfamiliar person enters her visual field (see Figure 2-3). Separation anxiety and wariness of strangers are so common among infants of seven months and above that some psychologists have assumed that they are two sides to the same coin—the coin being the infant's attachment to the caregiver. Rene Spitz, for example, argued that the infant shows distress at the sight of strangers because this sight reminds the infant that the caregiver is not present.[44]

The notion that separation and stranger anxiety are somehow related in infancy is an intriguing hypothesis, but it does not account for the many times that infants have been observed to show fear of strangers in their caregiver's presence.[45] Although in some instances the infant's separation from her caregiver may explain her wariness of strangers, in many other instances this

---

[40] Piaget, 1963; Escalona, 1973; Bretherton & Bates, 1979.
[41] Robertson, 1953; Sroufe & Waters, 1977; Ainsworth, Blehar, Waters, & Wall, 1978.
[42] Bowlby, 1960.
[43] Schaffer, 1963; Bowlby, 1969, Vol. 1.
[44] Spitz, 1950.
[45] Sroufe, 1977.

Figure 2-3. Wariness of strangers. The response of an eight-month-old baby to a stranger's attempts to communicate.

Source: T.G.R. Bower, *A Primer of Infant Development.* San Francisco: W.H. Freeman, 1977, p. 51. Photos by Jennifer G. Wishart. Reprinted with permission.

wariness must have additional and different causes. Harriet Rheingold and Carol Eckerman have argued that fear of strangers is an unpredictable event of uncertain meaning: "Infant reactions to strangers are unreliable, unstable, inconsistent, and incompatible with unequivocally observed affiliative relations."[46] Further, they note that studies have shown that the age at which stranger anxiety first appears varies much more widely than the writings of Spitz and others would indicate. Alan Sroufe, on the other hand, has countered that the data on age of onset *are* coherent if one takes into account differences in scoring procedures used by various investigators.[47] Sroufe argues that clear-cut attachment and stranger wariness appear at about the same time because they both require the cognitive capacities of distinguishing between persons and realizing the permanence of persons (see above). But attachment and wariness are also connected with one another in more complex ways. Infants who are securely attached to their caregivers may indeed act less wary of a stranger when in the presence of their caregivers, as Sroufe's own research has shown. This is an indication that the infant's emotional state benefits from the *secure base* provided by her caregiver. Under other circumstances, with an absent caregiver or a particularly intrusive stranger (who tries, for example, to pick the infant up), the infant will be wary. Infants show wariness by crying, expressions of fear, or by a number of other less intense indications that they are in a state of emotional discomfort.

[46] Rheingold & Eckerman, 1973.   [47] Sroufe, Waters, & Matas, 1974.

Assessing Attachment: The Strange Situation

The *strange situation* is an experimental technique that Mary Ainsworth has designed to study the interplay of stranger wariness, separation anxiety, and attachment in the course of an infant's everyday exploratory behavior. Prior to Ainsworth's work, psychologists had attempted with some limited success to "measure" infants' attachments to their caregivers. Most notably, some investigators assessed the strength of infant attachments by observing their infant subjects' responses to seven common short-term separation situations. Among these were the baby being left alone in a room by the caregiver, being left in a baby carriage or a crib, being put down from the caregiver's arms, and being "passed by" while sitting in a chair or a crib.[48] Here the intensity of a baby's separation protest was the measure of attachment to the caregiver. The idea was that separation protest, beginning at about seven months, was the clearest signal of an infant's attachment. Further, it was assumed that the stronger and more frequent the protest, the greater the attachment.

The problem with this as a measurement technique is that infants who are secure in their attachment do not always show intense signs of separation anxiety when the caregiver leaves for short periods of time. Such infants are at least as attached as those who show severe upset, and probably more so. Mary Ainsworth concluded exactly this in her extensive study of twenty-three Ugandan infants in their natural setting:

> In particular, I do not believe that the degree of disturbance in minor separation situations may be used as an indication of how strong or intense the attachment is. The seven Ugandan babies whom I classified as insecure-attached seemed to be more intensely and more consistently disturbed by minor separation situations than the sixteen babies classified as secure-attached, but I do not believe that they were more strongly attached—merely more insecure. When ill, babies in the secure-attached group were "clingy" and behaved much like the insecure-attached. Were they more attached to the mother when ill or merely more insecure?[49]

Ainsworth's conclusion was that separation anxiety cannot serve as the sole criterion for a measure of infant attachment. Rather, a multiple measure, sensitive to a number of signs of attachment, is needed. From this conclusion came the strange situation, certainly the most widely used measure of infant social development.[50]

The strange situation is so designated because it places an infant in an unfamiliar setting with a stranger, both in the presence and in the absence of the infant's caregiver. The physical setting is an experimental room with three chairs, one for the child, one for the child's mother, and one for the stranger. The child's chair is surrounded by toys. The child is exposed to this setting in eight episodes, each of which lasts about three minutes (except the first, which

[48] Schaffer & Emerson, 1964a.   [50] Ainsworth & Bell, 1970.
[49] Ainsworth, 1967.

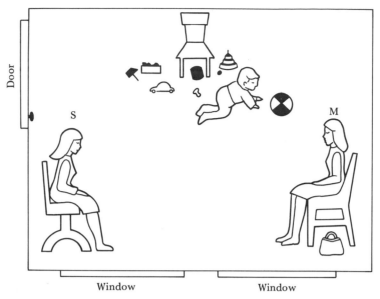

Figure 2-4. A Diagrammatic Sketch of Ainsworth's Strange Situation.

Source: M. Ainsworth, M. Blehar, E. Waters, & S. Wall, *Patterns of Attachment.* Hillsdale, N.J.: Erlbaum, 1978, p. 34. Reprinted with permission.

lasts only thirty seconds). During episode 1, the mother and baby are first introduced to the experimental room. During episode 2, the baby explores the room with the mother present. During episode 3, the stranger enters, talks to the mother, and then approaches the baby. During episode 4, the baby and the stranger are left alone in the room together. During episode 5, the mother returns and the stranger leaves, so that the baby is reunited with the mother. During episode 6, the baby is left alone in the room. During episode 7, the stranger enters the room, and the baby is alone with the stranger. During episode 8, the mother again returns and the stranger leaves (see Figure 2-4).

Ainsworth's strange situation, therefore, exposes a child to three potentially upsetting experiences: separation from the caregiver, contact with a stranger, and unfamiliar surroundings. The episodes are arranged so that the effect of these experiences may be observed separately and also together, since during episodes 4 and 7 both occur simultaneously. The sequence of episodes in the procedure is fixed so that it can present to the infant a *cumulative* stress experience. This is a key to the assessment: the infant may become progressively more and more upset as the sequence of strange events unfolds. Finally, and most importantly, the child's reactions to separation and stranger presence may be viewed in the context of the child's willingness to explore the unfamiliar environment. That is, it is possible to determine how seriously the cumulating stress experiences affect a child's natural tendency to explore and play with the toys and other objects in the strange situation.

In a study of one-year-old infants and their mothers, all from middle-class

American homes, Ainsworth found three distinct patterns of responding to the strange situation[51] (see Table 2-1). The largest group of infants (almost 70 percent of Ainsworth's sample) were classified as Group B and had a securely attached pattern of behavior. These infants actively explored the new environment when in the presence of their mothers, and they showed no distress at the novelty of the situation. Upon reunion with their mothers after separation, the infants greeted them with positive expressions of feeling. They did not necessarily cry when the mother first left the room. Rather, they often seemed to realize that the mother would still be accessible to them if they needed her. In general, these infants used their mother as a secure base from which to explore the room and interact with the stranger. Even when they became distressed after the mother left (which generally occurred after the second separation, during episode 6), these group B children were able to recover quickly by actively seeking contact with the mother on reunion and maintaining this contact for some time. These babies also showed very little negative emotion when the mother returned, but rather welcomed the mother with affection and delight. They were relatively easy to comfort, even by the end of the experiment when they were most upset, and they quickly returned to exploration of the room after they were comforted.

In contrast, a sizable minority of Ainsworth's sample (about 20 percent) actually *avoided* their mothers during the reunion episodes. This was a dramatic contrast, since it is during the reunions that the Group B children showed greatest positive feeling and proximity seeking toward their mothers. The avoidant babies, on the other hand, not only did not seek contact with the mother during reunion, but sometimes looked away from her when she approached. This is a phenomenon called *gaze aversion* and is a common response to an approaching stranger, but hardly to a returning mother. The avoidant infants—Group A—also were not particularly upset upon initial separation from their mothers. They did become distressed after being left alone for a while, but this distress was comforted as easily by the stranger as by the child's mother. Even their play with toys often showed an emotionless, superficial, and rigid quality.

Finally, a third group of children were quite distressed upon every separation from the mother, but were difficult to comfort upon reunion. In fact, these children resisted comfort and contact from their mothers, even though (unlike the Group A children) they did show considerable separation anxiety. Their behavior showed an angry ambivalence, in the sense that they objected to being left alone, but they refused to be consoled when rejoined with their mothers. On the one hand, they were overly preoccupied with the mother, and on the other hand, they could not be consoled by her. They seemed to experience a lack of confidence in other people (including the caregiver), as well as in new situations. These Group C children were the ones least likely to play with the toys in the room or to interact with the stranger. They even became upset

[51] Ainsworth, Blehar, Waters, & Wall, 1978.

Table 2–1 Three Patterns of Infant-Caregiver Attachment

	Group A *Anxious/Avoidant* *Attachment*	*Group B* *Secure* *Attachment*	*Group C* *Anxious/Resistant* *Attachment*
Infant Exploration	*Independent exploration*	*Exploration from secure base of caregiver*	*Poverty of exploration*
	1. readily separates to explore during pre-separation	1. readily separates to explore toys	1. has difficulty separating to explore; may need contact even prior to separation
	2. readily explores	2. readily explores	2. wary of novel situations
	3. little affective sharing	3. affecting sharing of play	3. little affective sharing
	4. affiliative to stranger, even when caregiver is absent (little preference); no avoidance of strangers	4. affiliative to stranger in mother's presence	4. wary of strangers
	5. distress as easily comforted by stranger as by caregiver	5. readily comforted by caregiver when distressed (promoting a return to play)	5. not easily comforted by caregiver or by stranger
Reunion with mother	*Active avoidance upon reunion*	*Active seeking of contact or interaction upon reunion*	*Difficulty settling upon reunion*
	1. turns away, looks away, moves away, ignores	1. seeks caregiver; knows caregiver will be there if needed	1. may show striking passivity
	2. may mix avoidance with proximity	2. if distressed, immediately seeks and maintains contact, which is effective in terminating stress	2. may simply continue to cry and fuss
	3. avoidance is more extreme on second reunion	3. if not distressed, shows active greeting behavior (happy to see caregiver and strong initiation of interaction)	3. may mix contact seeking with contact resistance (hitting, kicking, squirming, rejecting toys)

Source: Adapted from L. Alan Sroufe, Infant-caregiver and patterns of adaptation in preschool: The roots of maladaptation and competence. Presented at the Minnesota Symposium, October 22, 1981. To appear in M. Perlmutter (Ed.), *Minnesota Symposium in Child Psychology*, Vol. 16, in press.

upon first entering the unfamiliar room in the presence of their mothers. They also refused to return to exploration of the room after reunion.

Of Ainsworth's three patterns of attachment behavior, only the Group B pattern shows an ability to use the mother as a secure base from which to explore the world. The two other patterns, A and C, show an inability to do so, each for its own distinct reasons. These reasons derive from the unique nature of each attachment pattern. It is not correct, according to Ainsworth, to call one pattern "more" or "less" attached, as these are qualitative, not quantitative, differences in mother-child relations. In many ways, a pattern B relation is optimal, but this is because of its security and other qualities, not because it is more intense.

Infant behavior in the strange situation demonstrates that attachment to a caregiver cannot be assessed simply by the magnitude of a child's separation anxiety when the caregiver is not present. How much a child cries when left alone is not directly related to how well attached the child is to the mother. Nor can attachment be measured by how negatively an infant reacts to an approaching stranger: Group B babies were often quite friendly toward the stranger in Ainsworth's situation. In fact, "how much" type of questions are not at all appropriate to the notion of attachment, as noted above: this is because it is the quality of attachment that is crucial, not the quantity. Well-attached children often will not cry or protest very strongly when left alone for brief periods of time. They are also easily comforted by the caregiver when they do become upset. Such children actually show considerable independence from the caregiver, in that they are able to explore strange objects and interact with strange persons on their own. But their exploratory activity is greatly aided by the security of their attachment. "Security" here does not mean "strength," but rather a feeling of confidence that the caregiver will be there when needed. The other patterns described by Ainsworth—both Group A and Group C—were not necessarily weaker attachment patterns, but were certainly poorer quality ones.[52] Ainsworth's analysis of patterns rather than strength of attachment has been called an *organizational approach* to infant behavior.[53]

[handwritten margin note: Erikson's "trust"— into early anal phase.]

Long-Term Developmental Consequences of Attachment

We know from the observations of Bowlby, Ainsworth, and many others that attachment to a caregiver is a major part of children's early social lives. We know, too, that attachment has important implications for children's early affective experience and that the quality of children's attachment to their caregivers is linked with their propensity to explore the world around them, including other persons in that world. We might suspect therefore that the

[52] Some psychologists have wondered whether these patterns can be reliably recognized (Gewirtz, 1972b; Weinraub, Brooks, & Lewis, 1977), but a growing body of research has replicated these patterns and has clearly established the reliability and validity of Ainsworth's measure (Sroufe & Waters, 1977; Waters, 1978; Waters, Wippman, & Sroufe, 1979).

[53] Sroufe & Waters, 1977.

quality of children's attachments in the first years of life has something to do with how well children develop socially, emotionally, and intellectually.

When John Bowlby, reporting to the World Health Organization in 1951, first claimed that early disruptions of a mother-child relation could have long-term, deleterious effects on the child's later development, his claim seemed speculative at best.[54] Now, three decades later, Bowlby's assertion is widely accepted by both professionals in the child-development field and by the popular media. Medical, legal, and educational practices have been accommodated to children's early attachments, with the greatest attention directed at respecting and continuing the caregiver-child bond throughout the child's early life. Some critical revisions in Bowlby's initial conception have been suggested by contemporary writers. But such revisions notwithstanding, a large body of empirical evidence has confirmed Bowlby's basic claim that successful early attachments are necessary precursors to future psychological growth and adaptation.

Bowlby's original concern was with the effect on the child of repeated, long-term separations from the mother. (Bowlby was quite specific in writing of the mother, rather than of caregivers generally.) Drawing on observations by Robertson,[55] Bowlby described three types of reactions shown by children when separated from the mother. (These reactions, of course, occur only after a clear "phase 3" attachment has been established, after about seven months of age.) The first type of reaction, called *protest*, is the most dramatic but least harmful to the child. The child cries, clings, or calls to the mother upon her pending departure. The second type of reaction, called (perhaps a bit melodramatically) *despair*, occurs after a week or so of the mother's absence. During the period of despair, a child enters into an inactive and withdrawn state resembling mourning: a listless, muted type of behavior that suggests a feeling of hopelessness and sadness at the mother's continuing absence. This state, suggests Bowlby, still does not have long-term consequences for the child, however miserable the child may feel at the time. It is the third type of reaction, called *detachment*, that holds such dangers. Detachment may begin after a few weeks of separation, and increases upon subsequent separations from the mother. On the surface, it seems like quite a normal state. The child perks up, no longer despairing at the mother's absence, and seems bright and cheerful once again. There is a "settling in" to the new routine with mother now gone, and a renewed interest in toys and food. But this renewed interest does not easily extend itself to other people. In fact, even when the mother returns, the child is likely to greet her apathetically, ignoring or rejecting her advances. According to Bowlby, the child in this state defends against being hurt further by disrupted attachments to others. The defense takes the form of refusing to reestablish an attachment. The more often the child experiences detachment, the more likely the child is to make such a refusal.

---

[54] Bowlby, 1951.

[55] Robertson, 1952.

One reviewer has compared the dangers of detachment in Bowlby's theory to the harmful effects of radiation poisoning: each dose accumulates until deadly damage is done, and even small doses can adversely affect future health.[56] In the case of detachment, it is the child's ability to establish future social relationships that is at stake, as well as all the aspects of psychological well-being that are endangered by social isolation. How closely, we must now ask, has psychological research supported this view of detachment and its risks?

Michael Rutter, a British psychiatrist, has conducted two landmark reviews of the major empirical studies pertaining to the effects of maternal deprivation.[57] His conclusion is that there is substantial evidence to support Bowlby's position that maternal deprivation may have lasting adverse effects on children, but not always in the way that Bowlby imagined. Rutter documents a number of social, intellectual, and emotional disturbances that have been shown to result from early shortcomings in children's relations with their caregivers. These disturbances include intellectual retardation, conduct disorders during behavior with adults and peers, and failures to respond to others with positive affective feelings. But Rutter doubts that all of these adverse consequences can be attributed to one particular parent-child problem, such as extended separation. Rather, the evidence indicates that there are a cluster of possible impoverishments, conflicts, and other adversities in children's relations with their caregivers, and each type of adversity is associated with a particular kind of childhood disturbance.

Rutter distinguishes between four different types of "adversities" that may befall a child's relations with his caregiver. The first is an interference with the attachment behaviors that children under normal circumstances display in the presence of the caregiver. This adversity may indeed follow from separation, although not always. If children have secure ties to the caregiver to begin with, or if they engage in positive social interactions with another caregiver during the separation, they are less likely to experience disrupted attachment with the original caregiver upon reunion.[58] Separation, therefore, is only a partial cause of disrupted attachment behavior. Other causes are within the child, the parent, or the circumstances of the separation.

The second type of caregiver-child adversity is disharmony and conflict between caregiver and child. This is not at all a consequence of separation, but rather stems from discord in the interactions that do take place between caregiver and child. The third type of adversity is the lack of meaningful cognitive and linguistic experiences that may result from an impoverished social environment. Such a lack of stimulation may as likely be encountered in an unfortunate home condition as in a separation. The crucial factor here is not the separation from a caregiver but rather the nature of the social interactions —rich or impoverished—that are available for a child. Finally, the fourth type

---

[56] Hogan, 1975b.
[57] Rutter, 1972, 1979.

[58] Robertson & Robertson, 1971; Ainsworth, Blehar, Waters, & Wall, 1978.

of adversity is insecure attachment with the caregiver. This insecure attachment is of the type that Ainsworth described in her identification of children who exhibited avoidant or ambivalent attachment behaviors. Again, such a problem stems more from the nature of the caregiver-child interaction than from separation in itself. Either a noninteractive parent or a "difficult" and "noncuddly" baby can contribute to the failure to establish early secure relations between the two. Babies who are relatively unresponsive due to illness or to temperamental tendencies often have difficulty participating in the early social interactions that lead to secure attachments.[59] We shall further explore the issue of temperamental tendencies in the next chapter.

Rutter's analysis looks beyond separation as the primary cause of disturbances arising from deprivation in caregiver-child relations. More important than separation in and of itself, Rutter suggests, is the quality of the child's social interactions, both in the presence and in the absence of the caregiver. If the child is institutionalized for an extended period, the crucial issue is the availability of high-quality social experience in the institution.[60] If the child's family goes through the separation of a divorce, the crucial issue is whether or not the child was exposed to lengthy and intense family squabbling prior to and during the divorce. Further, the child herself can be seen as one (though not the sole) active determiner of the character of social interactions. Seemingly from birth, some children have more difficulty than others in engaging people in interactions that lead to attachments. At the other extreme, some children seem almost invulnerable to the adversities associated with one or another kind of caregiver deprivation.[61]

Rutter is quite specific in linking each of his types of caregiver-child adversities with a particular kind of subsequent behavioral disorder. The first type of adversity, interference with attachment behavior, leads to the acute distress syndrome that Bowlby described after observing the three phases of separation reaction that children display during extended stays at hospitals. The second type of adversity, family conflict and disharmony, leads to conduct disorders in a child's subsequent social relations. The third type of adversity, the lack of meaningful social experiences, leads to intellectual retardation. And the fourth type of adversity, insecure early attachment, leads to an *affectionless psychopathology*, or the inability to respond with positive emotions to other people. Table 2-2 outlines Rutter's system of cause-effect relations.

Clearly, Rutter's position implies that early caregiver-child relations are important signals of strengths or weaknesses in children's future social and intellectual development. Some evidence for this comes from a study in which infants at eighteen months were observed in the strange situation and classified according to the quality of their attachment behavior.[62] Ainsworth's categories (Groups A, B, C, as described above) were used for this classification. The

---

[59] Brown & Bateman, 1978.
[60] Rutter, 1972.

[61] Rutter, 1979.
[62] Matas, Arend, & Sroufe, 1978.

Table 2-2 Lasting Consequences of Different Types of Adversities in Caregiver-Child Relations during Infancy

Nature of caregiver-child adversity	*Antecedent conditions to adversity*	*Behavioral disorder in child's later development*
1. Interference with attachment behavior	Separation, coupled with (1) poor quality social interactions during the separation and (2) vulnerability on the part of the child	Acute distress syndrome (e.g., severe psychological reactions during extended hospitalization)
2. Conflictual interpersonal relations	Family conflict, caregiver-child disharmony	Conduct disorders in interactions with adults and peers
3. Lack of meaningful social experiences	Impoverished social environment, little or no social stimulation	Intellectual retardation
4. Insecure early attachment	Characteristics of caregiver (coldness, noninteractiveness) combined with characteristics of the child ("noncuddliness," passivity, behavioral difficulties associated with particular temperaments, premature birth, illness, etc.)	Affectionless psychopathology

Source: Based on M. Rutter, Maternal deprivation 1972–1978: New findings, new concepts, new approaches. *Child Development*, 1979, *50*, 283–305.

infants were then observed when they were two years old, during a free-play and a subsequent clean-up session, and in the course of working at four problem-solving tasks. As predicted, the infants assessed as securely attached (Group B) at eighteen months were the ones who were most cooperative, persistent, and effective during the sessions six months later. They were also more enthusiastic about engaging in the new behavior required by the tasks. Interestingly, those in the securely attached group did show some oppositional behavior (protest, refusal) when asked to switch from free-play to clean-up, but they cooperated very well with their mothers when they needed their mothers' help on the problem-solving tasks. This is clearly a sign that the securely attached children were more capable of adaptive social behavior than the nonsecurely attached children, many of whom showed noncompliance with adults in all situations.

The above study shows direct continuity in infants' social adaptation across a six-month time span. But, although six months is a fairly sizable portion of a two-year-old's life, this still represents a narrow time span in relation to human development. Studies across a broader age span have also provided evidence for such continuity, although in a less direct manner. For example, Dorothy Tizard has studied children reared in institutions from infancy to the age of eight.[63] She has shown that children who have had little opportunity to form stable attachments with caregivers are in some respects maladapted later in life and in other respects not so. Intellectually, by ages five through eight, their performance on I.Q.-type tests does not seem to suffer significantly. But these children did show frequent clinging behavior as late as four years of age, were overly attention seeking around adults, and rarely had close relationships with others. This was even true of children who were "late-adopted" at age four or so: although the late-adopted children were able eventually to form attachments to their new parents, they nevertheless showed signs of the same social difficulties that were found in the other institutionally raised children who remained in institutions. As in the aforementioned study, the data here also confirm the continuity between the quality of early attachment and later social adaptation. But the continuity in the Tizard studies did not pertain to intellectual functioning, only to the child's ability to establish social relations. Of course, as Rutter points out in his review of Tizard's findings, impaired social functioning can have a deleterious effect upon intellectual growth, even if the child's I.Q. scores are not affected. For example, children with difficulty cooperating with adults are not likely to benefit as fully from schooling as are more socially competent children. Moreover, some evidence collected by Mary Main and her colleagues suggests that even children's cognitive development may be directly tied to infant attachment, at least in the early years of life.[64]

---

[63] Tizard & Joseph, 1970; Tizard & Rees, 1974, 1975; Tizard & Hodges, 1978.

[64] Main, 1973; Main & Londerville, 1978.

There is also evidence that links the quality of early attachment to children's peer-group behavior in the preschool years.[65] One study provided particularly powerful evidence for this link because it was a *prospective* study.[66] That is, the quality of attachments was assessed when the infant subjects were fifteen months of age; predictions were made concerning which subjects would later show the greatest competence with peers, and then these predictions were tested over two years later by observing the subjects (now three-and-a-half years old) during peer play situations. As predicted, children who were assessed as securely attached at fifteen months were popular and well adjusted in the peer group at three-and-a-half years. Other children sought their company, they participated frequently in peer activities, they often acted as group leaders, and they were sympathetic to peers who were in distress. In contrast, children assessed as insecurely attached at fifteen months were socially withdrawn at three-and-a-half years. Further, the two sets of infants differed on a number of personality variables. Those in the securely attached group were more forceful, self-directed, and curious at three-and-a-half years than their insecurely attached peers. As we shall see in subsequent chapters, these are all early signs of *ego strength*. In contrast, those in the insecurely attached group were described at three-and-a-half years as "unaware," "spaced out," and apathetic in their personal manner.

The quality of a child's early attachment behavior, therefore, does indeed have important long-range developmental implications. This does not mean, however, that all aspects of the child's future life are determined once and for all by the caregiver-child relation. Some aspects of later life—future social behavior, certain personality characteristics—seem more tied to the quality of early attachment than are other aspects of later life. Even more importantly, there is increasing evidence that certain deleterious effects of early caregiver deprivation—particularly cognitive effects—may still be corrected by later intervention.[67] Indeed, some psychologists have argued forcefully that a child's potential for development remains intact surprisingly late in life, whatever the adverse blows of early experience.[68] Although we would certainly hope this is true, there is by now no question that poor early care places children at risk personally and socially for years after infancy.

Psychological research has confirmed Bowlby's original view of the long-lasting importance of early attachment to the development of the child. But this research has brought us away from the notion that the lasting influence of early attachment derives from a single psychological process. Rather, we now see a number of processes at work in the formation of early attachments; and we consequently see several different reasons why the nature of a child's early social relations continues to be of significance for the child's behavior and development long after infancy.

---

[65] Lieberman, 1977; Waters, Wippman, & Sroufe, 1979.
[66] Waters, Wippman, & Sroufe, 1979.
[67] Kagan, 1976.
[68] Kagan & Brim, 1981.

Of the processes implicated in the formation of early attachments, we must include the following: (1) social interaction and communication between caregiver and child, in which the infant plays an active role from the start; (2) the affective needs of the child, particularly the need for "felt security"; (3) the biological needs of the infant, including need for food, shelter, and protection; and (4) the infant's intellectual needs for stimulation and interesting environmental experience. All of these contribute to the forming of close relations between infant and caregiver, and the failure of the infant's caregiving environment to provide any of these can be seriously disruptive to the infant's development. Of the developmental consequences of deprivation in caregiver-child relations, we may point to the following quite distinct outcomes: impaired future relations with adults and peers, personality disorders, affective imbalances, and failures to maximize one's intellectual potential. None of these outcomes is an automatic result of early caregiver-child adversities. Some children may be more vulnerable to such adversities than are others, and fortuitous later life circumstances may reverse some of the effects of the early deprivation.

The Role of the Father

The quality of an infant's early attachment does not depend solely on the child's relations with a single caregiver, such as the child's biological mother. In particular, the father can play a major role in supplementing, mitigating, or even substituting for the mother's influence, depending upon the family's needs and circumstances.

Until now, we have viewed the infant's early social life through a narrow lens. This lens has placed a single relation—the infant with his primary caregiver—in sharp focus, but has left the rest of the infant's social world obscure. This view may have helped us gain an initial understanding of the infant's most intense and consequential relationship, but even this understanding cannot be complete without broadening our focus to include more of the infant's social network. For in actuality no relationship, however important, exists in a vacuum. The caregiver-infant relationship is an inextricable part of a *family system* that usually includes a father, as well as other members. These family members interact with one another in multiple and diverse ways, creating a web of direct and indirect mutual influence. In terms of the father and his role, this means that not only does the father have his own important relationship with the infant, but also that the father has an influence upon the way the mother influences the infant.

How close is the father's own relationship with the infant? The popular stereotype, of course, is that the father is often a distant, secondary figure in the family and the mother is unrivaled as a love object in the eyes of the infant. But this is probably not the case.[69] Michael Lamb made home observations of

[69] Lamb, 1977a, 1977b.

typical families in which the mother usually was the caregiver. In observations made when the infants were in their first year, Lamb found no differences in the babies' preferred attachment figures: "babies were 'equally attached' to both parents."[70] He then made further observations of some of the same babies when they were in their second year. Also, Lamb added to his sample some other babies between the ages of fifteen to twenty-four months. Again, he found no signs that the infants favored the mother as an attachment figure. In fact, although the infant girls showed no trend either way, infant boys actually showed a preference for interacting with their fathers. Thus, the fathers had become particularly attractive as attachment figures and as playmates to their sons. Lamb interprets this as an indication of the importance of the father-son relation for the son's early gender identification.[71]

Lamb has also found that fathers interact with their infants somewhat differently than do mothers. As Lamb puts it, "fathers were more likely to initiate physically stimulating and idiosyncratic types of play."[72] Mothers, on the other hand, tended toward more conventional and less physical play centering around toys. K. Allison Clarke-Stewart has amplified this picture of differences between mother-infant and father-infant interaction, finding that fathers played with their infants in a more vigorous and physical manner than did mothers.[73] Also, father-infant interactions were more rapid and unpredictable than those of mothers. In contrast, mothers played with their children more quietly, more often through verbal than through physical means.

Aside from the father's own interaction with the infant, he has another, less direct, influence upon the infant's social life. This is through his relations with the mother. Research has consistently shown that mothers interact differently with infants when in the presence of fathers than when not.[74] The most consistent finding is that the mother interacts less intensely with the infant: that is, her rate of infant-directed behavior diminishes to a marked degree. Fathers, too, engage less with their infants when with the mother than when alone. Although this finding does not tell us much about the exact interpersonal dynamics that occur between the mother-father-infant triad, it does show that a third person's presence makes a significant difference in the infant's social environment. Most importantly, it indicates that the family is a *system* of interacting individuals that exert mutual influence upon one another. There are many roles that a father could play within this system: he could distract the mother from proper caregiving, for example; or he could mitigate the effects of irresponsible or abusive acts on the part of the mother. All of these contingencies, and many others, require further research before we are to adequately understand their causes and consequences. For now, we must simply take note of the demonstrated fact that through their participation in the family system, fathers play both a direct and an indirect role in their infants' lives.

---

[70] Lamb, 1980, p. 29.
[71] Lamb, 1980.
[72] Ibid, p. 35.

[73] Clarke-Stewart, 1978, 1980.
[74] Lamb, 1977b; Waters, Wippman, & Sroufe, 1979.

Three main conclusions come out of the research with fathers and their infants: (1) In most families, the father is as salient an attachment figure as the mother; (2) Fathers play more physically, more vigorously, and more unpredictably than do mothers; and (3) When fathers and mothers are together, the interaction between either parent and infant is less intense than when either parent is alone with the infant. Further research has replicated all of these findings. One concerned investigator took special care to conduct his family observations under the most unobtrusive conditions possible. He had suspected that previous research results might have been artifactual due to investigative conditions that overly manipulated parents and infants, leading to unrepresentative behavior. Consequently, he observed forty families (a large number for such studies) in relatively natural and "psychologically pure" home conditions. His conclusion from his observations was that "contrary to my initial suspicions, the results of these (prior) researches are robust and provide a generally accurate picture of the family system during infancy."[75]

Beyond Attachment: The Development of Communication between Infant and Adult

Infant-adult social interaction is important for other reasons beyond its contribution to the establishment of attachments. These other reasons can be identified if we shift our focus beyond attachment to the more general phenomenon of communication between infant and adult. Aside from helping the infant establish attachments, communication is important in itself and plays many other roles in the infant's developing collection of social and cognitive skills. We shall not engage here in a lengthy discussion of these other consequences of communication and its development. Such a discussion would embroil us in the entire complexity of issues surrounding children's intellectual, symbolic, and linguistic capabilities, all being beyond the scope of this book. But, in order to indicate some ways in which social interaction and intellectual functioning are intertwined at the start of life, we will look at some aspects of infant-adult communication.

One role of communication between infant and adult is as a precursor to the infant's later acquisition of verbal language. As indicated at the beginning of this chapter, some researchers have linked the child's language development to the earliest forms of *interactional synchrony* between mother and newborn. While such hypothetical connections remain speculative pending longitudinal evidence, it is perfectly plausible that certain prelinguistic exchanges between infants and adults do establish for the infant a conceptual base upon which actual language is later built. These early prelinguistic exchanges have been called *protocommunication* in the psychological literature.[76] Such exchanges include some aspects of full-fledged communication, such as turn-taking and a shared interest in maintaining the interaction, but they cannot be called

[75] Belsky, 1979.   [76] Fafouti-Milenkovic & Uzgiris, 1979.

communication *per se*. This is because there is not yet an intentional transmission or receipt of information on the part of the baby. Protocommunication is embodied in simple acts like giving and taking, showing and pointing, imitating and gesturing. It may well be a necessary developmental precursor to the acquisition of verbal language at the end of infancy and is certainly the context in which infants are introduced to the possibility of shared meaning between themselves and others (see, for example, the photographs of early imitation presented in Figures 2-1 and 2-2). Shared meaning, of course, is the heart of any language system, and it is difficult to see how linguistic capability could be mastered without a grasp of its possibilities.

There is no question that protocommunication develops rapidly in the first months of life, even prior to the infant's first experimentations with words. Imitation, signaling, and other behaviors with protocommunicative significance increase in frequency and intensity throughout infancy. Such increases are due to developmental changes in the infant's behavior. The tendency of the mother to imitate the infant does not change—rather, it is the infant who becomes more imitative with age.[77] Not only does the frequency and intensity of protocommunication increase during infancy, but so too does the quality of protocommunicative acts. For example, protocommunication becomes intentional as the infant's cognitive abilities develop, finally reaching the status of full-fledged "communication."[78]

Other developments in infant-adult protocommunication are best described as a substitution of new patterns for old ones and have implications for the infant's relations with the entire surrounding world. For example, face-to-face reciprocal interactions of the "turn-taking" variety peak in frequency and intensity at about four months of age. After this time, there is less face-to-face interaction between infant and adult, but a new mode of interaction emerges: social exchanges that incorporate an object or an external task.[79] Gradually, the infant's social interactions with adults include playing with a toy or exploring a new part of the world. Initially, the adult with whom the object is shared must be a familiar person, but before long the infant can interact in this manner with unfamiliar persons as well.[80] By the end of the first year, infants are able to share objects or tasks with adults in a purposively cooperative manner (by which is meant, to quote from Trevarthen, "each of the subjects is taking account of the other's interests and objectives in some relation to the extrapersonal context, and is acting to complement the other's response").[81]

With the development of the social capacity to share external tasks and objects with adults, a whole range of opportunities becomes available to the infant. Most important, the infant now has access to the adult's knowledge of the external world. Infant-adult communication begins to have a profound influence on the course of the infant's cognitive development, because the infant

[77] Pawlby, 1977.
[78] Bretherton & Bates, 1979.
[79] Hubley & Trevarthen, 1979.
[80] Fafouti-Milenkovic & Uzgiris, 1979.
[81] Hubley & Trevarthen, 1979.

has developed means with which to sustain and extend adult-child communication to include an external focus. This is one of the many ways in which social interaction, even in its earliest manifestations, reaches into all aspects of human functioning.

Peer Relations in Infancy

In the tumultuous Europe of World War II, Anna Freud and Sophie Dann were able to witness a "natural experiment" in early peer relations.[82] Six German-Jewish infants, orphaned shortly after birth by Hitler's gas chambers, were sent to the same concentration camp, Theresianstadt in Moravia. These children, all of whom were between the ages of six months to a year, were placed in the care of a conscientious but overworked staff in the camp's Ward for Motherless Children. The food and medical treatment were adequate, but there were no opportunities for sustained interaction of any kind with adults. Nor were there toys or other available playthings. Rather, the infants had only each other for companionship and stimulation.

When Theresianstadt was finally liberated by the Russians, the six children—now approximately three years of age—were flown to England, where they eventually came under the care of Sister Sophie Dann. In consideration of the children's almost lifelong association with one another, it was decided to keep them together in their new home. Sister Dann, collaborating with the psychoanalyst Anna Freud, immediately undertook to record systematically the children's behavior in relation to one another, as well as the children's reactions to the new adults in their lives. In this manner, Freud and Dann were able to document the continuing effects on the social lives of six children who were raised during infancy in the unusual condition of rich, stable peer relations, combined with irregular and impoverished adult interaction.

It was immediately clear to Freud and Dann that the six children had formed deep attachments to one another. The children's attachments were quite narrowly focused, extending neither to adults nor to other children beyond their own group:

> The children's positive feeling were centered exclusively in their own group. It was evident that they cared greatly for each other and not at all for anybody or anything else. They had no other wish than to be together and became upset when they were separated from each other, even for short moments. No child would consent to remain upstairs while the others were downstairs, or vice versa, and no child would be taken for a walk or on an errand without the others. If anything of the kind happened, the single child would constantly ask for the other children while the group would fret for the missing child.[83]

---

[82] Freud & Dann, 1951.

[83] Ibid, p. 131.

In contrast, the children's initial relations with new adults had quite the opposite quality. The children were unfriendly to the point of overt hostility. Tantrums, screaming, bad language, and other expressions of anger would greet any attempt by adults to establish social contact with the children. The six children would tolerate adults only while the adults were providing them with basic needs, such as food or clothing. For other kinds of social intercourse, the children turned only to one another.

Interestingly, although the six children showed strong and enduring attachments to each other, in many ways their relations among themselves were quite different from relations usually found between adult attachment figures and infants. For one thing, the six children were surprisingly democratic with each other. No one child, including the oldest, assumed leadership for any extended period of time. Instead, the children would take turns at being leader: one child would tell the others when mealtime began and ended, another child would take the initiative in inventing and organizing group games, and so on. Also, the children were exceedingly sympathetic to one another's distress, and shared responsibility for each other's welfare. The attachments that these children showed in their peer relations were unlike the unilaterally dependent attachments that children normally express toward their caregivers. Rather, the six children expressed their mutual attachments in the context of equal relationships, much as would emotionally bonded peers of any age.

After a few months, the children did begin to establish positive relations with the adults in their new home. The positive relations at first were modeled after the peer interactions that the children experienced with one another, rather than on more usual types of caregiver-child interactions:

> The children's first positive approaches to the adults were made on the basis of their group feelings and differed in quality from the usual demanding, possessive behavior which young children show toward their mothers or mother substitutes. The children began to insist that the members of the staff should have their turn or share; they became sensitive to their feelings, identified with their needs, and considerate of their comfort.[84]

By the end of their first year in England, the children had all showed at least the beginnings of normal relations with adults, including the dependent and possessive qualities (along with signs of separation distress) that the children's initial positive interactions with adults had lacked. Typical child-adult attachments clearly were forming, although these still lacked the intensity and stability of the children's continuing attachments to one another.

The Freud and Dann study attests to the potential power of infant peer relations. In normal family conditions, this potential is never fully exploited. Rarely are infants forced to rely upon peers for their major source of sustained social interaction. In fact, even as a secondary source of social stimulation,

---

[84] Ibid, p. 142.

regular peer contact is largely unavailable to most infants: one group of experts on infancy has estimated that no more than 20 percent of middle-class American parents provide their infants with frequent peer experience.[85] It takes, then, a highly unusual occurrence to test the full potential of peer interaction in the social development of the infant. Freud and Dann had access to such an unusual occurrence, and their data demonstrate that infants at least as young as six months of age can indeed provide each other with the social stimulation essential for normal growth. Further, they do so in a remarkably sensitive and egalitarian way.

What is also striking in the Freud and Dann study is not only the stable and intense personal relations to one another that the six children had established by the time they were three, but also their capacity eventually to form positive relations with new adults. It seems that the attachments that the children were able to establish with one another through all the years of adversity had also enabled the children to maintain their capacity for social relationships with others. Of course, we must also consider the possibility that these infants may have had prior attachments to adults, unbeknownst to Freud and Dann.

The children did show some hostile initial reactions to new people, as well as some other minor psychopathological symptoms (such as unusual oral-gratification needs and high degrees of masturbation). But by and large, the six children came through their catastrophic experience remarkably unimpaired. Unlike other war orphans that the authors had seen, these children showed no grave social, personality, speech, or intellectual deficits. "They were neither deficient, delinquent, nor psychotic."[86] Socially and emotionally they were caring, cheerful, and affectionate, at first only with each other, then later with their adult caregivers. Intellectually, they were bright and open to new learning. They were able to learn a new language (English) with an ease that surprised even their most optimistic teachers. We cannot say that these infant peers were able to provide one another with wholly "secure attachments" in the manner that adults could, since it is impossible to imagine infants performing all the caregiving and communicative acts that mature and responsive adults are capable of. Still, the infants did manage to keep one another socially and psychologically intact, and this in itself is a remarkable testament to the possibilities inherent in infant peer relations.

Developmental Studies of Infant-Infant Interaction

Sustained infant peer relations are not commonplace in normal family circumstances. Not only is this true of Western family life in modern-day society, but it has also been true throughout the course of human history. This

[85] Lewis, Young, Brooks, & Michalson, 1975.   [86] Freud & Dann, 1951, p. 168.

is probably because they are not required for the biological survival of the child. Actual biological survival aside, the psychological value of infant peer relations (that is, their potential for contributing to the child's emotional and intellectual well-being) has been evident only in highly unusual life circumstances, such as those witnessed by Freud and Dann. Under normal circumstances, infant peer relations have never appeared to have much adaptive value, psychologically or socially. Behavioral research often ignores uncommon phenomena whose adaptive significance is uncertain. Perhaps for this reason, few investigations on infant-infant interaction were attempted in the first five decades of scientific research in child psychology. In fact, only in the past ten years has the development of infant peer relations been studied systematically and frequently.[87]

Within this relatively new area of inquiry, there is some controversy concerning the interpretation of findings on infant peer interactions. The dispute is between those who emphasize the sophistication and mutuality of infant peer interactions and those who do not. In many ways, as we shall see, the dispute is a matter of emphasis. Both sides agree that, during the second year of life, toddlers do begin engaging in some instances of extended, reciprocal social exchanges with their peers. Some investigators, however, claim that such instances are so rare and situationally specific that they tell us little about infants' social capabilities. Others believe that such behavior does indeed reflect a critical area of social competence that develops in most toddlers. As we shall see, both parties to this dispute agree on the data, but disagree on the developmental significance of those data. For our purposes here, we shall attempt to blend both sides of the controversy into a balanced account of infant peer relations.

All observers agree that infants show little special interest in one another during the first six months of life. When placed close to one another, infants as young as two or three months may look at and even touch one another, but only in the same manner that they use to explore any novel object.[88] Between six and nine months, infants show a more particularized interest in peers, smiling at each other's vocalizations and following one another around rooms (see Figure 2-5).[89] But it is not until nine months or so that infants engage in peer behavior that some have called truly social. At this point, infants begin offering and taking objects from one another.[90] Soon thereafter, infants have been observed to play primitive peer games, like run-and-chase or peek-a-boo.[91] By the second year of life, infants take turns with one another in play, intentionally imitate one another's behavior, and even engage in short "conversations," although not always with the use of intelligible language.[92]

Once infants do discover the social potential of their peers, they seem to do so with increasing eagerness.[93] One study of infants from ten months to two

[87] Mueller & Vandell, 1978.
[88] Buhler, 1933.
[89] Bridges, 1933.
[90] Vincze, 1971.

[91] Eckerman & Whatley, 1977.
[92] Eckerman, Whatley, & Kutz, 1975.
[93] Holmberg, 1981.

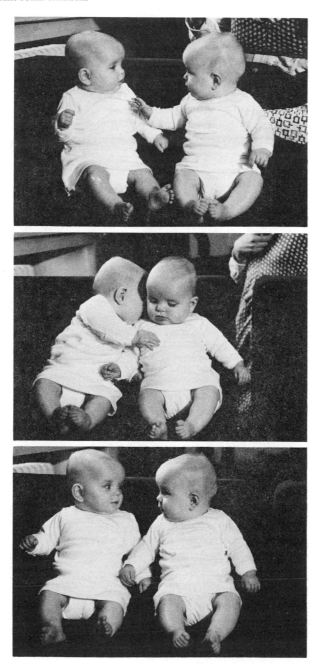

Figure 2-5. Seven-month-old Twins Interacting with One Another. Twin babies usually become closely attuned to each other when quite young.

Source: T. G. R. Bower, *A Primer of Infant Development*. San Francisco: W. H. Freeman, 1977, p. 57. Photos by Jennifer G. Wishart. Reprinted with permission.

years of age found that, when placed in a room with both their mothers and another infant, infants preferred playing with their peers to playing with their mothers.[94] The younger infants in this age range (the ten-month-olds) were shown to direct more looks and following behavior to their peers than to their mothers. The older infants (the "toddlers" between one and two years of age) were shown to converse with, imitate, and exchange toys with their peers more frequently than with their mothers.

The only infant behavior that has been found consistently to be directed more toward mothers than toward peers is tactile contact like touching, holding, and hugging.[95] By the second year of life, infants prefer to engage in *proximate* behaviors (like touching) more with their mothers than with their peers; but, given the opportunity for peer interaction, they engage in *distal* behaviors (looking, imitating, vocalizing) more with peers.[96] Commentators have pointed out that even the rare study not replicating this conclusion provides no evidence in contradiction of it.[97] Again, we see in the vast majority of these studies further confirmation of the (often untapped) social potential of infant peer relations.

The Quality of Infant-Infant Interaction

Despite the studies that show infant peer interaction, there are those who believe that such interaction in the second year of life has been much overrated. For example, Wanda Bronson points out that, in all of the infant and toddler studies thus far, the actual *incidence* of peer interaction is strikingly low.[98] Further, she writes that the *quality* of infant and toddler peer interaction should not be called "mutual" or "reciprocal," as several writers have done. Generally, she believes that these investigators' own data have shown that infants and toddlers rarely sustain interactions with one another beyond brief "bursts" of activity. On the rare occasion when they do so, it is usually to fight over a mutually desired toy. This can hardly be considered the stuff of intimate social relations!

Bronson's own observations of toddler peers revealed very few behavioral *contact chains* (that is, sustained, sequential exchanges in which the two peers modify their activity in order to respond to one another's behavior). Most of the "chains" that she did observe were disputes over the same toy, an event that Bronson considers to be a "special case of early social behavior." Contact chains of a more positive sort, centering around games or prosocial communication, were extremely rare. Bronson did observe, however, a small but noticeable increase in these positive types of peer interaction toward the end of the toddlers' second year.

---

[94] Rubenstein & Howeds, 1976.
[95] Lenssen, 1975.
[96] Lewis, Young, Brooks, & Michalson, 1975.

[97] Lamb, 1980.
[98] Bronson, 1981.

In addition to Bronson's critique, we should note that peer interactions during infancy have none of the exquisite qualities of adult-infant interaction that we discussed at the beginning of this chapter. To the contrary, research consistently has shown that social interactions between infants lag behind adult-infant interactions developmentally, remaining in many respects less sophisticated throughout all of infancy. Nothing like the mother-child reciprocity reported by Brazelton, Stern, and others has been found in infant peer relations. Yet the Brazelton and Stern findings on mother-child interaction extend down to the early weeks of life. Commenting upon this discrepancy, Edward Mueller and Deborah Vandell have written:

> The parents [in the Brazelton and the Stern studies] were always available for engaging their infants' eyes. Their "mother love" made them into almost perfect engagement-affording creatures to their largely incompetent offspring. . .The situation vis-à-vis peers is very different. Even if an *en face* position could be sustained, which is doubtful given weakness of neck musculature, the biological rhythms of attention and withdrawal would prevent all but random synchronies in their gaze. Therefore, purely on the basis of relative affordances, it is possible to conclude that normal parent-infant engagement will occur prior to normal peer engagement.[99]

Even by toddlerhood, there is still a developmental gap between the two types of interactions. Vandell compared mother-toddler and toddler-toddler interactions and found that initial attempts to interact were far more likely to be successful between mother and child than between child and child and that the interactions that did take place were significantly longer in the mother-toddler case.[100] Once again, such differences between adult-infant and infant-infant interactions no doubt stem from the greater ability of the adult to sustain an interaction with an infant by acting in ways that are complementary to the infant's behavior. Mothers are certainly more likely to be responsive to their infant than are other infants. Vandell's data directly confirm this, since mothers were found almost without fail to respond to their toddler's attempts to initiate an interaction, whereas toddlers were quite irregular in their responsiveness to one another.

A further contrast between adult-infant and infant-infant interactions may be seen in the infant's first constructions of social games with others. Jerome Bruner and his colleagues have studied the genesis of the peek-a-boo game between adult and child.[101] Infants as young as six months can be seen to play this game with adults, although initially the infant's role is limited to that of the observer who is delightfully surprised by the "peek-a-boo." By the end of the first year, however, infants may assume the role of the superior in their games with adults; not long into the second year, they freely switch back and forth between the two roles. This shows a sense of "role reversal" in the infants' interactions with the adult. In peer relations during the first two years

---

[99] Mueller & Vandell, 1978, p. 317.   [101] Bruner & Sherwood, 1976.
[100] Vandell, 1976.

of life, role reversal seems to be a much rarer phenomenon. Mueller and Lucas described three stages of social interaction that they observed among groups of toddlers in free-play settings.[102] Only at the final stage of interaction did infants show role reversals in their play with one another. Although Mueller and Lucas did not report data regarding the relative frequency of stage 3 interactions in their toddler groups, it is clear from a further report by Mueller and Brenner that such behavior is rarely seen in toddlers younger than eighteen months to two years.[103] Similarly, Catherine Garvey has shown that, in children's verbal play with peers, role reversals are a relatively late development.[104] In fact, in Garvey's study, role reversals in children's verbal interactions with one another were not found until three or four years of age. This, of course, is in marked contrast to the infant-adult role reversals observed by Bruner in infants not long after their first birthday.

The Mueller and Lucas stages of toddler peer interaction also demonstrate another contrast between adult-infant and infant-infant interaction: the different roles played by objects in the development of these two types of early social relations. We have already seen that initial parent-child interactions require no object to bring the two parties together. Although the baby bottle and the feeding situation may provide one context for a mother's social engagement with her infant, there are many others as well, for example, the times when the mother simply holds or plays with the infant directly. The notion that mother-infant attachment derives from more "primary" objects of need such as food has been thoroughly discounted by recent accounts of both animal and human social relations. Further, Trevarthen's research (summarized earlier) indicates that mother-child interactions that incorporate objects do not appear until well after other, more direct, communication sequences between mother and infant have been established.

The early development of peer interaction, as studied by Mueller and Lucas, seems quite different. They, along with a number of other researchers working independently, have asserted that initial peer contacts between infants take place around objects of mutual interest, rather than through direct communication or play with one another. This also accords with Bronson's findings concerning toy possession, noted above. Mueller and Lucas's stages of toddler peer interaction apply to toddlers between the ages of one and two. Their first stage is one of "object-centered contacts":

> The prevalence of object-centered contacts during the initial meetings of a play group of 1-year-olds may be explained by (their) relative deficiency in peer-appropriate strategies. Having had experience with objects, 1-year-olds with no peer experience are far better prepared to act effectively on objects than on their age mates. Whereas object-centered contacts reflect the toddler's lack of peer-appropriate stategies, the simultaneous exploration of common objects by two or more children provides more opportunity to gain more understanding of their peers.[105]

[102] Mueller & Lucas, 1975.
[103] Mueller & Brenner, 1977.

[104] Garvey, 1974.
[105] Mueller & Lucas, 1975, p. 229.

In Mueller and Lucas's view, objects provide a ground for initial peer contact; and, by so doing, they afford infants an opportunity to get to know one another. In this manner, object contacts lead the way toward more reciprocal and interactive peer encounters. For example, two toddlers may be drawn together by an interesting toy that can only be used by one child at a time. Initially, the children are aware only of the toy, ignoring the other child's presence. But to gain access to the toy, the children are forced to take turns with one another. This is a rudimentary system of social exchange, and participating in such an exchange acquaints a child with one means of regulating peer relations. Thus, the somewhat accidental peer interaction established by the object contact generates a social experience that helps the child develop more advanced ways of interacting with peers.

At stage 2 of toddler peer interactions, toddlers directly show mutual interest in one another's activities. They actively respond to each other's behaviors, and then, in turn, respond to the responses of the other. In this manner, extended interaction sequences are built up. Reciprocal activities like turn-taking are pursued for their own sake, rather than simply as means to get to a desirable object.

Mueller and Lucas's third stage of infant peer interaction has been described above. At this stage, children participate in role reversals with each other: "Thus the child who offered an object in turn received one, and the child who received an object offered one."[106] Because role reversals require some understanding of the other's point of view, as well as some flexibility of behavior, they are the most advanced of the toddler peer interactions observed by Mueller and Lucas.

A longitudinal study of toddlers by Mueller and Brenner confirmed empirically much of the stage progression outlined by Mueller and Lucas.[107] Toddlers at twelve months of age engaged in object-centered contacts during 92 percent of their peer interactions, whereas by eighteen months of age, toddlers engaged in such contacts only 69 percent of the time, a significant decrease. Replacing the object-centered contacts in the older infants' interactions were peer-centered exchanges of a more socially developed nature. However, even the oldest toddlers in the Mueller-Brenner study still were engaging most of the time in object-centered interactions with their peers. Although the relative frequency of this primitive type of peer interaction had decreased with age, it still predominated in the toddlers' group play through the end of their infancy. This was again confirmed in a further study showing that "shared meaning" in toddlers' interactions revolves mainly around toys and issues of possession, a finding not unlike the conclusions reached by Bronson, noted above.[108]

In sum, two differences between infant interactions with adults and with peers have been found in recent research: (1) infants engage in sophisticated

---

[106] Mueller & Vandell, 1978, p. 597.
[107] Mueller & Brenner, 1977.
[108] Brenner & Mueller, 1982.

forms of reciprocal social interaction with adults long before they do so with peers; and (2) initial infant-infant interactions, unlike initial infant-adult interactions, rely on objects as vehicles for social exchange. Now it may well be that the second difference is at least partly connected to the first one. In other words, the relative lateness of infant-peer interaction may be related to the centrality of the object in initial peer encounters. In fact, infants show a marked increase in their eagerness to explore objects at about nine months of age.[109] It seems more than coincidental that this is also the time when, according to Trevarthen, objects are incorporated into mother-child communication sequences and that the first peer object-centered contacts appear. The infant's increasing awareness of the external world may not only afford the infant more extended communication channels with the parent, but it may also open up (though inadvertently at first) the pathway to peer relations. The child's interest in objects may derive at least partly from the increasingly powerful communication system emerging from the parent-child relation. No doubt the causal influences work both ways: the child's interest in objects fosters the growth of social interaction centered around objects at the same time as the child's increasingly sophisticated social communications with the parent encourage a greater interest in objects.

In normal circumstances, infants rarely exploit their full potential for establishing social relations with peers. Fortunately, the catastrophic situation witnessed by Freud and Dann seldom occurs in contemporary Western society, and perhaps unfortunately, most parents do not go out of their way to arrange sustained peer experiences for their infants. Because the studies summarized here were all done with modern-day Western children, it is impossible to determine how much they tell us about the potential developmental course of peer interaction in other life circumstances. Perhaps in other social conditions, there would not be such a marked lag between infant-infant and adult-infant interaction. Perhaps objects would not play such a central role in facilitating initial interactions between infants. (Remember, peer relations among Freud and Dann's six war orphans flourished even when, as young infants, the six were placed together in an environment lacking toys.) To explore the true potential of infant-infant relations, we must await fundamental changes in our social arrangements. Until then, our scientific understanding of infants will be constrained by the limits of our child-rearing practices and our family-home environments.

Facilitating Peer Interactions among Infants

If we, individually as parents or collectively as a society, decide it worthwhile to encourage our infants to interact more with their peers, recent research has provided us with some guidelines concerning how such greater interaction may be facilitated. Societal changes, such as the increasing use of

---

[109] Piaget, 1954; Vandell, Wilson, & Buchanan, 1980.

infant day care, indeed may impel us to take such guidelines seriously: this may be our best means of providing our infants with maximally rich social experience even while absent from their parents for long stretches of working time.

The nature of the infant's physical setting has been found to influence the extent to which infants will interact with one another. Above all, a familiar environment is conducive to infant peer interactions. This means that infants tend to be more interactive with peers in their own homes than in strangers' homes and that the more they become familiar with a new setting, the more they are likely to become socially oriented to their peers.[110]

Toys can encourage peers to initiate interactions with one another. Sometimes these initial interactions may have a somewhat negative affective tone, as when two infants fight over the same toy. This is a main point in Wanda Bronson's critique. It has been reported that infant conflict is only found when there are play materials that interest both infants.[111] The condition for maximal conflict is when there is only one toy available for two infants. Such conflict, of course, is accompanied by some negative feelings on the part of the infants. But, from a developmental point of view, such conflict is not all negative. The turn-taking and sharing that it forces have major implications for the infants' early social development. It is through such episodes, often accidental and unpleasant, that infants may acquire the initial social experiences that enable them to learn about the characteristics of peers and peer relations. This is not to say that such learning could not take place without object play or object conflict. Certainly the Freud and Dann report of the six object-deprived but highly interactive orphans is evidence to the contrary. But it is clear that toys can be a useful, if not a necessary, medium for early peer interaction and that even initial negative interactions around toys may have positive developmental consequences.

Perhaps the major influence on infant peer interaction (not unlike many other kinds of social interaction) is the nature and number of the infant's social partners. Studies conducted by Michael Lewis and his colleagues suggest that an infant is more likely to interact with an infant his own age than with an older child. Lewis concludes that "play with older children might be too threatening for infants, whereas play with those who have more equal capacities and skills is less threatening, hence is more facilitating for subsequent peer interactions."[112]

Amount of experience with peers also influences infant peer interactions. Mueller and Rich compared toddlers who had had four-and-a-half months of peer experience with toddlers who had had little or no peer experience.[113] Both groups interacted with the same frequency, but the experienced infants interacted with greater social sophistication. That is, the experienced children were more likely to engage in reciprocal or complementary social behavior (as in

[110] Mueller & Vandell, 1978.

[111] Maudry & Nekula, 1939.

[112] Lewis, Young, Brooks & Michalson, 1975, p. 58.

[113] Mueller & Rich, 1976.

role reversals) and to build up extended social interactions by coordinating one social act with another (such as looking and vocalizing, offering and sharing a toy, and so on). Therefore the quality, but not the quantity, of the infants' peer play was improved by prior peer experience. These findings apply to an infant's prior experience in general, and not simply to the specific playmate with whom the infant was observed to be interacting. There is also some evidence that infant peers who are familiar with each other are more likely to interact than those who are not. In particular, acquainted peers are more likely to touch, smile at, seek proximity with, and generally act "friendlier" to each other than are unacquainted peers.[114] Again, the differences in the quality of interactions between infant "friends" and "non-friends" are more striking than are the differences in the quantity of interactions.

Finally, observers have consistently found that infant-peer relations are generally conducted in groups no larger than pairs.[115] Not only are peer dyads the overwhelming norm during infancy, but it seems that they are also the best forum for infants to develop social interaction skills. Deborah Vandell followed six toddlers for six months as they participated in both pairs and in larger groups.[116] She found that during the dyadic encounters, the toddlers increasingly interacted in more developmentally sophisticated ways throughout the six-month period. Their peer interactions were more extended, complex, complementary, and socially coordinated. In the larger group settings, however, there were no developmental advances in the infants' peer interactions. Reflecting on the advantages of dyadic over larger group encounters for infants, Mueller and Vandell write, "The dyad may help the infant to focus his behavior on a social partner. In the group situation, the numerous peers may divert and distract the infant from the attention needed for successful interaction."[117]

Summary

Infants are participants in social relations from the start of life. Although they probably do not do so intentionally, infants initiate and respond to social interaction with caregivers almost from the moment of birth. Initially, the infant's means of initiating social interaction are limited to crying, sucking, and other expressions of discomfort and hunger. Although crude and undirected, such nonconscious means of initiating interaction have assured infants of survival within the human community for countless generations. In addition, infants in the days and weeks after birth have been shown to respond with particular intensity to social interaction and communication from adults. Newborn infants move their bodies in synchrony with their parents' voices,

[114] Lewis, Young, Brooks, & Michalson, 1975.

[115] Bronson, 1975; Mueller & Vandell, 1978.

[116] Vandell, 1976.

[117] Mueller & Vandell, 1978, p. 602.

they maintain eye contact with adults at regular intervals, they smoothly and rhythmically build up long periods of attention in other people, and they "take turns" in reciprocally exchanging vocal sounds and gestures with their parents. Much of the well-timed and well-patterned turn-taking in adult-newborn social exchanges is no doubt due to the adult's sophisticated manner of maintaining reciprocal interactions by injecting sounds and gestures at appropriate intervals in the "conversation." Nevertheless, the infant's responsiveness and active participation in such early *protocommunications* is undeniable evidence of the infant's early social disposition.

Before long, infants develop new and more powerful ways of initiating interaction with their caregivers. To crying and sucking are added such means of signaling and approaching the caregiver as smiling, babbling, cooing, clinging, and following. The cluster of behaviors that infants use to contact their caregivers has been called *attachment behaviors* because of their common function of bringing the infant into proximity with a caregiver. Some writers have claimed that the overall goal of seeking proximity with a caregiver is biologically based in the infant's constitution, and that it is this inherited goal that explains the universality of attachment behaviors in the early months of life. Others have emphasized the infant's emotional need for *felt security* as the guiding factor in the infant's attempts to seek proximity with an attachment figure.

Developmentally, infants progress through four phases in their attachments to their caregivers. During the first eight to twelve weeks of life, infants indiscriminately promote contact with others through babbling, crying, looking, smiling, and so on. This is called the *preattachment* phase because the infant has not established bonds with particular people. The next phase, *attachment-in-the-making*, takes place from the end of phase 1 until seven months to a year. The infant now begins focusing on familiar persons and expends special efforts in seeking proximity with her primary caregiver. The phase of *clear-cut-attachment* is next, from the end of phase 2 until the second or third year of life. The infant may protest at the impending departure of the primary caregiver, but, if securely attached, will be able to use the caregiver as a base from which to explore the world. The fourth phase, which extends from the end of phase 3 onward, sees the beginning of a fully communicative caregiver-child relation in which the two share each others thoughts, feelings, and goals. An experimental technique called the *strange situation* has been used with success to assess the quality of attachments demonstrated by one-year-old infants. Individual differences between infants' patterns of attachments to their mothers have been identified and connected with the infants' ability to explore the world and interact with other people.

The nature of a child's early relations with his caregiver has long-range consequences for the child, in particular with regard to the child's later social development. Such consequences, however, are neither absolute nor irreversible. The shock of early, long-term separations from the caregiver can be alleviated by good-quality social relations with other people during the time of the separation. A good-quality caregiver-child relation prior to the separation can help. Many others beyond the primary caregiver can also fulfill the infant's attachment-related needs. Later experience can do much to remediate the effects of early caregiver-child adversities. There is no one-way, cause-and-effect relation between children's early experiences with their caregivers and their later life experiences. Nevertheless, children are not infinitely plastic, and early attachments do count. A good caregiver-infant relation provides the foundation for the child's subsequent psychological growth, and an unfortunate relation may have continued, multiple adverse influences on the child well beyond the time of infancy. Although early attachment does not establish an irrevocable legacy, it can provide a preview of later strengths and weaknesses in a child's interactions with the world.

Adult-infant social interactions have a meaning beyond the infant's need for secure attachment figures. Among other things, they provide a forum for the child's development of communication and language skills. At the end of the infant's first year, adult-infant interactions often incorporate external objects or tasks. Through sharing a toy or a game with an adult, the infant gains access to some of the adult's knowledge of the world. In this manner, the extension of adult-infant interactions to include object-focused communications goes hand in hand with the infant's increasing awareness of the external world.

When given the opportunity, infants can conduct rich social relations with peers as well as with adults. Sustained infant-infant interactions begin well after sustained adult-infant interactions. The point at which peers commonly begin interacting with one another in an extended, natural manner is the subject of current dispute in the research literature. But there is no question that peer relations lag behind adult-infant relations in closeness and sophistication. This lag is no doubt due to the superior abilities of adults to maintain exchanges with infants by carefully gauging their responses to infants' social behaviors. But once infants begin interacting with other infants, they do so eagerly, sometimes preferring play with infants over play with their own parents. There is even some evidence that, in extreme circumstances, infant-infant relations can substitute for adult-infant relations in providing infants with essential social stimulation. In such cases, the infant-infant relations still maintain their peer flavor, being more democratic and less dependent than normal caregiver-child relations.

In modern-day Western society, infant-peer relations often begin with accidental (and usually negative) contacts fostered by a mutual interest in the same object. Such *object-centered contacts* encourage infants to develop rudimentary social interchanges such as turn-taking and sharing. Soon infants pursue peer interactions for their own sake. At the end of infancy, sophisticated social behaviors like *role reversals* begin to appear in infants' peer play.

Although parents do not encourage infants to interact with other infants with any great regularity, research has provided us with guidelines on how to facilitate infant peer relations. Infants interact with one another most readily in familiar settings and in the presence of sharable objects. They interact most easily with peers of their own age and with peer "friends" with whom they are already acquainted. Most importantly, their social exchanges take place primarily in pairs; larger groups distract their interactional attention.

Chapter 3

Infant Individuality
and the Origins of Self

As with sociability, the roots of individuality go all the way back to the beginning of life. Theoretically, it could be no other way. Even at day 1, there must be something upon which subsequent development through the life span is based. As Heinz Werner is reputed to have said, "Something is not growing out of nothing!"[1] The challenge for the developmental psychologist is to recognize the rudimentary initial "versions" of lifelong capacities and to chart the developmental links between early and later behaviors—despite how different from one another these behaviors may appear at first glance.

In this chapter, we shall discuss the first signs of individuality in the newborn and shall follow the subsequent development of individuality and "self" through the end of the infancy period. This will prepare us for further

---

[1] Werner's remark was made in reference to the once-fashionable psychoanalytic notion that humans are born without rational facilities and only later become oriented toward making sense out of reality (Wyss, 1973). With the advent of the "ego psychology" school of psychoanalysis, this notion was abandoned in favor of the view that even young infants had mechanisms, albeit primitive ones, for perceiving and knowing the real world outside themselves. The lifelong continuity of psychological development was thereby established in psychoanalytic theory.

discussions of personality and social identity in the childhood and adolescence chapters.

The individual and social aspects of a person's development influence one another in a number of ways. Examples of this can be seen early in infancy. Chapter 2 documented the two-way nature of interactions between adult and child even at the start of life. The newborn infant is an active (though not fully intentional) participant in social interactions, initiating contact with the caregiver through crying, and maintaining contact through gazing, synchronized bodily movements, and other signs of social responsiveness. As more advanced behavioral capacities develop, the infant becomes an active participant in more sophisticated types of social exchange. In an important sense, therefore, the infant helps determine the character of the social interactions in which she engages; the same may be said of the child and the adult throughout life. Chapter 2 presented the developmental side of the infant's contribution to her own social experience, showing how infants participate in different types of social relations as they grow older and that their own developing skills and capacities influence the manner of this participation. Consequently, we conclude that the infant's own developmental state determines to some extent the nature of her social experience.[2]

The point *not* made in Chapter 2, but instead saved for the present chapter, is that *individual* differences between infants also influence the nature of the social interactions that the infants experience. From birth onward, individual infants approach and conduct interactions with parents and others in widely varying ways. Such individually based variations have multiple consequences for the social lives and the subsequent social and personal development of the individual infants. Although a child's social self is by no means preprogrammed at birth, neither is the child born as a figureless lump of clay, interchangeable with any other lump. Even at the beginning of life, certain individual characteristics may lead an infant to undergo a certain type of social experience, and this in turn may predispose the infant to develop in one rather than another direction. Constitution at birth is not destiny, but neither is it wholly plastic, blank, or slatelike, to mix a few of the popular metaphors.

We shall, therefore, begin our discussion of infant individuality with a consideration of early individual differences that seem to have important social and personal consequences for infants. Later in the chapter, we shall discuss another aspect of infant individuality: the early construction of the self. Certainly these two aspects of individuality are related, since the self is, in part, based upon one's awareness of the ways in which one is unique—that is, different from others. But at least conceptually these two aspects of individuality are distinct, and they have spawned different theoretical and research traditions. The first has been deemed the study of "differences among selves," the second the study of "the development of self in relation to others."

[2] Green, Gustafson, & West, 1980.

Infant Individual Differences and Their Social Consequences

Infants vary in a number of ways, but before we discuss these variations, two cautionary notes are in order. First, even if we observe variation between infants very early in life, this does not necessarily mean that it is due solely to biogenetic factors. Personal tendencies generally emerge in the context of social relations at the beginning of life as well as later: if an infant shows a unique way of behaving, this uniqueness most likely is manifested, and probably arose, in interactions with someone else. As we saw in Chapter 2, the infant is open to social influence from the start. There are few, if any, individual differences in behavior that have not been, in part, formed through social interaction.

Our second cautionary note concerns the stability of the individual differences that are found in infancy. As we shall see, some investigators claim to have found enduring patterns of behavior that are detectable as early as six months of age. Others, however, have reported great variation and little consistency between infants' early characteristics and their later behavior.[3] Some have asserted that, where there is stability in an infant's behavior over time, this is due primarily to stability in the persons with whom the infant interacts.[4] In other words, it may be stability in the *caregiver's* characteristics, rather than in the infant's, that leads to consistency in the infant's behavior over time. Others have emphasized more the *interaction* between caregiver and child, claiming that it is this, and not individual characteristics of either person, that retains a stability over time.[5] We shall not resolve this controversy here, but we shall consider both sides and shall be cautious in drawing our conclusions.

Responsiveness to Social Interaction

A small but consistent body of research has shown that infants often differ dramatically from one another in their responsiveness to social interaction. Such differences, in turn, may effect the infant's relations with his caregiver for better or for worse. In their study of parent-child attachment, H. Rudolf Schaffer and P. E. Emerson observed that some babies could be described as "cuddlers" and other as "noncuddlers."[6] The cuddlers were those who showed pleasure and were easily comforted by the parents' hugs. The noncuddlers were more active, wiry, and resistant to physical contact. Not surprisingly, the cuddlers received warmer and more affectionate treatment from their parents than did the noncuddlers. Schaffer and Emerson believe that the cuddliness of an infant exists prior to parental treatment and is not merely a result of it. Michael Rutter has also reported that babies with certain predispositions receive better treatment in their families than do others.[7] For example, children with irregular sleeping habits, unfastidious eating patterns, and frequent

---

[3] Sameroff & Chandler, 1975; Sameroff, 1978; Waters, 1978.

[4] Blehar, Lieberman, & Ainsworth, 1977.

[5] Emde, 1980.

[6] Schaffer & Emerson, 1964b.

[7] Rutter, 1978.

negative moods were far more likely to draw parental criticism than were their more pleasant peers. Of course, as noted above, babies might *become* more or less cuddly or pleasant as a consequence of early handling. Neither study, however, has clearly established a direct causal connection between infant characteristics and parental treatment.

Michael Lamb and his colleagues have designed procedures for assessing individual differences in infant sociability.[8] Dimensions measured by this scale include social responsiveness, cooperativeness, and general emotional tone. Lamb reports that infants vary to a moderately large degree in their scores on this measure, and that the measure itself is reasonably reliable.[9] On the basis of these findings, Lamb refers to infant sociability as a trait, indicating his belief that this is a personal characteristic that can be used to distinguish individuals across different contexts.[10] Nevertheless, test-retest correlations for this measure were not significant over a one-year period.[11] This sheds some doubt on the temporal stability of this "trait."

Temperament

Some infant individual differences with social consequences do seem to be surprisingly stable throughout the early years of life. In an ambitious nine-year research project called the New York Longitudinal Study, Alexander Thomas, Stella Chess, and Herbert Birch followed the temperamental development of 138 infants from when they were born through their elementary school years.[12] The researchers focused on nine aspects of temperament that can be observed in very young infants: (1) activity level, (2) rhythmicity (or regularity) of behavior, (3) distractibility, (4) approach or withdrawal when confronted by a new experience, (5) adaptability to change, (6) attention span (or persistence), (7) intensity of reaction to stimuli, (8) threshold of responsiveness (or amount of stimulation needed to evoke a discernible response), and (9) quality of mood. On the basis of parent's observations of their own children taken at regular intervals throughout the first ten years of the children's lives, Thomas, Chess, and Birch have concluded that the original characteristics of temperament tend to persist in most children over the years. Table 3-1 illustrates some of these temperamental continuities.

Clearly, many of the temperamental differences that distinguish young infants from each other have social implications in infancy as well as later in childhood. A highly active child will initiate and conduct different sorts of social interactions with parents and peers than will a less active child, and likewise for each of the other categories of temperamental differences. Particularly striking implications of temperament can be seen in the social interactions of children who show certain combinations of temperamental characteristics.

[8] Stevenson & Lamb, 1979; Lamb, 1981, 1982.
[9] Lamb, 1982, p. 218.
[10] Ibid., p. 214.

[11] Ibid., p. 218.
[12] Thomas, Chess, & Birch, 1968; Thomas & Chess, 1977.

Thomas and his colleagues have suggested three combinations that especially affect children's relations with the social environment. Children who are very regular and adaptable and who show positive moods and positive approaches to new experience are considered "easy" children. These are the children who have few behavioral problems and get along well with parents and friends from the time of infancy onward. Children who are relatively inactive, slowly adaptable, and who show slightly negative moods, mildly intense reactions, and withdrawal in new situations are considered "slow to warm up." These are the children who are shy, indifferent, or negative upon first contact with others, but who soon act in ways that are indistinguishable from their "easy" peers. Children who are irregular in their eating and sleeping habits, who withdraw in new situations, who are slowly adaptable, intense in their reactions, and negative in their moods are considered "difficult" children. Many such children encounter criticism and other negative reactions from parents, as the Rutter study cited above indicates. Also, these children seem more likely than others to have behavioral problems in home and school. In Thomas, Chess, and Birch's sample, 23 percent of the difficult children were in the researcher's "behavior problem" group, as opposed to 4 percent of the other subjects.

The New York Longitudinal Study has been criticized because its methodology relied heavily on parental and teacher observations for the assessment of subjects' temperamental characteristics.[13] The main concern has been that parents and teachers may not be able to make unbiased judgments about the children with whom they are intimately involved. The researchers attempted to answer this concern by doing further empirical work. Members of the original research team independently observed about a fifth of the children in the study, both when the children were infants and when they had grown to school age. The researchers' own assessments compared favorably with those of the parents and teachers. The researchers interpret this as an indication that, far from being invalid or unreliable, parental and teacher ratings were particularly accurate because the parents and teachers had extended opportunities to become familiar with the children and their temperamental dispositions.

There is another sense, however, in which the results of the New York Longitudinal Study may be open to criticism. Because parents, teachers, and other adults (members of the research team included) make up the social world with which the child must interact, it is clear that the same people (or at least people from the same social milieu) who assessed subjects' temperaments in this study were those with whom the subjects did or did not have behavioral problems. For this reason, it is impossible to determine from this sort of data the precise relations between children's temperamental characteristics and the nature of their social relations. Were the adults who assessed temperament and those who decided which children had behavioral problems simply responding to the same thing twice in the subjects? Many of the characteristics of "difficult" children may themselves be seen as "problems" to adults. Or did the

---

[13] Lamb, 1978.

Table 3–1 Temperamental Continuities

Temperamental Quality	*Rating*	*2 months*	*6 months*
ACTIVITY LEVEL	HIGH	Moves often in sleep. Wriggles when diaper is changed.	Tries to stand in tub and splashes. Bounces in crib. Crawls after dog.
	LOW	Does not move when being dressed or during sleep.	Passive in bath. Plays quietly in crib and falls asleep.
RHYTHMI-CITY	REGULAR	Has been on four-hour feeding schedule since birth. Regular bowel movement.	Is asleep at 6:30 every night. Awakes at 7:00 A.M. Food intake is constant.
	IRREGULAR	Awakes at a different time each morning. Size of feeding varies.	Length of nap varies; so does food intake.
DISTRACT-IBILITY	DIS-TRACTIBLE	Will stop crying for food if rocked. Stops fussing if given pacifier when diaper is being changed.	Stops crying when mother sings. Will remain still while clothing is changed if given a toy.
	NOT DIS-TRACTIBLE	Will not stop crying when diaper is changed. Fusses after eating, even if rocked.	Stops crying only after dressing is finished. Cries until given bottle.
THRESHOLD OF RESPONSIVE-NESS	LOW	Stops sucking on bottle when approached.	Refuses fruit he likes when vitamins are added. Hides head from bright light.
	HIGH	Is not startled by loud noises. Takes bottle and breast equally well.	Eats everything. Does not object to diapers being wet or soiled.

Source: Adapted from A. Thomas, S. Chess, & H. Birch, The origin of personality. *Scientific American*, 1970, *223*, 108–9. Reprinted with permission.

Table 3–1 (Cont.)

1 year	2 years	5 years	10 years
Walks rapidly. Eats eagerly. Climbs into everything.	Climbs furniture. Explores. Gets in and out of bed while being put to sleep.	Leaves table often during meals. Always runs.	Plays ball and engages in other sports. Cannot sit still long enough to do homework.
Finishes bottle slowly. Goes to sleep easily. Allows nail cutting without fussing.	Enjoys quiet play with puzzles. Can listen to records for hours.	Takes a long time to dress. Sits quietly on long automobile rides.	Likes chess and reading. Eats very slowly.
Naps after lunch each day. Always drinks bottle before bed.	Eats a big lunch each day. Always has a snack before bedtime.	Falls asleep when put to bed. Bowel movement regular.	Eats only at mealtimes. Sleeps the same amount of time each night.
Will not fall asleep for an hour or more. Moves bowels at a different time each day.	Nap time changes from day to day. Toilet training is difficult because bowel movement is unpredictable.	Food intake varies; so does time of bowel movement.	Food intake varies. Falls asleep at a different time each night.
Cries when face is washed unless it is made into a game.	Will stop tantrum if another activity is suggested.	Can be coaxed out of forbidden activity by being led into something else.	Needs absolute silence for homework. Has a hard time choosing a shirt in a store because they all appeal to him.
Cries when toy is taken away and rejects substitute.	Screams if refused some desired object. Ignores mother's calling.	Seems not to hear if involved in favorite activity. Cries for a long time when hurt.	Can read a book while television set is at high volume. Does chores on schedule.
Spits out food he does not like. Giggles when tickled.	Runs to door when father comes home. Must always be tucked tightly into bed.	Always notices when mother puts new dress on for first time. Refuses milk if it is not ice cold.	Rejects fatty foods. Adjusts shower until water is at exactly the right temperature.
Eats food he likes even if mixed with disliked food. Can be left easily with strangers.	Can be left with anyone. Falls to sleep easily on either back or stomach.	Does not hear loud, sudden noises when reading. Does not object to injections.	Never complains when sick. Eats all foods.

child's temperament somehow *lead* to the problem—a conclusion that the researchers themselves suggest? Because the judgments about temperament and behavioral problems in this study arise from sources with similar orientations, there is no way to decide between these alternatives.

Temperament and social interaction. However much a child's distinctive temperamental characteristics establish a basis for uniqueness and individuality in the child, the ultimate significance of these temperamental characteristics to the child, as an individual and as a member of society, will be determined by the ways in which these characteristics influence the child's interactions with other persons. There is nothing objective or predetermined about the social effect of a particular temperamental characteristic. In one social context, for example, high levels of activity may be prized as "vigor," "lustiness," or "liveliness"; in other social contexts, they might be devalued as "restlessness," "hyperactivity," or "aggressiveness." How a disposition is received affects the very meaning of the disposition in both an individual and a social sense. One study, in fact, showed that some mothers actually behave *more* affectionately to infants that they perceive as difficult, apparently to placate them.[14] Other studies have shown that "difficult temperament" is a concept whose meaning varies widely from parent to parent, and whose exact behavioral significance for any particular child is quite uncertain.[15] For reasons such as these, it is impossible to speak of temperament as a fixed objective trait with a stable social value.

Thomas, Chess, and Birch are careful to write of temperament as a "phenomenological" construct, implying that its meaning is at least partly in the eyes of the beholder. And even beyond its meaning, they write, temperament is socially determined, although not entirely so. Thomas and his colleagues do believe that there is some genetic component to temperament, and therefore that there is an objective biological grounding for a young infant's distinct disposition. They cite studies of infant twins as evidence for this genetic component.[16] The researchers also acknowledge hormonal and other physical influences experienced by the infant prenatally as another important factor. But they emphasize, above all, that temperament is formed by multiple influences, including social ones, that operate at the start of life as well as later in development:

> Temperamental individuality is well established by the time the infant is two to three months old. The origins of temperament must therefore be sought in. . .genetic, prenatal, and early postnatal parental influences. Once temperamental individuality is established, it cannot be considered immutable as development proceeds, any more than any other characteristics of the growing child. Whatever their role may be in the origin of temperament, environmental influences may very well accentuate, modify, or even change temperamental traits over time.[17]

[14] Bates, Olson, Pettit, & Bayles, 1982.   [17] Thomas & Chess, 1977, p. 153.
[15] Bates, 1980.
[16] Rutter, Korn, & Birch, 1963; Torgersen, 1973.

An even stronger statement asserting the interactional nature of temperament has been made by Robert Emde.[18] Emde reasons that the data collected
by Thomas and his colleagues tell us more about the parent-child relation than
about the child because: (1) the data were derived from parental reports and
tell us mainly about parental perceptions of their children, and (2) the behavior
that the parents observed always took place in the context of the parent's
presence. For these reasons, Emde believes that Thomas, Chess, and Birch
may have discovered "interactional traits" between parents and children,
rather than temperamental dispositions of the children as individuals:

> I believe that Thomas et al. may have tapped a more complex *interactional* system
> in demonstrating their developmental continuities; perhaps they have discovered
> enduring interactional traits. Perhaps what has been referred to as "infant temper-
> ament" refers to fundamental adaptational modes; to dynamic equilibria charac-
> terizing parent-infant relational systems over the course of development.
> Individual differences of infants are not stable in any simple way; perhaps there
> are relational "constants" that will give us a research handle on developmental
> continuities.[19]

Whether or not we fully accept Emde's speculations, Thomas, Chess, and
Birch's data enable us to see the two-way relations between temperament and
social interaction. An infant's temperamental characteristics influence the
nature of his social life, and the infant's temperamental characteristics are, in
turn, interpreted and influenced by others.

The average child and temperamental differences. Temperament is a
concept that implies broad patterns of behavior and affect, such as those
described by Thomas, Chess, and Birch's temperamental categories (activity
level, mood, and so on). Each of these categories implies a general tendency of
infants to act and to experience their feelings in a certain consistent manner
over time. The work of Thomas and his colleagues indicates that infants may
indeed be distinguished from each other on the basis of such categories,
although this is mostly true for extreme cases. That is, infants assessed very
high or very low on activity, adaptiveness, and so on, are the ones best described
by Thomas, Chess, and Birch's system. But most infants fall somewhere in the
middle on all of the categories of temperament. For these "average" children,
the findings of the New York Longitudinal Study were far less clear than for
the extreme children. For example, it was not as evident that the temperamental characteristics of the average children were as stable over time as they were
for the extreme children. Consequently, few predictions could be made about
the social behavior and development of the average children. In short, the
descriptive and predictive value of Thomas, Chess, and Birch's broad-based
categories of temperament was mainly in application of the categories to the
extreme cases in the sample. Other researchers who have studied general,
"patterned" individual differences in infants have reported similar results.[20]

[18] Emde, 1975.   [20] Kagan, 1971.
[19] Ibid. p. 23.

Individual Differences in Specific Social Behaviors

Another approach is to look at more specific types of infant behavior, such as crying, looking, or vocalizing. For systematic observations of such behaviors, trained researchers are needed, ideally with the additional aid of modern-day film or videotape equipment. It is difficult to ask parents to assess their children's behavior on categories more minute than those used by Thomas and his colleagues: in this regard, too, the parental assessment methodology of the New York Longitudinal Study has its limitations. But several recent observational studies have focused on infant behaviors that can be defined more concretely and specifically than the nine broad categories of temperament. Such studies have found that most infants vary greatly from one another in the ways in which they perform specific behaviors like crying or looking. Further, these specific behaviors have predictable social consequences that follow from the different ways in which individual infants perform them.

In newborns, crying is the behavior most likely to instigate interaction with the caregiver. Researchers have found that most interactions between mother and infant during the first month of life are initiated by the infant's cries.[21] In a study of individual differences between newborns at birth, Anneliese Korner has reported wide variations between infants in both the length and frequency with which they cry.[22] Korner concludes, "With such individual differences in crying, it is reasonable to infer that an irritable infant initiates interaction with his mother more than a placid baby. The overly placid baby who, in the long run, may be in greater need of stimulation, may receive less, purely by virtue of his peacefulness. The newborn may be viewed, in part at least, as the determiner of how much stimulation he receives." [23]

Differences other than crying also have been found in newborn babies' behavior at birth. In a series of studies, Korner found some babies to be far more alert and visually responsive than others.[24] Given the importance of the infant's gaze in maintaining social interactions, these early differences in visual alertness certainly must affect the quality of an infant's first relations with his caregiver.[25]

Infants also differ in their auditory responsiveness, as well as with respect to a number of other behavioral and sensory abilities that may affect their social interactions. T. Berry Brazelton has designed a Neonatal Behavioral Assessment Scale that measures a wide range of visual, auditory, and motor abilities in newborn babies. He and his co-workers have reported substantial individual differences between newborns on such measures.[26] These differences endure for at least several months after birth and include not only visual and auditory alertness but also aspects of behavior that are observable *only* during social interaction. For example, Brazelton's scale distinguishes infants

[21] Bell, 1974; Lewis & Rosenblum, 1974, Vol. 1, Introduction.
[22] Korner, 1971.
[23] Ibid., pp. 618–19.

[24] Korner, 1974.
[25] Stern, 1977.
[26] Brazelton & Collier, 1969; Brazelton, 1973.

on their "cuddliness" (whether the infant resists being held, or lies passively in the adult's arms, or actively grasps the adult and molds to the adult's arms). In light of Schaffer and Emerson's evidence (pp.71–72), it seems likely that an infant's initial degree of cuddliness could have profound effects on the caregiver-child relation all throughout infancy.[27] Other items on the Brazelton scale that reveal important differences between newborns include consolability and irritability. From Brazelton's own case studies, we have ample evidence that these dimensions of newborn behavior can have a powerful effect on caregiver-child relations. Brazelton has described one extreme case in which an eager and well-intentioned mother was rendered almost helpless in the face of an irritable and nonresponsive newborn.[28] The baby would vacillate between intense, nonconsolable screaming and deep sleep. Only severe physical restraint could calm the baby, who then would revert to his inaccessible sleep state. Eventually, the mother became so depressed out of a feeling that her baby was "rejecting" her that she was forced to seek psychotherapeutic help.

The Effect of an Individual's Physical Endowment

Aside from temperament or behavior, the infant's unique physical endowment is another aspect of infant individuality that has immediate and marked consequences for the infant's social interactions. Even normal infants vary greatly in size and shape from one another.[29] Such variations may indeed influence basic components of early interaction, such as how the baby is held. Babies born with physical deformities or other birth defects are particularly likely to experience unusual social interactions. A common theme in reports on the psychological effects of birth defects is that such babies are often "socially stigmatized" by parents and peers alike.

Infant blindness presents some special obstacles to social interaction.[30] Comparing a stranger's sympathetic reactions to films of a normal baby with films of a blind baby, Selma Fraiberg writes:

> . . .the blind baby on the screen does not elicit these spontaneous moods in the visitor. Typically, the visitor's face remains solemn. This is partly a reaction to the blindness itself. But it is also something else. There is a large vocabulary of expressive behavior that one does not see in a blind baby at all. The absence of differentiated signs on the baby's face is mirrored in the face of the observer.
>
> What we miss in the blind baby, apart from the eyes that do not see, is the vocabulary of signs and signals that provide the most elementary and vital sense of discourse long before words have meaning.[31]

Blind infants do have ways of initiating social interaction, but these ways are somewhat different from those of sighted children. For example, the first smiles of a blind infant come in response to the sounds of human voices, rather than to the sight of human faces. Most interestingly, blind infants are more

[27] Schaffer & Emerson, 1964b.
[28] Brazelton, 1961.
[29] Tanner, 1974b.

[30] Fraiberg, 1974, 1977.
[31] Ibid., p. 217.

likely to use hands than facial expressions to signal interest or recognition. Fraiberg's films reveal that blind infants as early as two months of age invite and sustain contact with their mothers by grasping or lightly fingering the mother's face and arms. By the seventh or eighth month, blind infants are able to express tactilely "an eloquent sign language of seeking, wooing, preference, and recognition."[32] The blind child's major problem is that his parent may not be able to "read" this language. For this reason, many blind infants have disturbingly little access to the early caregiver-child communication that is so important for the forming of attachments. Consequently these children may show impairments in their abilities to establish relations with others. Fraiberg reports that she has seen many blind children who have little emotional investment in persons by the second, third, or fourth year of life. Fortunately, parents can be trained to recognize the unique social cues of their blind infant. In families where this has been done, the infants develop in much the same manner as sighted children, reaching all the milestones of social attachment at approximately similar ages.

Sex Differences

Sex differences may also arise out of an infant's interaction with his or her parents. Behavioral research has found few differences between boys and girls solely attributable to biological sex. In their large-scale review of the literature, Eleanor Maccoby and Carol Jacklin report practically no firm sex differences that regularly show up in infants before age two or so.[33] Anneliese Korner has found boys to be born somewhat larger at birth than girls. Moreover, there is some tentative evidence that boys are somewhat stronger and more vigorous than are girls, whereas girls seem to be a bit more sensitive to physical stimulation, particularly around the mouth, than are boys. Such differences, however, are small in magnitude, and their behavioral implications, if any exist, are unclear. But there is one sense in which an infant's sexual endowment has immediate consequences, albeit in an indirect way. Research has shown that, from the time of birth, mothers treat boy babies quite differently than they treat girl babies.[34] Infant girls are talked to and gazed at significantly more than boys, whereas infant boys are held more than girls. Michael Lewis has summed up the major differences as being the mother's propensity to offer boys more close stimulation and to offer girls more distant stimulation.[35] Whether the same is true of fathers, or whether they treat boys and girls in the opposite manner, is not clear from current research. But since the mother is the primary caregiver in most cases, it is likely that most boy and girl babies experience some overall differences in parental treatment along these lines.

What could be the consequences of such differential treatment? Presently we have no conclusive answers to this question, but a case study of two infants by Sybil Escalona and H. H. Corman suggests that there may be profound

---

[32] Ibid., p. 228.
[33] Maccoby & Jacklin, 1974.
[34] Korner, 1973.
[35] Lewis, 1972.

consequences indeed to parental variation of this sort.[36] Before considering this account, let us point out that it is not always possible to infer general trends from such case studies, since this type of research focuses on only one or two subjects, and not on a broad sample. Sometimes the one or two cases under investigation are unusual in some regard. For example, in the Escalona and Corman study, it seems that normal maternal responses to sex differences were either nonoperative or reversed. John, the boy subject, received from his mother relatively high degrees of distant stimulation, and Mary, the girl subject, received high degrees of close stimulation. But despite this apparent divergence from general infant-rearing trends, the cases in this study are still intriguing because they offer us rare insights into the potential effects of distant versus close stimulation, as well as into other aspects of differential parental treatment upon developing infants. As in any case study, further studies with larger groups of subjects are needed in order to separate out all of the various influences that operate to create the interesting findings.

John and Mary were both born alert, moderately active, and healthy in all respects. Tests of perceptual sensitivity in the first weeks of life revealed no differences between the two infants other than Mary's slightly greater sensitivity to tactile stimulation (a difference that accords with one of the few substantiated infant sex differences noted above). But before long—by the end of their second month—the two infants began showing strikingly divergent patterns of responsiveness to the world. John became more responsive than Mary to stimulation received through the modalities of sight and sound, and he became more interested than she in inanimate objects as well as persons-at-a-distance (that is, persons not directly engaged in holding him). Mary, on the other hand, became more and more tactilely sensitive than John, showing an even greater interest than he in bodily self-stimulation and in persons (usually mother) who were holding or touching her. These differences endured, and in most cases increased, throughout the infants' first two years of life.

Escalona and Corman trace these differences in John and Mary's patterns of responsiveness back to basic differences in the ways in which their parents interacted with them from the time of birth. Both sets of parents were physically affectionate with their infants. But Mary's mother touched or handled her young baby *whenever* the two interacted. She would almost always use tactile means to contact her child, thus invariably drawing the infant's attention to her own and her mother's bodies during their interactions. John's mother, on the other hand, frequently initiated interaction by talking and looking at her baby without touch. John came to know his mother through sight and sound, as well as through touch during the early weeks of life. Further, as their relationship developed, John and his mother focused their interactions on toys and other aspects of the external, inanimate world to an increasingly greater extent than did Mary and her mother. The difference between the two types of parental treatment may be summed up as follows:

[36] Escalona & Corman, 1974.

whereas Mary's mother usually combined auditory, visual, and tactile approaches to her infant, John's mother often omitted the tactile part.

If this parental difference did, in fact, contribute to the differences between John and Mary as functioning individuals, its effect was profound indeed. Not only was Mary more attuned to her own body and its physical stimulation, but her relations with others were also markedly different from John's. Throughout the first year of life, Mary showed her greatest activity and achievements only when in the presence of her mother. When left alone, she became easily bored, playing in an "empty" and nonanimated fashion. John, on the other hand, heightened and extended his activity when left alone. While in the absence of his mother, he often showed his highest level of sophistication and interest in the world, seeking new opportunities for exploration and playing with eagerness and vigor. By the second year of life, the contrast between the two children sharpened further:

> Mary became increasingly dependent upon the presence and responsiveness of other people for pleasure and interest in activity. . . She constantly sought out other persons and it was as though even preferred toys, her doll, carriage, teddybear, and ball, gave pleasure to the degree that others acknowledged and participated in what she was doing.
> John also shared many games and activities with mother and other people. He also developed an intense and possessive relationship with mother. Yet, he spent an increasing proportion of time in pursuit of relatively independent play activity (animals, trucks, crayons, books, household objects, balls, strewing objects all about the floor, gleefully creating maximal disorder, etc.).[37]

In many respects, it seems that John's early upbringing has given him some important advantages over Mary. Cognitively, he is more prepared to learn about the outside world, particularly its inanimate parts, on its own terms. Socially, he seems better able to distinguish himself from others than is Mary, a necessity for both the development of autonomy and identity. But individual differences between persons often extend in many directions, and the cases of John and Mary's are more interesting than a simple argument for one type of upbringing over another. Mary, too, had her claims to superior competence. In particular, it was in the arena of social relationship that Mary proved to be particularly adept:

> All the familiar landmarks, from stranger-anxiety to separation-anxiety and relentless following; from the appearance of the semantic "no"[38] to the internalization of taboos and prohibitions and something like a sense of shame; and from simple reciprocal games to complex teasing and deliberate manipulations of others (such as playing one parent against the other to gain her ends); all developed in more differentiated form than we saw in John.[39]

Although manipulation and teasing of others may not seem like an admirable activity, it does show remarkable social sophistication for a two-year-old. This

[37] Ibid., p. 164.
[38] Spitz, 1965.
[39] Escalona & Corman, 1974, p. 165.

sophistication was what Mary had drawn from her pattern of early experience, and it represented her own source of personal strength.

Developmental Research on Infant Self-Knowledge

Much of what we know about self-knowledge, both with respect to the *I* and the *me*, comes from empirical studies conducted within the past decade, particularly from developmental research on infants.[40] It seems that psychologists have had an easier time studying the origins of human self-knowledge in its most rudimentary forms than in studying the more elaborate and complex conceptions of self that develop during childhood, adolescence, and adulthood (although we shall note a few important exceptions in later chapters). For the present, the recent flurry of infant self-knowledge research shall serve well to complete our view of infant individuality. We shall consider research that illuminates the infant's development of self-as-subject (the *I*), as well as research that illuminates the infant's development of self-as-object (the *me*).

William James predicted that the *I* aspect of self would prove elusive to empirical study, precisely because of its indeterminate nature. It is difficult to observe or characterize a phenomenon that may change unpredictably from moment to moment. Also, unlike the somewhat circumscribed nature of the self-as-object (which is mainly the collection of definitions that one constructs for one's self), the self-as-subject potentially incorporates all of a person's interactions with the world. The *I* enters into all of a person's experience, since it determines the unique nature of all the person's interpretations of events, people, and things.

Where do we begin studying such a dynamic and encompassing part of mental life? We may begin by isolating features of self-knowledge that are clearly necessary for the functioning of the self-as-subject. First, a sense of *separateness* from others is required. This means an awareness of one's own uniqueness as an individual, physically as well as emotionally and cognitively. Such awareness is necessary for a realization that one's experience in the world is one's own and nobody else's. Second, a *stable identity* over time and place is required. This means knowledge that one has a permanence that endures despite moment-to-moment changes in one's life circumstances. It also means an awareness of a fundamental sameness in the self, even as one takes on new characteristics. This sameness provides one with a sense of continuity in one's experience. This is the sense that it was *I* who, for example, fell off my tricycle thirty years ago, even though much about me has changed in the intervening years. These two elements of self-knowledge—the separateness and the stable identity of the self—are the basic ground upon which the self-as-subject operates. Without these notions, it would be impossible to organize one's personal experience in any meaningful sense.

[40] Lewis & Brooks-Gunn, 1979.

So fundamental are these elements of self-knowledge that we may fail to appreciate the considerable achievement that the acquisition of each represents. Studies of young infants, however, reveal that neither the notion of separateness nor the notion of stable identity should be taken for granted psychologically. Even such rudimentary forms as the realization that one is physically distinct from other people or that one's body retains its permanence from one moment to the next may be elusive for young infants. More sophisticated versions of these notions may not be worked out until late in life, as we shall see at the end of this book.

Contemporary Psychoanalytic Theories

Some of the most dramatic writing on the difficulties that infants have in grasping the separateness of self has come from the psychoanalytic tradition, in particular the work of Margaret Mahler.[41] Mahler, like other modern-day psychoanalysts, broadened and expanded Freud's original theory to include more of an emphasis on the interpersonal context of psychological development. Borrowing from a metaphor introduced by Freud, Mahler has described the initial psychological state of a newborn as akin to a bird's egg within its shell. According to this view, the newborn is, in effect, shut off from the external world by his exclusive focus on his own needs and feelings. Mahler calls this the *normal autism* of the newborn. In this primitive state, the young infant is so intensely oriented toward his own satisfaction that he does not distinguish between the different ways in which this satisfaction is achieved. Among other things, this means that the newborn cannot differentiate between his own and his mother's comforting of himself. "The effect of its mother's ministrations in reducing the pangs of need-hunger cannot be isolated, nor can it be differentiated by the young infant from tension-reducing attempts of its own, such as urinating, defecating, coughing, sneezing, spitting, regurgitating, vomiting, all the ways by which an infant tries to rid himself of unpleasurable tension."[42]

By the second month of life, according to Mahler, the infant recognizes that the mother exists as a means of fulfilling his needs. With this new awareness of mother as a separate object in her own right, the infant begins the long process of drawing the boundaries between others and the self. Mahler calls this process *separation-individuation*. The first recognition of mother as a means of self-gratification is only the beginning. Even after the infant is aware of mother as a physical being in her own right, the *psychological* boundaries between self and mother remain fuzzy for months. The infant projects his own subjective states outward to the mother and is aware of the mother only in relation to her effect on the infant's needs. Mahler refers to this as the undifferentiation of the *I* from the *not-I*. In his mind, the infant fuses his own activities and feelings with those of the mother, even though the mother is

---

[41] Mahler, 1968.　　　　　　　　[42] Ibid., p. 2.

recognized as a separate person. The infant assumes mother's thoughts are the same as his own, with his own thoughts still referring mainly to his own sensations and needs. Not until late in the first year of life does the separation-individuation process proceed to the point where the infant knows both his own physical and emotional uniqueness. The infant is then able to construct his own body image, as well as his own sense of emotional autonomy. Both help establish the bases for self-identity.

Mahler's work is useful in suggesting the formidability of the task that the infant faces in separating himself psychologically from his caregiver. Certainly the newborn must be confused at times about the means by which his needs are satisfied. Distinguishing between his own body and the external world (including his mother's body) may indeed be difficult, at least until the infant is able to associate his own sensations with his bodily parts. Further, it is plausible that infants often make the mistake of projecting their own psychological states onto others. How else is the infant initially to know the feelings and thoughts of others but in reference to his own?

Still, there are reasons to question certain metaphors that Mahler uses to describe the infant's absolute undifferentiation from his mother. Is "normal autism" an accurate description of newborn mental life? The research cited in Chapter 2 argues against this extreme characterization. Newborns do indeed seem able to respond selectively and appropriately to people. The roots of social interaction and communication can be seen in infant behavior as early as the first few days of life; and by the end of the first few weeks, the infant is an active partner to sustained social interchange with his parents. In short, the infant's earliest behavior in the presence of an interactive adult takes on a distinctively social flavor. This suggests that young infants have not only an awareness but also a special interest in other people. Therefore, they must be able somehow to distinguish between themselves and others.

Mahler's account of the infant's struggle to separate himself from the caregiver is a valuable contribution to the study of self-development. But it need not imply that in the beginning the newborn is psychologically confined to his own inner world. Even during the newborn period, the infant must be open to external influence, and this openness implies some initial awareness of the distinction between self and other. As noted in Chapter 2, it would be difficult to explain subsequent psychological development in the newborn without positing some rudimentary ability to recognize and to benefit from social interaction with others. A descriptive concept like "autism" does not capture this rudimentary ability, since autism implies an absolute inability to communicate with others. It suggests a closed rather than an open system. So, too, does the metaphor of the egg enclosed within its shell. Closed systems rarely change. As the infant years are among the most dynamic periods of life developmentally, we must therefore alter Mahler's metaphor a bit: there must be a crack in the shell.

Of course, no one knows for certain how infants experience the world. Any account of an infant's experience must be drawn by inference from some secondary data, since infants cannot inform us verbally of their percepts, thoughts, and feelings. Therefore, whether newborn babies experience a fusion with their mothers, or sense some distinction from the start, is a question that must remain open for conjecture.

Erik Erikson, another contemporary psychoanalyst who has extended Freud's theory in both social and cognitive directions, has also written about the infant's search for self-identity. His writings are in some ways closely compatible with those of Mahler. Erikson emphasizes the fused, symbiotic relation between newborn and mother, describing the infant's developmental task as a struggle to recognize the identity of the self as an individual.[43] This is similar to Mahler's thesis that the separation-individuation process occupies center stage in the infant's first year of psychoanalytic development. Like Mahler, Erikson also suggests that the infant is aided in making the distinction between self and mother through reference to his own sensations and the gratification thereof. Bodily sensations soon come to be seen as one's own, and the mother is quickly seen as an instrument for their stimulation and satisfaction. From this initial starting point, the distinctness and (subsequently) the autonomy of the self are developed.

One major difference distinguishes the writings of Erikson from those of Mahler. Erikson emphasized a particular mode of physical and psychological functioning as primary during the first year of life: the *mode of incorporation*. For Erikson, incorporation represents the breeding ground for infant psychological development. Metaphorically, it stands for the infant's incorporation of both physical nourishment and psychological information and stimulation from the world around her. In this sense, Erikson views the infant as being open and receptive to external events:

> Yet it is clear that in addition to the overwhelming need for food, a baby is, or soon becomes, receptive in many other respects. As he is willing and able to suck on appropriate objects and to swallow whatever appropriate fluids they emit, he is soon also willing and able to "take in" with his eyes whatever enters his visual field. His senses, too, seem to "take in" what feels good. In this sense, then, one can speak of an *incorporative stage*, in which he is, relatively speaking, receptive to what he is being offered.[44]

The emphasis on incorporation leads Erikson to extend his theory beyond the infant's struggle for self-identity to broader dimensions for psychosocial development. Since the young infant experiences the world through what she can "take in," it is of the utmost importance that both her nutritional and psychological needs be fulfilled regularly and reliably. If the infant's mother is responsive to such needs, the infant will develop the confidence to extend her incorporation of the world beyond the mother. According to Erikson, it is through satisfying her own incorporative needs that the infant experiences the distinction between self and mother.

[43] Erikson, 1968.   [44] Ibid, p. 98.

The central issue at this early age, according to Erikson, is one of *basic trust* in the world. "Babies," he writes, "are sensitive and vulnerable too." Their first experiences are crucial in determining whether or not they will develop this sense of basic trust: ". . .we must see to it that we deliver to their senses stimuli as well as food in the proper intensity and at the right time; otherwise their willingness to accept may change radically into diffuse defense or into lethargy."[45] This in turn would adversely affect all of an infant's psychosocial development, including the infant's attempts to see herself as a distinct person. Without trust in the world, there is little hope than an infant could feel the confidence in the self necessary to establish individuality and autonomy. For Erikson, therefore, individuation in infancy is only part of a larger struggle—the combined search for trust in the world and in the self.

In both Mahler's and Erikson's accounts, we can see a developmental connection between the caregiver-child attachment relation as discussed in Chapter 2 and the infant's search for self. Within the context of a secure attachment relation, the infant feels the confidence and trust necessary to temporarily separate from the mother and explore the world. The cycle of separating, exploring, and returning to mother expands to incorporate even more experience, and in the process, a sense of self is constructed. The infant's individuality, therefore, is but one of the many beneficiaries of a secure caregiver-child relation.

Erikson's view of infant individuation reveals some intriguing features in his general stage model for psychosocial development through the life cycle. For Erikson, all aspects of psychosocial development are to some extent intertwined at each stage of development, but each aspect has its own time of ascendancy at some period of life, which represents a *crisis*, or a "turning point" for the individual. With respect to each particular aspect of development, the individual faces either potential for growth and future strength (if the crisis is resolved successfully), or a vulnerability for maladjustment and future stagnation (if the crisis is not resolved). Adaptive psychosocial development means resolving each successive crisis as it arises during the stages of the life cycle. Resolving the crisis at any stage has implications both for the other aspects of psychosocial development that coexist with the crisis at that stage and for the resolution of all future crises as they appear in their own time.

We may illustrate Erikson's developmental model with reference to the individual's lifelong quest for self-identity, a quest which begins early in infancy. Like Mahler, Erikson has characterized the infant's progression toward self-identity as a movement from autistic isolation toward a recognition of the separateness and individuality of self and other (a recognition that Erikson calls *mutual recognition*). But although it is an important part of infant psychosocial development, self-identity is not the ascendant aspect of development during infancy. Rather, basic trust is. Identity does not reach its ascendancy until adolescence, at which time the *identity crisis* becomes the

[45] Ibid.

focus of psychosocial development. During infancy, the search for identity is secondary to the search for basic trust and is largely dependent upon the way in which the trust crisis is resolved.

Table 3-2 illustrates Erikson's view of the relations between lifelong development of identity and the major psychosocial crises as they appear from stage to stage throughout development. Note that the relations posited by Erikson are developmental ones. This means that all aspects of psychosocial development in Erikson's theory can be traced back to their roots in infancy. Further, they can be traced back in two ways. Along the diagonal of Table 3-2, each of the major life crises are ordered according to their position in the developmental sequence. This means that we can follow each successful resolution of crisis backward to the last successful resolution and forward to the next crisis. Along the vertical dimension each aspect of psychosocial development may be traced backward and forward to its earlier and later forms, both prior to and after the time when that aspect was in ascendancy during its own stage of crisis. Thus, the adolescent identity crisis may be traced back to infancy in two ways. In terms of its relation to the major turning points of life, it has its roots in the trust-versus-mistrust crisis of infancy, but it finds its closest representative during infancy in the infant's struggle for mutual recognition versus autistic isolation.

The potential power of Erikson's developmental model for clinical analysis and prediction should not be underestimated. When all the boxes in Table 3-2 are filled in, it becomes possible to follow the course of any psychosocial strength or maladaptation throughout development, both backward and forward in time. Predictions of future difficulty as well as inferences about past problems become possible. And by referring to the horizontal dimension of the table, one can form hypotheses about areas of difficulty that presently are correlated with a manifest problem in a person's life. An infant's refusal to eat may signify a failure of basic trust, which may in turn be associated with the infant's inability to communicate as a separate and distinct individual with the mother. The infant's failure to recognize her own distinctiveness may in turn be an early version of problems in autonomy and self-identity that will be encountered later in life if successful intervention is not undertaken.

We shall return to Erikson's multidimensional developmental stage model in later chapters of this book, particularly with respect to his analysis of identity development. For the present, we should note not only the potential power of his approach, but also some cautions about his methodology for collecting data and drawing inferences from that data. These same reservations also apply to Mahler's work. Both Erikson and Mahler rely upon a clinical methodology as the basis for their conjecture. And like all social-scientific methodologies, the clinical one has strengths and weaknesses that we must assess in order to evaluate the findings generated by the methodology. A clinical methodology relies upon case studies of clinical clients. During the case study, the client and the therapist together explore the client's interpretations of past and present events. From these interpretations, the psychoanalyst constructs a portrait of the client's history through the life cycle. There are, therefore, two

Table 3–2 Erikson's Stages of Psychosocial Development

	1	2	3	4	5	6	7	8
VIII Mature Age								INTEGRITY vs. DESPAIR
VII Adulthood							GENERATIVITY vs. STAGNATION	
VI Young Adult						INTIMACY vs. ISOLATION		
V Adolescence	Temporal Perspective vs. Time Confusion	Self-Certainty vs. Self-Consciousness	Role Experimentation vs. Role Fixation	Apprenticeship vs. Work Paralysis	IDENTITY vs. IDENTITY CONFUSION	Sexual Polarization vs. Bisexual Confusion	Leadership and Fellowship vs. Authority Confusion	Ideological Commitment vs. Confusion of Values
IV School Age				INDUSTRY vs. INFERIORITY	Task Identification vs. Sense of Futility			
III Play Age			INITIATIVE vs. GUILT		Anticipation of Roles vs. Role Inhibition			
II Early Childhood		AUTONOMY vs. SHAME, DOUBT			Will to Be Oneself vs. Self-Doubt			
I Infancy	TRUST vs. MISTRUST				Mutual Recognition vs. Autistic Isolation			

Source: E. H. Erikson, *Identity: Youth and Crisis.* New York: W. W. Norton, 1968, p. 94. Reprinted with permission.

features of psychoanalytic methodology that distinguish it from other research traditions in developmental study. First, most psychoanalytic descriptions of young children and infants are based upon the recollections of adult clients. Second, the therapist and the client cooperate in uncovering these recollections. Erikson calls this the mutuality of effort underlying the psychotherapeutic encounter, and he sees in this mutuality a special scientific virtue: ". . .scientists may learn about the nature of things by finding out what they can do to them, but. . .the clinician can learn of the true nature of man only in the attempt to do something *for* and *with* him."[46] The idea here is that in a social science, unlike in a physical science, the intentional and voluntary cooperation of the investigation's subject is needed for an accurate view of a subject's nature. The subjectivity necessary for the clinical method can be seen as both a strength and a limitation. We need to keep this subjectivity in mind when assessing any inferences drawn from such an approach (just as we need to keep in mind the limitations of any social-science methodology—and they all have their limitations).

The two traditional alternatives to the clinical methodology in child-developmental research are naturalistic observation and experimentation. Many of the infant sociability studies reviewed in Chapter 2 were conducted through naturalistic observation of infants' normal everyday behavior. Although appropriate for this area of study, naturalistic observation is of little help in investigating infants' self-knowledge. Clearly, it is easier to observe infants' behavioral responses to other people than to observe infants' understanding of themselves as separate individuals with stable identities. To accomplish the latter, techniques that challenge and probe an infant's knowledge are needed. The infant must be encouraged to express his latent knowledge about his own separateness and sense of identity in a manner that can be recognized and analyzed by an observer. Because in their normal, day-to-day behavior, infants rarely express such knowledge directly—and when they do, their behavior usually is ambiguous and difficult to interpret—we cannot learn much about infants' self-knowledge by simply watching them. For this reason, naturalistic techniques that do nothing more than record infants' spontaneous behavior are insufficient for the study of self-knowledge. What is needed are experimental techniques that force infants directly to deal with problems of self-identity.

Experimental Studies of Self-Knowledge

Recent work in infant development has indeed explored the origins of self-knowledge through experimental techniques. Unfortunately, researchers have been unable to devise techniques appropriate for infants younger than about six months. This is probably because it is difficult to communicate the demands of an experimental task to a very young infant. Thus, the state of a

[46] Erikson, 1964, p. 80.

newborn's understanding of self must remain conjectural until there are further advances in our infant-study techniques. With infants of six months and older, however, a number of researchers have found clever and revealing experimental techniques for exploring the development of self-knowledge. The most comprehensive set of experimental studies on infant self-knowledge has been conducted by Michael Lewis and Jeanne Brooks-Gunn.[47]

Lewis and Brooks-Gunn investigate infants' self-knowledge by testing infants' abilities to recognize themselves in three ways—in mirrors, in pictures, and on television. Each of these media is similar in that they all communicate through the visual mode, and so it is fair to say that Lewis and Brooks-Gunn's work is confined to testing visual self-recognition in infants. As the authors themselves note, it is possible that infants come to recognize themselves through other senses as well (hearing, smell, touch); but scientists have not yet found a way to explore these other potential elements in infants' self-knowledge. In each of the three visual media chosen by Lewis and Brooks-Gunn to test for infant self-recognition, there are some special features which the investigators exploit for purposes of systematic experimentation. Mirrors reflect a person's image in a way that is immediately contingent upon the actions of the person. In other words, whatever movements one makes are instantaneously reflected in the mirror. For this reason, a mirror image reveals the active, ever-changing quality of the self (at least insofar as the self's physical appearance is concerned). This is the aspect of self that we have been calling the self-as-subject, or the *I*, (Lewis and Brooks-Gunn make an identical distinction between self-as-subject versus self-as-object, except that their terminology is the *existential* self—the *I*—versus the *categorical* self—the *me*.) Of course, mirror images reveal how one looks as well as how one acts from moment to moment. In this sense, mirrors also reflect the physical self-as-object as well as the physical self-as-subject. But they are not limited to presenting only the static looks of a person. Pictures are limited in this way, since a picture image is in no way contingent upon a person's immediate actions. Lewis and Brooks-Gunn therefore took pictorial recognition to be a sign of categorical, or self-as-object knowledge, and took mirror recognition to be a sign of both existential (*I*) and categorical (*me*) self-knowledge.

In their T.V. experiments, the researchers were able to combine and separate in a controlled manner the different elements of visual self-recognition. For example, in one condition, infants watched T.V. images of their own current behavior. These in effect were mirror images of the infants presented on T.V. screens, and they were therefore immediately contingent upon the infants' actions. In a second condition, infants viewed T.V. images of themselves that had been recorded a week earlier. These images therefore looked like the infants but were noncontingent upon their current actions. In a third condition, the infants were shown T.V. recordings of another baby, so that in this experimental condition the infants viewed an image that neither looked like the

---

[47] Lewis & Brooks-Gunn, 1979.

self nor was contingent upon the activities of the self. The only condition that the investigators were unable to conceive of experimentally was a condition in which the T.V. image moved along with the activities of the infant viewer but in its physical features appeared dissimilar. Had the experimentors been able to present such a "contingent nonself" image, their infant subjects would have been tested with all the combinations of contingency, noncontingency, similarity, and dissimilarity of physical appearance. But even as is, findings from the researchers' T.V. study, when combined with findings from their mirror and picture studies, help unravel many of the threads in infants' development of both *I* and *me* self-knowledge.

How can we tell whether an infant recognizes herself in a visual image? Simple interest in the visual image is not a good index of self-recognition, since babies might find such images interesting for other reasons. Perhaps an infant is interested in babies' faces, not knowing that it is her own face that is being shown. Or perhaps an infant finds any mirror or T.V. images fascinating, regardless of their content. To use visual images convincingly to test for an infant's self-recognition, an experimenter must devise a way to elicit from the infant behavior that is explicitly self-oriented.

In their mirror-image studies, Lewis and Brooks-Gunn engaged their infant subjects in self-directed behavior by surreptitiously marking the infants' noses red. This was done by dabbing the infants' noses with red rouge during a typical (and thus altogether unnoteworthy) act of maternal nose-wiping. Once so marked, the infants were observed as they examined themselves in front of mirrors. Lewis and Brooks-Gunn looked for a wide variety of infant responses, including smiling at the mirror, touching the mirror, touching the body, pointing at the mirror, acting silly or "coy" in front of the mirror, and touching the mark on the end of their nose. The infants in the Lewis and Brooks-Gunn mirror studies ranged in age from nine to twenty-four months.

Infants at all ages in the mirror studies tended to direct more behavior toward themselves when their nose was marked than when it was unmarked. This means that, to some degree, infants in the entire age range of the studies knew that there was something different about themselves when they had a red nose. They showed this by smiling at themselves, touching their bodies, and pointing at their reflections to a greater degree than when their nose was unmarked. Thus, visual self-recognition in some form was found to be present in all age groups of the Lewis and Brooks-Gunn studies. But the developmental story of the mirror-study results is told in Figure 3-1. Here we can see that, when their nose was marked, infants aged fifteen months and older began specifically directing their behavior toward the mark, whereas younger infants did not. Although aspects of the younger infants' behavior showed that they did notice the rouge on their nose, only the older infants were able directly to indicate what was different about themselves.

From Lewis and Brooks-Gunn's mirror studies, therefore, we know that (1) infants at least as young as nine months show some visual self-recognition by an increase in bodily directed behavior in the red-nose condition; and (2)

But red nose could
interesting per se

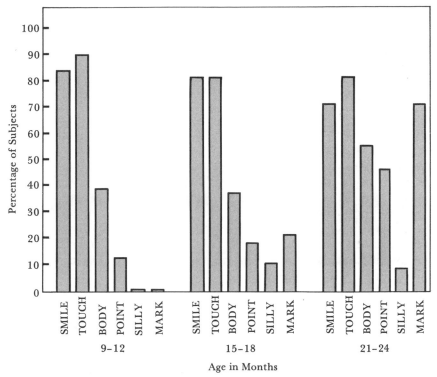

Figure 3-1. Infant Self-Recognition. The bars indicate the percentage of infants in the mirror studies who, at each age, showed by their behavior that they noticed a red mark on their nose.

Source: M. Lewis & J. Brooks-Gunn, *Social Cognition and the Acquisition of Self.* New York: Plenum Press, 1979, p. 68. Reprinted with permission.

after nine months, there is steady development in infants' abilities to identify specific changes (such as reddened noses) in their physical appearance. How do infants become able to recognize all the changing and unchanging features of themselves in a moving image? What clues do they go by? Is it the contingency of the image upon the self's actions that guides the infant, or is it rather the stable physical features like size and physical appearance?

Lewis and Brooks-Gunn's T.V. studies were designed to provide answers to these questions. As noted above, videotape technology enabled the researchers to separate for the purposes of experimentation some basic contingency and physical appearance features of moving visual images. Infants' responses to three types of T.V. images could be compared: (1) "live" images of themselves; (2) images of themselves videotaped one week earlier; and (3) images of another infant. In assessing their subjects' responses to the T.V. images, Lewis and Brooks-Gunn made special note of the infants' tendencies to imitate and to "play with" the image on the T.V. screen. In addition, the infants' facial and vocal expressions were recorded, as well as their movements toward and away from the image. Finally, one further condition was added in a follow-up study: on the T.V. screen, a stranger was shown sneaking up behind the infant. Would the real infant turn toward the stranger she had seen on the T.V. screen? Would the real infant do so in all three conditions (the "live" shot, the week-old shot, and the other-baby shot), or just in the appropriate one (the live shot)?

Subjects in the T.V. studies were the same ages as those in the mirror study (nine months and up), and the T.V. results nicely supplemented the mirror-study findings. Infants as young as nine months distinguished the live T.V. image from the others by playing with it more and by generally responding more positively to it than to the other images. In addition, infants at all ages in the study turned more often toward the approaching stranger in the live condition than in the other conditions. These findings indicate that initial visual self-recognition, present at least as early as nine months, is based upon the principle of contingency: when an image moves along with the self, it is possible at a very early age to recognize the self in that image. This explains the general self-recognition displayed by nine-month-olds when looking in mirrors. Other researchers have found signs of such self-recognition even prior to nine months, although their techniques do not confirm this as convincingly as do those of Lewis and Brooks-Gunn.[48]

Although the ability to use contingency as a clue to self-recognition is present as young as nine months, infants develop a greater responsiveness to contingency as they grow older. Lewis and Brooks-Gunn found a steady increase in infants' awareness of contingency through the second year of life. But the most striking developmental advance was not in the infants' use of contingency, but in their use of physical appearance in recognizing the self. To uncover this developmental advance, Lewis and Brooks-Gunn compared their subjects' responses to the noncontingent televised self-image (shot a week ago) with their subjects' responses to the televised image of another baby. It was not until fifteen months of age that infants distinguished their own pre-taped images from images of another child on the T.V. screen. When they were able to make this distinction, they smiled at and moved toward the other baby's image more than toward their own image, and they imitated and played with their own image more than with the other baby's image. These differences in behavior, which began at about fifteen months, increased further as the infants grew older. Lewis and Brooks-Gunn speculate that the infants of fifteen months and older were able to distinguish their own images from the other babies by referring to differences in the facial features of the two. This means that at about fifteen months of age infants begin to know what their faces look like. This conclusion is also supported by Lewis and Brooks-Gunn's mirror study, in which infants fifteen months and older were the only ones who showed specific awareness of their reddened noses.

It seems, therefore, that infants prior to fifteen months or so can recognize

[48] Amsterdam, 1972.

themselves only through contingency cues; not until the age of fifteen months, are they able to use facial and other physical features to distinguish themselves from others. Both of these abilities, of course, develop further throughout infancy. This developmental progression is confirmed by the findings of Lewis and Brooks-Gunn's picture study. By showing infants pictures of themselves and other babies, the researchers found the first clear recognition of self in infants aged fifteen to eighteen months. Since pictorial images are noncontingent upon a subject's actions, but do reveal facial and other physical cues, these age trends coincide with the age trends from Lewis and Brooks-Gunn's T.V. and mirror studies.

From the series of findings in the Lewis and Brooks-Gunn studies, we can infer that infants quite early develop a sense of self-as-subject (the existential self), but not until fifteen months or so do they begin developing substantial knowledge of self-as-object (the categorical self). Further, findings from the picture study suggest some of the basic categories that infants, beginning at fifteen months or so, use to identify themselves. These categories are gender and age. It seems that, when infants of fifteen months begin distinguishing themselves from others on the basis of noncontingent cues, they are particularly attuned to physical features associated with their sex and their age. They find it especially easy to tell themselves apart from opposite-sex babies and from older persons. The researchers believe that infants are able to discern the distinctive facial features that accompany sex and age: females have different-shaped faces (as well as different hair styles) than males, and babies have faces and heads *But also* that are shaped differently from those of older people. In their initial constructions of the self-as-object, infants focus particularly on facial features. Of all *data on movement rhythm.* facial features, those associated with gender and age are particularly apparent to infants as they begin constructing categorical knowledge of themselves.

There is still much that we have to learn about the development of self-knowledge in infancy. Because of limitations in their experimental methodology, Lewis and Brooks-Gunn's studies leave many questions unanswered. We do not know, for example, if visual self-recognition is a good index for infant self-knowledge in general, or whether other modes of self-recognition are equally (or more) important during infancy. Perhaps visual self-recognition is an adequate index of both the *I* and the *me* aspects of infant self-knowledge, perhaps for one but not the other, or perhaps for neither. We shall not know until other modes of infant self-recognition (touch, sound, smell) are experimentally probed. Also, even with regard to the visual mode of self-recognition, Lewis and Brooks-Gunn's measures were limited to those behaviors that they could readily observe. These included self-directed body movements and self-touching in the mirror study, imitating and turning in the T.V. studies, and vocalizing and pointing in the picture studies. Were these (and the other behaviors selected by the researchers) the best indicators of infant visual self-recognition? It is always possible that the infants knew more than they showed. A finer eye, or better observational measures, may have revealed a more sophisticated recognition at younger ages. But such constraints always accom-

Table 3-3 Development of Self-Knowledge in Infants

Age	Self-Knowledge
0–3 months	Interest in people, particularly babies. Emergence of distinction between physical self and physical other.
3–8 months	Recognition of self through contingency cues. Consolidation of self-other distinction.
8–12 months	Recognition of self through both contingency and categorical features of the self. Emergence of notion that self is permanent, with stable and continuous features.
12–24 months	Consolidation of basic self categories, such as age and gender. Self-recognition through categorical knowledge alone, independent of contingency cues.

Source: Based on M. Lewis & J. Brooks-Gunn, *Social Cognition and the Acquisition of Self*. New York: Plenum Press, 1979. Reprinted with permission.

pany experimental evidence. Until new techniques for infant research are designed, Lewis and Brooks-Gunn's account shall remain our best view into the development of self-knowledge during infancy. This account is schematized in Table 3-3.

As can be seen from Table 3-3, Lewis and Brooks-Gunn have described four major advances in infants' self-knowledge as it develops during the first two years of life. The first of these advances is seen in infants younger than three months. Since the infants in Lewis and Brooks-Gunn studies were all six months or older, the authors' description of this first infant self-knowledge advance is conjectural, based upon informal observation and outside sources in the psychological literature. From birth to three months of age, the initial organizing principle to appear in infants' self-knowledge is an unlearned attraction to the images of other people, and especially to the images of young babies. This attraction shows up in a young infant's fascination with mirror images, drawings, and pictures of faces, especially when the face is that of the self or that of another young infant.

The second advance, occurring between three and eight months of age, is the ability to recognize the self through contingency cues. Both the mirror and the T.V. studies demonstrated this ability, the essence of which is the understanding that the self is the origin and cause of the moving visual image that the subject sees in the mirror or on the T.V. screen. In this sense, the subject must realize that both the image's cause (the self's actions) and the image's effect (its movement) spring from an identical source—the self. This realization, the authors believe, is the organizing principle that sustains the infant's self-recognition during the period from three to eight months. Of course, this principle may extend beyond the visual mode into other modes not studied by the researchers. Very likely, the infant comes to similar cause-effect realizations with regard to the contingency effects of his own voice, his own touch, and his own smell, identifying the self in these cases with actions and results that are perceived through nonvisual sensory modalities.

small not all that contingent (variable). Also habituation

The third self-knowledge advance, occurring between the ages of eight and twelve months, is the association of certain stable categorical features with the self. The infant now can go beyond recognizing the self merely as the origin of paired causes and effects in the world and can begin constructing the self as a permanent object with enduring qualities. In this manner, the permanence of the self is realized and becomes an important organizing principle for the infant's knowledge of both self-as-subject and self-as-object.

Finally, the fourth infancy advance, occurring throughout the second year of life, is the defining of the self through categorical features alone, independent of any contingency knowledge that the subject may have. In defining the self categorically, infants make particular use of age and gender features. Other categories are soon to follow; and, as we shall see throughout this book, the process of self-definition and self-redefinition continues throughout life.

Summary

Developing socially means not only becoming integrated into society, but also differentiating oneself from others in society. One must establish one's own place in the social order, one's own identity and personality—in short, one's own unique sense of self. Whereas Chapter 2 discussed the social aspect of infant life, the present chapter described the development of the infant as a separate individual with a unique sense of self.

Infants are at birth different from one another in a number of ways. Some of these early differences have consequences for the infant's social life; these consequences, in turn, can magnify the importance of the initial differences. For example, some babies are born more active, wiry, and resistant to physical contact than others. This may make them less "cuddly" than their peers and may diminish the amount and quality of their contact with their caregivers. Even physical differences between individual infants—such as their size and gender—may affect the infants' social interactions with caregivers in a wide variety of ways.

Not only can individual differences between newborns affect the newborns' early social interactions, but these differences may affect children's social interactions well after infancy. Studies of temperamental differences between infants indicate that initial temperamental characteristics endure for years and often have predictable behavioral consequences as late as elementary school. For example, infants with regular habits, positive moods, and positive approaches to new experiences get along well with parents and peers from the time of infancy onward and encounter few behavioral problems when adjusting to school. Infants, on the other hand, who are irregular in their eating and sleeping habits, who withdraw in new situations, and who are negative and intense in their moods and reactions, often encounter criticism from their parents and are inordinately likely to show later behavioral problems at home and at school. But although early temperamental differences between infants may have a continuing influence upon the course of their lives, the crucial determiner of such influence is the way in which the infant's temperamental nature is interpreted, both by others and by the self. Individual differences only have a social meaning to the extent that they are viewed as being significant in some way. This applies to such individual differences as newborns' auditory and visual responsiveness, their physical endowment, their sex, and their propensity to cry and fuss. Case studies of individual infants have documented the dynamic interplay between initial infant characteristics and the particular social-environmental conditions that the infant encounters during the first few years of life.

The *self* is the construct through which individuals organize their knowledge of their own unique nature and distinctiveness. A sense of self relies upon the notions that one is separate from others and that one has a stable, permanent identity.

Psychoanalysts like Margaret Mahler and Erik Erikson have studied infants' self-development through clinical case studies and retrospective reports of reminiscing adults. They have portrayed the initial steps in self-development as a process of separating oneself from a state of fusion and symbiosis with the mother. In Erikson's multidimensional model of development, he has charted the genetic connections between the newborn's struggle for self-recognition and her later, lifelong search for self-identity. According to Erikson, the development of self-identity depends upon resolving various crises that occur sequentially throughout life. Successful resolution of each crisis leads the way toward confronting a new area of potential difficulty, and in this manner, working out an increasingly adaptive personality.

In contrast to clinical studies of infant self-development, experimental studies, such as those by Michael Lewis and Jeanne Brooks-Gunn, have focused on the development of infants' cognitive abilities, such as the ability to recognize oneself in visual images. In a primitive form, progress in such abilities can be seen as early as the first three months of life (although the experimenters themselves have not succeeded in directly studying infants younger than six months or so). By extrapolating from Lewis and Brooks-Gunn's experimental results, we can piece together a developmental account of how infants construct self-knowledge during the first two years of life. Findings from their studies confirm several important advances in both *I* and *me* aspects of an infant's self during this relatively brief period. Yet infancy marks only the beginning of the lifelong process of self-definition and self-understanding.

Chapter 4

Peer Relations and the Development of Prosocial Behavior

As children grow beyond infancy, peers become an increasingly important part of their social lives. It is in early childhood that peer relations first have a regular and major influence upon children's social development. While relations with adults still dominate the child's social world, a gradual shift in the relative significance of peers and adults has begun.

Soon after infancy, three psychological changes in children greatly influence the quality and scope of their peer interactions. First, everyday events begin more and more to take on symbolic significance to children. That is, the events represent something beyond themselves. The new symbolic significance not only alters the meaning of the events but also creates a world of new social-interactional possibilities between the child and others. Children's social play, as well as children's more serious role-taking activities, are chief beneficiaries of this new symbolic awareness. A second psychological change in early childhood is the awakening of a sense of moral obligation. This sense imbues simple peer activities like sharing and turn-taking with an intensity and regularity that were missing in the occasional infant versions of the same activities. A third psychological change is that children during the preschool years begin to view social interactions as part of a system of stable relations that continue beyond the immediate present. This means that peers begin to be seen as friends rather than merely as playmates or momentary companions. With these three developments, a new quality of mutuality emerges in young children's peer relations. The social-developmental consequences of these changes continue to multiply throughout childhood and beyond. This chapter will consider the particular manifestations of these changes in children's peer relations.

Social Play between Children

During early childhood, when social play reaches its apogee as an activity, it is most common between peers. This is perhaps because children find the activities of peers more easily duplicated than those of adults and thus are more likely to follow through on peer-initiated than on adult-initiated playful overtures.[1] Because social play in early childhood is typically a peer activity, it is discussed mainly in the present chapter. Of course, social play between children and adults also exists. To the extent that child-adult play differs in form and function from child-child play, it will be discussed in the following chapter.

Grown-ups typically refer to whatever children do with one another as "play," as in "Emily and Jesse are playing together," or "Why don't you play with your friends this afternoon?" In such phrases, any behavior counts as play. But careful observers have noticed certain properties in children's social play that distinguish it as a special type of activity, with properties all its own. In social play, children often suspend reality, much the same way that an author does while creating a narrative script. Children voluntarily assume different roles, taking turns in order to make up a game, a theme, or a story. Particularly among younger children, such roles are make-believe, and the story theme is heavily imbued with fantasy. The world of "pretend" dominates the world of reality, even when mundane events are being discussed. Consider the following example of playful dialogue between a two-year-old boy and a three-year-old girl, quoted by Catherine Garvey:[2]

Girl (*3 years, 3 months*)	**Boy** (*2 years, 9 months*)
(1) Say, "Go to sleep now!'	
	(2) Go sleep now.
(3) Why? (*whining*)	
	(4) Baby. . .
(5) Why?	
	(6) Because.
(7) No, say "Because." (*emphatically*)	
	(8) Because! (*emphatically*)
(9) Why? Because why?	
	(10) Not good. You bad.

[1] Eckerman, Whatley, & Kutz, 1975. [2] Garvey, 1977.

(11) Why?

(12) 'Cause you spill your milk.

(13) No, 'cause I bit somebody.

(14) Yes, you did.

(15) Say, "Go to sleep. Put your head down." (*sternly*)

(16) Put your head down. (*sternly*)

(17) No.

(18) Yes.

(19) No.

(20) Yes, okay, I will spank you. Bad boy. (*spanks her*)

(21) My head's up. (*giggles*)

(22) I want my teddy bear. (*petulant voice*)

(23) No, your teddy bear go away. (*sternly*)

(24) Why?

(25) 'Cause he does. (*walks off with teddy bear*)

(26) Are you going to pack your teddy bear?

This typical example of social play is different in many ways from the more serious exchanges that young children have with others (exchanges, for example, that focus on sharing a toy or performing a task). Most noticeably, the playful exchange is full of pretense. In the example above, the young girl pretends to be a baby while the boy pretends to be her parent. During this act of pretense, the children assume roles that are familiar to them and yet distinct from their everyday identities. Like actors in a play, the children assume the make-believe roles with full awareness of the pretend nature of their activity. The girl in this example indicates such awareness by occasionally stepping outside of the role to give the boy direction ("Say, Go to sleep. . .").

Defining Play

If social play is only one of many things that children do with one another, how can we recognize it when we see it? Intuitively, it is not difficult to sense the difference between the example cited above and an episode during which, for example, two children earnestly discuss what T.V. show to turn on. But precisely defining social play as a special kind of activity with properties all of its own is a troublesome task that has occupied social scientists for decades.[3] The first, and major, problem has been to decide what "play" (solitary *or* social) is. Here, two features of play have stymied scientists trying to arrive at a precise conceptual definition. First, any activity can be performed seriously or playfully, including talking with friends, tying one's shoelaces, eating, going to the bathroom, or engaging in sports. This means that it is very hard to derive

[3] Schlosberg, 1947; Bruner, Jolly, & Sylva, 1976.

behavioral criteria that distinguish the activity "play" from other types of activities. The second difficulty is that there are many different signs of play, but not all of them occur together during a playful episode. For example, laughter sometimes signals play, but not every playful incident contains laughter. Similarly with fantasy, pretense, role playing, endless repetition, and all of the other potential indicators of play.

Although these quirks of play have made it a difficult concept to define, it is still necessary for us to do so, particularly in a discussion of children's social development. This is because play is a unique part of human behavior and, as such, serves several critical and irreplaceable functions in social life and personal development. Further, any observer of children soon notices the pervasiveness of social play in their daily behavior. Certainly any activity so consequential, so striking, and so common needs to be defined and explained.

Play can be regarded as an *attitude* or an *orientation*, rather than as a particular type of activity in itself. A playful attitude may be directed at any conceivable event. Its polar opposite is a serious, reality-oriented attitude, which also may be directed at any event. The implication here is that it is only the child's attitude that determines whether or not the child is playing, and not the actual nature of the activity. For example, if a child takes a playful attitude toward activities or objects normally associated with work (chores, books, school things), the child is at play. If a child "works" at activities normally associated with playtime (practicing game skills to perfection, exploring toys curiously), the child is not playing but rather is being serious. In line with this manner of conceptualizing play, Susannah Miller has suggested that the word "play" is best used as an adverb, as in "The children playfully ran away from one another."[4]

What, then, is the difference between a playful and a serious attitude, and how can we tell them apart? Generally, in play one molds reality to conform to the desire and capabilities of the self, whereas in serious activity the opposite is true. Work activities are intended to bring the self in closer touch with the demands of the world, but during play the "coercions and sanctions" of reality may be ignored.[5] The child may transform the world to his or her own wishes, substituting his or her own rules for the regulations and limitations normally encountered in life.

A number of specific behaviors signal a playful state, although, as noted above, not all of these are present in any one playful episode. The following is a list of play markers that has been compiled from the writings of several scientists who have observed and analyzed children's play.[6]

1. *Play is pursued for the sake of pleasure, and is often accompanied by signs of pleasure* (laughing, relaxation). Although work may also result in pleasure, play is pleasure-seeking in a more immediate and direct sense. Related to this is the notion that play is a repetition of an

[4] Miller, 1968.
[5] Piaget, 1962.

[6] Piaget, 1962; Herron & Sutton-Smith, 1971; Garvey, 1977; Rubin, 1980.

activity "for its own sake" (rather than for a goal-directed purpose), which again implies the pleasure-directiveness of play.

2. *Play is creative and nonliteral.*   It consists of unusual and imaginative variation of old activities and skills. Such variation is not restricted by the usual reality considerations but is free to take its own course. The inventions of play have a quality of fantasy and are not directed toward new modes of adaptation to reality (such as the development of knowledge or ability).

3. *Play is free from major affective distress.*   Play does not normally occur when a person is in a state of fear, uncertainty, or other kinds of great stress. During overriding stress, play does not continue. Mild stress or conflict is either ignored in the course of play or resolved through fantasy solutions that are impossible in real life. This is because in play, the trouble of the world can be represented relatively painlessly. Hence, play has appeal as a safe forum for working out one's conflicts.

4. *Play is spontaneous and self-initiated.*   It is engaged in only under a person's own free will and is neither evoked nor controlled by the demands of others.

5. *Play is a repetition or elaboration of behavior already acquired.*   It does not directly involve learning, exploration, or information seeking, at least as a direct goal (although one by-product of play is that it indirectly offers an opportunity to develop and exercise skills). Rather, play consists of a continuation of behavioral patterns that are already established in a child's repertoire.

6. *Play is not principally governed by drives or by the pursuit of external goals.*   This is another way of saying that play is pursued "for its own sake," rather than for the purpose of adaptation. This criterion overlaps with several of the earlier ones, and again conforms to the notion that play consists of molding reality to the child's activity, rather than accommodating the activity to meet the demands of internal and external realities.

Both children and adults engage in many kinds of play, among which social play is only one variety. In addition to social play, there is self-centered play, focusing on a person's own body, and there is object play, focusing on some material aspect of the physical environment. Social play occurs in interaction with other people. Garvey has defined it as "a state of engagement in which the successive, nonliteral behaviors of one partner are contingent on the nonliteral behaviors of the other partner."[7] All of these types of play—self-

---

[7] Note that Garvey hinges her definition on the notion that play is mainly *nonliteral* behavior. This was one (number 3) of our seven markers of play above, though we included others as well for a more comprehensive definition. It also appears, however, that Garvey's use of "nonliteralness" as her main criteria is broad enough to include some of the other markers that we have listed. She cites, for example, laughter as one sign of nonliteral behavior (Garvey, 1974).

centered, object, and social—begin early in infancy and continue throughout adulthood. For example, self-centered play may be seen not only in the hand-waving and toe-tweaking of young infants but also in the playful body exercising (dancing, miming) of adults. The three types of play are present at all ages, but there is a shift in the relative frequency with which one engages in each type of play as one grows older.[8] In early infancy, a child spends the greatest part of playtime in self-centered play. Later in infancy, object play becomes more frequent, dominating other types of play. From childhood on, social play reaches its ascendancy. Developmental reasons for the shift will be discussed toward the end of this section.

Functions of Social Play

In a study of girls and boys ages three to five, Garvey was able to identify some of the special properties of social play during the early childhood years, when social play first becomes a common activity.[9] Using her criteria of nonliteralness and alternating contingency of behavior, Garvey found 158 episodes of social play in about nine hours of videotaped observations of children freely interacting. Social play, therefore, while frequent, was by no means the only (or even the predominant) type of interaction between children. Garvey analyzed the 158 social play episodes and concluded that they all reflected three types of competence that develop by early childhood. The first is the ability to distinguish reality from play, as is demonstrated by two children in an interchange such as "Really?". . ."No, just pretend." The second is an ability to abstract rules of social interaction; in particular, the rule of turn-taking during a play episode. This ability was frequently demonstrated by children giving directions to one another during social play, such as "You go next," or "Do it again." Third, children engaged in social play are able jointly to develop and vary a theme. In this sense, writes Garvey, "any episode of social play entails the exercise of *shared imagination.*"[10] It is almost as if children simultaneously act as playwrights and actors in their creation of a narrative script. The boy and girl quoted above as they exchange roles of parent and baby demonstrate how young children create and act out dramatic themes in this manner.

Garvey's analysis of children's social play draws heavily on the theory of the Russian psychologist Lev Vygotsky (1896–1934), who long ago proposed a connection between play and the development of symbolic abilities.[11] Vygotsky argued that the special feature of play is that it requires a child to reverse the normal relation between an action and its symbolic significance (or "meaning"). In most of a child's life, an action is simply what it stands for: a shove means "get away," a scolding means what it says, and so on. In play, however, actions take on a new significance, often quite divorced from their face value. A

[8] Parten, 1933; Buhler, 1935; Barnes, 1971; Eckerman, Whatley, & Kutz, 1975.
[9] Garvey, 1974.
[10] Ibid, p. 170.
[11] Vygotsky, 1976.

shove may be part of a ritual that invites a playmate to shove back, and a scolding may be part of a narrative theme that calls for a complementary role to be acted out. Further, not only do actions take on a new symbolic significance during play, but the symbolic significance actually dominates the action. This is what it means to interpret actions playfully rather than seriously. Thus, if one action in a play sequence does not succeed in preserving the play theme, another action may be substituted. It is the symbolic meaning of the play episode that is primary, rather than the specific actions themselves. It is less important to a playing child to utter particular words that a father might say than to maintain the role of father in a shared dramatic episode: if certain phrases do not work in conducting the play, others are tried.

Vygotsky wrote that, to a child, the rules of the play episode are a fundamental part of the symbolic meaning of that episode. In play, therefore, children show an unusual consciousness of rules underlying social interaction and directly mold their behavior to establish and conform to such rules. During play, of course, interaction rules are determined by the playing children themselves, rather than imposed by external social forces. The turn-taking rules that Garvey described are typical examples of rules that children themselves impose upon their own play behavior.

The example of self-imposed play rules that Vygotsky himself made famous was of two sisters "playing" at being sisters. In this example, two little sisters, aged five and seven, one day agreed to "play sisters." As they did so, their behavior changed remarkably from their normal sisterly conduct. It became stylized and self-conscious, acting out stereotypical versions of sisterhood roles. Vygotsky writes that the "vital difference in play" is that "the child in playing tried to be a sister." He continues:

> In life the child behaves without thinking that she is her sister's sister. She never behaves with respect to the other just because she is her sister—except perhaps in those cases where her mother says, "Give in to her." In the game of sisters playing at "sisters," however, they are both concerned with displaying their sisterhood; the fact that the two sisters decided to play sisters makes them both acquire rules of behavior. (I must always be a sister in relation to the other sister in the whole play situation.) Only actions which fit these rules are acceptable to the play situation.[12]

According to Vygotsky, therefore, play affords children unique opportunities to separate symbolic meaning from mundane events and to consciously manipulate rules of social interaction. Consequently, play assumes an enormous developmental significance in Vygotsky's theory. It is the realm in which children acquire their most basic human capacities: the abilities to think symbolically, to reason about what is possible rather than what is merely real, and to examine the underlying meaning of their own social behavior. Creativity, self-consciousness, and hypothetical thinking are therefore all connected developmentally to the "pretend" games of young children. Because of this critical developmental role, Vygotsky calls play the child's "zone of proximal

[12] Ibid., pp. 541–42.

development," meaning that play creates the conditions for the child's acquisition of new imaginative and social competencies. Vygotsky concludes that although play is not the child's predominant form of activity, it is nevertheless "the leading source of development in the preschool years." Many contemporary developmentalists have accepted and further explicated the connections that Vygotsky established between play, symbolism, and the development of social and intellectual knowledge.[13]

Aside from its developmental significance, the symbolic nature of play has an additional value to a child: it offers the child an opportunity to both stabilize and enrich his emotional life through varieties of expression not available in his everyday, reality-bound repertoire of activity. Since playful behavior has primarily a symbolic meaning, the consequences of this behavior do not directly affect the child's welfare. Children can take chances and express sentiments that would otherwise seem dangerous or threatening. Also, the range of themes for playful behavior is limited only by the child's imagination, and not by realistically realizable events. Through play, the child therefore is able to express otherwise unacceptable thoughts and feelings, and to explore the full range of imaginable experience.

It is this value of play that psychoanalysts have stressed in their writings. Freud himself described children's use of play to master conflictual events in their lives.[14] More recently, Lili Peller has followed Freud's lead in analyzing the symbolic content of play in terms of its emotional value to children. Peller writes that children's play is their attempt to "compensate for anxieties and deficiencies, to obtain pleasure at a minimum risk of danger and/or irreversible consequences."[15] This may happen in several ways, according to Peller. Faced with a difficult or unpleasant situation, the child at play can, without risk, try out imaginary ways to resolve it. In addition, a playful re-enactment of distressful scenes from the past may lead to mastery over the emotions initially experienced. The child may compensate for reality by correcting it, by changing roles in order to reverse the situation, or by changing the outcome in order to provide a "happy ending." Or the child may simply repeat an unpleasant episode over and over again, thereby lessening the impact of the initial experience. Through playful activity, the child is thus able to come to grips with his feelings and with the sometimes harsh realities of the world.

A related benefit of symbolism in play is the opportunity it provides for obtaining satisfaction of wishes that are not otherwise realizable. Through fantasy play, children may be cowboys, airplane pilots, teachers—or anything else they wish. Were play not available, children would always be bound by the realistic limitations of their abilities and could experience only frustration at the hands of these limitations.

A third benefit, according to psychoanalysts like Peller, comes through the "catharsis" of unpleasant or unacceptable emotional states. By playing out

---

[13] Huttenlocher & Higgins, 1978; Fein, 1979; Gardner, 1979.

[14] Freud, 1920.

[15] Peller, 1954.

scenes to their own advantage, children are able to neutralize fears and, in play, to do things that would not otherwise be dared. Playful expressions of anger or hostility—toward the child's mother, father, siblings—make it possible to vent these emotions without suffering potentially harmful consequences. Thus, the child playing with a doll can say, "Dolly has a nasty father. He never lets her play. Dolly's mother chose very badly," without losing father's affection. The child can even make mother "disappear" without really losing her.

A fourth emotional benefit of play cited by Peller is its role in the child's development of a positive self-conception. Children at play can set their own terms. They may create situations in which they are competent, thereby gaining a feeling of power over the environment. This feeling breeds confidence in real interactions with the world. In addition, turning from a passive to an active role during play encourages increasingly effective participation in the real world. Without this opportunity to experience feelings of power or competence in situations of the child's own design, self-confidence would be subject to the vagaries of success or failure in the far less accommodating atmosphere of the real world.

Because of its symbolic nature, therefore, play serves several vital functions in the life of a child. First, it offers the child an opportunity to develop and exercise the symbolic skills that make possible all creative and sophisticated processes of intelligence. Second, it offers the child an opportunity to represent sentiments that are normally difficult to express, thereby enriching and stabilizing the child's emotional life. Further, the social versions of childhood play serve yet another important developmental function, a function again related to the symbolic nature of play. While constructing make-believe roles for each other to enact, children engaged in social play gain a precious opportunity to coordinate their actions and intentions in a cooperative manner. In so doing, they join together in a creative experimentation with social roles and rules. The social-cognitive rewards of this cooperative effort should not be underestimated. During such instances of "shared imagination," children not only must learn to communicate effectively with others, but they also are forced to think reflectively about the very elements of social interaction—roles and rules. Social play is an enjoyable and self-conscious exercise in mutuality, and it offers children a chance to explore patterns of social interaction that they would rarely experience in real life. The child's social knowledge is certainly a primary beneficiary of such activity.

Developmental Phases of Children's Play

The many fruits of social play are apparent enough in the early childhood years, when the incidences of such play become increasingly frequent. But is the primary importance of the social forms of play confined to these few years, when they appear to flourish most dramatically? This is an intriguing developmental question that we have yet to consider. The heart of this question is the issue of whether social play is most representative of one particular period in a child's social development, and if so, why it is that early childhood should be this period. Related to this are questions of what leads up to and what follows from the waxing of social play in young children's lives, and what accounts for such transitions.

Psychologists who have studied the development of children's play have offered a number of reasons to explain why play becomes increasingly social in the period directly following infancy. In Piaget's theory, the "waning of egocentrism" during the early childhood years allows children to engage in cooperative activity, including social play.[16] (We shall discuss further Piaget's notion of egocentrism and the controversies surrounding it in the next section.) Piaget associates the onset of social play with the young child's developing cognitive ability to understand the point of view of another, and thereby to effectively communicate with the other. Piaget believes that children share points of view most easily with their peers, so that social play between children is one of the first examples of truly cooperative and reciprocal social interaction. By middle childhood, Piaget writes, children's social play becomes formalized and conventionalized. The result is the transformation of creative social play into "games with rules." Such games maintain their formats from occasion to occasion, and so individual children have less freedom to construct their own interactional patterns than they do in the dramatic "scripts" of earlier social play. In Piaget's theory, therefore, the processes of cognitive development and socialization account for both the increase of social play after infancy and its subsequent decline later in childhood. The cognitive advance that makes possible the taking of others' perspectives also makes social play possible, and the socialization advance that enables children to follow and respect conventional, shared rules marks the end of social play in its pure, unfettered form.

Piaget's developmental account is substantiated not only by his own informal observations, but also by data from several more formal observational studies of young children at play.[17] The earliest and most widely replicated of these studies was conducted by Mildred Parten almost fifty years ago.[18] Parten observed forty-two children between the ages of two and five during their morning nursery-school free-play time. She distinguished five categories that were evident in children's play[19] and ordered these categories in a scale of "social participation," with the latter categories representing more advanced

[16] Piaget, 1932, 1962.
[17] Smith & Connolly, 1972; Lowe, 1975; Rubin & Maioni, 1975; Rubin & Pepler, 1980.
[18] Parten, 1933.
[19] As with much research on children's "play," Parten's report does not indicate what, exactly, was considered play in the first place. Since researchers are not always explicit in their definitions of play —or, when they are, they often disagree with one another in their definitions —comparing results from different studies has been an enduring problem of interpretation. Parten's use of the notion "play" was more inclusive than our own definition, but how much more is uncertain. In any case, in discussing Parten's findings, we are assuming that there is considerable overlap between the "play" activities that she observed and the kinds of activities that we would call play, even though we can only speculate as to the exact extent of the overlap.

types of interactive behaviors. In quantifying her results, Parten weighted these categories with numbers that indicated "how much" social participation she believed each of these play categories represent. Parten's summaries are given below, in the order of their position on Parten's social participation scale, and along with the quantitative weights that Parten gave them.[20]

1. *Unoccupied behavior* (Weight: −3).   The child apparently is not playing, but occupies himself with watching anything that happens to be of momentary interest. When there is nothing exciting taking place, he plays with his own body, gets on and off chairs, just stands around, follows the teacher, or sits in one spot glancing around the room.

2. *Solitary play* (Weight: −2).   The child plays alone and independently with toys that are different from those used by the children within speaking distance and makes no effort to get close to other children. He pursues his own activity without reference to what others are doing.

3. *Onlooking behavior* (Weight: −1).   The child spends most of his time watching the other children play. He often talks to the children whom he is observing, asks questions, or gives suggestions, but he does not overtly enter into the play himself. This type of behavior differs from the unoccupied behavior in that the onlooker is definitely observing particular groups of children, rather than anything that happens to be exciting. The child stands or sits within speaking distance of the group so that he can see and hear everything that takes place.

4. *Parallel play* (Weight: 1).   The child plays independently, but the activity he chooses naturally brings him among other children. He plays with toys that are like those which the children around him are using, but he plays with the toys as he sees fit and does not try to influence or modify the activity of the children near him. He plays *beside* rather than *with* the other children. There is no attempt to control the coming or going of children in the group.

5. *Associative play* (Weight: 2).   The child plays with other children. The conversation concerns the common activity. There is a borrowing and loaning of play material, following one another with trains or wagons, and mild attempts to control which children may or may not play in the group. All the members engage in similar if not identical activity. There is no division of labor and no organization of the activity of several individuals around any material goal or product. The children do not subordinate their individual interests to that of the group; instead, each child acts as he wishes. By his conversation with the other children, one can tell that his interest is primarily in his associations, not in his activity. Occasionally, two or three children are engaged in no

[20] Parten, 1933, pp. 257–59.

activity of any duration but are merely doing whatever happens to draw the attention of any of them.

6. *Cooperative organized play* (Weight: 3).   The child plays in a group that is organized for the purpose of making some material product, striving to attain some competitive goal, dramatizing situations of adult and group life, or playing formal games. There is a marked sense of belonging or of not belonging to the group. The control of the group situation is in the hands of one or two of the members who direct the activity of the others. The goal as well as the method of attaining it necessitates a division of labor, the taking of different roles by the various group members, and the organization of activity so that the efforts of one child are supplemented by those of another.

Among her two- to-five-year-old subjects, Parten found parallel play to be the most frequent kind of play activity. But there were striking differences between the younger and the older children within this age group. These differences are clearly shown in Figure 4-1. For one thing, the incidence of parallel play declined with age, particularly in the period between two and four years. Along with this was a similar decline in children's solitary play. During the same age period, while solitary and parallel play were declining, associative and cooperative play were on the rise. Therefore, the older children in Parten's study were more likely than the younger ones to play in modes described by the more advanced categories of social participation. Another way of expressing this same result is the strong correlation (.61) that Parten reported between her social participation scale and the age of her subjects.

Parten's results are compatible with Piaget's developmental theory of children's play because they indicate that, with development, children are more likely to interact in a truly cooperative manner. Like Piaget, Parten suggests that, immediately after infancy, children's play is primarily solitary or "parallel" at best. Her notion of parallel play is a behavioral version of Piaget's notion of egocentrism, since both portray children as wrapped up in their own points of view, oblivious to the possibility of more direct interaction with those around them. Further, Parten also sees a shift from informal "associative" types of social play to more organized group activity by the end of early childhood. This shift is identical to the onset of "games with rules" that Piaget described. Parten's results have been replicated in a number of child-observational studies over the past fifty years, and her social participation scale has been incorporated into countless contemporary instruments for recording children's behavior in natural, free-play settings.[21]

A recent study by Roger Bakeman and John Brownlee has shed new light on parallel play and its significance for children's social development.[22] Using coding categories basically similar to Parten's scheme, Bakeman and Brownlee analyzed the free play of children at age three. The investigators then performed a sequential analysis of these free-play data and used a statistical

[21] Blurton-Jones, 1967; Smith & Connolly, 1972; Garvey, 1977.

[22] Bakeman & Brownlee, 1980.

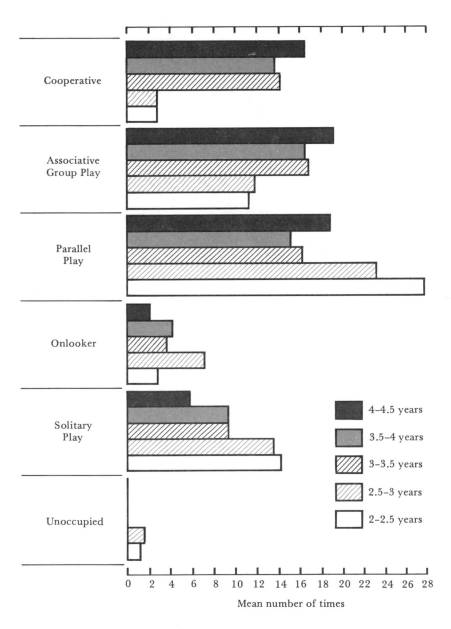

Figure 4-1. Social Participation and Age. The bars show the mean number of times each activity was engaged in at different ages. There were six children at each age level, and sixty observations were made on each child.

Source: M. Parten, Social participation among pre-school children. *Journal of Abnormal Psychology*, 1932, *27*, 260. Reprinted with permission.

procedure to calculate the probability that one type of behavior would follow another in sequence. This enabled Bakeman and Brownlee to determine that there was a strong probability that, in the course of a play session, a child's parallel play would be followed by associative or organized group play. It was improbable that parallel play would lead into solitary or unoccupied behavior. Bakeman and Brownlee conclude that parallel play may be used as a strategy by children who desire the company of others, but who do not have the social skills to directly initiate associative or group play. For these children, a brief episode of parallel play may serve as a transitional "warm-up" activity, orienting the child socially and leading to the cooperative play that the child actually desires. Age three—the approximate age of the Bakeman-Brownlee sample—may be just the time when children need such an orienting period. The authors conclude that "the movement from parallel play to group play may be more a matter of minutes than months, and that for the 32–42 month-old children observed here parallel play often functions in the stream of activities as a bridge to group play."[23] This conclusion points to the role of parallel play as a transitory social strategy more than as a developmental phase in the child's life.

Psychoanalysts like Lili Peller add still a further reason why play becomes more social and more cooperative during the early childhood years. The psychoanalytic account of children's play, as noted earlier, is particularly sensitive to the emotional value of the symbolism in play. In playing out a symbolic theme, a child can represent in a non-threatening way whatever troublesome or disturbing concerns she may have. Peller points out that the concerns of childhood change as children grow older because their social situations change in many important respects. Infants are largely confined to a social universe of intense interaction between themselves and their mothers. Soon, writes Peller, this universe expands to include other grown-ups (particularly the father), siblings, and peers. As the child's social universe changes, so do the areas of potential conflict and fear in her life. (So too, of course, does the possible range of persons with whom the child can construct a play theme, though this is not the focus of Peller's analysis.) With new conflicts and fears emerging in her life, the child must find ways of representing these new concerns through play. Turning to social forms of play, writes Peller, is one way for the child to fulfill this need. Thus, in psychoanalytic theory, new forms of play develop as a function of emerging life concerns that need to be represented symbolically in the themes of play.

Table 4-1 is Peller's survey of play activities from infancy through early childhood. The four "groups" of play that she lists correspond somewhat to Piaget's and to Parten's discussions of play development. From solitary play in groups 1 and 2, the child progresses to "early co-play" in group 3, and then to "organized co-play" in group 4. But in Peller's scheme, the progression reflects not only the child's developing social competence but also the changing emotional themes of childhood. In infancy, Peller cites anxieties over one's body as

[23] Ibid.

Table 4-1 Survey of Play Activities

	Central theme of play/object relations	Deficiencies anxiety (denied)	Social aspect	Play material	Secondary play gains
Group I	**Relation to Body** .... Anxieties concerning body	My body is no good. I am often helpless.	Solitary.	Extensions and variations of body functions and body parts.	Increased body skills and mastery. Initiation into active search for gratification.
Group II	**Relation to Pre-Oedipal Mother** .... Fear of losing love object	My Mother can— desert me; do as she pleases.	Solitary or with mother. Other children rank with pets, or things —not as co-players. Sporadic mirroring play.	Maternal play with dolls, stuffed animals, with other children, and mother herself. Peek-a-boo. Earliest tools.	Rage, anxiety mitigated; ability to bear delay, frustration. Initiation into lasting object relation.
Group III (*starts about 3 years*)	*Oedipal* Relations and defenses against them. .... Fear of losing love of love object	I cannot enjoy what grown-ups enjoy.	Early co-play. Attempts to share fantasy. Fantasy always social. Activity may be solitary or social.	Dollplay; wide variety of events, of father, mother images: pilot, nurse, magician, etc. Creative play, Imaginative play. Use of emblems, props, insignia.	Preparation for adult roles, adult skills. Co-play prepares co-work. Initiation into adventure, accomplishment.
Group IV (*starts about 6 years*)	*Sibling* Relations .... Fear of superego and superego figures	I am all alone against threatening authority. I cannot start all over again.	Organized co-play. Fantasy tacitly shared.	Team games. Board games. Organized games. Games with token armies	Dissolving Oedipal ties. Co-operation with brothers, with followers and leaders experienced as gratifying.

Source: Based on L. E. Peller, Libidinal phases, ego development, and play. *Psychoanalysis*, 1955, *3*(3), 3–12.

a primary theme, and naturally such anxieties are represented in self-centered, solitary play. A bit later, fear of losing love objects—first as related to the caregiver and then as related to the Oedipal figure—is the central theme that needs representing. This theme finds its most natural enactment in solitary play, in mother-child play, and in early forms of peer co-play. Finally, themes relating to moral (or "superego") anxieties are represented, according to Peller, in the organized play of middle childhood: team games, games with formal rules, and so on. It is noteworthy that the "play gains" that Peller envisions are a combination of gains in competence ("preparation for adult roles, adult skills") and emotional gains ("rage, anxiety mitigated"; "dissolving Oedipal ties"). Because of its emphasis on the emotional as well as the social and cognitive aspects of children's play, Peller's account is a valuable complement to any developmental theory of play.

The symbolic interactions of children's social play are symbolic interactions of a special kind. As we have stressed several times in this section, they are by definition a nonliteral and nonserious type of symbolic interaction, despite their very real benefits to the child's life and their very serious consequences for the child's social development. Other, more serious types of symbolic social interactions also appear with increasing frequency during early childhood. As in children's play, peer relations provide a natural forum for these other symbolic interactions. These shall be the subject of the following section.

Symbolism and Interpersonal Communication

Although symbolism and play have a developmental connection to one another, particularly in early childhood, symbolic activity also serves many serious purposes in human social encounters. The most important of these is symbolism's role in facilitating interpersonal communication. As we saw in the infancy section, communication (or at least protocommunication) is part of social life even during the first few months; but the flourishing of symbolic activity toward the end of infancy makes possible a powerful new form of dialogue and shared meaning between the child and others. Further, this new symbolic dialogue gives the child access to an extended range of social influences, opening the way for the child's further social development.

Mead's Significant Symbols and Role Taking[24]

George Herbert Mead, in his theory of the significant symbol, explicitly

[24] Role taking, like social play, occurs between children and adults as well as between children and their peers. Our discussion of role taking is placed in the present chapter for two reasons. First, as will be discussed later in this chapter, there is reason to believe that young children take the roles of their peers more easily and more effectively than they do with adults. This is not surprising, considering the greater similarity of children to one another than to adults and considering the generally cooperative and reciprocal nature of many peer interactions. Second,

asserted the importance of symbolic interaction for social exchange and communication. For Mead, significant symbols are gestures "which arouse in the individual himself the response which he is calling out in the other. . ."[25] A spoken word is a prototypical example of a Meadian significant symbol, since the speaker's interpretation of the word is fundamentally the same as the listener's.

The notion of symbolic interaction led Mead to attempt to explain how humans establish shared meaning in the course of communicating with one another. Mead's explanation was that individuals learn to "take the role of the other" as they interact with other persons. Through such *role taking*, individuals are able to find agreement between the meaning that the self and the other place on actions and events. The thoughts and understanding of the other can be anticipated, and the self's gestures may be adjusted accordingly, for optimal communication. In this way, a speaker knows that when he or she expresses a sentiment or idea, the meaning that is communicated is that which the speaker intended. Mead writes that this process of "mutual adjustment" is the basis for most human social interaction as we know it. Mead's theory, therefore, places the symbolic potential of human thought at the center of all advanced forms of social interaction, suggesting role taking as the social-psychological process through which symbolic interaction is carried out.

Role taking can be defined as mentally placing oneself in another's position: in popular terms, "putting yourself in someone else's shoes." It is the cognitive realization of another's point of view, an activity that also has been called "social perspective taking."[26] Mead assumed that the ability to take the role of the other was a uniquely human ability that developed sometime early in life. Further, he believed that there were two "general stages" of development, each of which reflected a particular type of role-taking ability. In the first type of role taking, a person simply takes the role of particular others with whom he comes in contact, getting to know each of their attitudes individually, through specific social acts. In the second type of role taking, the person comes to know the collective point of view of the "social group as a whole to which he belongs."[27] Mead called this collective point of view the "generalized other." A person's realization of the attitudes of the generalized other enables him to acquire societal standards and beliefs. In Mead's theory, therefore, role taking is central not only to the establishment of social relations and communication but also to the moral development and socialization of the individual.

Role Taking and Developmental Theory

Mead's writings contribute greatly to our understanding of social interac-

---

most developmental studies of role taking present children with tasks in which they are required to take the perspective of a peer. Although rationales behind such task choices are rarely presented, a good guess is that psychologists study children's role taking in peer contexts because this is where children take roles most naturally.

[25] Mead, 1934.
[26] Selman, 1976a; Kurdek, 1978.
[27] Mead, 1934, p. 54.

tion processes, although as John Flavell has pointed out, these writings fall somewhat short of being developmental theory.[28] Flavell notes that a developmental theory must outline the difficulties that children encounter in acquiring a skill like role taking, and it must analyze how children overcome these difficulties. Mead's writings acknowledge neither the problems that a person faces in attempting to take the role of another, nor the errors that persons (particularly children) often make in attempting to infer another's point of view. Without such an acknowledgment, it is difficult to study or describe children's progress as role takers in the course of their social development.

Flavell asserts that the main shortcoming in Mead's theory is that "his theoretical constructs (significant symbols and generalized others) are basically mechanisms for generating sameness, for creating individual homogeneity."[29] This is similar to the critique that we offered of both Baldwin and Mead's theories in Chapter 1. The critical problem is that not only are persons similar to one another in many respects, they are also different in important ways. In some cases, we can correctly predict that another person will respond to a word or a situation in much the same way as ourselves, and we can determine the other's point of view with direct reference to our own. Often, however, the other person's point of view will differ from our own in important ways, due to divergences in the life histories and mental orientations of ourselves and others. In such cases, role taking is a more complex and inferential activity. Opportunities for error abound. For example, it may be difficult for a rich person to anticipate a poor person's reaction to a material offer, or an older person to understand a younger person's communication needs. These and countless other cases of *perspective discrepancies* are the major obstacles to role taking and communication between people.

Perspective discrepancies pose an especially difficult problem for young children first learning to interact and communicate with others. A number of recent empirical studies have documented the mistakes and confusions with which young children often greet perspective discrepancies between people.[30] In one of the earliest of such studies, children were asked to tell stories from each of three pictured characters' viewpoints.[31] The youngest children (below age six or so) did not distinguish between the three characters' viewpoints, telling the stories in the same way for each character. Children a bit older could distinguish between the characters' viewpoints but could not relate them to one another: these children had each character tell his own story, but they did not coordinate the three separate stories into one coherent tale. Only among groups of subjects ages eight and above were there a sizable number of children who could both distinguish and relate perspectives of story characters.

A host of other experimental techniques have revealed children's problems in dealing with differences in social perspectives. Flavell and his colleagues designed a number of such techniques, ranging from relatively

---

[28] Flavell et al., 1968.
[29] Ibid., p. 15.

[30] Shantz, 1975.
[31] Feffer & Gourevitch, 1960.

simple picture-recognition tasks to more complex interpersonal games.[32] Among the simplest of these tasks is showing a child a two-sided card, with one side picturing a cat and the other a dog.[33] Does the child realize that the person holding the card is looking at something different than the child? When asked "What do I see?" by the experimenter, about half of a group of two-year-olds answered incorrectly on this task. Yet this is perhaps the simplest role-taking problem psychologists have devised. More complex perspective-discrepancy tasks reveal similar role-taking problems among older children. For example, children of elementary-school age had great difficulty giving helpful communicative messages to another child who was blindfolded.[34] They often forgot (or never realized) that persons without sight need more elaborate and action-oriented information than do people with sight. Other studies based on similar communication tasks have reported similar findings.[35] Finally, up to the adolescent years, children often show difficulty in dealing with different perspectives during games that require them to outwit an opponent. Here the problem is predicting what the opponent's perspective is, as well as figuring out how to have an influence on the opponent's perspective so that she will make a mistake. This kind of perspective-taking skill can be a lifelong accomplishment, as any frustrated poker player will know.

A developmental account of role taking must explain how children confront and overcome the conceptual difficulties presented to them by discrepancies between people's perspectives. As noted above, Mead's theory does not deal with the problem. Mead's role-taking theory was social-psychological, rather than developmental, focusing mainly on the connections between social interaction, symbolism, and role taking, rather than on the ontogenesis of any of these behaviors during the lives of individuals. For this reason, of course, we cannot reasonably expect Mead's theory to give us a full account of how children acquire such behaviors.

Egocentrism and Role Taking

A number of developmentalists, following Mead's lead, have focused on role taking as a central process in social interaction and communication and have studied children's acquisition of role-taking skills. Many of these developmentalists have incorporated into their studies some key concepts introduced by Piaget in his early work, particularly the notion of *egocentrism*. As we shall see, however, there has been serious contention about how helpful this concept is in describing children's social development.

Piaget himself never wrote of "role taking," but rather introduced some constructs, like egocentrism, that have provided a partial basis for contemporary accounts of children's role-taking abilities. In his early work, Piaget characterized primitive mental states (such as those typifying young children)

---

[32] Flavell et al., 1968; Masangkay et al., 1974.

[33] Masangkay et al., 1974.

[34] Flavell et al., 1968.

[35] Glucksberg, Kraus, & Higgens, 1975.

as egocentric and defined egocentrism as "the confusion of the self with the non-self."[36] Such a confusion implies a failure to recognize that others' perspectives are different from one's own, or, as we might say today, an incapacity to role take. In one early book, Piaget loosely wrote of a *stage of egocentrism* in which there is "behavior intermediate between individual and socialized behavior" when the child "plays in an individual manner with material that is social."[37] The stage of egocentrism yields in the course of development to a *stage of cooperation* characterized by differentiation and consequent reciprocal interchange between self and other.

\Parallel play is a perfect example of egocentrism in action. The child participates in a collective activity but remains embedded within his own point of view, confined to a focus upon his own behavior and thought.\ Piaget observed that even the conversations of young children often have this quality. Although the children exchange words, there is little sharing of ideas or communication of information. Rather, there is a "collective monologue" in which one child's words may be cues for the other child's reply, but in which there is no reciprocal exchange in any sense. These egocentric, non-dialogical "conversations" can sound quite odd to adult ears. The following is an example of four children talking together while making drawings:

> Child 1 (5 years, 11 months): It begins with Goldilocks. I'm writing the story of the three bears. The daddy bear is dead. Only the daddy was too ill.
>
> Child 2 (5 years, 11 months): I used to live at Saleve. I lived in a little house and you had to take the funicular railway to go and buy things.
>
> Child 3 (6 years, 10 months): I can't do the bear.
>
> Child 4 (6 years, 10 months): That's not Goldilocks.
>
> Child 1: I haven't got curls.[38]

No one who has spent time around young children doubts that they often engage in such noncommunicative discourse, but the developmental significance of such behavior is far from clear. Piaget initially believed that this nonreciprocal form of speech was an inevitable outcome of children's egocentrism, a cognitive limitation so pervasive that it colored every aspect of children's understanding and behavior. But a number of critics have pointed to problems in this analysis. For one thing, it was soon observed that the same children who engage in collective monologues with one another also, at other times, can communicate effectively and with full reciprocity.[39] Further analyses of Piaget's own data reveal considerably more communicative exchange, even among his youngest subjects, than Piaget acknowledged. The problem here may have been that Piaget's means of coding children's speech was too stringent, underestimating children's communicative competence.[40] In fact, contemporary research has shown that children as young as four can communi-

---

[36] Piaget, 1955.
[37] Piaget, 1932.
[38] Piaget, 1955, p. 21.

[39] Vygotsky, 1962.
[40] Gottman & Parkhurst, 1980.

cate non-egocentrically with each other.[41] They can even adapt their speech in order to take into account deficiencies in the listener's ability—using simplified speech patterns, for example, when talking to a younger companion.[42] If young children are able to interact so effectively, they must be able to role take in some meaningful way.

Does it make sense, therefore, to posit a general cognitive pattern like egocentrism that supposedly characterizes early childhood? An additional, though opposite, problem is that the confusion of perspectives which Piaget called egocentrism does not end when childhood is over. Adults, too, frequently do not take the role of the other in situations where such behavior is appropriate (or even necessary). Yet, these adults are cognitively far more sophisticated than even the children in Piaget's studies who had attained the "subsequent stage of cooperation." Is it accurate, then, to describe development beyond childhood as a decline of egocentrism? Egocentrism, whatever its worth as an analytic construct, does not seem to adequately describe a particular phase in children's social development.

Egocentrism as multidimensional. Recent experimental work on children's perspective taking sheds further doubt on the egocentrism construct when used to characterize the core nature of young children's thinking. Role-taking tasks of the type designed by Feffer, Flavell, and others reveal a wide variation in young children's abilities to take others' perspectives.[43] On some tasks, young children role take quite well, whereas on others they perform naively and egocentrically. The specific nature of the task seems to have a strong influence on how well the child will role take. Lawrence Kurdek, in a literature review, concludes that perspective taking must be considered a multidimensional construct.[44] Some tasks draw on certain facets of the perspective-taking process, others on different facets, and others (the most complex ones) on all of them together. By this line of reasoning, egocentrism should not be considered a unitary construct at all, but rather a manifestation of many separate confusions and cognitive limitations, all of which are task-specific. On some problems, therefore, children may not perform egocentrically, whereas on others, both children and adults will have trouble taking perspectives other than their own.

Various cognitive analyses of role taking have suggested a number of distinguishable components. For example, E. Tory Higgins has identified at least two: the ability to consider multiple "elements" in a problem, and the ability to "control the self" and the self's own perspective when considering a problem.[45] John Flavell has suggested some other isolatable components, all related to the ways in which children process information while making interpersonal inferences.[46] But for now, these analyses remain speculative.

[41] Garvey & Hogan, 1973; Gottman & Parkhurst, 1980.
[42] Shatz & Gelman, 1973.
[43] Glucksberg, Kraus, & Higgens, 1975.
[44] Kurdek, 1978.
[45] Higgins, 1980.
[46] Flavell, 1977.

Piaget himself came to recognize the deficiencies in his egocentrism construct, particularly when this construct was used to describe a period in development like childhood. In later writings on intellectual development, Piaget used the egocentrism notion to describe a variety of self-other confusions throughout life, rather than to characterize a particular "stage" of development. The way out of egocentrism in these later writings is through the process of "decentering" which enables the person to distinguish and take into account the various possible perspectives on any given problem. Used in this sense, perspective taking becomes a general strategy for considering information about different points of view. As a strategy, perspective taking is not tied to any stage of life, but rather it can potentially operate *in some form* at any time in life. The phrase "in some form" is significant here, particularly with respect to children's development. The question still remains, however, as to whether there are *different* strategies of perspective taking, some more effective and developmentally advanced than others. Do children use a better strategy as they grow older? Or is it simply that they use the same basic strategy more?

Egocentrism and spatial relations.   Piaget did not tackle the question of whether there are developmental advances—or stages—in children's perspective-taking strategies. Nevertheless, in some later work, he did describe certain developmentally staged concepts that are closely bound to the activity of perspective taking. In particular, Piaget's work on space describes children's developing ability to construct spatial perspectives that are different from their own.[47] The most well-known of Piaget's spatial perspectives tasks is the "three-mountains task," in which the child is asked to reconstruct the visual appearance of a three-mountains display from various points around the display. In administering this task, the experimenter places a doll at the various points and asks the child what the display looks like from the doll's point of view. The child's task is correctly to represent the doll's visual perspective.

Piaget outlines three main developmental stages in children's spatial perspective judgments. During the first, the child does not distinguish his own view on the array from that of others. In representing what another would see at various points on the array, the child merely reproduces his own visual perceptions. At the second stage, the child begins to differentiate his own viewpoint from that of others. The child realizes that a change in position will mean a change in perspective and consequently a different view. But the child cannot yet accurately construct the other viewpoints. Systematic errors are made because the child cannot preserve the position of the mountains relative to one another across changing viewpoints. Stage three represents a coordination of perspectives from all possible viewpoints on the visual array, enabling the child to preserve the original relation of the mountains to one another.

The stages that Piaget derived from children's responses to the three-

[47] Piaget, 1952.

mountains (and other) spatial tasks are certainly connected to children's perspective-taking ability. But the precise nature of the connection is not so clear. What has changed in a child who moves from stage 1 to stage 3 behavior? Is it the child's general ability to role take, or is it rather the child's knowledge of spatial relations like left-right and before-behind? Piaget's own analysis focuses far more on the latter than on the former. More specifically, Piaget conceives of the three-mountains task as a perspective problem in Euclidian space. As such, it requires the child to construct a system of spatial relations similar to a set of Cartesian coordinates; a horizontal left-right dimension must be coordinated with a vertical before-behind position. Further, on the three-mountains task these coordinated positions must be conserved relative to one another even as the visual perspective on them is transformed. In other words, in reconstructing other perspectives beyond his own, the child must retain the original positions of the mountains in relation to one another while recognizing that a change in perspectives also implies that certain visual transformations have occurred. Thus, as in so many Piagetian problems, the task requires maintaining basic constancies when there are apparent changes in reality.

In such an analysis, perspective taking is seen to develop primarily as a consequence of a specific task-related skill in which it is embedded. In other words, as the child progresses in her ability to understand spatial relations, she becomes increasingly adept at accurately representing a variety of visual perspectives that are different from her own. Extending this logic, she becomes increasingly able to recognize different social perspectives (what others think and believe) as she learns more about social relations and the nature of other people. Rather than portraying perspective taking as a general ability, the development of which leads to progressive changes in a wide spectrum of human behavior, such an analysis portrays perspective taking more as a many-faceted skill linked to a variety of specific conceptual achievements. Thus, there may be many types of perspective taking, all of which develop separately as a consequence of many types of learning (spatial, social, moral, and so on).

Even *within* a conceptual domain like spatial relations there may be task-specific features of certain problems that determine how well a child will role take. Researchers who have altered Piaget's three-mountains task in order to make it simpler, have been able to improve young children's role-taking performance significantly.[48] Similarly, changes in the nature of the task materials (three-dimensional versus two-dimensional displays, familiar versus unfamiliar objects) and in the opportunities given to subjects for manipulating the visual display can also aid children's perspective-taking performances.[49] In short, specific features of a problem can facilitate or hinder role taking even if the basic nature of the problem remains the same. This again suggests many influences on children's tendencies to role take, arguing against the notion of egocentrism as a unitary pattern, even within one well-defined area of knowledge.

---

[48] Borke, 1975.   [49] Ibid.

General cognitive egocentrism. Not all developmentalists hold to the view of role taking as a many-faceted skill. Some have continued in the line of Piaget's original formulation of egocentrism, believing general cognitive egocentrism to be a unitary force with deleterious effects on the entire range of young children's thinking.[50] These researchers have pursued the notion that perspective taking is a general ability underlying many aspects of children's social and intellectual behavior, and they have asserted that developmental changes in perspective taking are necessary for progress in children's personal, social, and moral judgment.[51] Along with this line of reasoning, role-taking has been seen as a conceptual ability in its own right, developing through its own series of stages as children directly confront the problem of understanding social perspectives in a diversity of social contexts.[52]

Robert Selman, for example, following earlier experimental work by Melvin Feffer[53] and John Flavell and his associates,[54] has formulated a developmental sequence of general role-taking levels.[55] Selman derives his sequence from children's responses to hypothetical stories and dilemmas in which different characters' perspectives are presented. For example, in one of Selman's stories, a child must decide whether to buy a puppy dog for a friend. The subject must describe each character's perspective and must discuss the similarities and differences between them, as well as the ways in which the different perspectives may influence one another. In children's responses to such dilemmas, Selman has found a series of five role-taking levels that span the period from childhood to adolescence (see Table 4-2). The first of these is level 0, which is *egocentric perspective taking* in the Piagetian sense. This is usually found in preschoolers. At this level, the child can identify certain thoughts and emotions in other people, but he confuses other person's perspectives with his own. The child does not realize that others can see a social situation differently from the way he does. Level 1 begins at about age five. At this level, the child understands that others' thoughts and feelings may be different from his own because they are in different situations or have different information than he does. At level 2, in middle childhood, the child is able to reflect on his own thoughts and feelings. The child can anticipate others' perspectives on his own psychological state and realizes that this anticipation influences his perspective on others. At level 3, late in childhood, the child can assume a third-person point of view. The child realizes that he can "step outside" a social interaction and evaluate the participants' perspectives according to criteria that none of them may share.

Selman's role-taking levels have been related empirically to the development of several types of social knowledge, especially moral judgment.[56] Such

[50] Rubin, 1973.
[51] Selman, 1976b.
[52] Selman & Byrne, 1974; Selman, 1976b.
[53] Feffer & Gourevitch, 1960.

[54] Flavell et al., 1968.
[55] Selman, 1976b, 1980.
[56] Selman, 1971; Kurdek, 1978; Selman & Jaquette, 1978.

Table 4–2 Developmental Stages in Role Taking

Stage	Age range*	Child's understanding
Stage 0 Egocentric Viewpoint	3–6 yrs.	Child has a sense of differentiation of self and other but fails to distinguish between the social perspective (thoughts, feelings) of other and self. Child can label other's overt feelings but does not see the cause and effect relation of reasons to social actions.
Stage 1 Social-Informational Role Taking	6–8 yrs.	Child is aware that other has a social perspective based on other's own reasoning, which may or may not be similar to child's. However, child tends to focus on one perspective rather than coordinating viewpoints.
Stage 2 Self-Reflective Role Taking	8–10 yrs.	Child is conscious that each individual is aware of the other's perspective and that this awareness influences self and other's view of each other. Putting self in other's place is a way of judging his intentions, purposes, and actions. Child can form a coordinated chain of perspectives, but cannot yet abstract from this process to the level of simultaneous mutuality.
Stage 3 Mutual Role Taking	10–12 yrs.	Child realizes that both self and other can view each other mutually and simultaneously as subjects. Child can step outside the two-person dyad and view the interaction from a third-person perspective.
Stage 4 Social and Conventional System Role Taking	12–15+ yrs.	Person realizes mutual perspective taking does not always lead to complete understanding. Social conventions are seen as necessary because they are understood by all members of the group (the generalized other) regardless of their position, role, or experience.

*Age ranges for all stages represent only an average approximation based on our studies to date.
Source: Based on R. L. Selman, Social-cognitive understanding: A guide to educational and clinical practice. In T. Lickona (Ed.), *Moral Development and Behavior: Theory, Research, and Social Issues.* New York: Holt, Rinehart, & Winston, 1976, p. 309. Reprinted with permission.

empirical relations do not, of course, indicate that role-taking advances *cause* progress in other areas, only that, as Mead believed, there is an important connection between role taking and many other forms of social intelligence. Moreover, the empirical evidence connecting levels of perspective taking with advances in moral judgment is not strong and has been challenged severely.[57]

Failing such evidence, should we speculate that role taking is indeed best described as an ability in its own right that follows its own developmental course, such as along Selman's sequence of levels? Or is it best described as a many-faceted process of considering social information that is normally embedded within specific social tasks? Should we continue using the construct of egocentrism to describe young children's confusion of self-other perspectives? At present, the weight of empirical evidence seems to be on the side of those who maintain the diversity and specific task-relatedness of role taking and who consider children to be egocentric only in some contexts but not in others.[58] On the other hand, as Carolyn Shantz has written, developmental psychologists may have to use the notion of egocentrism as a description of early role taking confusions, at least until a more accurate construct is found.[59] Otherwise we may lose sight of the fact that young children on many occasions do make role-taking errors of a kind that older persons normally never would.

Clearly, role taking assumes many different shapes, depending upon what aspect of the other's perspective one must consider in any concrete social situation. Is the child focusing on what the other is seeing? Feeling? Thinking? On the other in relation to the self or to yet other people? On peer others or adult others, on friends or acquaintances, siblings or unfamiliar others? There are reasons to believe that taking the role of the other is a different task, with different requirements, in each of these distinct cases.[60] Because a child will role take in one case is little indication that he can, or will, do so in another. It is for this reason that it seems best not to speak of role taking as a general "ability" that children "acquire," but rather as a frequently used process of considering perspectives other than one's own. It seems reasonable to suppose that the more frequently one uses the perspective-taking process, the more successful one will be at resolving social problems and the more one will benefit from others during social encounters.

The theoretical implications of this position are twofold. First, as noted above, it means that the performance aspect of perspective taking—that is, how well a person role takes on any occasion—is a function of conceptual abilities related to the occasion (or to the cognitive "task" posed by the occasion), rather than to a general perspective-taking competence. Social perspective-taking skill, therefore, would be determined by knowledge of persons, knowledge of self, knowledge of social relations, and so on, rather than a hypothesized "decentering" ability.

A similar position has been suggested by Martin Hoffman, who believes

[57] Kurdek, 1978.
[58] Borke, 1972; Higgins, 1980; Turiel, 1983.
[59] Shantz, 1983.
[60] Shatz & Gelman, 1973; Turiel, 1983.

that most empirical studies of role taking are really tapping children's "cognitive sense of other." [61] The developmental progress in role taking that these studies have documented, Hoffman writes, can be explained by the child's increasing knowledge of other people and their attributes. Hoffman describes four periods in the development of a sense of other, and he asserts that we can predict how well a child will take the perspective of another according to which developmental period the child is in. The four periods are:

1. Initial fusion between self and other *Freud*

2. Initial recognition (during infancy) of the existence and permanence of others *Piaget*

3. Development (from the end of infancy through the childhood years) of a sense that others have internal states, thoughts, and feelings that are different from one's own *Piaget / Mead*

4. Development (during adolescence) of an awareness that others have personal circumstances and life histories that influence their inner states

Hoffman's developmental descriptions are concordant with research findings from studies of "person perception" in children and adolescents.[62]

The second implication of this position is that role-taking development should be described as a continuous rather than a discontinuous phenomenon. This means that there are no "stages" or qualitative changes in children's role taking as they grow up. Such qualitative changes occur with respect to other conceptual achievements—such as in understanding spatial relations, social relations, other persons, the self, and so on. As such, these changes may influence the kinds of perspective taking that a child might do. But changes in children's perspective taking itself are not best described in qualitative, stage-like terms, as if perspective taking were an ability or conceptual structure reorganized in the course of development. Rather, developmental changes in perspective taking itself are more on the order of how often and how comprehensively the child considers the perspectives of others. These are "how much" questions that are not susceptible to a qualitative, structural analysis. This position, therefore, runs contrary to attempts like Selman's to define a developmental sequence of qualitatively distinct perspective-taking levels. Qualitative changes occur in the development of other conceptual understandings that often require perspective taking, but the child's perspective taking itself changes only quantitatively (that is, in amount of frequency) with age. Separate versions of this position have been suggested by Higgins and by Turiel, who both argue that processes like perspective taking should be viewed as information-receiving and computing strategies, and that perspective taking is not in itself reorganized in discontinuous fashion throughout development.[63]

---

[61] Hoffman, 1977b.
[62] Livesly & Bromley, 1973.

[63] Higgins, 1980; Turiel, 1983.

Prosocial Behavior

Perspective taking is a powerful strategy for interacting and communicating with others, but it can be used for good or for ill. Both love and hostility can be effectively implemented through role-taking strategies. In this sense, perspective taking is a morally "neutral" ability. In this section, we shall consider the positive uses of perspective taking: those that lead to kindness, sharing, and prosocial acts. When used in this manner, role taking generally includes an affective component called *empathy*—defined as a compatible emotional responding to another's feelings.[64] A sense of empathy provides a motivation for one to use social strategies like role taking in a prosocial rather than an antisocial manner.

Do children have a natural sense of decency toward one another? Popular views on this range from the romantic notion that children tend to be kind and sweet until corruptly molded, to the scenario in the novel *Lord of the Flies*, in which children shipwrecked on an island are seen to be uncaring, fratricidal barbarians when left to their own devices.

In fact, scientific observers of children's spontaneous peer interactions have reported that these interactions display a full spectrum of human qualities, from generosity to selfishness, from kindness to cruelty.[65] But not all types of behavior are represented with equal frequency, particularly among younger children. In one of the earliest systematic observational studies of young children's peer interaction, Lois Murphy found prosocial behavior among children—sharing, helping, sympathy—to be relatively rare (though certainly present) in the nursery-school years.[66] According to Murphy, aggressive and selfish interactions outnumber prosocial interactions by a ratio of eight to one. Other observational studies of preschool children have concurred with Murphy's findings.[67] This is not to say that young children on their own never cooperate with one another. As noted in Chapter 2, even infants engage in some spontaneous sharing and turn-taking when with peers. But, at least through the preschool years, prosocial interactions like helping and sharing are only an erratic aspect of children's peer activity.

With age and development, children tend more toward active, systematic cooperation with one another. Prosocial behavior becomes the dominant characteristic of stable peer relations, the norm rather than an occasional act. Sharing with peers, for example, increases dramatically between the ages of four and twelve.[68] So, too, do children's sympathetic and empathetic feelings for one another.[69] This section will consider some present explanations for these age changes. In addition, we shall consider some other influences on children's prosocial behavior aside from age and age-related growth.

[64] Hoffman, 1976.
[65] Murphy, 1937.
[66] Ibid.
[67] Whiting & Whiting, 1975; Yarrow & Waxler, 1976.

[68] Ugurel-Semin, 1952; Hanlon & Gross, 1959; Harris, 1971; Emler & Rushton, 1974.
[69] Green & Schneider, 1974; Rushton & Weiner, 1975.

Empathy

A child displays empathy when he reacts to another person's feelings with an emotional response that is generally similar to, or compatible with, the other person's feelings.[70] Many believe that empathy is a primary explanation for prosocial behavior.[71] This intuitively appealing assertion is based on the notion that a child's shared positive feelings for another's happiness motivate him to create the conditions for that happiness by acts of generosity, just as his shared negative feelings for another's distress motivate him to alleviate that distress through acts of help and kindness.

If empathy is indeed one major explanation for prosocial behavior and if, as noted above, children tend more toward prosocial behavior as they grow older, empathy itself must develop with age in children. What, then, accounts for the development of empathy in the child? In order to answer this question, it is necessary to separate out the various components of empathy, in the manner suggested by Norma Feshbach.[72] Feshbach writes that empathy has both an affective and a cognitive aspect. The affective aspect is the emotional response to the other's joy or distress. The cognitive aspect consists of assuming the other's perspective (role taking) and is related to discerning the other's emotional state.

In a comprehensive account of empathetic development and its consequences for altruistic and prosocial behavior, Martin Hoffman has suggested that mainly the cognitive component of empathy grows over the life span.[73] Purely affective empathic reactions can even be found in the newborn, as recent studies demonstrate.[74] From these studies, we know that infants as young as one day old become upset and cry sympathetically with another baby's cries. This, writes Hoffman, is empathic distress in its earliest form. Hoffman believes that such feelings of distress become the emotional basis for most prosocial behavior: "The sharing of positive emotions like joy and excitement may also contribute to helping behavior, but the connection is probably less direct because the empathic response to another's distress must be presumed to be primarily unpleasant."[75]

Although the affective component of empathy may be present at birth, the nature of the child's empathic response is transformed as the cognitive component develops. Much of this "cognitive" growth follows the increase in children's role-taking abilities that were described in the preceding section. Hoffman has analyzed the role-taking and the social-cognitive changes that contribute directly to empathic development (and thereby to children's prosocial behavior). He has described three general stages in developmental transformation of empathic distress through the process of social-cognitive growth.

---

[70] Feshbach & Feshbach, 1969; Hoffman, 1976.

[71] Hoffman, 1975; Mussen & Eisenberg-Berg, 1977; Staub, 1979, Vol. 1.

[72] Feshbach, 1977.

[73] Hoffman, 1975.

[74] Simner, 1971; Sagi & Hoffman, 1976.

[75] Hoffman, 1975, p. 613.

During the first stage, the "global" feeling of discomfort that newborn babies may feel when hearing the cries of others becomes a feeling of concern for another. This occurs between one and two years of age, when infants consolidate the notion that self and other are separate and permanent persons. The perspectives of self and other are still not reliably distinguished, but the infant realizes that the other is a person whose distress may need to be relieved. Hoffman's example of this stage is a thirteen-month-old infant who brought his own mother to comfort a crying friend, without realizing that the friend might be better comforted by his own mother (who was also available).

At around age two, children realize that others have inner states of their own, sometimes the same as and sometimes different from those of the self. This may seem early in light of the role-taking literature cited in the previous section, but Hoffman points out that many role-taking studies use tasks more complex than the simple role-taking requirements of a real-life empathic situation. The research that uses stripped-down measures—like the Flavell studies cited in the previous section—does indeed reveal role-taking skill among children as young as two. (Hoffman's point is in accord with our own claim that, since role taking has been shown to be a particularly task-dependent skill, it is best not to think of role taking as a general structure or ability that develops at one particular age and then permeates a child's social understanding.) When the two-year-old acquires this initial version of role-taking skill, the child becomes able to more actively and more appropriately attempt to relieve another's distress. First, the child can "put himself in the other's place and find the true source of the distress," and second, the child can make a "veridical assessment of the other's needs."[76] The child becomes more effective at both sensing and treating discomfort in a friend.

Stage 2 lasts from age two until about six years of age. Between ages six and nine, a third stage emerges. The basis of this third stage is the child's increasing awareness of the self and other as persons with continuing identities that transcend the immediate situation. Consequently, the child becomes concerned about the general condition of persons, rather than only about situationally caused distresses (although the child still does retain the ability to empathize with another's pleasures and pains of the moment). The child now becomes sensitive to the "general plight" of life's chronic victims—the poor, the handicapped, the socially outcast. This opens the way for a new domain of prosocial activity: the concerted effort to aid those less fortunate than oneself.

Hoffman has been able to marshal considerable empirical support for his view that empathic development is the source of altruistic and prosocial behavior.[77] But however compelling this view may be, other writers have stressed instead the influence of other variables beyond empathy as alternate explanations for the development of prosocial behavior in children. Among these other variables are the social context in which the child lives and the child's reasoning about issues that include but are not empathic considerations.

---

[76] Ibid., p. 616. [77] Hoffman, 1977b; Staub, 1979, Vol. 2.

Social-Contextual Influences on Children's Prosocial Behavior

Children grow up in particular family and cultural contexts. These contexts can vary widely from one another, both in behavioral choices that they offer a child and in the values that are stressed in child-rearing practices. The most striking differences between child-rearing environments have been documented by anthropologists comparing urban, Western cultures with rural, non-Western cultures. John Whiting and Beatrice Whiting's classic investigation of six cultures presented broad-based analyses of social-contextual differences between New England, Philippine, Kenyan, Mexican, Okinawan, and Indian home settings.[78] The Whitings were then able to link these social-contextual differences to behavioral variations that they observed in children growing up in these settings. The Whitings observed children ranging in age from three to fourteen.

In order to measure behavioral variations between children, the Whitings designed a "natural observation scheme" that enabled them to code children's social interactions during free play and other informal activities.[79] Many of the codes in the Whitings' observation scheme are related to prosocial behavior. For example, the scheme includes categories like "offers help" and "offers support," which are checked if the child shares food, toys, advice, or information with another. Such categories were consolidated during the Whitings' data analysis into a dimension that they referred to as "altruistic" behavior.

Children from three of the cultures—Philippine, Kenyan, and Mexican—were rated significantly higher in their altruistic behavior than children from New England, Okinawan, and Indian homes. What are the social-contextual factors in these cultures that may have contributed to such a behavioral difference in the children? The clearest distinction between the two sets of cultures is that children in the former three are more often needed for household chores and family responsibilities. In these mainly rural societies, mothers often spend their time working in the fields, and consequently, they have less time for housework than women in more urban cultures. Children are therefore required to baby-sit with younger siblings and to perform household duties on a regular basis. Such frequent helping activity, carried out with the earnestness associated with an essential demand, clearly accustoms a child to behave prosocially with others. A further indication of this process is the Whitings' finding that the last-born children, as well as the "only children," in these families were less inclined toward helping behavior than first-born children. This again suggests that children who have the most experience with being helpful and with caretaking responsibilities are likely to be the most prosocially oriented.

A similar pattern of social influence has been discovered in other studies of rural and urban cultures. M. C. Madsen, for example, presented a cooperative game to children from a variety of cultural settings, including small South

---

[78] Whiting & Whiting, 1975.　　　　　　　[79] Ibid.

American, African, and Asian communities as well as urban, middle-class communities in the same countries.[80] Madsen consistently has found children from the smaller urban communities to be more cooperative with one another during the game than their big-city counterparts. Madsen also reports similar differences between Israeli kibbutz children and children raised in Tel Aviv and Haifa.[81] Madsen's explanation for these differences, concordant with the Whiting and Whiting findings, focuses on the greater need for a child's help in rural society. For this reason, Madsen believes, families in rural cultures encourage cooperativeness and generosity in their children and discourage conflict and competitiveness.

Reviewing the data from cross-cultural studies of children's prosocial behavior, Paul Mussen and Nancy Eisenberg-Berg have concluded that "children are likely to develop high levels of prosocial behavior if they are raised in cultures characterized by (1) stress on consideration of others, sharing, and orientation toward the group; (2) simple social organization or a traditional, rural setting; (3) assignment to women of important economic functions; (4) members of extended families living together; and (5) early assignment of tasks and responsibilities to children."[82] These five characteristics are by no means independent of one another; rather they are closely interrelated, at least in the cultures investigated by the Whitings and by Madsen. For example, when women serve essential economic functions, children often are called upon to take up some of their household tasks and responsibilities. This is particularly true of poorer, rural families who cannot afford servants. In such cases, parents no doubt find it necessary, in the course of child rearing, to stress cooperative values to their children. Mussen and Eisenberg-Berg's summary, therefore, reveals a many-faceted system of cultural influences that predisposes children from traditional, rural environments toward more prosocial behavior than children from complex, technological backgrounds.

An intriguing question is whether a complex society that consciously emphasizes values of cooperation and sharing in its political dogma would have an influence on its children similar to that found in traditional, rural societies by anthropologists. Examples of such modern societies might be found in big cities of Communist countries like China or the Soviet Union. (The rural sections of these countries—particularly in China—would share so many characteristics of typical traditional culture that any analysis of political-values impact would be confounded.) Although this intriguing issue has never been directly investigated, Urie Bronfenbrenner's study of socialization practices in the Soviet Union suggests that sociopolitical influences may indeed be possible.[83]

Bronfenbrenner describes a number of means through which Soviet parents and school authorities attempt to inculcate "communistic" values like cooperation and sharing in their children:

---

[80] Madsen, 1971.
[81] Shapiro & Madsen, 1971.
[82] Mussen & Eisenberg-Berg, 1977.
[83] Bronfenbrenner, 1970.

From the very beginning stress is placed on teaching children to share and to engage in joint activity. Frequent reference is made to common ownership. . .collective play is emphasized. Not only group games, but special complex toys are designed which require the cooperation of two or three children to make them work.[84]

Also, as in more traditional societies, Soviet children are encouraged to take responsibility for their younger siblings and friends. Teachers expect older students to tutor younger ones on schoolwork and parents expect siblings to support one another if personal difficulties arise. In this manner, socialistic ideals are translated into behavior directives for children in their everyday social interaction. Bronfenbrenner believes that such directives inevitably must have a positive effect on children's sense of responsibility and consideration for one another. But as Mussen and Eisenberg-Berg have commented, further comparative data from the Soviet Union and other cultures must be collected before Bronfenbrenner's case is convincingly established.[85] Whether the politically inspired behavioral directives are having their intended effects (or other unintended effects) upon children's development is not yet known.

Fair Exchange and the Child's Sense of Justice

It does not take very long for an observer of children's social interactions to hear the outraged cry of "That's not fair!" Even children as young as two will reveal a sense of fairness, at least in its breach, when denied a share of a cookie or a turn on a swing.

This sense of fairness indicates an early belief that peer interactions should be governed by certain prosocial regulations. As such, it is among the first signs of moral awareness in the child. By "moral" we mean a respect for obligatory social regulations based upon principles of justice.[86] Young children's conceptions of fair exchange clearly meet these criteria.

Interestingly, many who have written extensively on children's moral judgment have overlooked children's fairness exchanges.[87] These theorists have placed the developmental roots of morality in a childhood stage of unilateral obedience to adult authority, as if justice were a notion understood only by the adult. Such writings do tell us something about the nature of early adult-child relations, and as such, they will be discussed in the next chapter. Also, these theories are our best guide to moral development during adolescence and adulthood, and in this regard, they will be discussed in the final chapters of this book. But in overlooking children's rich and active understanding of fairness, kindness, and other prosocial notions, they have not only failed

---

[84] Ibid., p. 21.
[85] Mussen & Eisenberg-Berg, 1977.
[86] This notion of morality has long been accepted in the Western philosophical traditon (Aristotle; Kant, 1951; Rawls,

1971). We shall begin with this notion in our discussions of children's moral development, although alternative formulations will be discussed later in this book.
[87] Kohlberg, 1969; Rawls, 1971.

to locate the origins of morality but have inaccurately conveyed the nature of children's social behavior—particularly children's peer-oriented behavior.

It was Piaget who first suggested that children typically engage in two moralities, not just one.[88] The first is an adult-oriented morality of unilateral respect for adult codes and sanctions. We shall discuss this further in the following chapter, along with the rest of Piaget's moral judgment theory. But the other morality of the child, according to Piaget, is a peer-oriented morality of cooperation and exchange between children and their playmates. Piaget believed that both moralities exist side-by-side in children's behavior and that initially each was simply applied to one or another class of social relation, adult-child or child-child. Thus, in early childhood, adult-child relations are typically unilateral, with power and authority in the hands of the adult; whereas between children, relations are more reciprocal, cooperative, and equal. But eventually, according to Piaget, the cooperative standards of peer morality replace the unilateral authoritarian standards of adult-oriented morality in all of the child's moral judgment, and reciprocity becomes the norm of all moral interactions. In Piaget's theory, therefore, the true developmental roots of morality are to be found in reciprocal peer exchanges like sharing, even though during early childhood such behavior exists alongside (and is in some ways dominated by) less cooperative and more unilateral interactions with adults.

Development of a child's sense of fairness. If sharing, reciprocal exchange, and the sense of fairness are so central to the beginnings of morality in the child, their early developmental course is of critical importance for the child's present and future moral development. In a series of studies on children's *positive justice* conceptions, William Damon has charted the growth of fairness and sharing notions in children ages four through twelve.[89] Positive justice focuses on conflicts involving the distribution of goods and benefits: for example, an issue in childhood positive justice is how one should divide up goods, toys, and food among playmates. Excluded in positive justice are all "retributive" fairness concerns, such as what kind of punishment best suits a misdeed. Positive-justice reasoning, therefore, is that aspect of moral judgment that determines solutions to prosocial problems like with whom one should share, what, how much, and how often one should share, who deserves an award or a reward, and so on.

Damon used two types of techniques to investigate the development of children's sense of positive justice. The first was an intensive, probing interview that included hypothetical dilemmas, as well as direct questions about fairness. This procedure was introduced to child developmental research by Piaget in his studies of children's physical-world conceptions, and it is known by the label that Piaget originally gave it, "the clinical method." In Damon's adaptation of this procedure, children ages four through twelve were presented

---

[88] Piaget, 1932.   [89] Damon, 1975, 1977, 1980.

with dilemmas of the following sort: A classroom of children spent a day making crayon drawings in school. Some children made a lot of pictures, some did not; some drew well, others not so well; some were lazy, others diligent; some well-behaved, others not. Some children were poor, some were boys, some girls, and so on. The class then sold the drawings at a school bazaar. How should the proceeds of the fair be fairly distributed? Should the kids that did the best get more? What about the poor kids? The lazy ones? The well-behaved? Should girls get more than boys? Children's answers to these and other questions were probed extensively with challenges, counter-suggestions, and follow-up questions (like "why?" and "why not?") in order to elicit as much reasoning as possible from each child.

Damon found that the development of children's positive-justice conceptions could best be described in a sequence of age-related levels. These levels were confirmed not only by cross-sectional studies of children at various ages between four and twelve, but also by longitudinal studies in which individual children's reasoning could be observed as it changed over a period of years.[90] In addition, others using Damon's procedures have found the same developmental progression in Israel, Europe, Puerto Rico, Canada, and several other sections of the United States.[91] Damon's positive-justice levels are summarized in Table 4-3, along with approximate age norms for their appearance. In addition, beneath each level is a sample of reasoning scored at that level, given here as a means of illustrating the developmental sequence.

The levels summarized in Table 4-3 describe children's reasoning about hypothetical positive-justice dilemmas and questions. One wonders if this type of reasoning has anything to do with children's real-life social behavior. Does a child's verbal responses to a positive-justice interview indicate how the child will act when faced with a real-life sharing problem? In order to investigate this question, Damon used a second technique in which children were placed in an experimental situation modeled after his hypothetical positive-justice dilemmas.[92] In this situation, four children were asked to make bracelets for the experimenter and then were given ten candy bars as a reward. The children's real task was to decide among themselves how fairly to split up the reward. As in the hypothetical stories, the experimental situation was arranged so that different children had different justice claims. One child had made the most bracelets, one child was at a disadvantage because the other children were older, the children differed in size and sex, and so on. The main question of interest was, would children's behavior in this "real-life" situation change with age and development in the same way as did their reasoning on hypothetical positive-justice dilemmas—that is, in accord with the sequence of levels summarized in Table 4-3?

The results of this experiment indicated that there is indeed some connec-

---

[90] Damon, 1977.

[91] Larson & Kurdek; 1979; Simons & Klassen, 1979; Enright, Manheim, & Franklin, 1980; Enright & Sutterfield, 1980; Levine, 1980.

[92] Damon, 1977; Gerson & Damon, 1978.

Table 4–3 Early Positive-Justice Levels

Level 0-A: (Age 4 and under): Positive-justice choices derive from wish that an act occur. Reasons simply assert the wishes rather than attempting to justify them ("I should get it because I want to have it").
Level 0-B: (Ages 4–5): Choices still reflect desires but are now justified on the basis of external, observable realities such as size, sex, or other physical characteristics of persons (e.g., we should get the most because we are girls). Such justifications, however, are invoked in a fluctuating, after-the-fact manner, and are self-serving in the end.
Level 1-A: (Ages 5–7): Positive-justice choices derive from notions of strict equality in actions (i.e., that everyone should get the same). Equality is seen as preventing complaining, fighting, "fussing," or other types of conflict.
Level 1-B: (Ages 6–9): Positive-justice choices derive from a notion of reciprocity in actions: that persons should be paid back in kind for doing good or bad things. Notions of merit and deserving emerge.
Level 2-A: (Ages 8–10): A moral relativity develops out of the understanding that different persons can have different, yet equally valid, justifications for their claims to justice. The claims of persons with special needs (e.g., the poor) are weighed heavily. Choices attempt quantitative compromises between competing claims.
Level 2-B: (Ages 10 and up): Considerations of equality and reciprocity are coordinated such that choices take into account the claims of various persons and the demands of the specific situation. Choices are firm and clear-cut, yet justifications reflect the recognition that all persons should be given their due (though, in many situations, this does not mean equal treatment).

Source: W. Damon, Patterns of change in children's social reasoning: A two-year longitudinal study. *Child Development*, 1980, *51*, 1011. Reprinted with permission.

tion between children's real-life behavior and their hypothetical reasoning about positive justice, but that this connection is at times weak and somewhat tenuous. First, Damon found that children's *reasoning* in the experimental situation (that is, what they said about dividing up the candy bars) did conform to the developmental positive-justice sequence. That is, the older children reasoned at the higher levels and the younger children at the lower levels, just as on Damon's hypothetical interview. But when direct comparisons were made between children's reasoning in the two contexts—real-life versus hypothetical—it was found that children often tended to reason somewhat lower in the real-life conflict. Damon speculated that this was because the lower levels are more self-oriented, and the temptation of actual candy bars in the experimental situation influenced children to think of their own self-interest in addition to fairness. If so, self-interest had only a partial influence: children's real-life reasoning rarely lagged more than one level backward from their hypothetical reasoning. This suggests that there were limits to the extent to which the children would forget fairness in favor of their own self-interest. The two interacted, with both playing a role in the child's real-life reasoning.

This interactional blend of self-interest and justice was also evident in children's actual conduct choices (what they actually did with the candy) during the experimental situation. In some ways, the children's choices could be predicted from their levels of hypothetical justice reasoning. For example, children at the lowest levels (generally the four- and five-year-olds) tended to give more candy to themselves than did children at the higher levels. Children at the higher levels tended to reward the younger, "disadvantaged" child more than did lower-level children. These findings were in accord with the development of positive justice as described in Damon's positive-justice sequence. Often, however, children acted in ways that were as much tied to their self-interest as to their notions of justice. For example, children at *all* ages tended to favor themselves somewhat more than others, although—and this is the important point—this self-favoring tendency was most pronounced among lower-level children. Thus, we again see the interaction between justice and self-interest. Similarly higher-level justice reasoners found different ways of being self-favoring than did lower-level reasoners. For example, at the higher levels, children would tie modest claims for extra candy to how many bracelets they had made, whereas at the lower levels, children made bolder claims (asking for as many as seven out of the ten candy bars) on the basis simply of their own wishes.

It seems from Damon's study, therefore, that children's reasoning in real-life social situations develops with age much the same as does their reasoning on hypothetical interviews. But reasoning has only a partial influence on their actual social conduct. Also influential are the nature of the situation (which in this case included the tempting presence of real candy), the child's understanding of his own self-interest within that situation, as well as a number of other interacting social and cognitive variables.

Friendship and the Development of Stable Relations between Peers

All of the behaviors discussed thus far in this chapter—social play, role taking, empathy, prosocial behavior, fairness—are typical of children's social interactions beginning at about age two. Many of these behaviors are most evident in children's peer interactions, which is why they were presented in this chapter. Although adult-child interactions share some of the same characteristics as child-child interactions, a child's social exchanges with adults generally are better described by other qualities, as we shall see in the next chapter.

The reason that children's peer interactions normally demonstrate different qualities than children's interactions with adults is that social relations between children serve different purposes and reflect different mutual expectations than do social relations between children and adults. That is, children

But father as playmate

usually seek each other out for companionship, affection, and common amusement, whereas children and adults normally establish relations based upon the child's need for protection, care, and instruction. Little wonder that the two sets of interactions often differ qualitatively.

How do children's peer interactions contribute to their continuing social relations with other children? The archetypical peer relation, at least among children in contemporary Western societies, is friendship. Friendship is a social relation based upon affection (or "liking") and serves such purposes as providing companionship and mutual support. Because friendship is certainly the most common relation between peers in our culture, most child developmentalists studying children's relationships have chosen it as their focus. Our question about the social-relational significance of children's peer interactions, therefore, may be profitably phrased in the following manner: In what way do children's peer interactions contribute to establishing and conducting friendship?

Often, research bearing upon this question has taken the form of interviews with children about their understanding of friendship.[93] In such research, children are asked questions like "What is a friend?," "How do you make friends?," "How do you know that someone is your friend?," and "What would make you not want to be friends with someone any more?" A number of investigators have posed such questions to children ranging in age from four to fifteen. Generally, the results of the various interview studies have been similar with respect to the developmental trends they have uncovered. These results indicate that the relational meaning of friendship is not fully appreciated until the end of childhood.

In one interview study of 130 children ages six through fourteen, James Youniss found that six- and seven-year-olds speak of friends as playmates with whom they share goods and physical activities.[94] Nine- and ten-year-olds, on the other hand, speak of friends as persons who respond to one another's needs. For these older children, friends support one another when in trouble, comfort one another when hurt or lonely, and help one another with problems. There is, therefore, a development of the notion that friendship implies continuing responsibilities that transcend specific interactions like sharing and playing. Youniss concludes:

> The younger the child, the more likely that interpersonal understanding will be in the form of rules about interactions. For example, friends should share; they should not hurt one another. The older the subject, the more clearly the relation will be understood as an integrated system of rules. This means that interactions are understood as to their implications for the relation itself. This also means that the relation is known as an ongoing thing whose continued existence depends on the type and sequencing of interactions that the friends participate in and generate.[95]

In Youniss's view, therefore, children develop the ability to conduct

---

[93] Bigelow, 1977; Selman & Jaquette, 1978; Bigelow & LaGaipa, 1979; Berndt, 1981.

[94] Youniss & Volpe, 1978.
[95] Ibid. pp. 6–7.

stable, long-standing relations with friends by acquiring notions like responsibility, mutual support, and reciprocal help. The peer interactions of early childhood are not in themselves enough to maintain a continuing friendship relation. Activities like play come and go without long-range implications for their participants. Peer interactions become part of true friendships when they are organized around a sense of shared responsibility and commitment. In Robert Hinde's scheme, the interactions then become part of a pattern with a larger relational meaning.

Several other studies have found similar changes in children's developing conception of friendship. Brian Bigelow, for example, found that Scottish first-graders mostly mentioned common activities when writing essays about friends.[96] These six-year-olds rarely mentioned behavior indicative of loyalty or commitment. But by age twelve (sixth grade and up), Bigelow's Scottish subjects frequently wrote of loyalty and commitment as basic criteria for friendship. The age trends documented by Bigelow, therefore, are comparable to those reported by Youniss, even though they were derived from a study in another country.

Development of the Understanding of Friendship

According to Bigelow, there are three stages in the development of children's understanding of friendship. At stage 1, friendship is seen as a common activity among peers who like each other and who are in "propinquity" (geographical or physical closeness) with each other. At stage 2, the notions that friends must admire one another and that such a mutually positive attitude must last over time are added. Stage 3 friendship, emerging toward the end of childhood, includes notions like mutual acceptance, loyalty and commitment, genuineness, common interests, and potential for intimacy.

A similar description of children's friendship development has been offered by Robert Selman as part of a general analysis of *interpersonal understanding* in the childhood years. Selman's stage model is derived from data gathered by means of the clinical interview method. Subjects are asked to respond to dilemmas about typical problems and conflicts encountered by friends. For example, in one dilemma a girl must choose between going to a show with a new friend or keeping a promised date with an old friend. Questions probe subjects' conceptions of how friendships are formed, how they are maintained, and how they are terminated. In children's answers to these questions, Selman found much the same progression that Youniss and Bigelow observed in their subjects. Selman formulated a developmental sequence that closely follows the logic of Bigelow's stages, with some additional distinctions and elaborations. Selman's sequence also portrays a movement from the early childhood notion of friendship as momentary interactions to the late childhood

[96] Bigelow, 1977.

notion of friendship as a stable, intimate relation implying trust and commitment.

Perhaps the clearest confirmation of the developmental trend in children's friendship understanding has been provided in a study by Thomas Berndt.[97] Children from kindergarten to grade six were asked a series of open-ended questions about friendship, and each response was coded in one of eight possible categories. Among the categories were play and association, attributes of a friend, behavior of friends, intimacy or trust, and loyal support. Berndt found that children at all ages referred to friendship as entailing play and association, and believed that friends should behave prosocially with one another. But the older children tended far more to mention intimacy, trust, and loyal support as criteria for friendship. Berndt offers the following analysis of this age change, as illustrated by two children's complete responses to the question, "How do you know that someone is your best friend?" The first child is in kindergarten, the second in the sixth grade:

> Child 1: I sleep over at his house sometimes (*play or association*). When he's playing ball with his friends he'll let me play (*prosocial behavior*). When I slept over, he let me get in front of him in 4-squares (*a playground game—prosocial behavior*). He likes me (*defining features*).

> Child 2: If you can tell each other things that you don't like about each other (*intimacy*). If you get in a fight with someone else, they'd stick up for you (*loyal support*). If you can tell them your phone number and they don't give you crank calls (*aggressive behavior*). If they don't act mean to you when other kids are around (*loyal support*).

Unlike Bigelow and Selman, Berndt prefers not to describe the developmental progression in children's friendship conception as a sequence of stages. This is because Berndt's data reveal that early friendship notions like play and association are not rejected when later notions like intimacy and loyal support emerge, but rather exist side-by-side with the later notions in children's thinking. Many types of stage-like development do not share this pattern, but rather reflect a hierarchical organization in which earlier behavior becomes transformed, and therefore replaced, by new behavior at a later stage. As we shall see in later chapters, in moral development new beliefs often replace old ones, rather than simply adding on to them. Similarly in cognitive development, new understanding about number, to pick one of many examples, substitutes for the child's previous understanding rather than simply expanding it.[98] If friendship understanding does not develop in a similar way, as Berndt's data seem to indicate, it may not follow a course best described by hierarchical stage models of development. If this is true, a less traditional use of the stage notion may be called for.

The studies on children's friendship thus far discussed have focused on children's verbal conceptions of friendship, rather than on children's actual

---

[97] Berndt, 1981. [98] Piaget, 1965.

behavior with their friends. Most studies into the development of friendship have, in fact, been limited in this way because of an exclusive reliance on verbal interviews with children as a research methodology. Verbal interviews are an effective means of investigating age changes in children's orientation to their world, but with interview data alone we can never be sure whether these age changes are reflected in children's daily behavior, as well as in their social cognition. At the present time, the study of friendship development, and of social-cognitive development in general, is seriously lacking data on developmental changes in children's real-life behavior.[99]

A rare exception to this is the recent work of John Gottman and Jennifer Parkhurst.[100] Gottman and Parkhurst made home observations of young children between the ages of three and six as the children were at play with both friends and new acquaintances. From their findings, they were able to draw some informative and even surprising conclusions about early friendship development.

First, the friendships of the younger children in their study were characterized by frequent fantasy and the playing of extended fantasy roles. Older children's friendships were more focused on their actual present activities rather than on make-believe roles. This finding corresponds to the work on children's play discussed at the beginning of this chapter. As we saw then, narrative and pretend play are at their height in the period just following infancy, and then they decline soon after that. Children's social play becomes, in effect, more organized, more literal, and more "serious" with age.

Second, younger children showed greater communicative clarity with their friends than did the older children. The younger children, to a greater degree than the older children, were responsive to requests for information or explanation from their friends. In addition, they were more likely than older children to discuss the reasons for their disagreements and to purposefully avoid disagreements whenever possible. When a serious squabble had begun, however, younger children had more difficulty de-escalating it. It seemed, therefore, that the younger children took particular care to avoid disagreements, or to explain them away immediately, because of an awareness that disagreements have unmanageable, adverse consequences for their friendships. If true, this shows a formidable real-life social awareness in very young children, an awareness that has not surfaced in verbally based studies of children's social cognition.

In general, Gottman and Parkhurst conclude that the young children in their study created a "climate of agreement" for one another. They did so in part by avoiding disagreement, and in part by drawing frequent social comparisons between themselves and their friends. These comparisons communicated a sense of solidarity between the friends, according to Gottman and Parkhurst. This is because social comparisons can establish a common ground between two people. Examples range from a simple dialogue such as "I'm doing mine

[99] Shantz, 1983.   [100] Gottman & Parkhurst, 1980.

green"/ "I'm doing mine green too," to the following, more elaborate interchange:

> G: Know how many things I am?
> J: How many?
> G: A studier, and an ordinary dancer, and an Indian, and a dinosaur trainer. How do you think that is?
> J: Ah, when I grow up I'm going to be all those things. I'm going to be a fireman, a policeman, and a rocketship man, and a dinosaur person.[101]

The older children in Gottman and Parkhurst's study did not frequently emphasize solidarity with one another through drawing social comparisons. Rather, they showed a greater tolerance for differences, as well as for disagreements. This developmental difference may reveal something about the nature of young children's "egocentrism": that it has a *positive*, as well as a negative side. As Hermione Sinclaire-de-Zwart has pointed out, egocentrism can lead one to behave and feel like one is highly similar to others. This, in turn, can enhance one's sense of unity with others. Among the young children in Gottman and Parkhurst's study, such a sense of unity clearly led to harmonious friendship interactions in most instances. Of course, the toleration of differences is also a positive achievement, and we must recognize this as a developmental advance on the part of the older children. But we come away from the Gottman and Parkhurst study with the sense that even children's earliest friendships can be remarkably communicative and close.

Summary

Children's peer interactions are transformed soon after infancy by three changes in their psychological capacities: their growing awareness of the symbolic significance of everyday events, their emerging sense of moral obligation, and their increasing ability to view social interactions as part of a system of continuing, stable social relations.

The flourishing symbolism of early childhood can be seen in children's play and role-taking activities. Play is a nonliteral, pleasurable activity that is distinct from serious, reality-oriented behavior. In social play with one another, young children not only distinguish reality from playfulness, but they also develop imaginative themes and consciously establish rules for their social interactions. Play is therefore a primary training ground for both creativity and social development. It enables a child to experiment with social roles and social rules, and to cooperate with others in the process. In addition, play has many beneficial emotional consequences for young children, such as allowing children opportunities to express "unacceptable" fears and conflicts, to gain a sense of mastery over themselves and their environment, and through fantasy, to satisfy wishes that are otherwise unobtainable. As children grow older, their

[101] Ibid.

play becomes increasingly associative and organized, reflecting a development in their ability to participate socially in group activities.

Role taking—the mental placing of oneself in another's position—is central to all forms of human communication. There is evidence that children engage in primitive forms of role taking very early in life. But when children are confronted with perspectives that are different from their own, they often have difficulty reconstructing those perspectives. They often assume similarity where there is none, and thus they make errors such as neglecting to give another person a special sort of information required by the other's unique point of view. Also, children's spontaneous speech often suffers from a peculiar noncommunicativeness that Piaget called "egocentrism."

At the same time, young children in other contexts are capable of remarkably subtle and adaptive language use, indicating that children are not totally egocentric in all regards. Further, although as they grow older, children do improve their abilities to understand others' perspectives, such improvement does not occur all of a piece. Rather, the rate of improvement varies widely with the specific nature of the social problem that requires role taking. For these reasons, psychologists have argued about how best to characterize role-taking development in childhood. Whereas some have proposed that role-taking skill develops as an ability in itself and then is applied to other aspects of social thinking, others have suggested that role taking is a strategy that need not itself change during the course of development. From this latter point of view, what does change is the child's understanding of important social issues and problems. As such understanding grows, the child is able to use it to construct the perspectives of others in a variety of social contexts.

Children not only develop the abilities to play and communicate with one another during childhood, but they also make marked progress in their tendencies to interact kindly and fairly with one another. Sharing, giving, helping, and other types of "prosocial" behavior become increasingly evident, particularly among peers, as children grow older. A child's sense of empathic identification with another's troubles changes from a simple emotional reaction of sympathetic distress to a generalized concern about the plight of those in unfortunate life conditions. A child's sense of justice changes from focusing on the desires of the self to considering equality, merit, need, reciprocity, and compromise as fundamental elements in problems of fairness. There is evidence that growing up in societies that emphasize shared responsibility and the consideration of others may facilitate the development of a prosocial orientation in the child. There is also reason to believe that prosocial behavior between peers in childhood is an important precursor to later moral development.

Peer interactions like social play and sharing may be viewed as part of a system of ongoing peer relations. The archetypical childhood peer relation is friendship. With age, children develop a conception of friendship as a continuing, stable relation that has significance beyond the immediate interchange. Several studies have found that children's ideas about friendship evolve from an early focus on the exchange of material goods and activities to a later emphasis on notions like intimacy, loyal support, trust, and common interests. Although the earlier notions do not disappear, by the end of childhood there is an appreciation of friendship as a psychological relation in which intimacies (interests, secrets, problems), rather than only playthings, are exchanged, and in which there is a mutual commitment that preserves the relation over time. Observations of children's real-life friendship interactions indicate that even young children communicate well with their friends, creating a climate of agreement and a sense of solidarity in their interactions. Older children, on the other hand, are better able to tolerate differences and disagreements in their friendships.

Chapter 5

Adult-Child Relations and the Transmission of Culture

A child's need for protection, nurturance, and communication from adults does not end with infancy. Throughout the childhood years, adults continue to provide children with guidance and services essential to children's physical and psychological growth. A child looks to adults for food and shelter, instruction and advice, companionship and affection, even discipline and control. In return, children offer adults obedience, help, and cooperation, as well as many emotionally gratifying opportunities for intimate and caring interactions. It is clear, then, that there is reciprocity in adult-child relations. But it is reciprocity of an asymmetrical kind, the kind of reciprocity that we have called *complementarity*. Children and adults both have expectations of one another, but these expectations are not identical: often children want things from adults that adults do not want from children, and vice versa. Further, in many ways the child's needs in the adult-child relation are greater than the adult's, because they are essential for the child's present survival and future development.

The Two Social Worlds of the Child

Because of this asymmetry in adult-child relations, some characteristics of adult-child relations differ dramatically from basic characteristics of children's peer relations. In an adult-child relation, the source of power and constraint is usually the adult. *Cooperation* on the part of the child often means obedience and respect for the adult's authority. The adult guides, directs, and tutors the child. The child sometimes seeks, sometimes resists, but usually acquiesces to such direction. In comparison, peer interactions normally are more directly reciprocal in a symmetrical way. Cooperation between peers means sharing or helping: only rarely does it mean following or obeying. This is not to say that adult-child relations are in every respect undemocratic, or that all adult-child relations are the same in this regard. Nor is it to say that all peer relations are constituted according to the ideal of equality. But on the whole, adult-child interactions recognize and maintain the one-way authority relation between adult and child, whereas peer interactions normally deal with authority, if at all, in only a playful manner (see Chapter 4).

For these reasons, several child psychologists have characterized the adult-child relation as one of *unilateral constraint*, and the peer relation as one of *mutual respect*.[1] This is no doubt too simple a characterization, for it ignores the many nonconstraining interactions that take place between adults and children. It also suggests that only children have respect for other children. Nevertheless, this characterization does point to the undeniable fact that adult-child relations generally respond to different needs than do children's peer relations; and that, due to differences in these needs, adult-child interactions often are not as equal, as democratic, or as reciprocally symmetrical as are children's peer interactions.

Perhaps the best way of framing this distinction has been suggested by Willard Hartup.[2] Hartup has written of the "two social worlds of childhood," referring to the adult versus the peer world. Hartup acknowledges the differences that we have just cited, in particular, the greater mutuality and cooperation of peer relations versus the greater protection and constraint (and thus the more authoritarian flavor) of adult-child relations. But Hartup makes a further point concerning these two different "worlds" that children live in. The two, writes Hartup, are connected in a developmental sense, in that adult-child relations prepare a child in many ways for participating in peer relations.

Indeed, we have already reported evidence for this in Chapter 2. There we looked at how secure caregiver-child attachment in infancy paves the way for positive peer relations during the preschool years. Not only do securely attached children spontaneously get along well with their peers, but their caregivers are particularly likely to encourage them to develop peer relations.[3] Thus, children's peer and adult relations are fundamentally tied together in the course of the child's development.

Despite their developmental connectedness with one another, the two types of relations do play somewhat distinct roles in the social development of

[1] Piaget, 1932; Sullivan, 1953; Youniss, 1980.

[2] Hartup, 1979.

[3] Lieberman, 1977; Waters, Wippman, & Sroufe, 1979.

children because of the qualitative differences between them. In the last chapter, it was suggested that peer relations are particularly implicated in the development of sharing, fairness, kindness, and other types of prosocial behavior. In this chapter, it will be suggested that adult-child relations have a particular link with another aspect of the socialization process: the transmission of cultural standards, values, and rules to the child. Children, of course, play an active role themselves in this process, as we shall see when we discuss the *social-psychological mechanisms* of cultural transmission. And as we saw in Chapter 4, peer interactions like play offer children a chance to practice and experiment with the social rules and regulations of their culture. But it is the adult world—in the family, in the school, and in other societal institutions —that initially presents the constraints and embedded values of the social order to the child.

This need not be done harshly or against the will of the child. Even though our stereotypical view of adult constraint is the kind of scolding encountered by a disobedient Huck Finn, there are many more supportive ways in which socialization is implemented. Mary Ainsworth has commented that, in a securely attached caregiver-child relation, socialization occurs from "within," in the sense that the child actively seeks and accepts the adult's guidance.[4] In support of Ainsworth's contention, there are studies showing that securely attached children are easily compliant in the face of adult authority.[5] We should realize, therefore, that socialization need not mean a process in which a powerful adult forces cultural standards on an unwilling child. This certainly happens on occasion, but is only one of many ways that adults influence their children. We shall describe a number of such ways in this chapter.

To illustrate some typical differences between children's peer and adult interactions, we may compare the peer play dialogue quoted in Chapter 4 with some recorded dialogues between teachers and children. These dialogues were collected by Nancy Much and Richard Shweder in an observational study of social interaction between teachers and students at a Chicago elementary school.[6] The authors note the "cultural control message" that they believe is implicit in each teacher's statements.

1. Madeline comes to school after a day's absence.

   Teacher: Madeline, we missed you yesterday. Where were you?
   Madeline: See, my mother and dad didn't want me to come to school because they both slept late.
   Teacher: Oh, they had vacation yesterday?
   Madeline: Yeah.
   Teacher: Well, I guess that's a good excuse.

   Cultural Control Message: Children are expected to be in school every day.

[4] Ainsworth, 1978.
[5] Stayton, Hogan, & Ainsworth, 1971;

Matas, Arend, & Sroufe, 1978.
[6] Much & Shweder, 1978.

2. Some nursery-school children have gotten their clothes wet and are changing into extra pairs of trousers kept by the school. They are in a dressing area with a double door that opens separately above and below. Gary, Abel, and Edith stand around the open top half of the door. Edith stands on a chair looking through the door. Gary and Abel peek over the top.

Vickie: You silly dummies...you're all peeking. We're getting dressed, you guys. We're still getting dressed.
Teacher (*approaching*): What's wrong? Are you changing clothes?
Vickie: Yes.
(*Teacher closes the door.*)
Edith *(to Gary)*: Keep that locked. Now don't open it.
Vickie: Don't look, now, don't look!

Cultural Control Message: One must not watch while others undress.

3. The teacher has greeted Fred as he came in the door. Fred did not respond. The teacher walks over to Fred.

Teacher: Fred, Fred, Fred, you were so busy you didn't hear me say "Hi, Fred." (*She takes Fred's chin in hand.*) Just say "Hi," then I'll know we saw each other.

Note: The teacher's "accusation" contains an account, "you were so busy..."

Cultural Control Message: One is expected to return a greeting.

4. Agnes shows the teacher fresh paint on her shirt.

Agnes: Look what Clifford did.
Teacher *(to Clifford)*: Why did you do that?
Clifford: What?
Teacher: Paint her shirt.
Clifford: I didn't paint her shirt.

Cultural Control Message: One must not damage the personal property of others.

The teachers in these episodes clearly are conscious of social regulations like school-attendance standards, dress codes, greeting conventions, and property rules. The teachers also seem aware of their role in administering these regulations in the schoolroom setting, as well as of their role in instructing children about the existence and meaning of the regulations. This instruction is not always direct or explicitly didactic in form. Often the teacher simply acknowledges the regulation by a suggestive comment or a leading question (examples 1 and 4, respectively). But the teacher's guidance, however indirect or disguised, is tangibly present. There is none of the nonliterality that we witnessed in children's peer enactments of social interaction rules. In making this comparison, we should note of course that the Much and Shweder study did not attempt to establish an adult-child database similar to the peer dialogues quoted by Garvey. Our comparison, therefore, is merely for the sake of illustration and has not been confirmed by systematic sampling procedures.

Parents are the child's primary source of instruction concerning values and rules of the culture, at least through the early and middle childhood years. Virtually all parents attempt in some way to socialize their children, but there are wide variations in how this is done. Parents, of course, often disagree with one another on how children should act and on what they should be like. We therefore might expect parents to differ in their conscious goals for their children. But even beyond parents' conscious intentions, parents also differ in their styles of interacting with their children. Observers of parent-child relations have recognized a number of distinguishable patterns of child rearing that vary from household to household. These child-rearing patterns are embedded in the everyday verbal and nonverbal exchanges between parent and child. Often parents themselves are not aware that these interactions represent one or another distinct child-rearing style. But the implications of particular patterns of parent-child interaction for children's personal development can be profound, as we shall see in the following section.

Child Rearing

Child-rearing trends come in and out of vogue at different times throughout history. During some historical periods, prevailing voices have advocated treating children pretty much like adults, warning against "coddling" or "spoiling." At other times, children have been considered to be special in their needs and abilities, and experts of the day have suggested permissiveness and warmth in the handling of children.

Historians have traced back to the child-rearing practices of the Middle Ages, when, according to one historian, there was so little recognition of children as special people that "the idea of childhood did not exist."[7] Records of medieval Europe reveal that children were inducted into adult occupations shortly after weaning, with no time set aside for play or tutoring. Even the paintings of that period blur the distinction between children and adults by failing to capture the special physical features of children's faces and demeanor. The only recognized difference was size: otherwise, these little people dressed, acted, and were seen to be just like anyone else. In time, however, Rousseau and his followers portrayed childhood as a blessed and idyllic period deserving care and respect from adults.[8] The permissiveness-restrictiveness cycle was in full swing. Some noteworthy episodes stand out: the early "will-breaking" advocated by some of our Puritan forefathers,[9] the claims of behaviorist John Watson that overly affectionate parents raise children with weak personalities,[10] and the postwar "permissiveness" revolution attributed to Dr. Benjamin Spock.[11] The cycle continues to the present day, with the child-rights movement of the early 1970s leading to the parental responsibility reaction of the 1980s.[12]

Of course there is never uniformity in parents' behavior during any period of history. Despite prevailing historical currents, there is always varia-

[7] Ariès, 1965.
[8] Rousseau, 1763.
[9] de Mause, 1974.

[10] Watson, 1919.
[11] Spock, 1947.
[12] Farson, 1974; Wald, 1979.

tion in the actual practice of individuals. At the present time, perhaps the full range of child-rearing practices is represented in our own Western society. But the historical trends do highlight some potential differences in how parents perceive and treat their children. Such trends lead us to wonder about the consequences of these differences. Do changes in parental philosophy and practice alter the nature and outcome of children's development? This intriguing question has been the focus of a number of child-development investigations over the past forty years. Before we look for answers to this question, however, we must attempt to characterize more carefully the range of variation in parents' child-rearing behavior.

Permissive Versus Restrictive Child Rearing

"Permissive" versus "restrictive" is an intuitively appealing way to dichotomize parental child-rearing attitudes, but the extent to which a parent is permissive or restrictive does not in itself tell us enough about the parent's relations with the child. In order to make inferences about behavioral consequences of parental child-rearing patterns, other dimensions must be added to the permissiveness-restrictiveness dichotomy. This is because permissiveness or restrictiveness is meaningful as a child-rearing variable only in combination with other mitigating factors, such as the extent to which a parent communicates openly with a child, the warmth of the home environment, and the severity of punishment with which the parent greets a misdemeanor. Although some of these may be correlated to some degree, they do not always go together in the same way. It is the particular patterns or combinations of these factors that have predictable influences on the child-rearing process.

As an example of this point, an early study of children's aggression by Robert Sears, Eleanor Maccoby, and Harry Levin found that *both* the permissiveness and the punitiveness of parents must be considered if relations are to be found between parental practice and children's behavior.[13] The researchers interviewed 379 mothers of five-year-olds about their past and present treatment of their children. One series of questions dealt with the parents' reactions to their children's aggression, such as:

> Sometimes a child will get angry at his parents and hit them and kick them or shout angry things at them. How much of this sort of thing do you think parents ought to allow in a child of (his, her) age? How do you handle it when (child's name) acts like this?

There was wide variation in parents' answers to these questions. Many parents were both permissive of their child's aggression and nonpunitive when it occurred, as in the following reply:

> Mother: I think he's at the age right now where you're apt to get quite a lot of it. I think as they get a little bit older, you can stop and reason with them, but right now I think that they get pretty angry at times and they do say things. And

[13] Sears, Maccoby, & Levin, 1957.

afterwards, they're sorry for it, so I let him say it and it's over with, and afterwards I might say, "You weren't very nice to Mummy," and he'll generally admit it.

Others were nonpermissive and highly punitive:

Mother: They should never allow him to hit them back. If he hits them, they should hit him right back. If you let him get away with it once he will always want to get away with it.

Interviewer: How do you handle it when he acts like this?

Mother: If he hits me I hit him back twice as hard, and if he does it again, I just get my paddle I have, and I give it to him again, and then he stops.

Interviewer: How do you handle it if he is deliberately disobedient?

Mother: I take off his clothes and he's in for the day and he's not to play with anything—not even his toys or anything that belongs to him—he's not to touch anything—he's to leave things alone and stay in bed.[14]

Although frequently parents who were nonpermissive were also punitive when faced with their child's aggression, this was not always the case. Sears and his co-workers found a number of parents who would not tolerate aggression, but who tried to stop it through nonpunitive means such as persuasion. There were even some mothers who were tolerant of aggression and yet punitive when it occurred, a somewhat surprising combination. The authors describe this "permissive/punitive" pattern in the following way: "In this latter group were some mothers who felt they *should* allow their children to display aggression; but they could restrain their own impulses to suppress the child's aggression only so long, and then they would blow up. When the punishment came, it was likely to be severe."[15]

The investigators compared mothers' statements about their own parental reactions to the mothers' reports of their children's aggressive behavior. Of course, in each case there is a strong possibility that mothers gave inaccurate accounts: mothers may be biased observers of both their own and their children's behavior. If this study were done today, in the age of videotape technology, direct observations of the mothers and their children likely would be taken as a check on the reliability of the mothers' reports. In any event, the findings that Sears and his co-workers reported in this early study were intriguing despite the shortfalls in their methodology.

Sears and his co-workers found that high permissiveness does relate to children's aggression, as we might expect. But this does not tell the whole story. The extent of parents' punitiveness also has an effect, but this time in the opposite direction of our common-sense intuitions: the more punitive the parent, the *more* aggressive the child. Because of this, the combination yielding the most aggressive children was high permissiveness and high punitiveness, and the combination yielding the least aggressive children was low permissiveness and low punitiveness. Parents who are opposites in both their permissive-

---

[14] Ibid., pp. 353–54.   [15] Ibid., p. 357.

Table 5-1 Styles of Child Rearing and Children's Aggressiveness

	High punitiveness	*Low punitiveness*
High permissiveness	most aggressive children (group 1)	moderately aggressive children (group 2)
Low permissiveness	moderately aggressive children (group 3)	least aggressive children (group 4)

Source: Based on R. R. Sears, E. E. Maccoby, & H. Levin, *Patterns of Child Rearing.* Evanston, Ill.: Row Peterson, 1957.

ness and their punitiveness (groups 2 and 3 in Table 5-1) have children who are similar in the extent of their aggressiveness.

The Sears, Maccoby, and Levin findings may be plausibly interpreted in a number of ways. The authors believe that parental permissiveness encourages children's aggression because it creates expectations that the expression of aggressive tendencies is acceptable behavior. For a different reason, punishment also encourages aggression: the authors speculate that punishment increases the child's frustration, thus working against its intended purpose.

Such interpretations, of course, assume that the parents' behavior has a one-way causal effect on the child without significant reciprocal influence or feedback. Most child-rearing studies have assumed a similar causal direction in favor of the parent's influence upon the child. This is a natural assumption, considering that (1) the parent has the greater power, and (2) the parent was there first. But it should be noted that other causal effects in the parent-child relation are also possible. For example, the child's aggressiveness may influence the parents' child-rearing style, just as the parents' child-rearing style may influence the child's behavior. Temperamentally aggressive children may engender punitiveness in mothers who normally would be lenient. Such might be the case of a child who, through repeated misdeeds, forces a parent to finally deal harshly with the problem. Similarly, a child's attitude and behavior may determine how permissive a mother *believes* she is (and thus how a mother answers a researcher's interview about child rearing). A mother who is rarely confronted with her child's misbehavior may believe that she is nonpermissive, whereas in reality she has never been really tested. A mother with a highly aggressive child, on the other hand, may be forced to accept the notion that she tolerates such behavior, even if her tendencies with a less aggressive child may have been not to permit aggressiveness.

Child's Own Disposition and Child Rearing

Richard Bell has reinterpreted the findings from a number of socialization studies in exactly this manner.[16] He has argued that children's temperamental

[16] Bell, 1968.

characteristics determine how aggressive or compliant they will be, and that parents adjust their disciplinary practices accordingly. In other words, Bell believes that parents use whatever method of child rearing that works best with their particular child. Children with certain temperamental dispositions respond well to certain disciplinary techniques; children with other characteristics respond well to other techniques. Thus, in Bell's analysis, correlations between parental practice and child behavior indicate a causality in the opposite direction than socialization studies generally imply. Rather than showing that certain parental practices cause certain patterns of child behavior, Bell claims these correlations show that certain patterns of child behavior call for particular child-rearing practices, and that parents generally respond in an appropriate manner.

Bell's argument may be too one-sided in favor of the child's influence, no doubt understating the enormous degree to which parents determine the nature of the home environment. The correlational studies that Bell reinterprets can be argued either way: since they show nothing more than a simple association between parental and child behavior, the causal direction is a matter of conjecture. This is in part Bell's point, that the direction of causality in favor of the parent has too often been inappropriately inferred from data that can tell us nothing about causal directions. But, by the same logic, Bell's claims in favor of the child are equally unsupported by the correlational data that he reinterprets.

Recently, however, there have been a few studies providing more direct empirical evidence in support of Bell's claims. In one such study, Joan Grusec and Leon Kuczynski asked mothers of children aged four through eight to describe their means of disciplining their children.[17] Twelve distinct types of child misbehavior were presented to the mothers, and the mothers were asked to respond to each. The types of child misbehavior included a child taking money from his mother's purse, a child ignoring calls to dinner, a child ignoring warnings of danger, and children hurting others both physically (pushing a peer off a tricycle) and psychologically (making fun of a senile old man).

The mothers' chosen discipline techniques were "determined more by what the child did than by some consistent child-rearing approach on the mother's part."[18] For example, mothers chose power-assertion techniques (such as threats of punishment) for dealing with most of the misdeeds, but they chose reasoning and discussion for the misdeeds that caused psychological harm to others. Often mothers said that they would discipline a child with multiple techniques, such as power assertion followed by reasoning. These findings shed doubt on the notion that parents have consistent disciplinary patterns which they uniformly apply, whatever the nature of their child's behavior.

Such evidence certainly supports Bell's contention that children have an

---

[17] Grusec & Kuczynski, 1980.   [18] Ibid., p. 1.

effect on their parent's child-rearing practices. But it does not imply that parental behavior is totally, or even primarily, shaped by the child. As we saw in the attachment literature, and as we shall soon see in other child-rearing studies, parents do have their own distinctive ways of interacting with their children, and these ways make a difference for the child's social development. As we shall see time and again throughout this book, parents have an uncontested role as the major influence in their children's lives, and parents vary widely in how they exert this influence. But the arguments by Bell and others in favor of children's effects on parents have added an important qualification to this statement: a parent does not operate in a vacuum. The child is an active participant in the parent-child relation, and the child's own distinctive characteristics contribute to the family atmosphere.

Democracy and Control in Child Rearing

The Sears, Maccoby, and Levin study demonstrates that permissiveness/nonpermissiveness is only one of several significant dimensions in a parent's child-rearing style. In itself, the extent of a parent's permissiveness does not tell us much about the child's behavior because the consequences of parental permissiveness vary according to how permissiveness is combined with other dimensions such as punitiveness. Beyond punitiveness, there are several other child-rearing dimensions. The two that have been most frequently studied are "democracy" and "warmth" in the parent-child relation.

The ground-breaking investigation of democracy in the home was conducted by Alfred Baldwin over a ten-year period in the 1940s.[19] Baldwin followed the development of sixty-seven children from birth through the school years. The children were observed regularly in both home and school settings, and parents were interviewed and observed with their children every six months. On the basis of these interviews and observations, both children and parents were rated on a large battery of behavioral scales. These scales were defined by adjectives such as sensitivity, affectionateness, nonconformity, cruelty, impatience, sense of humor, leadership, and so on, through a wide range of behavioral characteristics. Using factor-analytic techniques, Baldwin clustered these variables into a few general factors that he believed were central to the issue of how parent-child relations influence the child's socialization. On the parental side, Baldwin's two general factors were control and democracy. Control is the factor closest to the permissiveness-nonpermissiveness dimension: "It emphasizes the existence of restrictions upon behavior which are clearly conveyed to the child. . .(and) the lack of friction over disciplinary decisions."[20] Democracy, on the other hand, emphasizes the openness of communication between parent and child. In democratic relationships, policies are arrived at by mutual agreement, reasons are given for disciplinary actions,

---

[19] Baldwin, 1948, 1955.　　　　[20] Baldwin, 1948, p. 130.

and the child's active consent is sought whenever parental decisions concerning the child must be made.

> Democracy is characterized by a high level of verbal contact between parent and child, appearing as consultation about policy decisions, as explanations of reasons for the family rules, and as verbal explanation in response to the child's curiosity. Accompanying this flow of verbal communication is a lack of arbitrariness about decisions. . . .[21]

As in the case of permissiveness and punitiveness, all combinations of control and democracy were possible and did appear in Baldwin's sample: controlled and democratic homes, uncontrolled and democratic homes, controlled and undemocratic homes, and uncontrolled and undemocratic homes. By examining the child-behavioral correlates of each combination, Baldwin was able to separate out the differing effects of control, of democracy, and of the various patterns of the two in combination with one another. Some key results of Baldwin's study are summarized in Figure 5-1.

With control held constant, democracy is related to variables that suggest an active, assertive child. That is, children from democratic homes tend to be more aggressive, fearless, and curious than other children. In a negative sense, they are also more disobedient and more cruel than children from undemocratic families. With democracy held constant, control is related to conformity in a child. It decreases negative aspects of behavioral nonconformity such as quarrelsomeness, negativity, and disobedience; but it also decreases some positive aspects of nonconformity such as originality, assertiveness, and tenacity. The optimal combination, therefore, seems to be high democracy and high control, since the adverse effects of each may be compensated for by the positive effects of the other. One unfortunate combination is high control with lack of democracy, since this is related to a lack of curiosity, assertiveness, originality, and fancifulness in a child. Despite the gains in conformity to cultural demands that this pattern achieves, the impairment of a child's personal initiative would seem too great a sacrifice. Another unfortunate pattern is high democracy with low control, related to unruliness and lack of discipline in a child.

The results of Baldwin's study suggest that democratic child rearing, when tempered by judicious parental control, can facilitate the development of a planful and inventive child who takes an active part in his own socialization. The implication is that democracy without control, or control without democracy, both have their distinct dangers: the former in encouraging rebelliousness and other excesses of nonconformity, the latter in discouraging spontaneity and assertiveness. Again, we see that qualities like permissiveness or restrictiveness in a parent's behavior are only a part of a complex picture, and their effects cannot be meaningfully predicted outside of the pattern of child-rearing variables with which they are entwined.

Finally, we must once again caution that each child's own unique pattern

[21] Ibid., p. 131

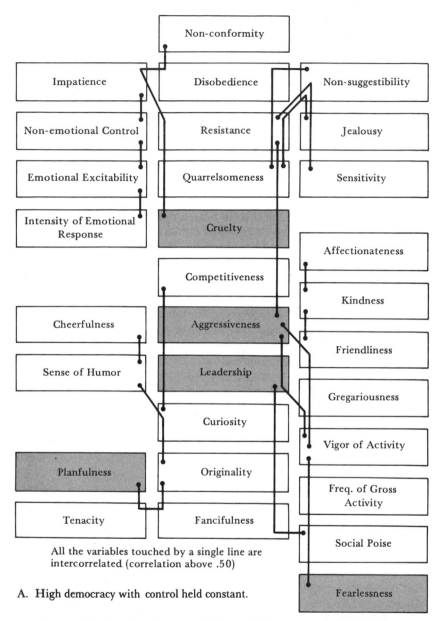

All the variables touched by a single line are
intercorrelated (correlation above .50)

A. High democracy with control held constant.

Figure 5-1. Some Influences of Parental Democracy and Control upon
Children's Behavior.

Source: A Baldwin, Socialization and the parent-child relationship, *Child Development*, 1948, *19*,
130, 132. Reprinted with permission.

of activity is another critical variable whose influence cannot be determined in
studies only designed to assess the one-way causal consequences of parental
behavior on the child. Perhaps temperamentally active and assertive children

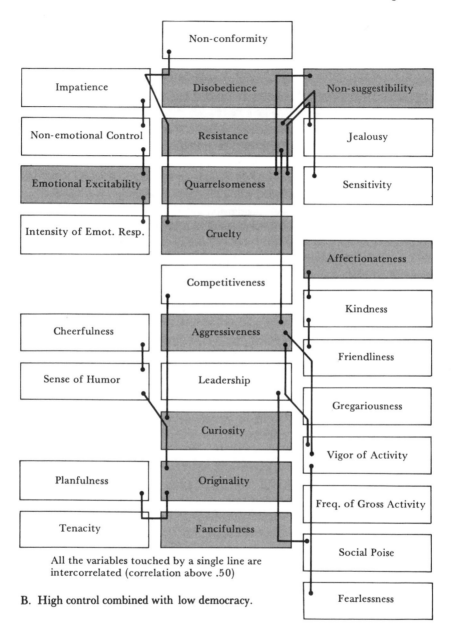

All the variables touched by a single line are intercorrelated (correlation above .50)

B. High control combined with low democracy.

play some role in provoking parents to treat them democratically. Baldwin's findings indicate only an association between parental style and children's behavior. To determine the extent to which one directly influences the other, a more elaborate sort of experimental research paradigm must be used. Lacking such experimental data, it is wise to remain open to the possibility that there are bidirectional causal effects between parents' and children's behavior. That is, just as parental treatment may encourage certain kinds of behavioral outcomes in children, so too children's behavior may lead parents to engage in certain kinds of child rearing.

Authoritarian, Authoritative, Permissive, and Harmonious Child Rearing

Baldwin's ground-breaking investigation set the stage for further refinements in the study of parental control, permissiveness, and democracy. In a comprehensive series of child-rearing studies, Diana Baumrind traced the relations between several patterns of parental behavior and children's success in adapting to their everyday activities.[22] Baumrind began her research program by identifying a cluster of adaptive traits that she assumed all parents wished to encourage in their children. Baumrind called this cluster of traits *instrumental competence.*

> . . .instrumental competence is defined by social responsibility, independence, achievement orientation, and vitality. By *social responsibility* is meant behavior which is friendly rather than hostile to peers, facilitative rather than disruptive of others' work, and cooperative rather than resistive of adult-led activity. By *independence* is meant behavior which is ascendent rather than submissive, purposive rather than aimless, and self-determining rather than conforming. By *achievement orientation* is meant behavior in which the child seeks rather than avoids intellectual challenge and problem solves persistently and efficiently rather than inefficiently and impulsively. *Vitality* refers to the child's level of biological energy and vigorous appearance.[23]

Baumrind was then interested in defining the parental behavior patterns that might be associated with instrumental competence (or its lack) on the part of children. She began by looking at four dimensions of child-rearing behavior: *parental control, clarity of parent-child communication, maturity demands,* and *nurturance.* The first two dimensions are similar to Baldwin's general factors of control and democracy, respectively. Baumrind considered *parental control* to be a "measure of strict discipline," displayed in the parent's active attempts to influence the child's behavior so that she will conform to parental standards. *Clarity of parent-child communication* means the extent to which a parent solicits the child's opinions and feelings when family decisions are made, and also the extent to which a parent offers the child reasons for punitive or restrictive measures whenever such must be taken. *Maturity demands* refers to any parental pressure or encouragement to perform well in the intellectual, social, or emotional sphere. This is the classic exhortation of "Live up to your abilities!" that children often hear from the adults in their lives. *Nurturance* means warmth and involvement in caretaking, or the extent to which the parent expresses concern for the child's well-being and pleasure in the child's accomplishments.

Like the other researchers whose work has been discussed in this section,

---

[22] Baumrind, 1967, 1973, 1977.   [23] Baumrind, 1973, p. 4.

Table 5-2 Baumrind's Patterns of Parental Child Rearing

Pattern	Control		Clarity of communication		Maturity demands		Nurturance	
	High	Low	High	Low	High	Low	High	Low
Authoritarian	✔			✔	✔			✔
Authoritative	✔		✔		✔		✔	
Permissive		✔	✔			✔	✔	

Source: Based on D. Baumrind, Child care practices anteceding three patterns of preschool behavior. *Genetic Psychology Monographs*, 1967, *75*, 43–88.

Baumrind found that the importance of parental child-rearing practices lies not in single behavioral dimensions but in combinations and clusters of these dimensions. From clustering in various ways the initial four dimensions described above, Baumrind put together three main patterns of parental child-rearing style: *authoritarian, authoritative,* and *permissive* (see Table 5-2). Parents high in control, low in clarity of communication, high in maturity demands, and somewhat low in nurturance were labeled *authoritarian.* Parents high in control, high in clarity of communication, high in maturity demands, and high in nurturance were called *authoritative.* Parents low in control, high in clarity of communication, low in maturity demands, and moderately high in nurturance were called *permissive.* Parents, of course, rarely represent only one of these types in their behavior: normally parental behavior is more varied and less stereotypical than this would suggest. But according to Baumrind, the predominant child-rearing behavior of most parents can be described by one or another of these major patterns. Therefore, this typology can be used to distinguish between different parents' child-rearing interactions with their children.

Baumrind's authoritative pattern most closely coincides with Baldwin's optimal combination of control with democracy. Indeed, Baumrind's results, like Baldwin's, strongly favor this authoritative cluster of dimensions. Authoritative parents tend to have children high on all measures of instrumental competence. They were self-assertive, independent, friendly with peers, and cooperative with parents. Both intellectually and socially, they demonstrated success, enjoyment, and strong motivation toward achievement. Children with authoritarian parents, on the other hand, tended to be withdrawn, showing relatively little vitality and eagerness in their daily activity. In addition, they were shy and generally uneasy around peers. Girls raised in an authoritarian manner were particularly dependent upon their parents and lacking in achievement motivations, whereas boys showed more than ordinary degrees of hostility. Interestingly, many of these less-than-ideal characteristics were also found in children of permissive parents. Although apparently opposite in their intended effects, authoritarian and permissive parental practices are both associated with a lack of instrumental competence, self-reliance, vitality, and self-control on the part of children. Permissively reared children, however, were more positive in their moods and showed more vitality than did children of authoritarian families.

How can we explain the similar child-behavior correlates of two such opposite child-rearing patterns? Baumrind believes that both authoritarian and permissive parents shield their children from stress, the former through restricting the child's opportunities for initiative, the latter through not forcing the child to confront the consequences of his own actions. Since both types of parents are overprotective, each in their own way, their children fail to develop assertiveness, self-reliance, or tolerance of life's disappointments and frustrations. In contrast, writes Baumrind:

> Authoritative parents value self-assertion, willfulness, and independence and attempt to facilitate children's attainment of these goals by assuming active and rational parental roles. Their children, on the whole, are socially responsible because their parents impose demands that are intellectually stimulating (that is, their expectations are demanding and clearly communicated but not unrealistic), as well as moderately tension producing (inasmuch as firm discipline necessarily results in occasional clashes of will).[24]

In such speculations, Baumrind assumes particular parental child-rearing styles create fortunate or unfortunate characteristics in their children, rather than the other way around. Once again, we would caution that current data tell us nothing about the direction of influence in parent-child relations. We still must entertain the possibility that children play some role in shaping their parents' interactional styles.

One indication that a child's personal nature does much to determine the quality of a parent-child relation comes from an empirical footnote to Baumrind's investigations. In the course of categorizing parents according to the three predominant child-rearing patterns, Baumrind and her co-workers noticed that some families did not fit into this scheme. The parental treatment of children in these families would be called neither authoritative, authoritarian, nor permissive with any accuracy. Most of these parents, Baumrind believed, could be typed as *nonconformists*, since they tended to be skeptical about the prevailing values of contemporary Western society.[25] Although these parents did not fit into one of the three main patterns, they could be rated on the same cluster of dimensions that make up the main patterns: nonconforming parents were low in maturity demands and high in clarity of communication, yet they were more controlling than conventionally permissive parents. They disliked authority and authoritarianism but still actively attempted to influence their children's beliefs and behavior. Interestingly, this pattern of child rearing was associated with different characteristics in boys than in girls. Girls in nonconforming families resembled children of authoritarian and permissive parents, but boys managed to be independent and achievement-oriented, like the children of authoritative parents. Somehow the child's sex interacted with the parent's nonconforming style in a way that influenced the effects of this

---

[24] Ibid, p. 21. [25] Ibid., p. 14.

style. Baumrind speculates that nonconforming parents treat their sons differently than they do their daughters. Sons in such families meet with firmer control, since they are seen as future agents of a male-oriented society. Daughters, on the other hand, are seen as potential female victims of this society, as "pawns of forces beyond their control"; for this reason, their parents are reluctant to handle them with firm discipline or control. Whatever the reason for the difference between boys and girls of nonconforming families, these children provide some initial indication that children's own characteristics (in this case, sex) determine to some degree the nature of parental child-rearing styles.

An even more intriguing indication of this point comes from yet another group of families that Baumrind had trouble placing within her initial categorical framework. This group was very small, consisting of only eight families out of ninety-five in the study sample.[26] In these families, Baumrind reported, the issue of control was moot. Although parents from these families rarely exercised control, they "seemed to *have* control in the sense that the child generally took pains to intuit what the parent wanted and to do it."[27] For this reason, Baumrind's observers could not rate these parents on the control dimension, and the eight families were put into a new category called the *harmonious pattern*. This pattern was distinguished by an atmosphere of harmony, equanimity, and rationality in parent-child interactions. Accordingly, values like power, achievement, control, and order were de-emphasized in favor of congeniality and fairness in human relations.

The children in harmonious families play as important a part as the parents in achieving the benign family atmosphere. The harmony would soon break down without the child's "intuiting" (as Baumrind calls it) the parent's wishes. Without this intuitive spirit of cooperation on the part of the child, the harmonious parent would soon be forced to exert authoritative or authoritarian control, or the pattern would simply degenerate into permissiveness. The fine line between harmonious and permissive patterns is demonstrated in the following quotes from one of Baumrind's interviews with a harmonious parent. Note that the parent relies on her daughter to provide much of her own control. With a different child, the parent would either need to adopt child-rearing practices with firmer modes of authority, or she would need to foresake the notion of control altogether. The child's own sense of balance saves her parent the necessity of making this choice.

Interviewer: Describe Nina.

Mother: She's strong-tempered, which comes up because she's always been taught that her opinions are valid. So if you disagree with her, she'll stand there and argue all day if she feels differently. But all of the things that make her hard to deal with are again the same things that make her very appealing. She's a very individualistic person. She tries very hard to please people and to communicate with people and to amuse them, but she's not a follower, really. And she doesn't

[26] Baumrind, 1971.   [27] Ibid., p. 99.

need other people—she's not dependent, really. Psychologically she's not dependent on other people—I don't think she feels so, although she knows she couldn't do a number of things herself.

Interviewer: How do you feel when she disobeys?

Mother: If you use the term disobeys, that sort of conjures up a negative feeling. Oftentimes she just doesn't think the way I do. It's just a difference of opinion. But I figure to a certain amount that I've been here longer—walked around on the earth longer, so I know more. Which isn't particularly valid either.

Interviewer: What do you do when Nina disobeys?

Mother: I don't know. I don't ask her to do a heck of a lot, really. Usually it gets done. We go and do it together, or—if she's really dead-set against it, she won't do it completely on her own. If she feels that from her standpoint it's not something she's required to do, whether it makes sense to me for her to do it, she won't do it. I really dislike punishing her. Punishing her comes down to—most of the time—doing physical things. And I have a strong distaste for that so I conk out. That's probably why she's so headstrong too. . .

Interviewer: What decisions does Nina make for herself?

Mother: She makes all her own decisions and then we argue about them. She really does. She decides all her own things. She decides her clothes, what she'll eat; but they're sort of in the context of what's happening. She goes to the store and she decides what she'll wear by what she'll see. Or if she gets dressed in the morning, she'll decide what she'll wear by what she can see around her.[28]

A number of other child-rearing studies have confirmed Baldwin and Baumrind's basic findings concerning the importance of control, communication, maturity demands, and nurturance in the home. Generally, parents who consistently maintain control in a democratic manner have children who are competent, nonaggressive, self-reliant, and high on self-esteem.[29] Parents who have high expectations for their children and make what Baumrind calls "maturity demands" on them have children who are competent, nonaggressive, sociable, and altruistic.[30] Parents who are warm and nurturant have children who are altruistic, considerate, friendly with peers, compliant with their parents, and high in self-esteem.[31] On the other hand, parents who are authoritarian, cold, or overly permissive have children who often lack these character strengths: that is, children who are intellectually and socially ineffective; children who lack empathy and self-confidence; children who are aggressive, cruel, or disobedient; and children who demonstrate negative moods, apathy, dependence, and difficulties in self-control.[32]

These child-rearing studies provide us with correlational evidence of relations between parental style and children's behavior. On the basis of these studies, we may begin to speculate about how certain types of parent-child interactions help foster the development of certain behavioral patterns in

[28] Ibid, pp. 101–2.
[29] Bee, 1967; Coopersmith, 1967; Patterson, 1976; Emmerich, 1977; Maccoby, 1980.
[30] Whiting & Whiting, 1973, 1975; Edwards & Whiting, 1977.
[31] Coopersmith, 1967; Hoffman & Saltz-

stein, 1967; Patterson, 1976; Zahn-Waxler, Radke-Yarrow, & King, 1979.
[32] Coopersmith, 1967; Hoffman & Saltzstein, 1967; Block, 1971; Feshbach, 1974; Maccoby, 1980.

children; and, conversely, how certain types of activity on the part of the child may, in part, shape the child-rearing patterns of parents. As noted several times in this section, correlational data cannot help us decide on the extent to which the parent influences the child *versus* the extent to which the child influences the parent. Nor can the evidence from these correlational studies explain for us the exact mechanisms of social influence through which parent and child shape one another's behavior. Do parental child-rearing practices work through the direct induction of skills and competence; through indirect means such as modeling, observation, or imitation; through motivational sequences of reward and reinforcement; or through more subtle social-psychological processes, such as the molding of one's behavior to conform to one's self-attributions? All of these mechanisms of behavioral change have been suggested in one theory or another, though they are quite different from one another in their hypothesized consequences for the child. We shall return to a discussion of these mechanisms later in this section. For now, let it simply be said that the child-rearing studies described in this section suggest that parent and child influence each other, but they do not define the direction of this influence nor the manner through which this influence is realized. For such further definition of the social-influence process in the adult-child relation, we must go beyond correlational data to more experimental types of studies.

But first, as a prelude to discussing mechanisms of change in the child-rearing process, it will be helpful to place the child firmly back in the process. As suggested a number of times above, traditional child-rearing studies tend to slight the role of children in their own socialization, since the studies are built on the unilateral assumption that parental practice determines the nature of the child, rather than vice versa. Although they cannot rule out the latter possibility, these studies are usually interpreted as if the former were the true causal course of events. (Note the language that Baumrind, as a typical example, uses in the passage quoted earlier concerning the "effects" of authoritative parenting upon children.) Richard Bell and others have tried to redress this imbalance by claims in the opposite direction, and by demonstrating empirically how children can influence their parents' chosen disciplinary techniques. But there is another kind of data that also shows children as having active influence on the parent's mode of exercising authority, and even presents the parent-child relation from the child's own point of view. Examining such data at this point will help us regain a necessary balance in our further discussions of parenting and its relation to children's social development.

The Child's Viewpoint on Parental Authority and Control

The most direct way to investigate the child's viewpoint is through clinical interview procedures such as those described in the previous chapter. In a series of studies, William Damon used such clinical interview techniques to explore children's conceptions of parental authority.[33] Children between the ages of four and twelve were presented with hypothetical stories of the following kind:

> This is Peter (Michelle for girl subjects), and here is his mother, Mrs. Johnson. Mrs. Johnson wants Peter to clean up his own room every day, and she tells him that he can't go out and play until he cleans his room up and straightens out his toys. But one day Peter's friend Michael comes over and tells Peter that all the kids are leaving right away for a picnic. Peter wants to go, but his room is a big mess. He tells his mother that he doesn't have time to straighten his room right now, but he'll do it later. She tells him no, that he'll have to stay in and miss the picnic.[34]

After hearing this and other stories, children were asked a number of probing questions that required children to address two issues related to parental authority: the legitimacy of leadership and the rationale for obedience. Legitimacy is the basis of a person's right to lead or to command. For example, children were asked why the mother or the father had the right to tell them what to do—that is, what qualities do they have that make them special in this sense? The rationale for obedience is the issue of why (or why not) one should obey someone else's command in the first place. A typical question concerning this issue was, what would happen if Peter decided to disobey his mother and go to the picnic anyway?

Damon found that children of all ages generally believe that obeying one's parent is important, but their reasons for obedience and their understanding of parental leadership legitimacy change dramatically as they grow older. Damon charted a sequence of developmental levels that describe children's authority conceptions between the ages of four and twelve. These levels are summarized in Table 5-3.

In general, the progression is as follows: at the earliest level, the child believes that he obeys because he wants to. Parents are obeyed because they tell you what you want to do. Commands that conflict with your desires do not have to be listened to. At the next level, the reality of punishment is grasped. You obey in order to avoid unpleasant consequences. The next level infuses parental authority figures with attributes like physical strength and all-encompassing power that legitimize their commands. You obey mother because she is bigger and stronger, and because she will inevitably find out if you disobey. At the next level, parental command is legitimized by superior virtues like being smarter, and obedience is considered an exchange: the parent has done much for the child in the past and so deserves respect. Toward the end of this progression, you consider it in your best interest to listen to parents. This is because parents have had more experience than children, and they know what is best for you. But when the parent is wrong, it becomes possible to disagree, because the child is now seen as having the fundamental rights of an equal in the relationship. Finally, at the last level, obedience becomes a matter of choice, based upon a temporary and voluntary deferral to someone who cares about

---

[33] Damon, 1977, 1980.   [34] Ibid.

Table 5-3 Children's Authority Conceptions

Level	Approximate age range	Authority legitimized by:	Basis for obedience
0-A	4 yrs. and under	Love; identification with self.	Association between authority's commands and self's desires.
0-B	4–5 yrs.	Physical attributes of persons.	Obedience is a means for achieving self's desires.
1-A	5–8 yrs.	Social and physical power.	Respect for authority figure's power.
1-B	7–9 yrs.	Attributes that reflect special ability, talent, or actions of authority figure.	Authority figure deserves obedience because of superior abilities of past favors.
2-A	8–10 yrs.	Prior training or experience with leadership.	Respect for authority figure's leadership abilities; awareness of authority figure's concern for subordinate's welfare.
2-B	10 yrs. and above	Situationally appropriate attributes of leadership.	Temporary and voluntary consent of subordinate; spirit of cooperation between leader and led.

Source: Based on W. Damon, Patterns of change in children's social reasoning: A two-year longitudinal study. *Child Development*, 1980, *51*, 1011.

your welfare. You obey your mother because she cares about what is good for you and can be helpful. If, in a certain situation, you know more than mother, she should be the one to listen to you.

In both cross-sectional and longitudinal studies, Damon has found that, with age, children regularly advance through these levels of understanding parental authority. The best evidence for this was a longitudinal study in which Damon followed individual children ages four through ten over a two-year period of time. By the end of this period, almost all children had advanced along the sequence by one or two levels, and none had moved backwards.[35] This indicates that the development of children's authority understanding is somewhat independent of specific family backgrounds, school experience, or other social-contextual variation. Rather, it is more the result of each child

[35] Ibid.

actively working out the principles of authority and obedience in order to make sense of this important aspect of social experience.

Because a child's conception of parental authority develops according to its own logic and at its own pace, we must consider the definite possibility that it exerts its own distinct influence upon a parent's child-rearing behavior. Here, then, we have a tangible basis for positing the child's effect upon the parent: as the child's understanding of parental authority changes with development, no doubt parental practice must accommodate to these changes. This accommodation at times becomes easy and at times difficult, depending upon the nature of the change and the way in which the parent reacts to the change. But parents who are at all sensitive to their child's thinking will recognize, in some way, the social-cognitive changes in the child's authority understanding, and they will adjust their behavior accordingly. In this way, the child and the parent both shape the interaction between them. Further, these interactions, and the parent-child relation in general, evolve as the child and the parent both adapt to the child's social-cognitive growth.

Mechanisms of Adult-Child Influence

Although children help determine the nature of their interactions with adults, this does not negate the fact that these interactions have a powerful influence upon children. In fact, such influence very likely is the major force in children's social development.

This section will examine the psychological mechanisms through which children's behavior and development are influenced in the course of adult-child interactions. The main questions are: How and why do these interactions have such an important influence? What aspects of children's behavior and development are most affected by such interactions? Are moral conduct and the acquisition of sex roles affected? If so, to what extent are parent-child interactions responsible for the child's morality and the child's sex typing? Finally, is it true that adult-child interactions have developmental effects that are different from those brought about by children's peer interactions?

Observation and Imitation

The most direct explanation for a parent's influence upon a child is that the child naturally tends to imitate the parent's behavior. This explanation, of course, also accounts for behavioral similarity between parent and child. The principal exponent of this explanation is Albert Bandura, whose social learning theory provides a detailed account of observational learning processes during child development.[36] Bandura and his colleagues have studied children's observation and imitation of adult models in a wide variety of experi-

[36] Bandura, 1977.

mental situations. In one well-known set of experiments on aggression, children watched an adult beat up a Bobo doll and then had the opportunity to do the same (see Figure 5-2).[37] In an experiment on moral reasoning, children were exposed to the moral judgments of a model and then were asked to respond to the moral dilemma themselves.[38] From these and other experimen-

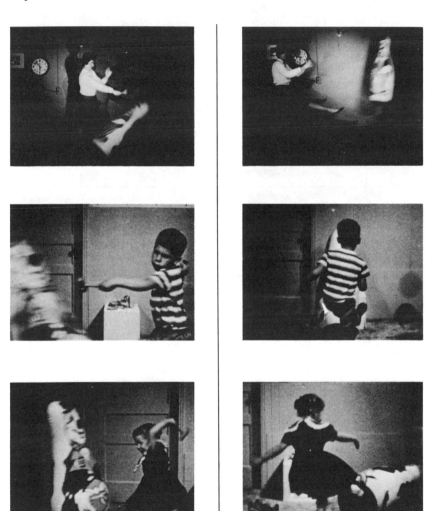

Figure 5-2. Observation and Imitation. The children first observe the model strike the doll with a hammer and then observe the model kick the doll. Subsequently, they copy both of the model's acts.

Source: A. Bandura, D. Ross, and S. A. Ross, Imitation of film-mediated aggressive models. *Journal of Abnormal and Social Psychology*, 1963, *66*, 8. Reprinted with permission.

[37] Bandura, Ross, & Ross, 1961.   [38] Bandura & McDonald, 1963.

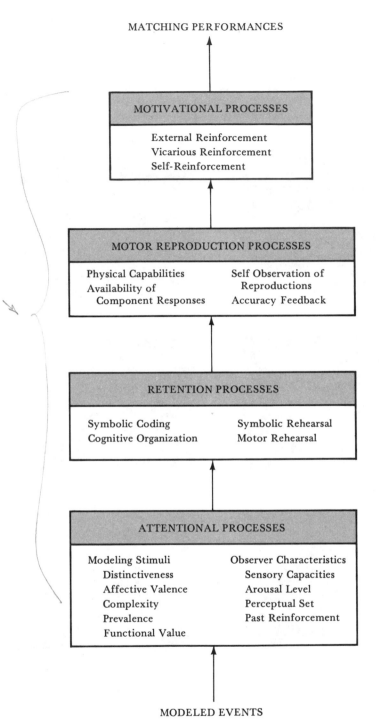

MATCHING PERFORMANCES

MOTIVATIONAL PROCESSES

External Reinforcement
Vicarious Reinforcement
Self-Reinforcement

MOTOR REPRODUCTION PROCESSES

Physical Capabilities
Availability of
  Component Responses

Self Observation of
  Reproductions
Accuracy Feedback

RETENTION PROCESSES

Symbolic Coding
Cognitive Organization

Symbolic Rehearsal
Motor Rehearsal

ATTENTIONAL PROCESSES

Modeling Stimuli
  Distinctiveness
  Affective Valence
  Complexity
  Prevalence
  Functional Value

Observer Characteristics
  Sensory Capacities
  Arousal Level
  Perceptual Set
  Past Reinforcement

MODELED EVENTS

Figure 5-3. Observational Learning. Processes of attention, retention, motor reproduction, and motivation govern observational learning and imitation, according to the social learning analysis.

Source: A. Bandura, *Social Learning Theory*. Englewood Cliffs, N.J.: Prentice-Hall, 1977. Reprinted with permission.

tal demonstrations, Bandura abstracted the principles behind the modeling process that he believes accounts for most human learning: "Fortunately, most human behavior is learned observationally through modeling: from observing others one forms an idea of how new behaviors are performed, and on later occasions this coded information serves as a guide for action."[39]

Although the observational modeling process proposed by Bandura is direct, it is by no means simple. Children do not exactly copy the behavior of models in mirror-image fashion. Rather, there are a number of component processes that determine when and whether a child will imitate a particular model on a particular occasion (see Figure 5-3).

The first set of these processes, the *attentional processes*, are implicated in the child's initial apprehension of the behavior that is to be imitated. The model's behavior must have certain characteristics, such as perceptual distinctiveness and affective salience, if the child is to notice it. In addition, the observing child must choose to carefully direct his attention to the behavior. The second set of processes, called the *retention processes*, enable the child to derive meaning from the observed behavior. The child codes and interprets the model's behavior according to whatever cognitive categories the child has developed, and in this way, finds a behavioral pattern in the observed stimuli. This pattern will structure the child's imitative response. The third set of processes, the *motor reproduction processes*, determine how well the child actually reproduces the model's behavior. Translating an intention to imitate into action requires physical skills. Each child's particular capabilities and limitations will influence the extent and accuracy of the child's modeling. Finally, the fourth set of component processes are the *motivational processes*. These derive from the rewards that the child obtains, or anticipates, for imitating the model. Some of these rewards come from external sources, such as when the parent approves of the child's behavior. Others come from the self, as when one is proud of one's own accomplishments. Such motivating reinforcements determine not only whether the child will imitate the model in the first place, but also whether the child will continue to reproduce the model's behavior in the future.

As an example of Bandura's modeling theory, let us take the common case of a child observing his father drive a car. If the child is very young, he will give only a crude approximation of his father's driving behavior, for several reasons. First, the child does not know how to carefully "watch" the father drive, and he misses many of the important details of the father's performance (process 1). For example, the child may not observe the father step on the brake or turn on the directional signal. Second (process 2), the young child does not know how to interpret the father's actions in terms of automobile-driving categories. The child may notice the father turn the steering wheel but may not be able to connect this act with the car's moving to the left. Third (process 3),

---

[39] Bandura, 1977, p. 22.

the child may not be strong enough, big enough, or well-coordinated enough to manipulate the car's equipment. Finally (process 4), there are neither external nor internal incentives for a young child to seriously master automobile driving. Children are not allowed to drive, even if they could. The result is that the child may playfully mimic the father's actions, either in the father's car itself or with one of the child's own toys; but the child will not truly reproduce the father's automobile driving. Only as he develops the skills and incentives outlined in Bandura's four component processes will the child begin to learn driving by observing the father's example.

The strength of Bandura's analysis is that it accounts for the interaction between children's developing abilities and the tutorial influence of models whom the children encounter as they grow older. But Bandura's emphasis on modeling as the major source of such influence has encountered severe criticism from many child developmentalists. Martin Hoffman, for example, has identified a number of major problems in Bandura's social learning theory.[40] The most important of these is that modeling as a learning process can lead only to similarity between the child's behavior and that of others. This means that, if Bandura is correct in his emphasis, conformity must be the end point of development. But conformity is not an adequate developmental goal in any area of development. With respect to morality, for example, conformity can lead to evil as easily as it can lead to good. Stanley Milgram's demonstration that people can unjustly harm others out of a sense of conformity and obedience to authority is but one of many indications of this.[41] In fact, conformity is not only inadequate as a goal of moral development, but it also does not typically characterize moral development during any period of life. Moral "novelty" can be seen in the sometimes bizarre beliefs of young children, in the idealistic theories of adolescents, as well as in the visionary statements of prophets and saints. The same can be said of any sphere of development: people at all ages often respond creatively to new social situations as they arise, and conformity is but one of many behavioral patterns that must be explained. A theory predicated on the assumption that developmental progress means increasing conformity to selected models cannot account for the development of flexible and inventive adaptation to the world. *But how flexible are we?*

Identification

Sigmund Freud introduced the notion of identification in order to explain how young children learn to control their antisocial impulses.[42] In Freud's view, all children experience feelings of both sexuality and hostility toward their parents. In the case of boys, the mother is the target of sexual desire; and the father, envied because he possesses the mother, is the target of hostile impulses. Freud called the archetypical situation of boys the *Oedipal complex*

---

[40] Hoffman, 1970, 1971.
[41] Milgram, 1974.
[42] Freud, 1922.

because it parallels the dramatic situation created by Sophocles in his classic play *Oedipus Rex.*[43]

The child's early feelings of sexuality and hostility toward his parents do not exactly lead him to be welcomed into the bosom of his family. To the contrary, wrote Freud, the child becomes quickly aware that the open expression of these feelings may lead to the loss of his parents' love. The child's realistic solution is to repress the feelings. But the child's mechanism for effecting realistic solutions (the child's *ego*) is weak in comparison to the sexual and hostile impulses (the *id*) that must be suppressed. That is, the ego needs some help in order to control the antisocial aspects of the child's dispositions. This help comes by way of the mechanisms of the identification process (the *superego*).

As a permanent solution to the continuing problem of antisocial impulses, the child identifies with the parent and incorporates the parent's moral standards. These standards become the child's own, "internalized" as part of the child's new superego structure. As such, they will function autonomously throughout life, in effect enabling the child to punish himself whenever he does wrong. Thus, by the end of the Oedipal period—by age four or five at the latest —the child has adopted from his parents an energized set of moral rules that will guide his conduct throughout life. Although this moral system may be modified during later periods of development, the major part of its shape and substance is formed during the period of initial parental identification.

The notion of identification, as Freud intended it, implies more than the modeling of another's behavior or capabilities. Rather, it implies the wholesale incorporation of another's beliefs, attitudes, and rules of conduct. It means the sharing of another's state of mind, more than the copying of another's behavior. Whereas modeling may add to one's repertoire of actions and skills, identification necessarily transforms one's personality.

Because identification implies such wholistic transformations in personality, there is reason to question its very existence. In fact, is it reasonable to believe that a child's moral character is permanently shaped by a cataclysmic conflict resolution at age five? Or that the child is able to assimilate the totality of his parents' moral standards at this early age? Many psychologists doubt, first of all, that such major, lifelong changes in personality take place so suddenly or so wholistically.[44] Second, many developmentalists believe that the acquisition of complex cognitive systems like morality is a constructive process in which the child plays an active role. Like Bandura's social learning theory, the Freudian identification theory assumes that during socialization, the child passively adopts the moral beliefs of others. As we shall see, there are alterna-

---

[43] The early affective experience of girls, according to Freud, is more complex and varied than that of boys, and consequently the identification process takes a more convoluted route. Freud, in his writings, did little to illuminate the female pattern of identification. Instead, he chose to explicate the more direct course of male identification, and to treat the female case as a somewhat less effective variation of this process (Freud, 1933).

[44] Langer, 1969; Crain, 1980.

tive views of socialization that take the child's own input into this process more seriously.

Empirical evidence for Freud's identification theory has been hard to come by. Large-scale investigations by Robert Sears and his colleagues found no consistent pattern in children's tendencies to be similar to their parents, despite the sex of child or parent, the nature of the child-parent relation, or any other variable the investigators could think of.[45] Surveying the identification literature, Martin Hoffman concluded that there was no support for the assertion that morality is internalized because children fear the loss of parental love.[46] In addition, Hoffman found no relation between children's identification with their parents and children's use of moral standards to evaluate their own behavior, nor between identification and children's feelings of guilt over wrongdoing.[47]

Despite its lack of empirical support, the Freudian notion of identification continues to have appeal for psychologists attempting to explain important similarities between parent and child. Modeling has seemed too piecemeal a procedure to account for the many complex patterns of behavior and belief that children seem to acquire from their parents. Morality is not the only such pattern; sex-role identification is another. To many, it has seemed intuitively more plausible to explain a child's adoption of sex-typed conduct and values by a wholistic process like identification with the same-sex parent than by a succession of behavioral imitations of many persons throughout childhood. This is because a child establishes one and only one sex role (male or female) during childhood, and it is difficult to explain this kind of cognitive commitment without some notion of total identification with one person. Certainly, a series of unpatterned imitations with a variety of models cannot account for sex typing, since a child imitates adults of both sexes while growing up.

For reasons like this, identification has been retained in contemporary theories of social development, although several of Freud's key assumptions have been altered. For example, the "status envy" theory posits that any person who controls an intensely desired resource may serve as a subject for the child's identification.[48] The mother's love, as in Freud's Oedipal situation, is only one of several possible resources that children intensely desire. Others include material possessions, instrumental competence, and mastery over the environment. The assumption here is that the child takes on the characteristics of the model in order to command the model's coveted resources.

More recent accounts of identification.   Jerome Kagan has presented the most elaborated version of identification theory, combining Freud's original notion with selected principles from social-learning theory.[49] Kagan, like Freud, treats identification as a wholistic "acquired cognitive response" rather than as a similarity in particular overt behaviors between child and model. In

[45] Sears, Maccoby, & Levin, 1957; Sears, Rau, & Albert, 1965.

[46] Hoffman, 1983.

[47] Ibid.

[48] Kagan, 1958; Whiting, J. W. M., 1960.

[49] Kagan, 1958.

other words, identification is a belief in similarity and an intention to increase that similarity, and not simply isolated instances of similarity produced by individual imitative acts. The first step in identification, according to Kagan, is the child's perceived desire for resources (goal states) that the model possesses. For Kagan, the two desired goals that motivate identification are mastery and love. Next, "the wish to command the goal states of M (the model) leads to the desire to possess the characteristics of M because S (the child) believes that if he were similar to M he would command the desired goals."[50] Kagan then invokes principles of reinforcement to explain how the identification is maintained. The child is rewarded by his identification in two ways. First, once the child associates the model with the desired goal states, the expectation is created that any similarity to the model will itself be rewarding: "The identification response (i.e., 'some of the characteristics of the model are mine') is reinforced each time S perceives of it and is told that he is similar to M."[51] Second, the child is rewarded because, in adopting the model's thoughts and behavior, he actually manages to acquire for himself some of the resources associated with the model: "The S must not only perceive similarity between S and M, but also must experience some of the desired, affective goal-states of M."[52]

Kagan's formulation has been widely used to account for products of identification such as sex typing, although it does have its weaknesses, both empirically and theoretically. Empirically, it must encounter the same criticism as Freud's original theory: there is virtually no support for the existence of identification, other than intuitions about one's own experience. The only available experimental evidence comes from modeling studies by Bandura and others.[53] But these are studies of isolated imitative events, rather than enduring identifications that result in a transformed state of mind. In addition, aside from its lack of empirical support, Kagan's formulation may be theoretically implausible as well. This is because it assumes that children at an early age are capable of the following sorts of cognitive operations: Assumption: Daddy possesses a variety of valued resources (love of mother, mastery, possessions) because he has certain attributes (maleness, personality features, beliefs). Deduction: Therefore, if I acquire similar attributes, I too will capture these resources. From the work of Piaget and others, we know that this type of logical reasoning is rare during the preschool years.[54] Yet, it is during these early childhood years that sex typing, initial moral values, and other products of identification are acquired. Such theoretical contradictions lead us to question the explanatory value of this type of identification model.

A more radical revision of the identification concept has been suggested by Lawrence Kohlberg in an analysis of children's sex-role development.[55] Kohlberg not only reformulates the processes through which identification occurs, but he also dramatically devalues its role in the child's acquisition of

[50] Ibid, p. 299.
[51] Ibid.
[52] Ibid.
[53] Bandura, Ross, & Ross, 1961, 1963;

Bandura & Walters, 1963.
[54] Piaget & Inhelder, 1969a, 1969b.
[55] Kohlberg, 1966.

new behavior. This is because Kohlberg believes children do not copy most new behavior from others but rather actively acquire it on their own. Identification is a by-product rather than an instigator of this process.

Kohlberg begins with the assumption that children constantly attempt to make sense out of the world and their place in it: this is the cognitive expression of children's need to adapt to their environment. It is because of this beginning assumption that Kohlberg has called his theory "cognitive developmental." Part of the child's cognitive effort is the search for identifying features of the self. We shall discuss the details of this search during childhood in the next chapter. For now, the important point is that Kohlberg's theory places this cognitive effort *prior* to the process of identification with others. In other words, Kohlberg believes that before the child establishes an identification with another person, the child must make some judgments about the nature of his or her own distinguishing characteristics. Gender, according to Kohlberg, is the most cognitively accessible characteristic of self, since it is detectable in several overt physical attributes (dress, hair length, genitals). In this sense, Kohlberg is in agreement with Michael Lewis and Jeanne Brooks-Gunn (see Chapter 3), who have found that gender is one of the first properties of the categorical self that children come to recognize. Kohlberg believes that by age four or five, children have established their gender identity in a content, nonchanging way ("I am a boy, and I shall remain a boy"). In light of Lewis and Brooks-Gunn's research, we might even push this accomplishment back a year or two from Kohlberg's estimation.

Once the child constructs a stable gender identity, Kohlberg writes, the child spontaneously develops sex-appropriate values and standards. This follows from the child's "natural" tendency to "value positively objects and activities that represent his gender identity because his gender identity is part of himself."[56] The assumption here is that young children judge as "good" anything directly associated with the self. Kohlberg takes this to be an axiomatic feature of human behavior, barring pathological deviations.

After the child has established gender and its associated sex-appropriate values, the process of identification with same-sex persons is ready to begin. Kohlberg's general principle is this: ". . .for a boy with masculine interests and values, the activities of a male model are more interesting and hence more modelled."[57] A boy, therefore, would most likely choose his father as a model because he recognizes gender similarity to the father in the first place. It is interesting to note that in Kohlberg's theory, a boy is more likely to imitate his older brother than his mother. Unlike Kagan's formulation, in which perceived similarity to a model is merely reinforcing, Kohlberg's theory holds that judgments of similarity instigate the entire modeling process. Kohlberg here owes a debt to Piaget, who asserted that children will imitate behavior already in their own repertoire long before they will imitate behavior that is genuinely

---

[56] Ibid., p. 111.   [57] Ibid., p. 114.

novel to them. In Piagetian terms, imitation based on reproductive assimilation (repetition of one's own activity) precedes that based upon pure accommodation (copying the world outside the self).[58]

But there is more to identification than modeling, as we noted above. The final step in Kohlberg's identification theory is the assertion that *emotional-affectional attachment* must join with modeling before real identification takes place. This often occurs because the desire to imitate a model "eventually leads to the desire to be near the model, and to obtain his approval, i.e., to obtain assurance that the self's behavior is like the model or conforms to his standards."[59] In this way, long-term modeling relationships generally breed emotional-affectional attachment, which in turn leads to identification proper. Therefore, identification as a state of mind develops from modeling as a consequence of the child's search for rewards like the model's attention. Further, Kohlberg believes that such rewards make a child dependent upon the model, which in turn intensifies the identification.

Kohlberg's radical reformulation of identification theory places the child's self-knowledge prior to modeling, and it places modeling prior to the child's search for social rewards (see Figure 5-4). This is the reverse order of the status-envy theories, which begin with the child's search for rewards and end with the child taking on new attributes of self from the model. From Kohlberg's cognitive-developmental perspective, imitation and identification cannot proceed from an initial desire to acquire attributes essentially foreign to the self,

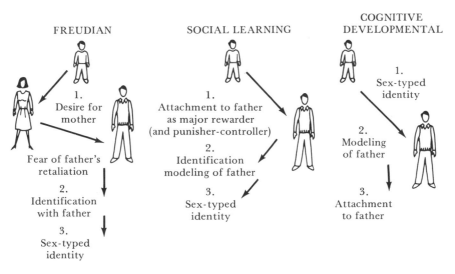

Figure 5-4.   Theoretical Sequences in Psychosexual Identification.

Source: L. Kohlberg, A cognitive-developmental analysis of children's sex-role concepts and attitudes. In E. Maccoby (Ed.), *The Development of Sex Differences.* Stanford, Calif.: Stanford University Press, 1966, p. 128. Reprinted with permission.

[58] Piaget, 1962.   [59] Kohlberg, 1966, p. 126.

because the child has no way of apprehending the existence or meaning of such attributes. Rather, the child initially desires to imitate acts and traits that already constitute a part of his self-definition, and then, in some long-lasting relationships, expands the scope of these imitations to forge a wholistic, emotionally charged identification with another person.

Kohlberg's identification theory avoids many of the problems in previous formulations: in particular, it makes no questionable assumptions about young children viewing identification as a means of obtaining a model's resources. Nor does it require the same kind of empirical verification that previous identification theories needed (and lacked). Unlike the other formulations, Kohlberg's theory does not predict that children incorporate wholesale their parents' behavior; rather, children begin by noticing the behavioral similarity that *already* exists, and the resulting identification is more of a cognitive and emotional bond than a desire to totally reproduce the model in oneself. Therefore, Kohlberg's view does not lead to the expectation that strong parent-child identifications will inevitably lead to consistent patterns of moral or sex-role behavior in the child. Consequently, the fact that Sear's and others' investigations fail to establish such relations provides no disconfirmation of Kohlberg's theory. In fact, Kohlberg cites exactly these failures, in addition to some new data of his own, as empirical support for his own view.[60] But Kohlberg's theory does leave some questions unanswered. For one thing, identification, if it does exist, is probably not limited to models of the same sex. To make the theory more general, other bases of interpersonal similarity beyond gender must be posited. But what are the limits of this extension? Does a child identify in some fashion with everyone who seems similar to the child in some way? Or are some bases of similarity, like gender, more compelling than others? Perhaps it is only those characteristics of self and other that are apparent early in childhood that provide the bases for stable, long-lasting identifications.

Finally, and most importantly, Kohlberg leaves unresolved the role played by identification, as he conceives it, in children's social development. As Kohlberg describes it, identification seems like little more than a synonym for attachment, except that it necessarily develops later than the initial version of attachment found between mother and infant. Yet Kohlberg also suggests that identification leads to a continuing modeling relation in which the child does acquire certain limited knowledge and behavior from the model. What is the extent, and what are the limits, of such identification learning? What does it contribute to a child's development? Although Kohlberg does not tackle this question in a positive sense, he is clear about what he believes identification does *not* do: in itself, it cannot account for the major conceptual and behavioral abilities that children acquire during socialization. That is, the major part of children's moral values, their sex-role standards, their social conduct, and their sense of self, do not derive from passive "copying" processes like modeling and identification. Rather, these social-developmental achievements are prior to,

[60] Ibid.

and often unconnected with, the child's identifications with others. For the developmental processes responsible for such achievements, we must look to mechanisms of social-psychological influence in which the child plays a more active and interactive role.

Attitude Change

Psychologists have described mechanisms of social influence that imply more direct interaction between adult and child than modeling or identification. These mechanisms consist of strategies for changing children's attitudes about their own behavior and consequently the behavior itself. For example, a parental goal might be to make a child realize that hitting his or her sister is wrong, so that the child next time will forgo any temptation to do so. Parents spontaneously employ a number of strategies to change their children's attitudes, generally for the ultimate purpose of improving the children's conduct in a moral sense. In order to assess the short- and long-term effectiveness of these strategies for attitude change, psychologists have reproduced a variety of the strategies under experimental conditions. In particular, four adult strategies for influencing attitudes have been experimentally studied: *power assertion, love withdrawal, informational internalization,* and *cognitive disequilibrium.* As the Joan Grusec and Leon Kucynski study cited earlier demonstrates, parents do not consistently limit themselves to one or another of these techniques, but they may in the degree to which they will rely on each.

Power assertion is simply the threat to punish if the child does not adopt a new attitude or behavior. This can be highly effective in the short term, particularly if the adult is present to enforce the sanction. But experimental evidence has shown that power assertion does not, in itself, lead to long-lasting, dependable attitude change. In fact, too much power assertion may have unintended countereffects. The clearest demonstration of this is the "forbidden toy" paradigm used by a number of investigators.[61]

In this paradigm, some children are asked not to play with a desirable toy under threat of a relatively mild sanction, and others are told not to play with the toy under threat of severe punishment. Neither group plays with the toy in the immediate situation. But when the children return to the laboratory on a later occasion, the children who experienced the severe threat are more likely to play with the toy, whereas the children in the mild-threat condition typically devalue the toy and refuse on their own to play with it. The extent to which parents assert their power to punish, therefore, does not determine the extent to which children will adopt behavioral or attitudinal directives. If anything, it seems that strenuous power assertions interfere with the process of influencing attitudes.

Love withdrawal is a more subtle and indirect means of forcing a child's

---

[61] Aronson & Carlsmith, 1963; Lepper, Greene, & Nisbett, 1973; Lepper & Greene, 1975.

compliance. It is implemented through direct expressions of disapproval ("I don't like you when you act like that"), or through indirect expression of coldness, disappointment, and disinterest (such as ignoring the child). In some ways love withdrawal is more permanently effective than power assertion. One recent study showed that love withdrawal is an effective means of gaining immediate compliance from children and is widely used by parents in response to all types of child misdeeds, including harm to persons, harm to property, and loss of self-control.[62] But despite its immediate effectiveness, love withdrawal still does not accomplish, in itself, the main goal of adult attempts to influence their children: having children adopt new, more "socialized" attitudes that children consider their own. That is, there is no evidence that love withdrawal leads to the "internalization" of genuine beliefs. Rather, love withdrawal leads only to limited changes in children's overt behavior. For example, it increases the likelihood that children will inhibit their anger and hostility toward others.[63] But it does not lead to the adoption of new moral standards and beliefs that children will maintain on their own, apart from consequences having to do with their parents' approval.

Empirical evidence for this has been provided in a series of parental interviews and observations conducted by Martin Hoffman.[64] Hoffman compared three types of parental socialization techniques: power assertion, love withdrawal, and induction (which we shall call informational internalization, as below). Hoffman's findings concerning power assertion are consistent with the results of the forbidden toy experiment: he found power assertion to be a poor technique for instilling permanent change. Love withdrawal was somewhat intermediate between the other two in its effectiveness: it seemed to provide the child with more of a long-lasting motivation to improve his or her behavior than did power assertion, but it still did not lead children to commit themselves to moral principles that were functionally autonomous (that is, that operated on their own) in their parents' absence. The third technique, induction or informational internalization, accomplished this.

Informational internalization techniques are the most successful in permanently changing children's attitudes and behavior. Such techniques have one thing in common: they lead children to focus on the actual standards that their parents are trying to communicate, rather than on the disciplinary means by which parents enforce these standards. In other words, in a successful parental influence encounter, the aspect of the encounter most salient to the child will be the attitude or behavior that the parent tries to instill, rather than the parents' sanction against refusing to comply. In fact, in the most successful of such encounters, the child will forget the sanction entirely and will eventually even forget the parent's role in suggesting the new attitude. Instead, the child will attribute the attitude solely to the self, thus internalizing it wholeheartedly.

[62] Chapman & Zahn-Waxler, 1982. [64] Hoffman, 1967.
[63] Hoffman, 1967; Hoffman & Saltzstein, 1967.

Theoretical models accounting for the processes underlying such optimal internalization abound. We shall consider two of such models here: the minimal-sufficiency model as formulated by Mark Lepper[65] and the information-processing model proposed by Martin Hoffman.[66]

Lepper's model derives from a social-psychological tradition that has distinguished two processes of attitude change: *compliance* and *internalization*. Compliance means changing one's behavior in order to conform immediately to externally mandated standards. Internalization, on the other hand, means adopting these standards as one's own, both for the present and the future. Long-lasting behavioral change can only be expected with internalization, not with mere compliance. Social-psychological theory has hypothesized that compliance and internalization are fostered under different conditions.[67] The theoretical assertion is that tangible rewards and punishments promote compliance, whereas persuasion, argument, and reasoning promote internalization. But empirical research with children has suggested that this is only part of a more complex story, and that a further explanation may be needed for this assertion itself.

Lepper and his colleagues arranged two types of experimental situations to investigate the conditions under which internalization takes place. The first was a variation on the "forbidden toy" paradigm mentioned above.[68] In this experiment, Lepper followed the traditional procedure prohibiting children from playing with an attractive toy, using mild threats for some children and severe threats for others. Lepper replicated earlier findings that children in the mild-threat condition were less attracted to the toy in a subsequent session, and he also found that these children were more likely than those severely threatened to resist temptation in an entirely new situation. Lepper concluded that "prior compliance in the face of. . .relatively minimal extrinsic pressures, in general terms, seemed to increase subsequent internalization or private acceptance of the standards implicit in the adult's initial request; previous compliance in the face of more salient external pressures seemed to decrease later internalization."[69]

Threats and prohibitions aside, a similar relation was found between the positive rewards offered to children and children's likelihood of continuing a pattern of activity. In their second type of experimental situation, Lepper and his colleagues asked children to play with Magic Markers for a period of time.[70] Lepper knew that the children in his study found Magic Markers interesting, because the children were selected for the study by surreptitious observations that identified a group of children who clearly enjoyed this type of activity. Once in the experimental situation, the children were exposed to one of three reward conditions. Children in one group were told that they could win an attractive "Good Player" certificate by working with the Magic Markers,

[65] Lepper, 1983.
[66] Hoffman, 1983.
[67] Lewin, Lippett, & White, 1939; Kelman, 1958.
[68] Lepper, 1973.
[69] Ibid.
[70] Lepper, Greene, & Nisbett, 1973.

and in fact, they were awarded the certificate at the end of the session; one group was told nothing, but the children were awarded the certificate unexpectedly at the end of the session; and one group was simply asked to use the Magic Markers without any reward, expected or unexpected. Several weeks later, all three groups of children were again given a chance to play with the Magic Markers, but this time they were not explicitly urged to do so. The children who had obtained no previous reward for such play—the third experimental group—showed by far the greatest interest in using the Magic Markers again. Lepper concluded that "the use of unnecessarily salient extrinsic incentives. . .undermined children's intrinsic interest in the activity per se."

In order to explain the combined results of his studies, Lepper proposes a *minimal sufficiency principle* of socialization.[71] The principle states that the most effective means of changing a child's behavior in a long-term sense are those that are applied with just enough coercion or reward to engage the child in the new behavior, but not so much that the child finds the coercion or reward to be the most memorable part of the new experience. In other words, external incentives provided by the adult must be minimally sufficient to change the child's behavior without being more salient in themselves than the standards that the adult is trying to promote. Under these conditions, writes Lepper, the child's attitudes and behavior will be permanently transformed because the child will internalize the new standards.

Lepper uses his minimal sufficiency principle to explain the findings from previous socialization research by Baumrind, Hoffman, and others. For example, Lepper reconceptualizes Baumrind's distinction between authoritarian and authoritative parents as a distinction between parents who use overly sufficient coercive techniques versus parents who combine minimally sufficient techniques with reasoning and argument. Parents in the latter group —Baumrind's authoritative parents—establish the optimal conditions for their children to internalize socially appropriate standards. Thus, children with authoritative parents exhibit socially responsible behavior on their own initiative. In contrast, authoritarian parents foster compliance rather than permanent attitude change in their children. Permissive parents fail to provide their children even with the minimal coercions or rewards necessary to change their behavior in the first place. We shall see below how Lepper's model is also in line with findings from Hoffman's research.

The minimal sufficiency model accounts for the relative long-term effectiveness of subtle social influence techniques, especially when compared with more heavy-handed techniques like power assertion and love withdrawal. The heart of the model is the underlying assumption that children must be encouraged to attend to the behavioral standards that the parent wishes to communicate if internalization of these standards is to take place. Parental actions (like punishment) that draw the child's attention away from the standards themselves work against the internalization process. The key to

---

[71] Lepper, 1983.

success, according to Lepper, is to guide a child toward acting out the desired standards, through tactics that are not particularly noticeable to the child. The child will then focus on the standards themselves, as well as on the reasons behind them, and will ultimately incorporate the standards into his or her own attitudinal repertoire.

In his writing, Lepper also makes an important distinction between the child's acquisition of specific attitudes and standards (such as "Listen to the adult" or "Put away your toys") and coherent systems of belief (such as organized morality). Lepper believes that this theory is adequate for explaining how parents influence their children to adopt specific attitudes and standards, but that it is not adequate for explaining the long-term construction process that guides the development of more complex belief systems. We shall return to this point in our discussion of moral development.

Another version of an informational internalization model has been offered by Martin Hoffman in his attempts to explain children's moral development.[72] Hoffman believes that the "discipline encounter" is the central parent-child interaction responsible for the child's moral development. In a prototypical discipline encounter, the child acts in a way that adversely affects others, and the parent either stops the child's actions or punishes the child after the fact. In either case, the child will not be likely to repeat the unwelcome act in the parent's immediate presence. But will the child continue to refrain from this behavior when the parent is not around? This, writes Hoffman, depends upon the type of discipline encounter that the parent creates for the child.

Discipline encounters in which the parent mainly asserts power or withdraws love do not result in moral internalization, as research by Hoffman and others, cited earlier in this section, has demonstrated. If a discipline technique is to foster internalization, it must *induce* the child to anticipate the effect of behavior on others. Such *inductions* can take many forms, depending upon the situation and upon the age of the child. Here Hoffman argues, like Maccoby, that parents spontaneously vary their communications to children in accord with children's developing social-cognitive abilities. For example, an induction to a very young child will emphasize the direct effects of the child's actions: "If you keep pushing him, he'll fall down and cry." With an older child, the parent may focus upon the fairness of the child's actions in terms of the others' actions and intentions: "Don't yell at him, he was only trying to help." Or the parent may point to the psychological, rather than the physical effect of the child's actions: "He feels bad because he was proud of his tower and you knocked it down."

Inductions, therefore, nourish the child's concern for others, and they offer the child information about how his behavior can adversely affect others. This information helps a child better understand interpersonal causality (that is, the relation between the child's own act and the physical and psychological well-being of another), although, as noted above, the child's social-cognitive

[72] Hoffman, 1983.

maturity places some limits on the type of inductive information that the child is able to process. Hoffman therefore proposes an information-processing model in which the child's capacities for encoding and storing new knowledge provide constraints on the parent's communications, and in which the parent, working within these constraints, tries to expand the limits of a child's concern for others a bit further during each inductive discipline encounter.

But even inductions, according to Hoffman, do not in themselves socialize the child. This is because the child must pay attention to the message contained in the parent's induction, and the message alone will not suffice to motivate sustained attention. Hoffman believes that the child must be placed in an "optimum state of arousal" if the induced message is to effectively influence the child. This can be done by combining the induction with a mild amount of power assertion or love withdrawal. In other words, the inductive disciplinary technique places the message concerning welfare of others in the context of the parent's mild threats, disapproval, disappointment, or other moderately arousing parental sanctions. Without the sanction, the child will not be aroused enough to take the induced message seriously. If the punishment or love withdrawal is too severe, the child's arousal will be so great that it will interfere with the child's attention to the induced message.

Hoffman's theory is similar to Lepper's minimal sufficiency model, and it is compatible with the child-rearing research of Baldwin, Baumrind, and others. All these authors agree that the formula for long-lasting influence upon a child's behavior includes both parental control and parental communication to the child about the moral and personal significance of the child's behavior. The parental control must be effective but only mildly arousing in an emotional sense. Further, the parental communication must be adapted to the child's developing social-cognitive abilities, so that the parent's message is both informative to and understood by the child. Given such a seemingly complicated formula for socialization, it is encouraging that many parents reproduce it frequently in their parent-child interactions.

Conceptual Growth and the Child's Acquisition of Values

Psychologists in the tradition of Piaget (often called cognitive developmentalists) have emphasized the conceptual growth that must take place if the child's social and moral attitudes are to permanently change. With Hoffman, they agree that parental communication cannot have much of an influence unless the child is able to understand it. But, in contrast to Hoffman and the other psychologists that we have cited in this chapter, cognitive developmentalists generally have concluded that even well-understood parental communication is only partially responsible for children's socialization. This is because many of the concepts and values central to a child's social development are acquired during social encounters with peers rather than adults.

Piaget himself found reasons to doubt the power of parental influence on children's social and moral attitudes. Piaget's conclusions were based on his investigation into children's rule-following behavior.[73] In this investigation, Piaget observed children of different ages as they were playing a common street game of marbles. He asked these children questions about the origins, meaning, and importance of the game rules that they were following. From his observations and interviews, he derived four stages in children's developing understanding of rules.

The first stage in children's development of rule conceptions is more a stage of play than of true morality, according to Piaget. The previous chapter described how, immediately after infancy, children engage in a great deal of symbolic play, during which they continually invent private rituals and games of make-believe. Piaget's first stage of rule following parallels this period of symbolic play in the life of a young child. The child will play at a common game like marbles, but in an idiosyncratic rather than a collective way. The child will invent his or her own rules, will change these rules at will, and in general will conduct the game according to his or her own private desires and fantasies. For example, the child may repeat over and over a private game like heaping marbles in a pile, rolling them across the room, heaping them again in another pile, and so on. The game does have regularities, and these regularities provide the developmental roots of later social rule following. But the game at this stage is strictly private, containing no collective element such as either cooperation or competition. During this early stage, the child does not distinguish regularities and rituals (such as repeating a private pattern of marble playing) from real moral rules (such as don't cheat). It is not until the second stage that the child develops a sense of *obligation* to follow rules.

During the second stage of rule following, beginning at about age five, children regard rules as external to themselves, as "handed down from above" by adults and other figures (including supernatural ones like God). Accordingly, children regard rules as permanent and sacred, not subject to modification for any reason. They value the letter of the law more than the human need for the law, denying, for example, that a game rule like the position of the starting line could be changed by agreement in order to make it possible for younger children to play. In other studies related to this same investigation, Piaget shows how this severe view of morality is manifested in other childhood moral judgments as well. For example, children at this stage value the consequences of an act more than the intentions behind an act: they commonly say that it is worse to break fifteen cups by accident than one cup with a mischievous purpose. Another example is that children at this stage often believe punishment to be inevitable after a wrongdoing, even if this means that God or nature will intervene. After telling a lie, they believe, they may well be hit by a falling branch or other catastrophe. Such judgments, writes Piaget, reflect the child's *moral realism*, a confusion between moral and physical laws. The child assumes that, like the law of gravity, moral rules are predetermined and permanent aspects of the world.

[73] Piaget, 1932.

At about age eight, the child begins to see rules as cooperative agreements. During this third stage, children understand that rules are useful means of regulating collective activity, but that any particular rule is somewhat arbitrary and changeable. Thus, one may modify a rule, provided that there is a consensus for this modification among those playing the game. This perspective implies that rules are co-constructed by equals for their own agreed-upon purposes, rather than that rules are introduced and enforced by a superior authority figure. This perspective is also related to the decline in children's moral realism: children now value "subjective" considerations (such as a person's intentions), and they see punishment as a human choice.

Finally, Piaget also makes brief mention of a fourth stage in children's rule conceptions, emerging at about age eleven. During this stage, children show interest in generating new rules to cope with all possible situations, even those that may never have occurred. This stage leads to an *ideological* mode of moral reasoning. The child's moral judgment now encompasses complex political and societal issues, rather than only personal and interpersonal concerns arising from their social relations. We shall return to this period of development in our chapters on adolescence.

Piaget's four stages of rules form a developmental sequence that represents continual improvement in children's moral understanding. By stage 2, children recognize their rule-following obligation, a significant advance over the first stage; by stage 3, they conceive of cooperation, equality, and reciprocity in rule following, all of which are central to the notion of justice. What can explain these developmental advances? Piaget's answer emphasizes the cognitive progress that children make during this period of development, linking this progress to specific types of social experiences that children encounter in growing up. Adults play only a limited role in such experiences.

On the cognitive side, Piaget views the child's advances as an example of his declining egocentrism (see Chapter 4). The child continually moves away from the limitations of his own perspective on the world, recognizing at first (during stage 2) that he has an obligation to conform to the will of others and next (during stage 3) that he may actively coordinate his perspective with that of others. In the process, the child increasingly realizes that others have points of view distinct from his own, and that these points of view must be reckoned with. At first, this means simply conforming to others' rules (stage 2), but eventually, this means working out cooperative compromises (stage 3).

The child's cognitive movement away from egocentrism, according to Piaget, is a function of the social interactions that he experiences. The recognition of obligation during stage 2 is fostered by the child's interactions with adults who constrain his behavior through commands. Piaget writes that such constraining social relations are based upon the child's "unilateral (one-way) respect" for the adult. In other words, the child accepts the adult's commands without question because he respects the adult as a superior, even endowing the adult with characteristics like omniscience and omnipotence. The positive contribution of adult relations is the child's sense of moral obligation, a sense that is necessary for the child initially to participate in a collective social life that is organized by rules. The negative feature of adult relations is that they do not allow the child to assert his own point of view. This is because the child does not enter into the relation as an equal, and therefore he cannot negotiate the nature or implementation of the rules with the adult. The child has no choice but to affirm the adult's authoritarian position and to suppress his own. This type of interaction cannot lead a child very far from egocentrism because he rarely has an opportunity to express a new point of view that is distinct from the prevailing point of view forced upon him by the adult.

In a peer relation, the situation is quite different; here, the child may engage in reciprocal exchanges with equals. These exchanges have many advantages over the constraining interactions of adult-child relations. One advantage is that the child can truly experience differences in perspectives; since neither party to the interaction has a special claim to truth or rightness (neither being considered superior), both parties are free to argue for the merits of their own opinion. Another advantage related to this is that the child then has a chance to experience cooperative interactions that are aimed at reconciling differences of opinion. This cooperative experience, according to Piaget, is essential for the child's moral growth because it introduces the child to notions like reciprocity, compromise, negotiation, and other elemental aspects of justice.

Piaget's conclusion, therefore, is that parents are only partially responsible for the cognitive changes central to a child's moral development. They do introduce children to the notion of obligation, and in this sense, the constraining adult-child relation plays a necessary role early in childhood. But cooperation and justice, moral concepts that are at least as important as obligation, are developed by means of a different type of social relation than that normally encountered in parent-child interactions. This different type of relation is intrinsically peer-oriented because it must be based upon a sense of mutual respect between equals, rather than on a sense of unilateral respect flowing from child to parent. It offers the child a procedure for co-constructing rules with others, rather than simply for following the rules already established. Most importantly, it enables the child to recognize legitimate differences between the perspectives of self and other, to accept these differences without suppressing either self or other, and to work out agreements that reconcile the differences to the mutual satisfaction of self and other. In short, it provides the child with the prototype of a democratic social relation.

Since Piaget's original investigation, a number of researchers have reported data that confirm and elaborate Piaget's point of view. James Youniss, for example, conducted extensive interviews with children about their views of child-child *versus* parent-child relations.[74] Youniss found that children generally interpret positive action within a peer context to mean reciprocal behavior like helping one another or exchanging intimacy, whereas they interpret

[74] Youniss, 1980.

positive action within an adult-child context to mean subservient behavior like obeying the adult. For example, children will say that in order to be "kind" to a friend you should share with the friend, whereas they will say that in order to be "kind" to an adult you should do whatever the adult says. Youniss concludes that the peer relation during childhood is based on principles of cooperation, whereas the child-adult relation is based on principles of complementarity. In other words, peers assume roles of equal status while interacting, whereas children and adults assume roles that, while complementary to one another, have unequal status. Youniss, like Piaget, believes that each type of relation serves its own function in the child's social development. The complementary nature of the adult-child relation fosters in the child a respect for those aspects of the social system that are beyond the child's reach; or in other words, an attitude of conformity to the societal rules that the child must accept. This is certainly an essential element in the socialization of any citizen, since there will always be aspects of the *status quo* to which one must defer. But in addition to respect for the social system, one should also develop a rationale for that respect, and this rationale should include moral principles like fairness and mutual concern for one another's welfare. Such principles will also provide a just basis for changing the status quo when necessary. For Youniss, as for Piaget, it is the cooperative nature of the peer relation that is responsible for fostering these principles.

Of course, the distinction between peer and adult-child interactions is not always clear-cut. By no means are peers always cooperative with one another, and many in fact treat each other in as authoritarian and constraining a manner as does any adult. Conversely, adults often approach children with an attitude of mutual respect and often attempt to interact reciprocally and cooperatively with them. The difference between the two types of interactions is one of degree rather than of absolute divergence. Yet, it is a real difference. Despite an adult's intentions toward a child, the adult-child relation is almost always limited by the responsibility that the adult must assume for the child's welfare. This responsibility means that the adult is sometimes called on to enforce rules and sanctions, at the very least for basic protective reasons, such as keeping the child away from danger. Because the adult must sometimes occupy an authoritarian role, the adult-child relation is less likely to reflect a sense of cooperative agreement among equals than do relations among peers. This may change as children grown older and require less protective guidance from their parents. At such a time, the adult-child relation may be restructured so that it assumes the characteristics of a peer relation. Until then, however, adult-child interactions have their own particular strengths and limitations that enable them to serve an essential, though not all-encompassing, function in the child's social development.

The Social and Cultural Context of Adult-Child Relations

There are some commonalities in adult-child relations all over the world:

for example, in every known human society, adults protect and nurture children, command and discipline them, and provide important emotional attachments for them.[75] Consequently, adult-child relations are universally similar in at least two ways: first, adults are necessary for children's growth and survival, psychologically as well as physically. Second, and partly as a consequence of the first, adults occupy the position of social power and authority in the adult-child relation.

Despite these basic commonalities, adult-child relations are not universal in all of their features. As Baumrind, Baldwin, and others have shown, there is a great deal of individual variation in how adults and children interact with one another, even in middle-class American society. When we look at societies and cultures that differ significantly from our own, we find large-scale, systematic variation in patterns of interaction between adults and children. Along with this interactional variation, we find profound differences in children's behavioral and developmental patterns as well.

In this section, we shall discuss adult-child relations in social contexts other than middle-class American society. Although the great majority of socialization studies have been set in our own middle-class culture, there have been a few empirical investigations of adults and children living under different social conditions. Some of these have examined cultures and nationalities around the world, whereas others have examined subcultures within our own society (such as lower socioeconomic groups). These investigations have not only offered us insight into diverse patterns of socialization but they have also deepened our understanding of social-contextual influences within our own culture. We shall begin this section with a discussion of cultural and subcultural variation and shall end it by identifying some institutions and other societal influences that provide a context for adult-child relations within our own culture.

Cross-Cultural Variations

The most extensive comparisons of family life in different cultures around the world have been provided by the cross-cultural research of Beatrice and John Whiting and their colleagues.[76] The implications of this research for children's prosocial behavior have been summarized in the previous chapter. But the research also tells us something about how cultural differences in parent-child relations may influence children's social behavior. For example, John Whiting's early research found that in most non-Western cultures, parents placed much less value on their children's independence and self-assertiveness than in our own society.[77] In traditional family life, babies are weaned later and children are isolated less often than in contemporary Western

[75] Whiting & Child, 1953; Werner, 1979; Munroe, Munroe, & Whiting, 1980.
[76] Whiting & Child, 1953; Whiting, B.,

1966; Whiting & Whiting, 1975.
[77] Whiting & Child, 1953.

life. Parental values stress the interdependence of persons with others in the community, rather than the independence of persons from one another. Children are encouraged to be part of the functioning community, rather than to excel over others.

Recent research by Beatrice Whiting and Carolyn Pope Edwards has found that such cultural differences are even sharper for girls than for boys.[78] In several African and Asian communities, Edwards and Whiting found that parents frequently asked their daughters to spend time with infants and younger children. This, according to the researchers, encourages the girls to adopt a highly nurturant attitude toward others. In our society, children normally spend their free time with peers, except during specially rewarded occasions like baby-sitting. Parental expectations in traditional societies may be an important reason for both the greater cooperative orientation and the sharper sex differences found among children of these societies.

The Whitings have also found far more frequent attention-seeking behavior among children in our own society than among children from non-Western societies.[79] This finding is particularly revealing when combined with comparative data presented by Robert LeVine.[80] LeVine reports that parents in African and other non-Western cultures do not use praise as a means of reinforcement for their children's appropriate behavior. Rather, the appropriate behavior is expected. Parents respond only when this expectation is violated: that is, they punish a misdemeanor but do not reward a good deed. This pattern, of course, differs greatly from typical middle-class American practice. For the purpose of socializing the child's behavior, however, it seems to work well enough:

> . . .most of the learning in certain African societies—and in a great many other rural communities—takes place without praise or explicit approval as a reinforcer. Children in those societies observe and imitate, getting corrective feedback when necessary and no feedback when they perform correctly. Their motivation is taken for granted and their rewards, if any, are diffuse and vicarious rather than direct and personal. This form of socialization seems to work so well in the acquisition of socially valued skills that one begins to wonder if our own use of praise as a reinforcer is entirely superfluous.[81]

LeVine believes that there is only one major difference in the results of the two child-rearing patterns: the reinforcement-through-praise practice engenders the attention seeking found among children in Western society. That is, the Western parent's praise, according to LeVine, does not increase the likelihood of appropriate behavior from the child, but it does increase the child's tendency to explicitly demonstrate that behavior in the parent's presence. In addition, it leads the child to engage in attention-seeking behavior generally, even away from the home.

LeVine believes that, in our system of values, the attention seeking of American children is a "mixed blessing." Clearly, it can be an annoyance,

---

[78] Edwards & Whiting, 1980.
[79] Whiting & Whiting, 1975.
[80] LeVine, 1977, 1980.
[81] LeVine, 1980, p. 80.

diverting adult energies away from more genuine and substantive interactions with children. But it also represents an expression of self-confidence and self-assertiveness. These are not only virtues in our society, but they may even be necessary for the child's future competence and personal agency.

These are the very values that Baumrind built into her notions of instrumental competence. In a less achievement-oriented culture, these values may be antithetical to adaptation. But in our society, parents tolerate (and even encourage) early manifestations of them, even in distracting behavior like attention seeking, out of an intuitive sense that they represent orientations that are well-adapted to our culture. This intuitive sense is shared by child-rearing experts like Baumrind who believe that self-assertion and self-confidence are an essential part of American children's social competence.

Subcultural Research

Cross-cultural comparisons often seem to imply that life within any one culture is fairly homogenous. But this is hardly the case for most contemporary technological societies. Within the United States, for example, there are a large number of distinguishable subcultures, each with their own life styles and systems of values. Some of these subcultures are based upon religious heritage, others on ethnic heritage, others on occupational or economic status. Some preliminary ethnographic work has described differences in family patterns found in some of these subcultures. For example, one study has analyzed the parental values and child-rearing practices of families living in California communes and has found wide variation both between different types of communal groups and between these groups and conventional American nuclear families.[82] This type of subcultural ethnographic work is not yet far enough along to inform us about the influences of diverse adult-child relations on children's social development. But there is one type of subcultural research that has reached this point. This is comparative research on social-class differences in socialization. Such research has generated widespread attention and controversy, no doubt because of its pressing social-policy implications.

The most substantial body of comparative research on parent-child relations in lower *versus* middle-class families focuses on the type of language that parents use with their children. Basil Bernstein's influential but controversial research introduced the notion that lower-class parents speak to their children in a different linguistic code than do middle-class parents.[83] Lower-class parents use a *restricted code* of speech, which means that they limit their verbal exchanges to direct expressions of concrete statements and commands. Middle-class parents, on the other hand, use an *elaborated code* consisting of complex syntax, conditional statements, and the expression of abstract ideas. Although both sets of parents speak the same language (English in the case of Bernstein's subjects), they select differently from the linguistic forms available to them.

---

[82] Eiduson, 1979.   [83] Bernstein, 1970.

The notion of *code* implies that each set of parents uses their own principles of linguistic selection.

Clearly, the elaborated linguistic code of the middle class is best adapted for communicating the standards and rationales that underlie a parent's commands and sanctions. As Lepper and Hoffman have shown, this kind of full communication is essential if a long-lasting internalization is to take place. The restricted code, on the other hand, goes no further than to direct or prohibit the child's actions ("Go to bed now"; "Stop hitting your sister"). Without offering the child reasons for these commands (such as "...so you won't be tired tomorrow"; "so you won't hurt her"), this code provides the child with no information with which he can construct his own permanent standards. Instead, use of this code can only draw a child's attention to the commands or sanctions themselves. The restricted code, therefore, gives a parent access to very little beyond power assertion as a child-rearing technique.

Bernstein has linked this social-class difference in language to a number of cognitive and social differences between lower- and middle-class children.[84] For example, Bernstein reports that lower-class children are less likely than their middle-class peers to consider intentions as a mitigating factor in conduct. In other words, on the Piagetian moral intentionality problem discussed above (Is it worse to break one cup with bad intentions or fifteen cups with good intentions?), lower-class children would be more likely than middle-class children to respond to the consequences (fifteen cups is worse). This, according to Bernstein, is directly attributable to the restricted linguistic code, which provides expression for concrete considerations like consequences, rather than abstract and indirect ones like intentions.

Bernstein's assertions have received some support from other investigations of social-class differences. Robert Hess and Virginia Shipman, in a large-scale study, also found that middle-class parents use an elaborated rather than a restricted code of speech.[85] Further, Hess and Shipman believe that the restricted language of lower-class parents is connected with important developmental deficiencies in lower-class children, with regard to cognitive as well as social abilities. They emphasize two particular features of the middle-class–lower-class language difference: (1) middle-class parents use *personal-subjective* statements ("Help me by being as good as you can"), rather than *status-normative* ones ("Act like other kids your age"); and (2) middle-class parents use *instructive* statements ("Let me explain how to do this to you"), rather than *imperative* ones ("Just do what I tell you"). In addition to Hess and Shipman's extensive study, several other studies also have replicated Bernstein's basic findings.[86]

Nevertheless, the work of Bernstein and his followers has been severely criticized by those who believe that it misrepresents lower-class speech pat-

[84] Ibid.
[85] Hess & Shipman, 1965.
[86] Labov, 1963; Deutsch, Katz, & Jensen, 1968; Heider, 1968; Krauss & Rotter, 1968; Deutsch, 1973.

terns. This alternative point of view asserts that lower-class dialogues are capable of communicating all of the subtleties and abstractions of middle-class dialogues. The problem is in the middle-class psychologist who misunderstands lower-class speech because he is unfamiliar with it. The most outspoken of such critics is William Labov, whose analysis of language among lower-class blacks has led him to the following conclusions:

> Unfortunately, these notions are based upon the work of educational psychologists who know very little about language and even less about Negro children. The concept of verbal deprivation has no basis in social reality: in fact, Negro children in the urban ghettos receive a great deal of verbal stimulation, hear more well-formed sentences than middle-class children, and participate fully in a highly verbal culture; they have the same basic vocabulary, possess the same capacity for conceptual learning, and use the same logic as anyone else who learns to speak and understand English.[87]

Labov believes that the "cultural deprivation" of lower-class children has nothing to do with parental instruction or linguistic codes, but rather with the educational and socioeconomic injustices that they inevitably encounter in our society. Research demonstrating the inadequacy of lower-class language, Labov writes, is contaminated by the middle-class biases that prevent an accurate reading of true lower-class linguistic capabilities. One problem is that middle-class researchers often do not understand lower-class dialect. Another is that lower-class subjects are often observed in situations where they feel ill at ease. This condition of discomfort in itself restricts their language use. Under different conditions, not accessible to the typical middle-class researcher, lower-class persons display language that is rich in complexity and abstraction.

Labov offers as an example of this problem the following actual comparison between two dialogues by the same eight-year-old black child. The boy's name is Leon, and the interviewer's name is Clarence Robbins (C.R.).

C.R. asks Leon some questions about television and gets responses that are restricted to single words or phrases:

> C.R.: You watch—you like to watch television?. . .Hey, Leon. . .you like to watch television? (*Leon nods*) What's your favorite program?
>
> Leon: Uhhmmmm. . .I look at cartoons.
>
> C.R.: Well, what's your favorite one? What's your favorite program?
>
> Leon: Superman . . .
>
> C.R.: Yeah? Did you see Superman—ah—yesterday, or day before yesterday: When's the last time you saw Superman?
>
> Leon: Sa-aturday . . .
>
> C.R.: You rem—you saw it Saturday? What was the story all about? You remember the story?
>
> Leon: M-m.
>
> C.R.: You don't remember the story of what—that you saw of Superman?

[87] Labov, 1979.

Leon: Nope.

C.R.: You don't remember what happened, huh?

Leon: Hm-m.

C.R.: I see—ah—what other stories do you like to watch on T.V.?

Leon: Mmmm???...umm... (*glottalization*)

C.R.: Hmm? (*4 seconds*)

Leon: Hh?

C.R.: What's th' other stories that you like to watch?

Leon: Mighty Mouse ...

C.R.: And what else?

Leon: Ummm ... ahm ...[88]

In a subsequent session, however, C.R. changed the social situation by (1) having one of Leon's friends present, and (2) introducing some "taboo" phrases that helped Leon feel less out of place in the interview situation. The contrast in Leon's language use is striking:

C.R: Is there anybody who says 'your momma drink pee'?

Leon: (*rapidly and breathlessly*) Yee-ah!

Greg: Yup!

Leon: And you father eat doo-doo for breakfas'!

C.R.: Ohhh!! (*laughs*)

Leon: And they say 'your father—your father eat doo-doo for dinner'!

Greg: When they sound on me, I say CBM.

C.R.: What that mean?

Leon: Congo-booger-snatch! (*laughs*)

Greg: Congo-booger-snatcher! (*laughs*)

Greg: And sometimes I'll curse with BB.

C.R.: What that?

Greg: Black boy! (*Leon—crunching on potato chips*) Oh that's a MBB.

C.R.: MBB. What's that?

Greg: 'Merican Black Boy!

C.R.: Ohh ...

Greg: Anyway, 'Mericans is same like white people, right?

Leon: And they talk about Allah.

C.R.: Oh yeah?

Greg: Yeah.

C.R.: What they say about Allah?

Leon: Allah—Allah is God.

Greg: Allah—

C.R.: And what else?

[88] Ibid.

Leon: I don't know the res'.

Greg: Allah i'—Allah is God, Allah is the only God, Allah

Leon: Allah is the *son* of God.

Greg: But can he make magic?

Leon: Nope.

Greg: I know who can make magic.

C.R.: Who can?

Leon: The God, the *real* one.

C.R.: Who can make magic?

Greg: The son of po'—(C.R.: Hm?) I'm sayin' the po'k chop God! He only a po'k chop God! (*Leon chuckles*).[89]

Labov cites this contrast as an example of how a culturally biased research design can turn a bright, verbal child into one who is monosyllabic, inept, and ignorant in the experimenter's presence. A culturally sensitive procedure would provide the researcher with a less distorted view, as in the case of C.R.'s second interview with Leon:

> The observer must now draw a very different conclusion about the verbal capacity of Leon. The monosyllabic speaker who had nothing to say about anything and cannot remember what he did yesterday has disappeared. Instead, we have two boys who have so much to say they keep interrupting each other, who seem to have no difficulty in using the English language to express themselves. And we in turn obtain the volume of speech and the rich array of grammatical devices which we need for analyzing the structure of nonstandard Negro English (NNE): negative concord (I 'on' play with him no more), the pluperfect (had came back out), negative perfect (I ain't had), the negative preterite (I ain't go), and so on.[90]

Like Labov, other developmentalists have spoken out against the "myth of the culturally deprived child." One thorough examination of available research on children's social-class differences concluded that ". . .much current theory concerning poor children's intellect is often misleading and incorrect: poor children do not suffer from massive deficiencies of mind."[91] Another writer has gone so far as to claim that lower-class life might offer children a better rearing environment than middle-class life because it offers children the opportunity to gain "realistic" insights concerning the importance of having social power.[92] Middle-class children, on the other hand, often suffer the consequences of naiveté when they leave the protection of their family homes.[93]

No one on either side of the social-class debate denies the adverse effects that poverty can have on children. Proper nutrition, medical care, economic and educational opportunity are all necessary for optimal physical and psychological development. Unfortunately, even in our affluent society, many families of the lower-class are not able to provide their children with some or all of the necessities.[94] Children from such economically deprived families would be at a

---

[89] Ibid.
[90] Ibid, p. 336.
[91] Ginsburg, 1972.

[92] Coles, 1967.
[93] Coles, 1975.
[94] Birch, 1968.

disadvantage in any culture, despite other possibly positive features of their family life.

But the issue of controversy is whether such economic disadvantages are also connected with psychological patterns unique to lower-class family relations, and thus ultimately, if these disadvantages are in the lower-class children themselves. Is poverty transmitted from generation to generation through ineffective patterns of child rearing? This is the implication of the research by Bernstein, Hess, and Shipman, and others in their tradition. Opposing those who believe that poverty is a result of inadequacies in the child rearing (or the children) of the lower classes are those who believe that the main problem of the lower classes is poverty itself, and that in other social and psychological respects, lower-class families and their children are as intelligent, vital, and well adapted to their world as are members of the middle class.

Any comparative research, cross-cultural or subcultural, must wrestle with the problem of values. Is it ever legitimate to say that one of the societies under study is operating better than another society to which it is being compared? By what criteria could we make such a claim? In cases where the contrasts with middle-class Western society appear sharp and invidious—such as a primitive tribal culture or an impoverished minority subculture—the middle-class researcher may be inclined to look for deficiencies in social behavior that explain (or at least are linked with) the culture's inferiority. Other social scientists have argued strenuously that one must resist this temptation, consciously preventing one's middle-class Western values from biasing one's conclusions. We shall return to this controversy under the topic of "cultural relativism" in Chapter 7.

The Influence of Societal Institutions in Contemporary Western Culture

Adults influence children's social development not only in the interpersonal relations that they establish with children, but also in the societal institutions that they create and maintain. Institutions like the family, school, and media directly affect the child's social experience. Further, these institutions constantly change as society evolves, so that a contemporary child's social experience differs in fundamental ways from that of children in other historical periods. Some of these changes are so fundamental that they have altered the social meaning and status of childhood itself. For example, until the seventeenth century, childhood was not recognized in Western society as a phase of life distinct from other phases. Paintings and writings from this historical period show that children were dressed and treated like small adults, and were expected to work (and to refrain from "frivolous" play) much like adults.[95]

One child-centered societal institution that has changed dramatically in recent times is the *family*. Changes both in family attitudes toward children

---

[95] Ariès, 1965.

and in the nature of family life have profoundly altered the conditions for children's social development. For example, parental attitudes toward discipline seem to change cyclically from severe to permissive every generation or so.[96] In this sense, child-rearing styles run in "fashions," which are likely to influence parent-child relations within that society. Similarly, family structure is affected by the contemporary social milieu. In recent American culture, for example, divorce is becoming increasingly frequent. Research has shown that the breakup of families can have serious consequences for children's social development. This is particularly true for boys, whose behavior at school and at home often deteriorates immediately following their parents' divorce.[97] Such immediate adverse effects may not develop into long-term problems, depending upon the disrupted family's success at restoring a sense of cohesion and equilibrium.[98]

School is another transformed societal institution that engages children for important periods of their lives. With the advent of universal schooling in the nineteenth century, school became an extended, long-term experience for children of all social classes. The socializing effects of this common experience have been apparent to educators for decades. Schooling communicates to children from diverse backgrounds the conventional norms and values of society-at-large.[99] It provides a training-ground for the acquisition of social and cognitive skills.[100] It also provides the child with a system of authority that supplements that which the child encounters at home. One researcher has found that children develop an understanding of school authority in a sequence that parallels the authority levels that Damon found in relation to children's conceptions of parent-child relations.[101] Taken in this light, schooling can be seen as an important reinforcer of adult-child relations in the home, adding depth and breadth to the child's knowledge of the social order and the child's own role in the social order's functioning. A theoretical model describing the developmental interactions between children's family and school experience is presented in Figure 5-5.

The most contemporary of societal institutions that influence children's development is *television*. Children in our society spend a significant proportion of their waking hours watching T.V.: American children's typical viewing time, according to several estimates, ranges from two to six hours per day.[102] Child developmentalists have wondered what all this T.V. exposure does to children. Consequently, a host of studies have investigated the effects of T.V. on children's cognitive and social development.

Findings from the T.V. research present a mixed picture. With regard to cognitive development, T.V. can present new informational content to children, particularly children from disadvantaged backgrounds who have had limited

[96] De Mause, 1974.
[97] Hetherington & Deur, 1971.
[98] Hetherington, Cox, & Cox, 1977.
[99] Dreeban, 1967.
[100] Goslin, 1965.

[101] Kutnick, 1980.
[102] Lyle & Hoffman, 1972; Liebert, Neale, & Davidson, 1973.

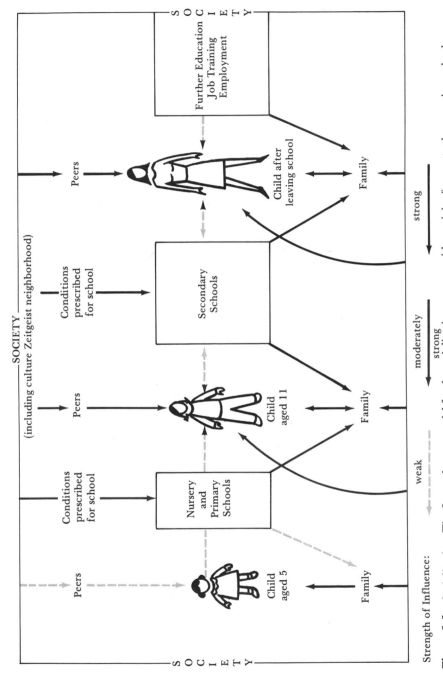

Figure 5-5.   Socialization. The figure shows a model for the socialization process, with special reference to the secondary school.

Source: H. Himmelweit & B. Swift, A model for the understanding of school as a socializing agent. In P. Mussen, J. Langer, & M. Covington (Eds.), *Trends and Issues in Developmental Psychology.* New York: Holt, Rinehart, & Winston, 1969, p. 159. Reprinted with permission.

exposure to preschool education.[103] But T.V. does little to alter children's basic cognitive abilities, at least in a positive sense.[104] In fact, some researchers believe that the overall cognitive effects of the medium are essentially negative: T.V. watching decreases children's attention span and takes time away from more developmentally beneficial activities like reading.[105] Probably the broadest consensus among child psychologists is that T.V. is a neutral growth experience, neither contributing nor taking much away from a child's intellectual abilities.[106] From this point of view, children get from T.V. only what they bring to it in attentional skills and knowledge; the passive exercise of watching T.V. neither adds nor detracts from children's cognitive strengths.

Similar overall conclusions can be drawn concerning television's effects on children's social behavior. A number of studies have shown that observing violence on T.V. (as on detective shows) will increase children's aggressive behavior, just as watching kindness on T.V. (as on "Mr. Rogers' Neighborhood") will increase children's prosocial behavior.[107] But such behavioral effects generally are short-term; and opposite effects of the same programs have also been shown. For example, one study found that children exposed to a broad array of violent T.V. programming actually displayed less aggression than peers whose T.V. exposure was severely limited.[108] Several other studies have found that the behavioral effects of T.V. depend not only on the nature of the programming but on the age and personality characteristics of the child viewing the program.[109] As in other areas of life, children only imitate what they comprehend and what they admire. These "mitigating factors" are more powerful determinants of children's behavior than the information received from any media presentation. Television can present ideas to children in a stimulating, dramatically powerful manner, but these ideas in themselves do not importantly influence children's intellectual or social development. In fact, what children do with these ideas is more a function of their intellectual and social development than of the ideas themselves.

Summary

Because children require protection and nurturance from adults, children's relations with adults have a different character than children's relations with peers. Although both adult-child and child-child relations are reciprocal, adult-child relations are asymmetrical (or "unilateral") in their balance of power and constraint. In other words, adults necessarily occupy positions of authority over children, whereas peers normally interact with one another as equals. This authoritative position leads adults to play a special role in children's social development: adults guide children's acquisition of cultural

---

[103] Ball & Bogatz, 1972.
[104] Stein & Friedrich, 1975.
[105] Collins, 1970.
[106] Liebert, Neale, & Davidson, 1973.

[107] Stein & Friedrich, 1975, pp. 208–9, 228–29.
[108] Feshbach & Singer, 1971.
[109] Collins, 1978, 1983.

standards, values, and rules of the social order. There are several different child-rearing techniques through which adults attempt to accomplish this. Research has shown some of these techniques to be more effective than others in influencing children to adopt culturally appropriate standards of behavior.

Studies of parental child-rearing practices have distinguished a variety of patterns in parents' disciplinary techniques. Parents differ from one another in their degree of permissiveness *versus* restrictiveness, in the amount of democracy that they allow in their family life, in their warmth and nurturance toward their children, in their clarity of communications toward their children, in their expectations for their children's maturity, and in control that they exert over their children's behavior. Parents low in clarity of communication, low in warmth, high in control, and high in maturity demands have been called authoritarian. Parents high in control, high in clarity of communication, high in maturity demands, and high in nurturance have been called authoritative. Parents low in control and maturity demands and high in communication and nurturance have been called permissive. In general, child-rearing research has linked the authoritative parenting pattern (particularly the combination of control and communication) with children who develop the "instrumental competence" necessary for successfully adapting to our society. Instrumental competence includes self-assertiveness, self-reliance, social sensitivity, and a sense of vitality. Authoritarian and permissive parents both seem to undermine children's instrumental competence, the former through restricting children's opportunities for initiative, the latter by allowing children to avoid the consequences of their own actions.

Psychologists who have analyzed the social-psychological mechanisms through which adults influence children's development have posited models that can explain these child-rearing findings. For example, the effectiveness of authoritative parenting can be explained by its intuitive reliance on mechanisms of informational internalization. Such mechanisms, called inductions by some and minimally sufficient discipline by others, combine a judicious amount of control with a comprehensible communication of the standards that the parent wishes the child to follow. The standards are justified in terms of their intrinsic value, rather than in terms of the prohibitions and sanctions that result from their violation. Mechanisms of parental control, like simple power assertion or love withdrawal, draw a child's attention to the disciplinary sanctions, rather than to the cultural standards that the parent is trying to communicate. For this reason, children are more likely to internalize and maintain standards that are introduced to them through parental inductions, rather than those introduced to them through disciplinary encounters where punishment is the most salient feature. This accounts for the relative ineffectiveness of authoritarian parenting. Permissive parenting fails for an opposite reason: not enough disciplinary control is established to direct the child's attention to the cultural standards in the first place.

In discussing adult-child relations, it is sometimes easy to forget that, despite the asymmetry of power in the adult's favor, the child too plays an active role in shaping the nature of the relation. Some children can force their parents into authoritarian modes of discipline, just as others can allow their parents to establish control in a relatively "harmonious" fashion. In addition, a child's personal characteristics, such as sex and age, to a large extent determine how the parent's actions will affect the child. Girls seem more vulnerable to certain non-authoritative child-rearing styles than boys, perhaps because in our society they have more difficulty establishing aspects of instrumental competence and self-assertiveness to begin with. As children grow older, their understanding of parental authority develops, and in the process, their expectations for parent-child interactions become transformed. If children are able to communicate these changing expectations to their parents, the parent-child relation will also transform itself, becoming more cooperative, consensual, and democratic.

But however democratic the adult-child relation becomes in some circumstances, it rarely achieves complete equality to the extent that typical peer relations often do. For this reason, some psychologists have hypothesized that adult-child and peer relations serve diverse socialization functions for the developing child. A sense of obligation toward rules and respect for the social order arise out of interactions with adults, whereas conceptions of justice arise more out of interactions with peers. In this manner, a child's active experience within different social relations contributes to the child's development of a comprehensive moral belief system.

Adult-child relations differ greatly across cultures, and possibly even across subcultures of a complex society. In some traditional cultures, such common parental techniques as reinforcement and praise are often omitted. Social scientists have connected this omission with the relatively infrequent attention-seeking behavior of children in traditional societies as compared with Western children.

Within our own society, some researchers claim to have identified social-class differences in parental speech patterns. Middle-class persons, according to these researchers, speak to their children in an elaborated code rich in abstractions and syntactical complexity, whereas lower-class persons speak in a restricted code limited to concrete statements and direct commands. If such differences exist, they could be connected with the greater tendency of lower-class parents to use power-assertion rather than informational-internalization disciplinary techniques, and thus with predicted social-developmental differences in their children. But several linguists have contested the validity of the lower-class/middle-class parental communication distinction, claiming that lower-class language expresses the same range of subtleties and complexities as does middle-class language.

Adults influence children's social development not only in the interpersonal relations that they establish with children but also in the societal institutions in which they engage children. Such institutions constantly change as society evolves, so that a contemporary child's social experience differs in fundamental ways from that of children in other historical periods. Three evolving societal institutions that influence children's social development are the family, school, and television. Each of these offers the child information and further experience with the adult world, although the extent to which each guides the child's social behavior depends on how each interacts with the child's intellectual and social development as a whole.

Chapter 6

Individuality
and Self-Development
during Childhood

THE last two chapters described the nature and growth of social interaction during childhood. In so doing, they emphasized the "sociability" aspect of childhood social development, first between children and their peers and then between children and adults. In the present chapter, we shall return to the other side of social development, the child's search for individuality and self-identity.

In this chapter, we shall follow the establishment of individual differences in personality through the childhood years, and we shall reexamine how gender and sex roles contribute to such differences. As in Chapter 3, we shall focus on those aspects of personality variation that have a marked impact on children's social interactions and social development. We shall return to Erikson's genetic model for his treatment of identity formation in childhood, using his conceptual framework to analyze one famous individual's childhood search for identity. Finally, we shall follow the development of self-knowledge into the childhood years, with a discussion of both the affective (self-esteem) and conceptual (self-understanding) manifestations of self.

Individual Personality Differences between Children

As early as infancy, as we observed in Chapter 3, a host of individual differences between children begin to emerge. Such differences in infancy range from physical differences such as size to behavioral differences such as activity level. Many of the behavioral differences are sharpened, intensified, or modified by a child's particular social environment. Even as fundamental a characteristic as temperament owes a debt to a combination of native disposition, social feedback, and individual interpretation. Because all people, including infants, are continually interacting with the social world, there is always a process of reciprocal influence between one's personality characteristics and one's social experience.

During childhood, this reciprocal influence between personality and social experience encompasses many new aspects of children's behavior. Individual differences between children multiply and become increasingly stabilized, leading to predictable variations in how children interact with others. Conversely, social experience (such as child rearing) begins to have observable and long-lasting effects on children's individual behavioral styles (as already suggested in Chapter 5). In this section, we shall consider the social implications of several types of individual differences between children. In particular, we shall examine dimensions of personality development such as ego-control and ego-resiliency, activity level, cognitive style, and sex role. Psychological research has shown these personality characteristics to exert especially profound influences on children's social lives. Such influences result both from the workings of these personality characteristics themselves and from the reactions of others in the child's social environment to these characteristics.

Several of the individual differences that we shall be considering influence a child's orientation to interpersonal engagement. This, in turn, may have snowballing effects in expanding or limiting the child's further opportunities for experiencing interpersonal events and for achieving greater interpersonal skill. An early inclination toward isolation and withdrawal, for example, may have negative snowballing effects that increase a child's social unease and inability. In fact, several studies have shown that children with poor social skills are often unpopular, apathetic concerning social relations, and low in self-esteem.[1] Much of the problem seems to be linked to these children's initial approach to social situations. For example, John Gottman and his colleagues have found that popular and unpopular children attempt entry into a group in very different ways. Popular children accommodate immediately to the group's activities without calling attention to themselves. If the group is playing a game, these children simply start playing along without further ado. Unpopular children, on the other hand, often make their presence explicitly known by requesting to play, being argumentative, or creating a fuss of one kind or

[1] Roff, Sells, & Golden, 1972; Gottman, Gonso, & Rasmussen, 1975; Asher, Oden, & Gottman, 1977; Putallaz & Gottman, 1981.

another. According to Gottman, they act continually like "newcomers"; in particular, they engage obtrusively in what Gottman calls "hovering" behavior. It is not difficult to see how the easygoing accommodating style of the popular children creates further opportunities for developmentally beneficial social experiences, in contrast to the awkwardly grating style of the unpopular children. This is the type of social-developmental consequence that could arise from individual differences in personality between children.

Ego-Control and Ego-Resiliency

In 1968, Jeanne and Jack Block initiated the most comprehensive longitudinal study of personality development yet attempted.[2] At that time, the Blocks began administering to 130 three-year-olds a massive battery of psychological tests and experimental procedures. In subsequent years, when the children turned four, five, seven, and eleven, they were given further comprehensive sets of psychological tests and procedures appropriate to their age. At the present time, the Blocks have reported findings concerning their subjects' personality development up to age seven. These findings provide us with unique information about the stability and social significance of key individual differences in children's personality characteristics.

In psychoanalytic theory, the "ego" is the set of personality structures that orient an individual toward reality. Generally, this means that the ego is responsible for modulating and controlling one's own impulses when necessary, and for devising strategies for satisfying those impulses in a manner that will not endanger the individual or society. This sometimes means forgoing certain impulses, finding less threatening ways of seeking gratification, or putting off the urge to seek immediate satisfaction. The ego operates by assessing the relationship between the individual's desires and social reality. Functions of the ego include perceiving threats and danger, delaying gratification, controlling impulses, and constructing safe, socially acceptable channels for impulse expression.

The Blocks accepted the psychoanalytic notion of the ego as central to an individual's personality development, but for the purposes of their study, they needed theoretical constructs that could be more precisely formulated and experimentally operationalized. For this reason, they condensed the psychoanalytic notion of ego into two constructs that they believe represent the core of ego functioning: *ego-control* and *ego-resiliency*. These two constructs serve as the focal points of the Blocks' longitudinal study. Through repeated testings and observations of children over a period of years, the Blocks have been able to document continuities in children's ego-control and ego-resiliency to both prior and subsequent patterns of social behavior.

Ego-control, in the Blocks' definition, is the "operating characteristic of an individual with regard to the expression or containment of impulses,

[2] Block & Block, 1980.

feelings, and desires."[3] As a dimension of personality, ego-control can be seen as a continuum ranging from *overcontrol* at one extreme to *undercontrol* at the other. Midpoints on the continuum are psychologically adaptive; the endpoints are less so. Ego-overcontrollers, write the Blocks, may be expected "to be constrained and inhibited, to manifest needs and impulses relatively indirectly, to delay gratification unduly, to show minimal expression of emotion, to tend to be categorized and overly exclusive in processing information, to be perseverative, nondistractible, less exploratory, relatively conforming, with narrow and unchanging interests, to be relatively playful and organized, and to be made uneasy by and therefore avoidant of ambiguous or inconsistent situations."[4] Ego-undercontrollers contrast sharply with overcontrollers on each of these dimensions. The Blocks describe undercontrollers as "expressive," "spontaneous," "distractible," "original," unable to delay gratification, "overly inclusive in the processing of information," having "many but relatively short-lived enthusiasms and interests," and living in an "ad hoc, impromptu" manner.[5]

Ego-resiliency means the extent to which one can modify one's level of ego-control to meet the demands of changing life situations. When necessary, the ego-resilient person can be highly planful and organized; but should spontaneity or originality be called for, such a person can temporarily "give up" some ego-control and adopt a more impulsive mode. The Blocks write that ego-resiliency is a "resourceful adaptation to changing life situations."[6] Unlike ego-control, ego-resiliency is positive in high degrees: along the continuum of unresilient-resilient, it is the resilient end, not the midpoints, that represents the most psychologically adaptive position. The Blocks describe the ego-resilient person as "resourceful before the strain set by new and yet unmastered situations, . . . engaged in the world but not subservient to it, and capable of both regressing in the service of the ego when task requirements favor such an adaptation and, conversely, of becoming adaptively organized and even compulsive when under certain other environmental presses."[7] In contrast, they describe the ego-unresilient person as being "brittle," "rigid," "repetitive," and unable to cope with stress or change.[8]

The Blocks have found that behavioral manifestations of ego-control and ego-resiliency can be reliably measured as early as age three and that they generally remain stable over the next few years of childhood. Further, and most significantly, a three-year-old's behavior in areas related to ego-control and ego-resiliency can predict important aspects of the child's social conduct at age seven. For example, activity level is one behavioral manifestation of ego-control; extremely active children are generally undercontrollers. The Blocks and a colleague found that children's activity levels remain stable between the ages of three and seven, and that a three-year-old's activity level is related to the child's peer-group behavior at least as late as age seven.[9] Highly active children

[3] Ibid.
[4] Ibid.
[5] Ibid.
[6] Ibid.

[7] Ibid.
[8] Ibid.
[9] Buss, Block, & Block, 1980.

tend to be more aggressive, more assertive, less compliant, less shy, and less inhibited in their play than do less active children. Like the Blocks, others have also found that highly active children tend to be frenetic, aggressive, overly domineering, and noncompliant with their peers.[10] But the Blocks were the first to convincingly demonstrate that this relation between activity level and social behavior in middle childhood is developmentally continuous with children's activity level as early as age three.

The Blocks also have documented several other developmental continuities related to ego-control and ego-resiliency. In terms of personality development, those who were undercontrollers at age three in later years were found to be more "energetic, curious, restless, expressive of impulse, . . .less constricted and less relaxed" than more ego-controlled children.[11] The undercontrolled children were also aware of their own distinct personality characteristics by age seven. They believed that peers would describe them as "less obedient," "less neat," and "lazy." As for ego-resiliency, children who were assessed as high on this dimension at age three later were found to be "able to recoup after stress, verbally fluent, less anxious, less brittle, less intolerant of ambiguity, and less likely to externalize or become rigidly repetitive or to withdraw under stress."[12]

In terms of children's social relations, early ego-undercontrol was found to be associated with later negative interpersonal behavior, such as teasing, manipulativeness, and aggression. Ego-overcontrol was associated with shyness in later years. Early ego-resiliency was associated with later positive interpersonal behavior, such as empathy, social responsiveness, and protectiveness. A combination of high ego control and high ego-resiliency at age three proved to be an especially adaptive pattern, resulting in "a high degree of socialization that fits and feels well, a relative absence of anxiety and intimidation in reacting to and acting on the world."[13] In contrast, high ego-control combined with a lack of ego-resiliency has a maladaptive pattern, both socially and personally. By age seven, such children appeared "victimized, immobilized, anxious, and overwhelmed by a world apprehended as threatening and unpredictable."[14]

These initial findings from the Blocks' ambitious longitudinal study have demonstrated that early individual differences in children's personalities can have long-continuing consequences for children's social and personal development. The Blocks believe that these early individual differences themselves have developmental roots both in the child's original temperamental differences and in the child's home environment. They suggest that overcontrol is fostered by families that emphasize structure and order, whereas undercontrol is fostered by families that are conflict-ridden and undemanding of the child.[15] Ego-resilience is fostered by families that are communicative, philosophically

[10] Battle & Casey, 1972; Halverson and Waldrop, 1973; Waldrop, 1976.
[11] Block & Block, 1980.
[12] Ibid.
[13] Ibid.
[14] Ibid.
[15] Block, 1971.

and morally oriented, and in which the parents are loving, patient, competent, and sexually compatible. Unresilience, in turn, is fostered by conflictual, discordant families that have little philosophical or moral concern.[16]

Cognitive Style and Children's Social Interactions

In the early days of psychology as an empirical science, studying perception generally meant studying the physiological and cognitive mechanisms that enable humans to make accurate judgments of the world around them. A "new look" at perception in the 1940s challenged the fruitfulness of examining such perceptual mechanisms apart from the personal characteristics and affective states of those engaged in the act of perceiving. This "new look" established once and for all the inextricable connections between one's perceptual judgments and the functioning of one's total personality. One series of studies emphasized the influence of one's needs, feelings, and attitudes upon one's perceptual judgment.[17] For example, one is more likely to notice a restaurant sign along the freeway when one is hungry than when one is not. Another series of studies, conducted by Herman Witkin and his followers, emphasized the influence of long-lasting personal dispositions upon one's perceptual judgments.[18] This line of work soon reached the point of describing "cognitive styles" that characterize the predominant ways in which individuals process information of all sorts. Ultimately, Witkin extended his model of cognitive styles into all areas of human functioning, including social interaction. Cognitive style became a means of distinguishing basic modes of apprehending the social as well as the physical world. It permeates one's orientation to one's life experience in all its variety, from early childhood on.

Witkin defined two basic cognitive styles: *field independence* and *field dependence*. These constructs evolved considerably during Witkin's thirty-year program of research. In the latest, and most comprehensive usage, field independence refers to "the tendency to rely primarily on internal referents in a self-consistent way," and field dependence to "the tendency to give greater credit to external referents."[19] Accordingly, field independence reflects a greater degree of differentiation between self and non-self than does field dependence. In a field-independent style, firm boundaries are drawn between oneself and the external world (which includes, most prominently, other people). Because of this strict polarity between self and others, strong internal frames of reference must be established. Without such internal standards, the field-independent person would have no place to turn for constructing judgments. The field-dependent person, in contrast, relies more readily on information provided by outside events and persons, since field independence assumes a closer connection between self and non-self to begin with.

[16] Sigelman, Block, Block, & Van der Lippe, 1970.

[17] Bruner, Postman, & Rodrigues, 1951.

[18] Witkin, Dyk, Faterson, Goodenough, & Karp, 1962; Witkin, Goodenough, & Karp, 1967.

[19] Witkin, 1978.

Many of the initial tasks designed by Witkin and others to test for field independence and dependence required subjects to restructure environmental information. These perceptual and cognitive tasks often favored those who could follow an inner sense of direction rather than the external environmental referents that were designed by the experimenter to be misleading. Therefore, field-independent people usually performed best in Witkin's early experiments. Because of this methodological bias, many have assumed that field independence is the superior of the two cognitive styles. This assumption is particularly easy for psychologists to make, because field independence is indeed associated with many of the cognitive problem-solving skills necessary for scientific thinking, such as actively manipulating and restructuring the world through symbolic thought processes. It is quite natural for intellectuals to endow their own way of thinking with a preferred status.

But extensions of Witkin's research into the social domain have revealed that field dependence too has its claim to superiority in certain areas of life. In a series of studies on group conflict resolution, Witkin and his colleagues found that groups with field-dependent members have less trouble reaching consensus than groups without them.[20] Field-dependent people are more accommodative to others than field-independent people, and thus they are more likely to find a common ground in a disagreement. In general, Witkin believes, this demonstrates the "greater tendency of field-dependent people to take account of others' views and to be attentive and sensitive to others' ideas and feelings."[21] This, in turn, is an indication of the overall "interpersonal orientation" shared by field-dependent people, an orientation that stands in contrast to the more distant, autonomous, and impersonal orientation of field-independent people. Witkin writes:

> Field-dependent people seek both physical and emotional closeness to others which, in turn, provides them with experience in interpersonal relations, whereas field-independent people prefer to keep others "at arm's length." Field-dependent people pay selective attention to social cues, in contrast to field-independent people who are relatively insensitive to such cues. Consistent with these differences are the characterizations of field-dependent and field-independent people that have been reported in the literature. Field-dependent people have been described as sociable, interested in people, wanting to help others, having a concern for people, knowing many people, and being known to many. Descriptions of relatively field-independent people have included individualistic, aloof, and concerned with ideas and principles rather than people.
>
> Finally, evidence is beginning to emerge that relatively field-dependent people may be more effective than field-independent people in getting along with others. Some of their characteristics make this difference reasonable. Thus, the preference of field-dependent people for interpersonal situations provides them with greater opportunity to participate themselves, and to observe others in social-interaction situations. Their more extensive exposure to people, together with their greater sensitivity to social information, may serve to build up a fund of behavioral expectancies useful in dealing with others. Field-independent people

---

[20] Witkin et al., 1974.　　　　　　[21] Witkin, 1978, p.18.

have been described in such terms as demanding, inconsiderate, and manipulative of people as a means of achieving personal ends; field-dependent people, in contrast, have more frequently been described as considerate, warm, friendly, tactful, and able to make others feel comfortable with them. Field-dependent people are also more apt to like others, and there is some evidence that they are better liked by others and are more popular as well. It is not difficult to see how these contrasting social attributes of field-dependent and field-independent people can contribute to a difference between them in ease of getting along with others.[22]

Witkin's findings have important implications for social development. Field-dependent people create their own opportunities for acquiring social skills through their easy access to other people. Because field dependence is an accommodative, other-oriented style, field-dependent people are likely to participate in and profit from a wide variety of social experiences. Field-independent persons, prone more to social isolation and conflict, may not reap the social-developmental benefits of social interaction as fully as field-dependent persons. On the other hand, as Witkin notes, field independence opens the way for a number of cognitive-developmental experiences that may elude field-dependent persons. In this view, the two cognitive styles are seen as fundamental modes of processing the world; each mode engenders a different set of interests and competencies. Field dependence leads toward interpersonal competence, whereas field independence leads toward competence in cognitive restructuring and active problem solving.

A child's cognitive style, therefore, may influence her orientation to the world early in her life. To the extent that a field-dependent style encourages a child to adopt an interpersonal orientation and to develop social competence, this may open up further opportunities for social experiences. This, in turn, should lead to increasing social skills that would further widen the child's social horizons, and so on, with snowballing effects. Conversely, an early orientation toward cognitive achievement may limit some children's social interests and experience, leading to a sense of unease and further withdrawal from social engagement. Cognitive style, therefore, can trigger off a chain of events with cumulative social-developmental consequences.

Differences in cognitive style, and in related interpersonal orientation, no doubt owe a major debt to family and societal child-rearing practices. We may recall Escalona's case study of John and Mary described in Chapter 3. The individual differences between these two children were along the same lines as those discussed by Witkin in his writings on field independence and dependence. John was an active structurer of his environment, strong in cognitive skills and in understanding the physical world. Mary, on the other hand, was interested more in other people than in objective knowledge, and she was relatively more advanced than John in all aspects of interpersonal competence. We do not know how either John or Mary would do on Witkin's cognitive-style tasks, even if they were old enough to take them. But Escalona's observations of these two children as they interacted with their respective parents

[22] Ibid., pp. 20–21.

provides us with a finely tuned analysis of how different modes of child rearing can lead to different sorts of cognitive orientation. In John's case, the parents constantly made John aware of objects and events clearly distinct from himself; whereas in Mary's case, objects and events were presented only in the context of social stimulation of the self, usually in the form of direct physical contact with others. It would not be surprising, then, to expect that John came away from his early childhood experience with a firmer sense of the boundaries between self and the outside world (including others), whereas Mary came away with a greater sense of the connection between self and others and a greater propensity to engage in social interaction.

Witkin believes, and has collected data to demonstrate, that particular forms of early childhood experience found in various cultures throughout the world are associated with one or another of his two cognitive styles. Some cultures, Witkin writes, encourage self/non-self segregation to a greater extent than do others. Such cultures are likely to foster field independence in their children. In particular, Witkin and others have found that *hunting* societies have child-rearing practices that encourage self/non-self segregations and hence have a greater proportion of field-independent children, whereas *agricultural* societies have the opposite child-rearing practices and fewer field-independent children. The field independence of hunters follows from the necessity of finding food in an environment that often appears visually homogeneous—an environment like the Eskimo's Arctic snowlands or the desert wastelands of the Arab nomad. Analytic attention to fine detail and an active restructuring of the environment are needed for hunters to survive. Parents train their children to have this orientation by such techniques as "imparting to their child a vocabulary which may be helpful to the restructuring process."[23] This may consist, for example, of a multiplicity of words for snow, sands, vegetation, and other seemingly identical physical phenomena. Agricultural societies, on the other hand, are often close-knit communities that require constant social communication, sharing, and harmonious interpersonal relations. As we saw in Chapter 5, parents in such societies often stress the interdependence of persons and cooperative values in their socialization training. "Critical here," writes Witkin, "is the encouragement of continued self-other connectedness which fosters the development of a field-dependent cognitive style and with it, the interpersonal skills and social characteristics likely to be useful in an agricultural setting."[24]

Field independence and field dependence need not be considered an absolute dichotomy, at least in terms of psychological reality. They are not mutually exclusive within any one person. In fact, Witkin and others have suggested that the most adaptive cognitive style may be a flexible blend of the two, whereby an individual may select the style most appropriate to a given life setting. This is called "mobility," and it has much in common with the

[23] Ibid., p. 35.   [24] Ibid., p. 36.

construct of ego-resiliency. A relatively "mobile" individual may develop both cognitive restructuring skills and interpersonal competence to an optimal extent. Even relatively mobile individuals, however, vary in the degree to which they favor field-dependent or field-independent orientations in the normal course of life. Research has shown that systematic variation of this type begins early in childhood and remains stable well into adulthood.[25]

Gender and Sex Roles[26]

When a sex difference is observed in young infants, it may be reasonable to speculate as to whether the difference is congenital or social in origin. Thus, the relatively greater sensitivity of newborn baby girls to oral stimulation likely can be attributed to genetic factors, whereas infant girls' relatively greater sensitivity to distant environmental cues probably arises from the manner in which the parents handle female versus male infants, as described in Chapter 3. Such speculations seem reasonable because young infants have had limited enough social experience that we may be able to determine whether there are any social factors in an infant's life to account, wholly or in part, for the acquisition of certain characteristics.

By the time of childhood, this is certainly no longer the case. Well before the age of three, the young child has been exposed to so much gender-related social feedback that any biologically "pure" behavioral sex differences—if ever they existed—have long since been elaborated, shaped, discouraged, encouraged, or otherwise modified by environmental influences. It is a simple fact, well documented in the psychological literature, that persons respond to boys and girls differently from birth onward.[27] Whether or not this differential treatment is based upon actual genetic differences in boys' and girls' behavior is no longer an issue by the time of childhood. The point is that such treatment exists and no doubt has its effects, and it is not possible to separate these effects from those of hypothesized gender-related genetic factors that no longer exist in anything like their original form. "Nurture-nature" questions concerning childhood sex differences are not, therefore, useful to address, and we shall bypass them entirely in this section. Rather, we shall assume that sex differences are created by multiple interacting influences, and we shall focus on how gender and sex roles influence individual children's social behavior.

There are two frequently observed features of children's free play that pertain to sex differences. First, boys play rougher than girls. Not only do boys engage more often than girls in mock "rough-and-tumble" games (tag, catch, roughhouse), but boys are also more prone to serious aggression, as manifested both in verbally and physically hostile behavior.[28] Second, both boys and girls

---

[25] Witkin, Goodenough, & Karp, 1967.

[26] In psychological literature, the term "gender" usually refers to one's biological endowment, whether male or female. "Sex role" refers to the social, psychological, and behavioral implications of gender.

[27] Korner, 1974; Frodi & Lamb, 1978.

[28] Smith & Connolly, 1972; Maccoby & Jacklin, 1974; Frodi, MacCaulay, & Thome, 1977; Barrett, 1979.

are more likely to play with same-sex than with opposite-sex peers.[29] These two features of children's free play emerge soon after infancy, and continue through middle childhood.

Eleanor Maccoby has suggested that these two sex-related features of children's social behavior may be connected.[30] Perhaps, she states, it is the qualitative differences between boys' and girls' social behavior that leads to sexual segregation in the playground, and she cites two recent laboratory studies of young children's social interactions as indications of this. In the first study,[31] pairs of unacquainted three-year-olds were observed at play by observers who were unsure of the children's gender (the children were purposefully dressed androgynously). Some of the pairs were same-sex. After compiling the observers' gender-blind behavioral ratings, it was found that (1) both boys and girls tended to direct more social behavior to their partners when in same-sex than in mixed dyads, and (2) the boy dyads were more likely to engage in grabbing, tugging, and other aggressive behavior than the girl dyads. Further, whenever a struggle broke out in a mixed-sex dyad, it was the girl who tended to withdraw or retreat to the nearest adult. Girls rarely acted this way in their own same-sex dyads. Maccoby concludes from this evidence that ". . .it seems that even at this early age children are already developing somewhat distinctive styles of play and that the play style makes a same-sex partner more compatible."[32] The "boyish" style—which has something to do with a quality of roughness—is appealing to other boys but makes girls wary. The less aggressive girlish style, on the other hand, makes other girls comfortable, but does not seem to be especially interesting for boys.

The second study that Maccoby cites centered around laboratory observations of four-year-olds at play in small, same-sex groups of three children.[33] Like the first study, this study found that boys and girls conduct their peer interactions quite differently. The male groups engaged in frequent roughhousing, wrestling, struggling over toys, and vigorous shouting and laughing. In contrast, the female groups engaged in very little physical tussling, but rather created systems of rules to regulate their interactions. When disputes arose over toys or taking turns, the girls would settle them by invoking the rules rather than by grabbing or hitting. Once again, we can see why young boys and girls may have an easier time dealing with same-sex peers.

The tendency of boys to engage in rougher types of play than girls has been found in cultures that diverge widely from our own, for example, African tribal villages and Asian island colonies.[34] In fact, Maccoby believes that it is practically a universal sex difference: ". . .the tendency of males to be more aggressive is perhaps the most firmly established sex difference and is a characteristic that transcends culture."[35]

[29] Serbin and Tonick, 1977; Maccoby, 1980.
[30] Maccoby, 1980.
[31] Jacklin and Maccoby, 1978.
[32] Maccoby, 1980, p. 215.

[33] DiPietro, 1979.
[34] Whiting & Whiting, 1973, 1975; Edwards & Whiting, 1980.
[35] Maccoby, 1980, p. 216.

There may be other sex-related characteristics of children's social behavior that transcend culture as well. Most important of these in a social sense is the relatively greater propensity of girls to be nurturant, particularly with those younger than themselves. The clearest findings concerning sex differences in children's tendencies to be nurturant come from the cross-cultural research of John and Beatrice Whiting and their colleagues.[36] In virtually all the cultures studied, girls as young as three years of age showed marked interest in caring for infants younger than themselves. Boys, in contrast, were generally interested only in playing with the younger child, and sometimes in bossing the younger child around or taking his possessions. This sex difference was sharper in some cultures than in others. In New England, the Philippines, and Kenya, for example, there was relatively little difference between boys and girls in this regard; whereas in India, Mexico, and Okinawa, girls were decidedly more nurturant than boys in a multiplicity of ways. The researchers attribute this contrast to differing socialization patterns in the various cultures. In New England, the Philippines, and Kenya, boys and girls were treated the same with respect to household and infant care responsibilities: in New England, neither boys nor girls were expected to help care for infants, whereas in Kenya and Okinawa, both were. In India, Mexico, and Okinawa, boys and girls were treated dissimilarly: "Girls, much more often than boys, were asked to do household tasks, to take care of infants, or to do work that kept them close to home and in the company of adult females."[37]

Sex differences in nurturance, therefore, may be sharpened by a cultural upbringing that places different demands on the two sexes. An optimal setting for fostering nurturance in children is one that gives children an opportunity to interact with those younger than themselves. Some cultures provide these opportunities more than others do. In Mexico, for example, research has shown that 25 percent of children's social behavior is directed at infants, whereas in New England only 3.5 percent is so directed.[38] One would consequently expect far more nurturance among Mexican children than among New England children, an expectation that is indeed borne out by the cross-cultural research of the Whitings and others (see Chapter 5). But the upbringings of children do not simply vary across cultures. Even within the same culture, different children may face different social experiences. Many cultures systematically offer different social experiences to girls than to boys. In such cultures, girls are often given many more opportunities to interact with infants than are boys. As a consequence, an orientation toward nurturance becomes the basis for a major sex difference in social behavior. "Thus, different cultural groups can magnify, minimize, or perhaps even eliminate, any sex difference in nurturance to the extent that they place girls and boys in the settings that promote the development of nurturant behavior."[39]

---

[36] Whiting & Whiting, 1973, 1975; Edwards & Whiting, 1980.

[37] Edwards & Whiting, 1980, p. 47.

[38] Ibid.

[39] Ibid., pp. 53–54.

Whether as widespread a sex difference as nurturance could be "eliminated" through cultural manipulations is a matter that present-day research cannot resolve. But the role of culture in encouraging and maintaining such a difference is clear. Further, it is also clear that some cultures, and some subcultures, encourage such a difference far more than do others. The extent to which this is advisable for the well-being of any given cultural group and of any individual within the group is an ethical issue of great contemporary concern.

Socialization patterns have a profound influence upon sex differences in children's behavior. As noted earlier in this section, gender-related social influence is a part of children's lives at such an early age, and in such a pervasive manner, that it is impossible to speak of "naturally occurring" sex differences in behavior once a child is beyond the first few months of infancy. But, although we cannot sharply distinguish social from congenital influences on children's sex-related behavior, we can examine more closely the mechanisms through which the social influence is effected. That is, we may ask how and why a young girl comes to act in a manner typical of females in her society, and a young boy in a manner typical of males.

Part of the answer to this has been provided by the socialization theories presented in Chapter 5. The phenomenon of "sex typing" can be viewed as one aspect of the "internalization" process. Accordingly, direct internalization mechanisms such as identification and imitation can be invoked to explain the child's acquisition of sex-appropriate behavior and attitudes. Many child psychologists, in fact, believe that sex typing is a prototypical example of internalization, the example among all others that most satisfactorily fits classic socialization constructs like identification. Freud, Sears, Kagan, Kohlberg, and Whiting have all accorded sex typing a privileged position in their accounts of the identification process; although, of course, all of these theorists have done so in their own particular way, as discussed in Chapter 5.

But empirical research has shown that internalization mechanisms like identification and imitation cannot provide a sufficient explanation for sex typing in children's behavior. It seems that, identification theories to the contrary, children do not prefer to imitate their same-sex parent over their opposite-sex parent. In addition, the extent to which a parent personifies a sex role in his or her own behavior has little to do with the extent to which a child's behavior is sex-appropriate. E. Mavis Hetherington reports that children, despite their gender, tend to imitate the dominant adult figure in the household.[40] This figure is usually, but not always, the mother, at least for children prior to school age. Since both boys' and girls' behavior often is firmly sex-typed before the age of six, Hetherington's finding argues against the theoretical assertion that children acquire sex-related behavior by selectively imitating their same-sex parent. In another study, investigators found no relation between the degree to which young children played with toys in a sex-appropri-

[40] Hetherington, 1967.

ate manner and the degree to which parents expressed sex stereotypes on a questionnaire.[41] Reviewing the available empirical evidence, Eleanor Maccoby and Carol Jacklin conclude that "there is very little relation between parents' own sex typing and that of their children."[42]

It is difficult, therefore, to accept explanations of sex typing based upon notions that emphasize the child's observation and direct imitation of the same-sex parent.

As in our Chapter 5 discussion of social influence upon children's behavior, we shall take a more inclusive and complex perspective on the internalization process, as do more cognitively oriented internalization theories (like attribution or induction theory). Indeed, there are ample indications that children's cognitions about gender and sex roles play a large part in their sex-typed behavior. Studies have shown that at a very early age, children actively attempt to understand the behavioral implications of gender and that as their understanding grows with age, they continually reexamine the importance of accommodating their behavior to society's sex-role stereotypes.

Children's Understanding of Their Gender and Sex Roles

There is no question that by age two children can distinguish between the class of males and the class of females. Some indication of this was offered by the self-recognition research of Michael Lewis and Jeanne Brooks-Gunn, described in Chapter 3. In a more direct study of children's early gender understanding, Spencer Thompson found that at twenty-four months, children consistently assign correct gender labels to pictures of males and females.[43] At this early age, children can use gender nouns (boy, girl, man, woman) accurately, though they have more difficulty with pronouns (him, her). Also (and somewhat contrary to Lewis and Brooks-Gunn's report), Thompson found that two-year-old children normally cannot apply gender distinctions to themselves, at least verbally. By the age of thirty months, however, children normally are adept at using gender-related pronouns as well as nouns, and at verbally identifying their own gender. At the end of the third year, children not only can identify gender differences but also show an awareness of cultural sex-role stereotypes. In other words, three-year-olds know that certain objects and certain activities "go with" one sex or the other. Thompson tested this by asking children to sort pictures of tools, clothing, appliances, and other common objects in feminine and masculine boxes. The three-year-olds in Thompson's sample regularly were able to sort the objects according to the sex-appropriateness of the activity associated with them. These children, therefore, not only knew their own gender but also some social-cultural implications of gender. Thompson concludes: "It appears that by 3 years of age children have accepted their gender label and that this can affect their sex role behavior."[44]

Other features of children's gender understanding develop soon thereaf-

[41] Smith & Daglish, 1977.
[42] Maccoby & Jacklin, 1974, p. 116.
[43] Thompson, 1975.
[44] Ibid., p. 347.

ter. By school age, most children have acquired a sense of "sex constancy."[45] This means that they understand that a person's gender does not change even if the person's appearance or behavior changes. In other words, the notion of gender is distinguished from the observable personal characteristics (hair length, dress, stereotypical behavior) usually associated with gender. Recognizing the permanence of gender relative to other personal attributes is a developmental achievement that may have important consequences for children's social relations. As noted in Chapter 5, Kohlberg claims that once children realize that they belong to the same stable sexual category as their same-sex parent, they will establish close affective ties with that parent, and possibly with same-sex others as well. This was the "emotional bonding" aspect of Kohlberg's identification theory. Experimental evidence for this was provided in a study in which researchers found that boys who had acquired a sense of sex constancy spent relatively more time looking at other males than did boys who had not yet acquired a sense of gender constancy.[46] This result has been replicated and extended to girls in subsequent research.[47]

In a direct study of how children view the consequences of gender for behavior, William Damon asked children ages four through nine for their opinions concerning the rightness or wrongness of sex-inappropriate acts.[48] For example, in one question, Damon posed the problem of a young boy who would rather play with dolls than with "boyish" toys. Another set of questions asked children for their opinions about wearing sex-inappropriate clothing (such as dresses for men), and another asked children about unconventional occupational choices, such as men becoming nurses and women becoming truck drivers. Damon found the following age-related progression in children's answers: At age four, children are willing to accept any deviation from the conventional norm for sex-appropriate behavior. This acceptance, however, seems based upon a lack of appreciation for the norm itself, or for the social sanctions attached to the norm. That is, a child will say that it is fine for a boy to wear a dress if he wants to but will show little recognition that this act violates a norm and may result in unpleasant consequences. By ages five to seven, children's attitudes take an abrupt turnaround. Now they consider it wrong to violate a sex-role convention, particularly because they believe they will be punished or shamed for such a deviation. Later in childhood, a liberalization of this attitude takes place. Children now recognize the reality of social pressure to conform to sex-role conventions, but they believe that individuals should have some personal leeway, despite the conventions. By the end of childhood, there is some knowledge of the formal social laws that prescribe equality between the sexes. Children use this knowledge to defend people's rights to make free choices concerning their own behavioral styles and occupations. Damon sees the development of these sex-role conceptions as one manifestation

[45] Emmerich, 1977; Kohlberg, 1966.
[46] Slaby & Frey, 1975.
[47] Ruble, Balaban, & Cooper, 1979.
[48] Damon, 1977.

of more general developments in children's social-conventional reasoning, an issue that will be discussed more fully in Chapter 7.

Advances in children's sex-role understanding directly affect how children apprehend and act upon the sex-role norms of their culture. For a young child, the issue is to be cognitively developed enough to recognize the norms. In fact, research has shown that, for preschool children, a child's degree of cognitive maturity is associated with the degree to which the child's behavior tends to be sex typed.[49] For older children, the issue becomes how to interpret the personal consequences of following or rejecting the norm. In many instances, it may be wise, and perhaps even valuable and gratifying, to perform conventional sex-typed behavior. In other instances, this may seem unnecessarily restricting for one's personal needs and inclinations. Determining an individual response to a widely held convention is as important a social-developmental task for children as is understanding the convention in the first place.

Personal Identity Formation in Childhood

During childhood, the search for identity continues, aided by new insights into the distinct nature of self. In constructing the groundwork for a self-identity, the child must establish a sense of similarity and difference between self and others. This sense is based upon some notion, however dimly defined, of the child's own personality characteristics. It is during childhood that deep and enduring personal dispositions stabilize, and psychologists can begin to assess children's "personality traits" or "character structure."[50] Children themselves implicitly make such assessments in forming their own unique sense of identity.

Erikson's Stages of Childhood Identity

No one has written more eloquently about the individual's lifelong search for identity than Erik Erikson.[51] On the basis on his clinical observations, Erikson has characterized the development of self-identity as a continuing drama that poses new personal challenges to the individual each time an old challenge is successfully met. The systematic plan of Erikson's genetic stage model was presented in Table 3-2. With reference to this model, it is possible to trace the development of identity from infancy through all the phases of life and to connect this continuing identity search with the other major psychosocial challenges of the life cycle. According to Erikson, one's identity does not become one's major psychosocial challenge until adolescence, but it is always an active concern, with important links to the dominant "crisis" of any particular life phase (see Table 6-1).

[49] Kohlberg, 1966; Conner & Serbin, 1977.
[50] Cattell, 1957; Kimble & Garmezy, 1968;
Gough, 1969.
[51] Erikson, 1968.

Table 6–1 Childhood Identity Formation

Stage	Dominant crisis	Identity crisis	Task with respect to identity formation	Conviction
First Stage (about first year)	Trust vs. Mistrust	Mutual recognition vs. Autistic isolation	Recognizing the separateness of self and other.	"I am what I am given."
Second Stage (about second and third years)	Autonomy vs. Shame & Doubt	Will to be oneself vs. Self-doubt	Believing that one controls one's own destiny.	"I am what I can will freely."
Third Stage (about fourth and fifth years)	Initiative vs. Guilt	Anticipation of roles vs. Role inhibition	Imagining a world of possibilities for the self.	"I am what I can imagine I will be."
Fourth Stage (about fifth year to end of childhood)	Industry vs. Inferiority	Task identification vs. Sense of futility	Developing a sense of competence	"I am what I can make work."

Source: Based on E. H. Erikson, *Identity: Youth and Crisis.* New York: W. W. Norton, 1968, p. 94.

In Chapter 3 we noted that, according to Erikson's theory, the infant's task with respect to identity formation is recognizing the separateness of self and other. This first sense of *mutual recognition* is cognitively based on an awareness that self and other are distinct individuals, and affectively based on a belief in one's own essential goodness and trustworthiness. Failure to develop a sense of mutual recognition may result in a continuation of the infant's primal sense of *autistic isolation*, in which neither the distinctions nor the interconnections between self and other are clearly understood. Although the conflict between mutual recognition and autistic isolation sets the stage for later challenges in the search for identity, during infancy it is secondary and somewhat derivative from the dominant crisis of trust versus mistrust.

Soon after infancy arises a new opportunity for further identity development. The dominant crisis of this stage is *autonomy versus shame and doubt*. This noble-sounding crisis is often played out in the mundane setting of the toilet. Through gaining control over when to "hold on" or "let go" of his feces, the child first experiences the possibility of autonomous free will. But with this possibility also comes a danger: failure to establish a sense of one's own control may lead to a lasting sense of shame and doubt, rather than of autonomy and free will. As in all psychosocial crises, environmental support is critical for a successful resolution: "The matter of mutual regulation between adult and child now faces its severest test. If outer control by too rigid or too early [toilet] training persists in robbing the child of his attempt gradually to control his bowels and other functions willingly and by his free choice, he will again be faced with a double rebellion and a double defeat."[52] Not only will the child miss an invaluable developmental opportunity, but in addition, he may lose faith in his own ability to "stand on his own feet."

The resolution of this childhood crisis has direct consequences for early identity development. At this age, the identity struggle consists of forging a "will to be oneself," rather than a sense of "self-doubt." The will to be oneself requires a belief in one's control over one's own destiny. Not only does this mean gaining a knowledge of how to effectively take care of oneself (including one's body and bodily functions), but also gaining "the very courage to be an independent individual who can choose and guide his own future." The developmental milestone of successful identity formation during this stage of autonomy, writes Erikson, is the child's belief that "I am what I can will freely."

The next childhood crisis begins at the end of year three and lasts until school age. This is the battle between *initiative* and *guilt* and corresponds to the Oedipal period described by Freud. Like Freud, at this stage Erikson sees the child becoming infused with a new energy and a new feeling of power. Also like Freud, Erikson believes that some of this energy is sexual in nature and directed toward the opposite-sex parent, and he believes that the development of a conscience (the Freudian superego) is necessary to control the dangerous

[52] Ibid., p. 109.

and antisocial impulses arising from this misplaced sexual desire. But unlike Freud, Erikson also cites other types of new childhood energy and power. Even more than sexual energy, Erikson emphasizes three developments as bringing about both the opportunity and crisis of this stage of initiative: "(1) the child learns to move around more freely and more violently and therefore establishes a wider, and, to him, unlimited radius of goals; (2) his sense of language becomes perfected to the point where he understands and can ask incessantly about innumerable things, often hearing just enough to misunderstand them thoroughly; and (3) both language and locomotion permit him to expand his imagination to so many roles that he cannot avoid frightening himself with what he himself has dreamed and thought up."[53] If the child experiences these new powers as means to positive achievements, if he learns to value the ambitions and goals that result from an awareness of these new powers, he will come away from this stage with a sense of initiative. If not, he will question his right to "intrude" upon the world through using his new powers. A sense of guilt will then accompany the natural surges of energy and aspiration that increasingly arise during these childhood years.

During this period, the identity quest revolves around the child's new ability to imagine a world of possibilities for the self. The child is now introduced to the notion of social roles through narrative play and fantasy, as discussed in Chapter 4. Accordingly, she can "try out" new possibilities for social action in the realm of make-believe and is constrained only by the limits of her imagination. Erikson also points out that bedtime stories play an important part in introducing children to the "big life" of heroes and ideal role models. All of these influences combine to offer children a chance to explore a virtually open world of role possibilities for themselves. If the child's sense of initiative predominates, the outcome for identity formation will be a positive "anticipation of roles"; if the child's sense of guilt predominates, the child's imagination will be squelched by "role inhibition." Optimally, the child will emerge from this stage with a sense of pride and purpose in expressing her new energies and fulfilling the promise of her new powers. The milestone for identity formation at this stage of initiative is "the firmly established, steadily growing conviction, undaunted by guilt, that 'I am what I can imagine I will be.'"

The final childhood stage in Erikson's theory brings to fruition some of the ambitious energy and imagined feats of earlier childhood. During this school-age stage of *industry versus inferiority*, children have the opportunity to acquire skills that enable them to achieve real accomplishments in the world. Erikson points out that children in all cultures are exposed to systematic instruction at this age, though not always in a formal school setting. The child's readiness for systematic, real-world instruction at the end of her playful period of expansive imagination, and the immediate adaptation of human culture to the child's new readiness, is evidence, Erikson believes, for the "wisdom of the

---

[53] Ibid., p. 115.

ground plan." In Erikson's view, children's psychosocial development and their social environments normally are quite sensitive to one another; all that is needed for an optimal unfolding of the genetic "plan" (the stages of psychosocial growth) is some supportive responsiveness, offered with some regularity, and in a noninterfering way, by the social environment.

According to Erikson, during the childhood school years work dominates the child's attention. The challenge during this period is to develop a sense of competence as a worker. This requires a chance to demonstrate that one can learn to use the tools of technology, applying them to problems that "count." If one comes away from this period with a belief in one's effectiveness as a learner and a worker, and with a positive affective orientation toward one's own accomplishments, a sense of industry will result. If not, a sense of inferiority may arise, discouraging further attempts to produce and excel.

For the child's identity development, the milestone of this stage is the belief that "I am what I can make work." Such a belief depends upon a successful resolution of the industry-inferiority crisis. Ideally, this resolution will offer the child a chance to select those skills and special talents that the child can call her own: a sense of particular competence to perform important tasks that "matter" to other people. This is what Erikson calls a sense of "task identification," opposed to which is this period's risk, an enduring "sense of futility."

Erikson's theory outlines how personal identity is formed through the life span. It portrays the general concerns and crises that individuals normally encounter during different periods of life, and it shows how the resolution of each crisis paves the way for dealing successfully with subsequent ones. In this sense, Erikson's stage model is a theory of normal personality development, despite its empirical origins in clinical observations. The model provides a means of analyzing problems in identity formation by comparing deviant paths against the optimal "game plan" that Erikson envisions. To date, this has been done only informally in Erikson's descriptive accounts of his own clinical cases, or of cases drawn from history—such as Martin Luther, Mahatma Ghandi, George Bernard Shaw, and William James.[54] But, as suggested in Chapter 3, the systematic nature of Erikson's model has potential for more precise and formal diagnostic use. Erikson has sketched out fundamental genetic relations between the successive tasks that arise during an individual's lifelong search for identity. Such a sketch could provide the basis for a powerful clinical-developmental assessment tool. We shall further explore the potentials of Erikson's theory in our chapter on adolescent identity, where we shall cite some empirical research based on his theory. In that chapter, one of the prime virtues of Erikson's theory will become immediately apparent: Erikson's stage model is one of the rare social development theories that connects the accomplishments and challenges of infancy and childhood with those of later life.

[54] Erikson, 1958, 1968, 1969.

Self-Esteem and Personal Control

Erikson's stage model is helpful in outlining the normal phases of identity development, but there are many aspects of individual variation in identity development that Erikson's model does not touch (or touches only indirectly through its potential for use in individual case studies). More systematic analyses of personality differences in children have focused on several aspects of children's self-identity. The oldest and most fully researched tradition of this kind is the literature on children's *self-esteem*. A more recent tradition, conceptually related to the self-esteem research, is the study of children's *sense of control* over themselves and their lives. Some of this line of research explores children's *impulsivity*, and some of it explores children's sense of personal agency, or *locus of control*, in their transactions with the world. Both of these research traditions are oriented toward personality as well as developmental factors. In other words, this research attempts to explain self-esteem and self-control differences between children, not simply in terms of their social-developmental maturity, but also in terms of the personality characteristics of individual children.

Self-esteem is an evaluative orientation toward the self, generally assessed in terms of its positive or negative value. In other words, self-esteem as a psychological construct is concerned with whether or not people evaluate themselves in a positive manner, and if so, the strength of their positive self-attitudes. Self-esteem research has not concerned itself with the conceptual bases for personal identity, nor the nature of self-understanding (see the following section, below). Consequently, in studying children's self-esteem, psychologists have designed scales to determine the quantitative degree of children's positive self-evaluations. This quantitative-assessment approach stands in contrast to the qualitative analyses of self offered by those psychologists who are more interested in children's formation of identity and self-understanding.

Historically, the quantitative approach to self-esteem has precedents dating back to William James's initial psychological analysis of the self-concept.[55] As described in Chapter 1, the self, according to James, consists of the *I* and the *me*. The *I* is the "self-as-knower," the aspects of self that continually organize and interpret experience in a purely subjective manner. The *me* is the self as known, or the self as object for knowing. As such, the *me* has a number of elements that James believed to be distinguishable both in theory as well as for the sake of empirical measurement.

The primary elements of the *me* were what James called the *constituents*. These constituents are the actual qualities that define the self as known. They include all the material characteristics (body, possessions), all the social characteristics (relations, roles, personality), and all the spiritual characteristics (consciousness, thoughts, psychological mechanisms) that identify the self as a

[55] James, 1892.

unique individual. James's suggestion was that each individual organizes the constituents of the *me* into a hierarchical structure, with "the bodily me at the bottom, the spiritual me at the top, and the extra-corporeal material selves and the various social selves between."[56]

But James did not end his analysis of the *me* with his outline of its cognitive constituents. He also discussed one affectively laden aspect of the *me*: self-appreciation (the feelings and emotions that the *me*'s constituents arouse). James believed that such feelings could be analyzed in two ways. First, like the constituents themselves, they could be described qualitatively: "Each [feeling] has its own peculiar physiognomical expression. In self-satisfaction the exterior muscles are innervated, the eye is strong and glorious, the gait rolling and elastic, the nostril dilated, and a peculiar smile plays upon the lips. . . ."[57] But the sum total of feelings about the self, James believed, could also be assessed quantitatively as well. To accomplish this, James proposed a particular formula designed to calculate the extent of an individual's self-esteem. James's self-esteem formula establishes a relation between the actualities and potentialities of an individual, so that the equation looks like this:

$$\text{Self-esteem} = \frac{\text{Success}}{\text{Pretensions}}$$

"Such a fraction," wrote James, "may be increased as well by diminishing the denominator as by increasing the numerator." [58] He then suggested various ways by which one could increase one's self-esteem, either by working harder to improve one's chance of success, or rethinking one's expectations for oneself.

Modern-day psychologists have focused on self-esteem far more than on any other aspect of the self. They have constructed dozens of instruments to measure self-esteem in children and adults, conducting literally thousands of studies in which self-esteem is a central variable.[59] Psychologists' interest in self-esteem no doubt arises from their belief in its importance to human social functioning. Many clinically oriented theorists take self-esteem to be the critical index of mental health.[60] Empirical research has linked high self-esteem to life satisfaction[61] and happiness,[62] and it has linked low self-esteem to depression,[63] anxiety,[64] and maladjustment.[65] Child psychologists and educators believe self-esteem influences both children's school performance and their social relations.[66]

Perhaps because there has been such widespread interest in measuring

[56] Ibid., p. 57.
[57] Ibid., p. 59.
[58] Ibid., p. 63.
[59] Wylie, 1961.
[60] Jahoda, 1958.
[61] Crandall, 1973.
[62] Bachman, 1970.
[63] Beck, 1967.
[64] Luck & Heiss, 1972.
[65] Kaplan & Pokorny, 1969.
[66] Wylie, 1961; Rosenberg, 1965.

children's self-esteem, there now exists a diversity of self-esteem assessment procedures for use with children down to about the age of eight. Some of these assessment procedures are quite global in nature and are aimed at tapping children's general sense of self-worth. One such technique, for example, asks subjects to respond to statements like, "On the whole, I am satisfied with myself" and "At times I think that I am no good at all."[67] In contrast, other self-esteem assessment procedures tap children's attitudes toward a range of specific self characteristics. One such instrument presents children with fifty statements of the following type: "I'm proud of my school work"; "I find it hard to talk in front of the class"; "I'm popular with kids my own age."[68] The children are asked to indicate whether each item is "like me" or "unlike me." With either type of measure, an overall self-esteem score can be calculated for any individual child. This score reflects the degree to which the child tended to answer items with a positive rather than a negative orientation. Children vary widely on such scores, and studies have shown that for most children such scores remain stable over time.[69] In other words, children with high self-esteem tend to stay that way for years, as do children with low self-esteem.

Positive self-esteem in children is associated with many of the same familial conditions that lead to independence, self-assertiveness, and instrumental competence. Researchers have found that children with high self-esteem come from homes in which the parents exercise control in a nonpermissive but democratic manner, communicate clearly with the child, and encourage the child to display affection and other emotions.[70] These are all similar to the child-rearing practices considered optimal by Baldwin, Baumrind, and others cited in Chapter 5. In addition to these familial correlates, self-esteem in children is also linked to their actual experiences with success or failure.[71] Children with low self-esteem are often those who really have had trouble in school, are unpopular, or act in embarrassing ways (like wetting their beds). In this sense, self-esteem reflects children's success in adapting to the world, as well as creating the conditions for successful (or unsuccessful) adaptation.

As noted earlier, psychological research has found self-esteem to be connected to mental health throughout life. In children, a particular correlate of self-esteem is assertiveness.[72] This is because positive self-esteem enables children to have confidence in their own judgments and actions, in social as well as intellectual endeavors. The author of one large-scale study writes that children with high self-esteem are creative in school and both independent and vigorous in peer relations:

> They have confidence in their perceptions and judgments and believe that they can bring their efforts to a favorable resolution. Their favorable self-attitudes lead them to accept their own opinions and place credence and trust in their reactions and conclusions. This permits them to follow their own judgments when there is a

[67] Rosenberg, 1979.
[68] Coopersmith, 1967.
[69] Coopersmith, 1967; Rosenberg, 1979.
[70] Wylie, 1961; Coopersmith, 1967.
[71] Rosenberg, 1979.
[72] Coopersmith, 1967.

difference of opinion and also permits them to consider novel ideas. . . They are more likely to be participants than listeners in group discussions, they report less difficulty in forming friendships, and they will express opinions even when they know these opinions may meet with a hostile reception.[73]

Perhaps the central dimension in childhood self-esteem, certainly related to assertiveness, is the sense of *control*. By control is meant a feeling of efficacy, or *personal agency:* a sense that one has some power, or causative effect, over the nature of self and the outside world. This does not mean absolute power, nor unilateral causation, but rather that one has some effect on the state of things within and outside oneself. Philosophers have long believed that this sense of control is the essence of self-concept, at least once the self-concept has been positively formulated. Charles Cooley, an early associate of James, Baldwin, and Mead, wrote that "self-feeling" (his phrase for self-esteem) was mainly linked to "ideas of the exercise of power, of being a cause. . . ."[74] According to Cooley, such ideas naturally arise in the course of self-development:

> The first definite thoughts that a child associates with self-feeling are probably those of his earliest endeavors to control visible objects—his limbs, his playthings, his bottle, and the like. Then he attempts to control the actions of the persons about him, and so his circle of power and self-feeling widens without interruption to the most complex of mature ambition.[75]

Control has two distinguishable aspects: control over oneself and a sense of efficacy over the outside world. Each of these types of personal control has been shown to have major impact on a child's social life and social development. In the psychological literature, self-control has been studied under the rubrics of *impulsivity*, and *self-regulation*, whereas a sense of efficacy over the outside world has been studied under the rubric of the *locus of control*.

Children vary widely in their ability to control their impulses. Some children tolerate the normal frustrations of life quite well. Others cannot bear any setback or delay in gratification, often responding with temper tantrums and other overtly aggressive behavior. Populations of children with "behavioral problems" are made up largely of children from this latter group. In *Children Who Hate*, a classic account of childhood emotional disturbance and its treatment, Fritz Redl and David Wineman describe such children as being "out of control."[76] These children not only act impulsively and hostilely on their own, but they have a contagious effect on others. They instigate out-of-control behavior in others and are easily distracted by others' instigations. The research of Jeanne and Jack Block, cited earlier in this chapter, showed that the manner in which children control their impulses can be a stable characteristic of their personalities. Treatment programs such as those designed by Redl and Wineman are by necessity lengthy and painfully slow in effect.

---

[73] Ibid., pp. 70–71.
[74] Cooley, 1912, p. 146.

[75] Ibid., p. 151.
[76] Redl & Wineman, 1951.

Learning control over one's impulses—generally called *self-control*—is an accomplishment that has many meanings and spans the course of life. It entails the balancing of one's own desires against the rights of others, as in the development of justice and morality. It also entails constructing future life plans that supersede immediate gratifications, deferring to certain social conventions and rules, respecting legitimate authority, and a host of other "socialized" acts which are taken up elsewhere throughout this book. But impulse control also requires a certain sense of self, a belief in one's own agency over inner and outer events in one's life. This belief in personal agency is the subject of a burgeoning psychological research area known as the *locus of control*.

Clinical psychologists have long known that some people feel far more in control of their own destinies that do others. Those who have a positive sense of influencing the major events in their lives have an *internal locus of control*. That is, they believe that their own inclinations and actions determine what happens to them, and therefore they feel responsible for their own success or failure. In contrast, people who feel essentially powerless over the course of events in their lives have an *external locus of control*. Such people often believe that life's important outcomes are in the hands of fate, or at least in the hands of other people. Clinicians have linked the powerless feeling generated by an external locus of control to physical inactivity, social isolation, and emotional depression.[77] Child psychologists have linked it to unpopularity and inadequate school performances in children.[78] One set of recent findings demonstrates that an internal locus of control is closely associated with high self-esteem in children, whereas an external locus of control is associated with low self-esteem.[79] This is consistent with the view, explicated above, that an essential component of self-esteem is a sense of personal control and efficacy.

An internal locus of control requires an expectation that the world is responsive to one's will. Children who have experienced a long history of nonresponsiveness from events and people in the world are clearly at a disadvantage in developing an internal locus of control. They may come to see life as a series of unsolvable problems and, in reaction, they may develop a mode of interacting with the world that Martin Seligman has called "learned helplessness."[80] Experimental evidence has shown that even normally optimistic people will become passive and depressed when continually confronted with problems that are beyond their control.[81] Persons who have experienced long periods of their lives in this way become permanently resigned to their own ineffectualness, "learning" to act helpless in difficult circumstances.

For children, the world may seen nonresponsive for many reasons. Parental indifference, peer hostility, the impersonality of school, all may confront

[77] Rotter, 1954.
[78] Rotter, 1966.
[79] Rosenberg, 1979

[80] Seligman, 1974.
[81] Seligman, 1975.

children with examples of unpleasant events that they cannot control. Robert Coles has documented the many ways in which all-too-common life difficulties like poverty rob children of the chance to discover the world's potential responsiveness.[82] But for most children, the world is also filled with events that children can influence. Most parents, peers, and school personnel do respond to a child's demands, wishes, and actions. Research has shown that the manner of such responding can make a large difference for a child's locus of control. One study found that parents who use a "suggestive" style of instructing their children ("Why don't you give this a try?") tend to have children with internal loci of control, whereas parents who use a "directive" style ("Here, do this!") tend to have children with external loci of control.[83]

A series of studies by Carol Dweck has shown that children who fail in school can be helped to succeed by encouraging them to believe that their failures are under their own control. Dweck gave difficult math problems to two groups of children. Both groups often failed to get the right answers, but the two groups were given different feedback on their performances. Children in the first group were simply told that they did not do well, the implication being that the problems were too hard for them intellectually. Children in the second group, on the other hand, were told that their papers were sloppy, that they did not spend enough time on the task, that they did not pay enough attention, or that they were not well-prepared—the implication here being that they did not try hard enough. Dweck found that children in the first group became apathetic about the math tasks and quickly lost interest when encountering further difficult tasks. Children in the second group increased their efforts and improved their subsequent performances.

Dweck believes that many children who chronically fail in school do so because they have learned to attribute their failures to factors beyond their control—to their own intellectual inabilities, for example. This is "learned helplessness" in the school setting. Further, in observations of actual schoolrooms, Dweck has found that teachers often contribute to children's sense of learned helplessness by unfortunate explicit and implicit messages to pupils.[84] Girls, in particular, seem to be the victims of such unfortunate messages. Teachers often assume that girls try as hard as they can in school, so that any failure stems from a deep-rooted incompetence rather than a lack of effort. In contrast, when boys fail, the teacher is more likely to blame motivational shortcoming, fooling around, sloppiness, inattention, and so on. Following Dweck's logic, we could connect this differential treatment of the sexes with the far greater incidence of perceived helplessness and depression found in women at all ages.[85] This would be another indication of the fundamental links between personal control, self-esteem, and positive mental health.

---

[82] Coles, 1967.
[83] Loeb, 1975.

[84] Dweck, Davidson, Nelson, & Enna, 1978.
[85] Dweck & Bush, 1976.

The Development of Children's Self-Understanding

Self-Understanding Distinguished from Self-Esteem

Because research on children's self-esteem concerns the degree to which children positively or negatively evaluate themselves, it does not capture the actual nature of children's self-conceptions. A research assessment of self-esteem determines only the direction (positive or negative) and extent (high or low) of children's self-evaluations. It does not inform us of the qualitative, cognitive bases for these evaluations. It does not tell us, for example, what aspects of self children at different ages believe to be most important in evaluating themselves. Nor does it tell us how children compile the variety of things they know about themselves into a coherent, organized self-definition. A typical self-esteem study does not distinguish between a child who positively values himself because he is a good baseball player and a child who positively values himself because he is a religiously moral person. This is because self-esteem measures do not systematically tap children's modes of defining and understanding themselves. For information about this latter issue, we must turn to studies of children's self-knowledge.

The work of Michael Lewis and Jeanne Brooks-Gunn, described in Chapter 3, showed how self-knowledge grows in important ways during the infant years. Erikson's writings on identity formation give us ample reason to believe that an individual's definition of self continues to be transformed all throughout the course of human development. We should expect that a thirty-year-old woman will define herself differently as an adult than when she was a little girl or a teenager. This is not simply because her life has changed, but also because different aspects of herself will be better understood, or seem more important, as she grows older. Not only, for example, may she have new social relationships (as a mother, a wife, and so on), but the very fact of social relationship may now take on a radically different meaning for her sense of self. Such changes are part of the continual construction of self-knowledge, and they may be considered the cognitive aspect of self-development.

Erikson's stage model shows how the challenges of identity formation change from period to period during the life span, but it does not offer an explicit analysis of how the self is actually known and defined at these different periods. In other words, Erikson tells us that during the school years, children must forge a positive sense of "task identification," but he does not explain how children conceptualize tasks in relation to their own abilities during this period, or how this conceptualization differs from children's earlier and later understanding of the tasks and abilities of self. For such an explanation, psychologists must directly study the development of children's self-under-standing.

Unfortunately, in developmental research, self-understanding has been strangely segregated from self-esteem. The two research topics have been investigated by psychologists from different research traditions, using different goals and different methods. To the disadvantage of both traditions, neither research line has been influenced by findings from the other. In particular, childhood self-esteem measures have been notoriously insensitive to the changing cognitive quality of children's developing self-understanding. Many critics have commented on this with concern, arguing that an instrument for assessing children's self-evaluations cannot be valid unless it adjusts for the different meanings that these evaluations, as well as the elements of self upon which they are based, may have for children at different ages.[86] Although some self-esteem instruments were designed with children especially in mind, and therefore are at least comprehensible to children, no scale in the current literature anticipates or "corrects for" developmental transformations in the conception of self.

In order to accomplish this, a childhood self-esteem measure would require a developmental model of self-understanding as a referent. This would enable the self-esteem researcher to determine the meaning and value of self-esteem test items to persons of various ages. Most importantly, it would enable the researcher to design a self-esteem inventory that reflects the major ways in which self-understanding is organized and reorganized throughout development. No such inventory can be conceptually valid without such an effort. Such a model would have to take account of children's changing emphases in their self-concepts; younger children emphasizing physical and active characteristics, adolescents emphasizing "inner" psychological characteristics (e.g., emotions and thoughts). It would also have to measure different aspects of the self-concept (e.g., physical, cognitive, and social) according to age. Several researchers have been sensitive to the problems inherent in designing self-esteem scales, but none have satisfactorily solved the problem.[87]

A developmental model of self-understanding is important for many reasons beyond the valid assessment of self-esteem. Recent studies in social-cognitive development have shown that social concepts require their own developmental analyses and cannot be reduced to global structures based upon logical or physical cognition.[88] Further, as this book has emphasized repeatedly, the self as a concept serves a unique and critical function in social understanding. Unlike concepts of relations (friendship, love, authority) or concepts of regulations (fairness, social rules, conventions), all of which serve to connect the individual with society, the concept of self plays a distinguishing role as well. In other words, among all the social concepts that help one understand one's integration into society, the concept of self provides one with an understanding of one's differentiation from others in society. In this way, it establishes the cognitive basis for one's identity as a unique individual, for one's special position, status, and role within the social network. Though not synonymous with personality, it is the conceptual underpinnings of it.

What constitutes knowledge of the self, and how does it differ from other types of social knowledge? In Chapter 1, we discussed some of the unique

---

[86] Keller, Ford, & Meachum, 1978; Brim, 1976; Harter, 1980.

[87] Rosenberg, 1979; Harter, 1980.

[88] Damon, 1977, 1979; Turiel, 1978; Flavell & Ross, 1981.

features of self, such as the *I-me* duality. Here we shall continue and expand upon that discussion.

The self is a psychological construct. It does not refer to anything tangible, observable, or even objectifiable. The sole determiner of a person's self is the person, subjectively selecting the critical processes and features that constitute his or her own self. Unlike the nature of one's personality, the nature of one's self is not a matter for consensual validation. That is, one could claim to have a charming personality and yet others, claiming a more objective knowledge, could disagree. In contrast, the self is one's own personal construction. Although others may offer feedback that a person may choose to incorporate into the self, the person is the sole arbiter of how to interpret this feedback. In constructing a self, the person has the power not only to decide upon the defining characteristics of self, but also to choose which categories of characteristics (physical, psychological, and so on) are to be considered, and how they are to be ordered. The self is a concept that, like any other concept, serves as a personal means of cognitively organizing part of one's life experience. A good definition of self has been offered by Sarbin:

> The interbehavioral field of the human can include perceptions and cognitions referable to objects in the external world, and perceptions and cognitions referable to his own body, to his own beliefs, his own statuses, and so on. . . The self is one such cognitive structure or inference. . . The self (in common with other cognitive structures) is subject to continual and progressive change, usually in the direction from low-order inferences about simple perceptions to higher-order inferences about complex cognitions.[89]

The self, then, is one psychological construct among many. But it is unique in at least one way. Alone among concepts, it is reflective: it "regards itself."[90] As Mead wrote, "It is an object to itself . . . (it is) both subject and object."[91] This characteristic led James to postulate the two main aspects of self, the *I* and the *me*. This dual, reflective nature of self has been outlined in Chapter 1.

Understanding Self in Comparison and Contrast with Understanding Others

There is a long tradition of psychological theory and research that asserts the similarity between understanding self and understanding others. Baldwin initiated this view in his discussion of the developmental processes that produce self-understanding. As discussed in Chapter 1, Baldwin believed that one comes to know the self only as one comes to know others, and *vice versa*. In other words, both self and others are discovered simultaneously, in the course of interactions between self and others. From such interactions, a person eventually makes inferences about the nature of self and others. Both types of

---

[89] Sarbin, 1962, p. 12.
[90] Mead, 1934.

[91] Ibid, p. 135.

inferences—self-inferences and other inferences—must be organized identically, since they share a common source in the social interactions that the person has experienced. In particular, Baldwin emphasized two interactional processes that ensure the similarity between self and other knowledge: *imitation* and *ejection*. Through imitation, one adopts for oneself the features that one observes in others; and through ejection (imitation projected outward), one endows the other with characteristics that one observes or feels in the self (particularly covert, unobservable characteristics like thought and emotion). So Baldwin wrote, "My sense of myself grows by imitation of you, and my sense of yourself grows in terms of myself";[92] and, elsewhere, "So the dialectic may be read thus: my thought is in the main, as to its character, a personal self, filled up with my thought of others, distributed variously as individuals; and my thought of others, as persons, is mainly filled up with myself."[93]

Baldwin's developmental theory has influenced many subsequent views on the relation between understanding of self and other. A number of empirical studies have demonstrated that, in many respects, the two types of knowledge develop in parallel fashion in the individual.[94] The most recent version of this notion has appeared in Michael Lewis and Jeanne Brooks-Gunn's research into infants' social cognition (see Chapter 3). On the basis of their studies, Lewis and Brooks-Gunn offered the following two principles: "Principle I: Any knowledge gained about the other also must be gained about the self. . . Principle II: What can be demonstrated to be known about the self can be said to be known about the other."[95]

But despite the important parallels pointed out by Baldwin and his many followers, there are also some obvious differences between self and other understanding. In fact, these differences may overshadow the similarities, leading us to question whether statements made by Baldwin and others have too strongly stressed principles of identity while neglecting actual distinctions between knowledge of self and other. For one thing, there is the distinction mentioned by Baldwin, between "that which is immediate and that which is objective." But Baldwin to the contrary, this hardly seems a minor distinction as far as the development of cognitive structures is concerned. It is difficult to imagine that the entire range of affect and cognition to which one has access in the "immediate" experience of self can be wholly and adequately represented through ejection or any other means for the sake of knowledge about others. Even given such attempts, the margin of error must be enormous. In other words, whatever one can surmise about the other's *me*, the other's *I* always remains more mysterious than one's own. An equally serious problem applies to the converse effort of gaining "objective" knowledge about the self. A person's perceptual orientation is "focused on the situation in which he is behaving, and he literally cannot see himself performing his actions."[96] In

---

[92] Baldwin, 1902, p. 21.
[93] Ibid., p. 32.
[94] Scarlett, Press, & Crockett, 1971; Lively & Bromley, 1973; Shrauger & Patterson, 1974.
[95] Lewis & Brooks-Gunn, 1979.
[96] Taylor & Fiske, 1975, p. 444.

contrast, a person often can observe others' actions with little difficulty. Researchers have found that "point of view does indeed markedly determine causal interpretations of social situations."[97] This permanent difference in perceptual orientations toward self and other seems certain to create differences in how self and other are conceived. In addition to all this, there may be profound affective differences between how one receives feedback on the self versus how one receives feedback on others. One is emotionally invested in the nature of one's own identity in a different way than in the nature of others' identities, and this may well lead to differences in how personal information on self and other is cognitively processed.

The small bit of empirical research that bears on this issue contains some indications that self and other may indeed be construed in significantly different ways. One study showed that a person is likely to attribute her own behavior in experimental situations to situational causes and free will, while the same person is likely to attribute another's behavior in the same situations to personality traits and dispositions.[98] This phenomenon has been replicated in a number of other ways. For example, people assess the applicability of a particular character adjective to themselves more easily and confidently than to other familiar persons.[99] People are also more likely to use categories referring to inner experience (such as motivation) when describing themselves than when describing others.[100] All these findings suggest that self-understanding has a distinctly different conceptual basis than other understanding.

Developmental Progression of Self-Knowledge during Childhood

Research on children's self-knowledge is different in character from infant self-knowledge research because children are able to communicate their self-conceptions verbally. Through the use of interviews and other verbal procedures, researchers have been able to probe children's conceptions of many psychological issues related to self. These issues include the nature of the self's basic components (including mind and body), one's awareness of self, one's definition of self, self in comparison to others, self in relation to others, and self-interest. From all of these diverse efforts, we can piece together a chronology of self-knowledge as it develops in the childhood years.

In a broad-based study of children's *naive epistemologies* (that is, their spontaneous philosophical analyses of the world), John Broughton asked children a number of open-ended questions concerning the self.[101] Broughton's questions were in the form of direct interrogations like, "What is the self? What is the mind? What is the difference between the mind and the body?" As is traditional in clinical interviews with children, Broughton probed the child's responses with a series of follow-up questions. From subjects' answers, Broughton derived a developmental progression of naive epistemology that

[97] Ibid., p. 438.
[98] Jones & Nisbett, 1971.
[99] Kuiper & Rogers, 1979.

[100] Lively & Bromley, 1973.
[101] Broughton, 1978.

covers the period from childhood through middle adulthood. In this book, we shall consider only the aspects of Broughton's outline that concern self-knowledge. In this chapter, we shall describe Broughton's two childhood levels; in later chapters, we shall take up his adolescent and adult levels.

In early childhood, according to Broughton, the self is conceived strictly in physical terms. The self is believed to be part of the body. Usually this means the head, although other body parts are also cited, including the whole body. Accordingly, the child confuses self, mind, and body. Because of this type of reasoning, young children typically express a number of peculiar opinions unique to this early level. For example, because young children believe that self and mind are simply parts of the body, they often say that any body may have a self and a mind, including animals, plants, and dead people. Further, since self is a body part, it can be described in terms of material dimensions such as size, shape, or color. Thus, children at this level distinguish themselves from others on the basis of their physical appearance and other material attributes: "I am different from Johnny because I have blond hair, different from that tree because I am smaller, different from my sister because I have a bike." Even the volitional aspects of self—that is, one's motivations and "free will"—are attributed to physical body parts. The child might say, for example, that the self is the brain, and the brain tells you what to do.

Later in childhood, at about the age of eight, Broughton's second level of self-knowledge emerges. Children now begin to understand the mental and volitional aspects of self on their own terms, removed from their direct links to any particular body parts. In other words, children now begin to distinguish between mind and body, although this distinction is not as finely articulated as it will be in the adolescent years. The beginning distinction between mental and physical enables children to appreciate the subjective nature of self. One is distinct from others, not simply because one looks different or has different material possessions, but because one has different feelings. The self's essential nature is therefore defined internally rather than externally and has psychological rather than physical attributes. Broughton quotes from a ten-year-old at this level: "I am one of a kind. There could be a person who looks like me or talks like me, but no one who has every single detail I have. Never a person who thinks exactly like me."[102]

Using different types of interview procedures, Robert Selman replicated much of Broughton's developmental progression.[103] Rather than asking children direct questions, Selman posed the following dilemma:

> Eight-year-old Tom is trying to decide what to buy his friend, Mike, for a birthday party. By chance, he meets Mike on the street and learns that Mike is extremely upset because his dog, Pepper, has been lost for two weeks. In fact, Mike is so upset that he tells Tom, "I miss Pepper so much that I never want to look at another dog again." Tom goes off, only to pass a store with a sale on puppies. Only two are left, and these will soon be gone.

[102] Ibid., p. 86.   [103] Selman, 1980.

Children are then asked whether or not Tom should buy Mike the puppy as a birthday present. Follow-up questions probe a number of psychological issues revolving around the perspectives of self and other. For example, sample questions are, "Can you ever fool yourself into thinking that you feel one way when you really feel another?" and "Is there an inside and an outside to a person?" From children's responses to this dilemma, Selman has outlined three childhood levels of "self-awareness."

Selman's first level, which he calls *physicalistic conceptions of self,* is almost identical to Broughton's first level. At this level, the child makes no distinction between inner psychological experience and outer material experience. In response to the Mike dilemma, children at this level typically will deny that a person's statements and behavior can be distinguished from the person's feelings: "If I say that I don't want to see a puppy ever again, then I really won't ever want to." Since the child is not aware of psychological experience apart from overt physical attributes and acts, the child views the self only in physical terms. The self's volitional tendencies are tied to specific body parts and derive strictly from the functioning of these parts. Selman writes that children at this level "often report that their mouth tells their hand what to do or that their ideas come from their tongue."[104]

Later in childhood, according to Selman, children recognize differences between inner and outer states, and they define the "true self" in terms of subjective inner states, rather than material outer states. Unlike Broughton, Selman believes that this developmental transformation in children's self-knowledge occurs in two levels rather than in one. First, writes Selman, by age six or so, children realize that psychological experience is not the same as physical experience, but they still believe that the two types of experience are consistent with one another. Then, by age eight or so, children realize that the self can fool oneself as well as others because of discrepancies between one's inner experience and one's outer appearance. Thus, Mike might really feel that he wants another puppy (psychological experience) even though he might say he doesn't (behavioral appearance). At this point, conscious deception becomes a possibility for the child because he is able to manipulate the relation between internal and external reality. He now sees that the self can monitor its own thoughts in a more direct way than others can. This means that one can put on a "facade" that others may not be able to penetrate. While the child admits that sometimes one's facade will fool the self as well as others, he is also aware that generally one has better access to one's own psychological experience than do others. This appreciation of the private, subjective nature of self, according to Selman, leads the child to a "reflective understanding that the self is capable of gaining inner strength by having confidence in its own abilities."[105]

Although Selman's three levels add some intricacies to Broughton's two-

---

[104] Ibid., p. 176.   [105] Ibid., p. 184.

level progression, the two researchers agree on the basic childhood shift from physicalistic to psychological conceptions of self. Research by Guardo and Bohan on the cognitive bases for self-identity in children ages six through nine provides further evidence of this shift.[106] Guardo and Bohan focused specifically on children's knowledge of four dimensions of self: humanity, sexuality, individuality, and continuity. Humanity refers to the sense that one has human qualities distinct from other life forms. Sexuality is the awareness of one's own gender and sex role. Individuality is the sense that one is unique in the world. Continuity refers to one's belief that one is connected with one's past and future self. Taken together, these dimensions provide the individual with a sense that he or she "is one being with a unique identity who has been, is, and will be a male (or female) human person separate from and entirely like no other."[107] The reader will recognize in this assertion the major elements of James's *I*. Concordant with James and his many followers, Guardo and Bohan approach the study of self with the point of view that the self is a psychological construct whose major function is to provide one with a cognitive sense of one's individuality. Guardo and Bohan's findings tell us how children between ages six and nine do this.

In order to test for children's sense of self, Guardo and Bohan asked their subjects if they believed that they could assume the identity of another being. Three types of beings were specifically mentioned by the interviewer: a pet (testing for "humanity"), an opposite-sex peer (testing for "sexuality"), and a same-sex peer (testing for "individuality"). The researchers' assumption was that if children believe that they can assume the identity of another being, they lack the dimension of self on which the question focused. In addition to these identity tests, the researchers tested for "continuity" by asking subjects whether they were the same persons in the past and future. Follow-up questions for all items were asked. For example, a typical probe question was, "Why do you think you could never become a dog?" In this manner, the researchers could determine not only whether the child had a sense of humanity but also the cognitive basis of that sense.

Guardo and Bohan found that all children in the six to nine age range had a definite sense of all four self dimensions. That is, virtually all subjects expressed belief in their own immutable humanity, sexuality, individuality, and continuity. This, of course, should come as no surprise to us, considering that Lewis and Brooks-Gunn found some awareness of at least the last three of these dimensions in infants younger than two. More revealing, from a developmental point of view, was Guardo and Bohan's finding that the conceptual basis for children's belief in these dimensions changes with age. Six- and seven-year-olds base their beliefs on their physical and behavioral characteristics. For example, a seven-year-old might say that it would be impossible to become just like a particular peer because that peer is shorter and not as good at basketball. Or the child might say that he will be the same as an adult because he will have

---

[106] Guardo & Bohan, 1971.   [107] Ibid., p. 1920.

the same name. Eight- and nine-year-olds use many similarly physicalistic notions, but they also add some psychological ones as well. For example, a nine-year-old might say that it would be impossible to assume a friend's identity because the friend has different likes and dislikes. Therefore, although Guardo and Bohan's study focuses more directly on the essential *I* dimensions of self than do Broughton's or Selman's studies, the main thrust of the findings from all these investigations is basically the same: during middle childhood, there is a developmental shift in self-knowledge, from physicalistic to psychological conceptions.

One recent study, however, has given us reason to modify the developmental sequence suggested by the writings of Broughton, Selman, and Guardo and Bohan. In this study, Keller, Ford, and Meachum showed that very young children (ages three to five) think of the self more in terms of activities than in terms of body parts or material attributes.[108] The researchers used several techniques to arrive at this conclusion. First, children were asked to spontaneously say up to ten things about themselves. Second, they were asked to complete the following sentences: "I am a _____. I am a boy/girl who _____." On these items, children responded most frequently with action statements such as "I play baseball" or "I walk to school." Body-image answers ("I am big" and "I have blue eyes") were far less common. In fact, other than action statements, which comprised over 50 percent of children's responses, no other category of response occurred more than 10 percent of the time. In a further confirmation of this trend, the researchers gave children direct choices between action and body-image statements. To do this, the researchers asked subjects which of the following types of statements subjects would rather have written about themselves: "Johnny has a nice face" or "Johnny can brush his teeth." Children overwhelmingly chose the latter type of statement, indicating again their preference for action descriptions of the self.

The results of Keller, Ford, and Meachum's study add a new dimension to our understanding of self-knowledge in early childhood. These results need not be taken as a contradiction of the "physicalistic" level proposed by the researchers cited above, as long as the notion "physicalistic" is conceived broadly enough to include physical actions, as well as body image and material possessions. In fact, this is in line with Selman's use of the word physicalistic: Selman's illustrative examples of his first self-awareness level include instances of children speaking about their actions. But this may be a too broad use of terms. For the sake of precise developmental description, it may be wisest to separate the notion of active self from the notion of physical self. In fact, in light of Keller, Ford, and Meachum's study, we might conclude that the active self predominates in the preschool years. This conclusion also accords with an earlier statement by Secord and Peevers, who claimed on the basis of free-response data that kindergarten children describe themselves almost exclu-

[108] Keller, Ford, & Meachum, 1978.

sively in terms of activities like play.[109] This may or may not be too strong a conclusion. Certainly we must give some recognition to Broughton and others' consistent evidence in favor of bodily and material self-definitions in very young children. Even if action does dominate self-knowledge at early developmental levels, it is clearly used along with more blatantly physical notions like body image and material possessions. It seems that elements of both active and physical self can be found in the preschool years. As long as we do not confuse action with other physicalistic notions, we can see that self may be conceived in multiple dimensions even in the early phases of development.

There are also reasons to believe that action continues to be an important element in older children's self-knowledge, only in a somewhat different way. In their study of children's free responses to self questions, Secord and Peevers report that even by third grade, children describe the self primarily in terms of activities.[110] But there is a new quality in the third-graders' active self-statements: Unlike preschoolers, who describe self in terms of its typical activities ("I ride a bike"), older children describe themselves in terms of their active abilities relative to others ("I can ride a bike better than my brother"). Secord and Peevers describe this as a shift from a focus on the self's habitual action to a focus on the self's action competencies. It indicates that children are now distinguishing themselves from others in comparative rather than absolute terms. That is, the issue is no longer what I do (or don't do), but what I can do well in comparison with others. This developmental shift serves the differentiating function of self, since it provides a sharper means of establishing one's differences as an individual.

A recent set of findings in social-psychological research confirms the developmental shift noted by Secord and Peevers. In a programmatic series of studies, Diane Ruble has investigated children's use of *social comparisons* in their self-evaluations.[111] The basic design of these studies was to give children a difficult task and then to offer them feedback on their own performance, as well as information about the performances of other children their age. Subjects were then asked for self-evaluations. Ruble found that children younger than seven made almost no reference to the information about other children's performances. Rather, they based their self-evaluation on the "absolute standard" of whether or not they completed the task. In contrast, children over age seven frequently compared their performance against those of others, and based their self-evaluation on such social comparisons. Concordant with Ruble's findings, other researchers have noted the same change in children's active self statements during middle childhood. Interestingly, two independent studies came to a remarkably similar quantitative conclusion: at around age seven, children's use of comparative competence notions in their descriptions of self and others triples.[112]

---

[109] Secord & Peevers, 1974.
[110] Ibid.
[111] Ruble, Boggiano, Feldman, & Loebl, 1980.
[112] Veroff, 1969; Ruble, 1983.

From the combined results of studies reviewed in this section, we can see the early use and later transformation of active knowledge of the self. In addition, we know that the self is often defined physically at early ages, and that psychological self notions emerge toward the end of childhood. There is also one further aspect of self-knowledge that can be found in children's statements: the social self. One researcher found that children as young as four sometimes describe themselves in terms of personality traits that have social significance.[113] For example, children call themselves "kind" or "nice," meaning that they act well with others. Further, by middle childhood, children consider that such social personality traits are a stable part of their self-definitions. Other researchers have noted that young children also refer to social group memberships in their self-descriptions.[114] A child might say, for example, that he is a boy scout or a Catholic. Although the social self does not seem to be as dominant during childhood as either the active or the physical self, it is occasionally present in the self-awareness of children at all ages. This again is an indication of the multiple bases of self-knowledge that exist during all phases of childhood development.

In our chapter on adolescent identity formation, we shall return to the subject of self-knowledge and its development. There we shall be able to tie together the threads of infant and childhood self-conceptions, forming a systematic genetic account. This will only be possible when we view the early developmental patterns in light of the major transformations and reorganizations occurring during the adolescent years.

A Case Study in Childhood Self-Development: The Autobiography of Jean-Paul Sartre

The development of individuality is best understood when considering the particulars of individual lives. Case histories of individuals not only exemplify and test general theoretical constructs but also offer new insights into certain human complexities that the general theoretical constructs may have missed. In Chapter 3, we saw the valuable potential of the individual case study in Escalona's analysis of John and Mary during their infant years. We shall now turn to a well-known childhood life history in order to both illustrate and amplify the theoretical assertions made in the chapter.

The case under examination is the early life of Jean-Paul Sartre, philosopher and playwright. At the age of sixty, Sartre wrote a retrospective account of his first ten years, documenting in careful detail the internal and external influences upon his initial life choices.[115] Because Sartre was well read in psychological theory, his retrospections are consciously directed at revealing

---

[113] Rotenberg, 1978.
[114] Livesly & Bromley, 1973.
[115] Sartre, 1964.

the critical psychological turning points of his unique personality. At the same time, Sartre tries to tell us his early life history in all its full, and not always theoretically tidy, complexity. The result is a blend of digested and undigested material, unusual both in its richness and its psychological insight. As a study in identity and self-formation, it surpasses in depth, continuity, and comprehensiveness any childhood case study currently in the psychological literature. Because of this, developmental psychologists often have turned to Sartre's autobiography for real-life illustrations of theoretical constructs. Robert White, for example, has used Sartre's life history to demonstrate White's notion of "self-dramatization" (the generation of dramatic self-images that influence one's life course).[116] Here we shall examine Sartre's life history as a means of demonstrating the processes of identity formation, self-development, and individuation during childhood.

The focal point of Sartre's autobiographical account is his construction of personal identity as a "man of letters." So central is this particular construction to Sartre's life history that his autobiography itself is entitled *The Words*, and its only two chapters are named "Reading" and "Writing." Sartre's description of his first ten years reveals a continuing but progressively evolving use of reading and writing as a means of defining his identity. Although the particulars of literary activity may be unique to Sartre and other writers-in-training, the general course of his childhood identity search conforms to the normative patterns outlined throughout this chapter.

Sartre entered his childhood years with unquestioned feelings of self-worth, a legacy of a devoted mother and a doting grandfather. His father died shortly after Sartre was born, and this event in itself bolstered Sartre's security in his mother's love and his own self-esteem:

> I was a good child: I found my role so becoming that I did not step out of it. Actually, my father's early retirement had left me with a most incomplete "Oedipus complex." No Superego, granted. But no aggressiveness either. My mother was mine; no one challenged my peaceful possession of her. I knew nothing of violence and hatred; I was spared the hard apprenticeship of jealousy... I am adored, hence I am adorable. What could be more simple, since the world is well-made? I am told that I am good-looking, I believe it... I know my worth.[117]

Sartre's feeling of unchallenged self-confidence provided him with a sense of goodness in the world and himself, not unlike that described by Erikson's notion of "basic trust." This sense enhanced Sartre's first experiments with entertaining others with words. As a young child, Sartre recalls delighting adults by his childish "words of wisdom," never failing to provoke admiration for even the silliest statements: "I pronounce true oracles, and each adult interprets them as he wishes. The Good is born in the depths of my heart, the True in the young darkness of my Understanding. I admire myself on trust: my words and gestures have a quality that escapes me and that is immediately

---

[116] White, 1972.   [117] Sartre, 1964, pp. 26–27.

apparent to grown-ups."[118] Here we see that Sartre's initial forays into creative language were colored by the tone of trust and self-confidence established during the infant years. In this manner, according to Erikson's framework, initiative follows from basic trust and autonomy. In Sartre's words, "I keep creating myself; I am the giver and the gift. . . I trust people."[119]

The initiatives of early childhood are often playful and symbolic, as discussed in Chapter 4. As noted above, Sartre makes frequent mention of his experimentations with words, both in social interaction with adults and in solitary play. His first fascination with books occurred long before he understood reading as a serious activity to be learned. Rather, the child Sartre used books much as other children use toys or dolls: as objects for pretend play and fantasy. Sartre describes long episodes of mimicking adults by pretending to read books. In this manner, his play with books was, at the same time, symbolic and imitative, revealing important childhood identifications that were beginning to influence his behavior.

As Erikson's theory indicates, the establishment of basic trust and secure attachments during infancy paves the way both for the playful initiatives of early childhood and for productive identifications with role models. Part of young Sartre's initial intrigue with books arose out of exactly such an identification. The role model was Sartre's doting grandfather, and Sartre's recollections clearly show how much his first bookish interests owed to this childhood identification:

> I began my life as I shall no doubt end it: amidst books. In my grandfather's study there were books everywhere. . . I would touch them secretly to honor my hands with their dust, but I did not quite know what to do with them, and I was a daily witness of ceremonies whose meaning soon escaped me: my grandfather, who was usually so clumsy that my grandmother buttoned his gloves for him, handled those cultural objects with the dexterity of an officiant. Hundreds of times I saw him get up from his chair with an absent-minded look, walk around his table, cross the room in two strides, take down a volume without hesitating, leaf through it with a combined movement of his thumb and forefinger as he walked back to his chair, then, as soon as he was seated, open it sharply to the "right page."[120]

Drawn to reading out of admiration for his grandfather's mysterious literary powers, the young child's attraction to books took on more than an intellectual flavor. There is a sensual and consciously erotic tone in Sartre's recollection of his first acquaintance with books:

> At times I would draw near to observe those boxes which slit open like oysters, and I would see the nudity of their inner organs, pale, fusty leaves, slightly bloated, covered with black veinlets, which drank ink and smelled of mushrooms.[121]

From such observations, the young Sartre developed a sense of shared affective experience between himself and his grandfather, spurring on even more intense and enduring identification around literary achievement. This

[118] Ibid, p. 31.
[119] Ibid, p. 32.

[120] Ibid., p. 40.
[121] Ibid., p. 41.

combination of a strong affective bond with an enduring identification has been noted by virtually every identification theorist discussed in Chapter 5. For Sartre, the combination was the source of a renewed self-confidence, as well as the source of an awakened motivation toward literary achievement:

> He was surely right, since he was a professional. I knew he was. He had shown me, on a bookshelf, a series of stout volumes bound in brown cloth. "Those, my boy, were written by grandfather." How proud I felt! I was the grandson of a craftsman who specialized in the making of sacred objects, who was respectable as an organmaker, as a tailor for Ecclesiastics. I saw him at work.[122]

Soon, however, the child Sartre perceived the need for real (rather than imagined) skill of his own. The playful initiatives amd symbolic identifications of early childhood were no longer sufficient for either maintaining or developing his sense of identity and self-worth. Actual competence, meeting the objective tests of real-world tasks, was required. For Sartre, this challenge was again met in the context of linguistic achievement, just as for other children it might be met in the context of athletics, crafts, music, mathematics, or a host of other individual ways. And for Sartre, as for all children, the challenge of acquiring serious competence was a gradual process, subsuming most of the childhood years. This is the period of life known in psychoanalysis as *latency*. According to Erikson, it is the time of the industry versus inferiority crisis, normally culminating in a sense of task identification that will provide a basis for successful identity formation during the adolescent years.

Sartre first acquired real skill when he learned to read. His family initiated the instruction, but soon Sartre was giving himself his own "private lessons." When he was finally able to read a grown-up book from beginning to end, Sartre for the first time experienced the pleasures and powers of genuine competence:

> I was wild with joy. They were mine, those dried voices in their little herbals, those voices which my grandfather brought back to life with his gaze, which he heard and I did not hear! I was going to listen to them, to fill myself with ceremonious discourse, I would know everything![123]

As Sartre himself notes, for him, this achievement had the same importance as learning to ride a bike, to work around the house, or to care for pets has for many other children. It was a forum for the expression and elaboration of his self-efficacy.

For Sartre as an individual, the early pleasure found in reading set the stage for a unique concentration of literary ability and motivation. Throughout childhood, Sartre would continue his search for competence and task identification in the linguistic arena. Reading soon turned into writing, and this provided Sartre with a firm foundation for childhood identity—a foundation, as it turned out, that would prove stable throughout his life. As soon as he began to write stories, the child Sartre envisioned himself as a "great writer." This

---

[122] Ibid., p. 43.   [123] Ibid., p. 48.

vision was reinforced by the reactions of his mother and grandfather, who treated Sartre as a budding genius. Visitors to the Sartre household were often shown the young prodigy working at his desk, and they were ostentatiously told not to disturb the boy in the act of creation. At this point, Sartre had no objective verification of his emerging talent (other than the flattery of his family); and in his later recollections, the author doubts that he had yet even developed such talent. Still, the positive feedback from others, combined with his own enjoyment of the activity, was enough to provide him with his childhood identity:

> I was beginning to find myself. I was almost nothing, at most an activity without content, but that was all that was needed. I was escaping from play-acting. I was not yet working, but I had already stopped playing... By writing I was existing...I existed only in order to write, and if I said "I," that meant "I who write."[124]

The sense of self emanating from this identity construction was both positive and autonomous. "I know joy," writes Sartre, "The public child was making private appointments with himself." In this manner, as noted earlier in this chapter, self-identity, self-knowledge, and self-esteem are linked. Self-identity serves the function of establishing one's individuality separate from others, as in Sartre's belief in his own special mission to write. Self-knowledge, particularly in its *I* aspect, enables one to construct a sense of self that is only partly determined by social influences. And positive self-esteem rests upon one's sense of control over one's own destiny, a sense that derives directly from one's success at constructing one's own personal identity.

Like any child, by age ten, Sartre had many challenges still to face in his search for a stable identity. In fact, as we shall see in Chapter 8, Erikson believes that the major crisis period of identity formation comes at the end of adolescence, the period of child identifications being no more than a necessary prelude to the main drama. In Sartre's case, his autobiographical account offers several indications of ways in which his childhood identity needed to be reformulated to meet the demands of adolescent social and personal life. For one thing, he had an unrealistic view of his own physical beauty, fostered by his adoring family. His physical self-conception needed to be revised so that he no longer expected to look like the figures in the romantic plays that he so admired. Second, he notes some incidents in which he was surprised to learn that a masculine identity implied sex-role requirements all its own. Third, and most importantly, he learned that literary success does not come easily or automatically. He reports some embarrassing failures at entertaining people with his words and stories as he grew older. As could be expected, his family and peers became more critical of his efforts once he was older, no longer lavishing praise simply on mimicry.

In order to retain his identity as a "great writer" while still maintaining

---

[124] Ibid., p. 153.

harmonious family and peer relations, Sartre was forced to decide that his writer's self must "remain incognito for a while."[125] Accordingly, he was able to participate in a normal series of childhood friendships while still retaining the notion that he had a special calling all his own. The special calling, as we know by now, would later reawaken to give the world one of its great literary figures.

We have discussed Sartre's autobiography in light of the main themes of this chapter—identity, self, and the search for individuality. Although Sartre certainly had an exceptional life, the course of his early social development reveals many of the same patterns that we find in children everywhere. The particulars may be unusual, but this is true for all individuals: such particulars are the "stuff" of individuality, whatever similarities there may be in the general process of individuation. The individuating aspect of social development may be seen as a construction of one's own particulars in a way that establishes one's own uniqueness while at the same time enabling one to find a mutually beneficial connection with the social order.

Summary

During childhood, several sources of individual differences between children begin to have especially broad social and personality consequences. Ego-control and ego-resiliency are personality dimensions that refer to one's manner of mediating between one's impulses and reality. By age three, children differ significantly from one another in their degree of ego-control and ego-resiliency. Both dimensions are stable over years of a child's life. In addition, research has found developmental continuity between both dimensions at age three and children's social behavior at least as late as age seven. For example, three-year-olds who show marked signs of ego-undercontrol tend to be aggressive, domineering, uninhibited, and noncompliant in their social play years later. Three-year-old ego-overcontrollers tend to become shy and socially withdrawn. Children assessed as highly ego-resilient at age three later become popular and particularly responsive to the needs of others. Children who are neither ego-resilient nor adequately ego-controlled at age three often later become immobilized and anxious, feeling victimized and helpless in their social encounters.

Two poles of cognitive style that also have social-developmental significance as early as childhood are field independence, in which firm boundaries are drawn between self and the external world, leading to a primary reliance on internal frames of reference; and field dependence, in which self and nonself are closely connected, leading to reliance on information provided by outside events and persons. Field-independent persons are individualistic, aloof, and concerned with principles more than personal matters, whereas

[125] Ibid., p. 217.

field-dependent persons are socially sensitive, concerned with others, and easygoing in social interactions. Research has linked these cognitive styles to culturally induced child-rearing patterns. For example, hunting societies orient children toward field independence by training them to make finely tuned descriptions of their environment. Agricultural societies, on the other hand, orient children toward field dependence by emphasizing communication, sharing, and close connections between self and others. Within modern technological societies, both types of child-rearing emphasis can be found, and children as young as five may show tendencies toward either field independence or dependence.

Gender is another source of individual differences with far-reaching social consequences. In children's free play, two sex differences between boys and girls have been commonly observed. First, boys play more roughly than do girls. Second, boys tend to play with boys, whereas girls tend to play with girls. These two sex-linked features of children's free play may be related to one another. Studies have shown that boys find the rougher style of their male playmates appealing, whereas girls in groups generally conduct their play peacefully, creating systems of rules to regulate their interactions. The tendency of boys to play rougher than girls may be a universal phenomenon.

Another socially significant sex difference that is found across cultures is the greater propensity of girls to be nurturant, particularly with children younger than themselves. Nurturance toward younger children is commonly found in girls as young as three, standing in stark contrast to boys, who generally confine their behavior to playing with and sometimes acting aggressively toward a younger child. This sex difference is sharpest in cultures that encourage girls to perform necessary household tasks at an an early age. In particular, in some societies, parents rely heavily upon their daughters for baby-sitting with siblings, and in these societies, the discrepancy between boys' and girls' nurturant inclinations is especially severe.

Although child-rearing practices certainly influence the acquisition of individual characteristics like cognitive style and sex-typed behavior, research has shown that direct internalization mechanisms cannot account for this influence. In relation to sex typing, for example, it has been found that the extent to which a parent personifies a sex role (male or female) has little to do with how sex-appropriate the child's behavior becomes. For a sufficient explanation of the sex-typing process, the child's cognitions about gender and sex role must be taken into account. At a very early age (at least as young as three) children recognize that gender has behavioral implications. As they grow older, children's understanding of sex-role conventions becomes increasingly informed and sophisticated, as social-cognitive research has demonstrated. Developing a sexual identity is a process of reconciling one's behavior with one's conception of sex role and its social implications.

Sexual identity is only one aspect of a child's total psychosocial identity. During childhood, a wide variety of new insights concerning the identifying features of self emerges. Erikson's stage model describes the child's transition through three successive childhood phases in the search for identity. Each phase of identity development is linked to a major psychosocial crisis that, according to Erikson, provides the dominant theme of that life period. Following from the infant resolution of the basic trust crisis (as a result of which the infant develops a sense of mutual recognition of self and other), the child confronts the childhood crisis of autonomy versus shame and doubt. Out of this crisis, in terms of the child's identity, the child forges a "will to be oneself." The next childhood crisis is initiative versus guilt, from which the child derives a positive "anticipation of roles" in an identity sense. The fruition of childhood identity comes during the next crisis, industry versus inferiority. From this crisis, the child develops a sense of task identification that enables him to establish an identity on the basis of beliefs that "I am what I can make work." At this point, the child is ready to enter adolescence with an identity firmly grounded in knowledge of his own particular competencies. This will be necessary to meet the challenges of the adolescent identity crisis.

A positive and well-organized psychosocial identity is contingent upon one's sense of self. The sense of self has two aspects, one affective and one cognitive. The affective aspect is called "self-esteem" and has been measured and studied in a large body of child research. In general, research has found positive self-esteem to be connected with a belief in one's efficacy and a sense of control over one's destiny. Family conditions that engender positive self-esteem in children include many of the same characteristics found to be optimal in the socialization research described in Chapter 5: clear communication between parent and child, democratic decision making, and the encouragement of emotional expressiveness. Researchers believe that low self-esteem in children adversely influences children's school performance and peer relations, generally interfering with their attempts to successfully adapt to their environments. Some psychologists claim that childhood self-esteem is the most revealing predictor of mental health later in life.

The cognitive aspect of self is called "self-understanding" or "self-knowledge," and it changes radically during the childhood years. For young children, physical notions predominate. Size, sex, age, and appearance are critical defining features of self during this period. In addition, and perhaps even more importantly, young children view themselves in terms of their active behavior and abilities: preschoolers often see themselves as someone who can ride a bike, help mommy with the dishes, and so on. Later in childhood, children show a greater awareness of their mental qualities, such as their ideas and desires. They also view their active abilities in a comparative light. It is not only important to them that they can play baseball, but also that they are good baseball players relative to others. This, of course, corresponds to Erikson's notions of task identification and special competence that develop from middle to late childhood. Finally, older children begin to define themselves in terms of their social relations and social group memberships. All of these trends in self-understanding development set the stage for the consolidation of self-knowledge during the adolescent period.

depends salience di upon such of mensions

Childhood individuality is best understood in the context of individual lives. One carefully documented childhood life history is that of Jean-Paul Sartre. Sartre's retrospections reveal many of the principles put forth by psychologists who have analyzed children's search for identity and self-definition. Although the particulars of Sartre's life are unique, the molding of these particulars into a stable personal identity follows a social-developmental pattern common to the individuation process in everyone.

Chapter 7

Adolescent Social Relations

THE shift from childhood to adolescence is marked by dramatic changes in all aspects of social life. Peer relations multiply and intensify, family relations are restructured, and the adolescent encounters a number of new demands and expectations in social engagements of every type. In addition, the adolescent begins to participate seriously, and almost as an equal, in the basic institutions of society-at-large, anticipating the day when he or she will acquire the full rights and responsibilities of a citizen.

This chapter will trace the development of peer, family, and societal relations during adolescence. Many have stressed the particular significance of the peer relation during the adolescent years, claiming that, at least in contemporary society, peer-group bonds replace family bonds in most respects. But others have argued that, despite the adolescent's increasing interest in peer relations, family ties still remain strong and critically important for most teenagers. This latter group claims that peer and family relations serve different, but equally essential, functions in adolescent social development. This is the same point made in the childhood section of this book, and we shall hold to it for the adolescent years as well.

Toward the end of the teen years, the adolescent begins directly to confront societal institutions such as the economic, legal, and political system.

No longer are social-institutional realities communicated solely through the family. The adolescent often looks for a job, must obey the law (or else assume the consequences), and is given some genuine political and legal rights (such as voting). For these reasons, the nature of society becomes an issue of major concern during adolescence. More so than at any previous period of life, the adolescent is exposed to the particular historical and social-cultural forces of the times. Adolescents themselves, with their expanding cognitive abilities and their emerging social and self-consciousness, are often acutely aware of these particular forces; their development cannot be understood without taking these forces into account. Further, societies constantly change, and each generation of adolescents confronts unique historical events. As a consequence, every cohort of youth shares certain formative experiences special to members of that cohort. These experiences, though not general across generations, are a critical part of growing up during every historical period, and they must be examined in any account of social development. Social scientists who study the particular historical influences on youth development are said to maintain a "life-course" perspective. In this chapter, once we have outlined some general features of adolescent social relations, we shall discuss some historical and social-cultural forces that have influenced the social development of particular generations of youth in recent times.

Adolescent Peer Relations

Two striking changes occur in peer relations during the teen years. The first of these changes is continuous with developmental trends in childhood peer relations: the nature and meaning of friendship continues to evolve, taking on new and more elaborate dimensions. The second striking change, however, is far less continuous with the peer interactions of childhood: some of the adolescent's peer relations suddenly become sexual in nature, and this sexuality begins to pervade many of the adolescent's peer heterosexual encounters.

Friendship

In the childhood section of this book, we saw that the nature of friendship changes as children grow older. During early childhood, friendship consists of sharing activities and material goods with a playmate. But later in childhood, friendship implies helping and trusting within a stable relationship. Thus, with development, children express a greater sense of mutuality in their friendships. During the adolescent years, this trend toward greater mutuality in friendships continues, aided by the emergence of new interpersonal needs and insights.

More than do younger children, adolescents speak about friendship as having two essential qualities: loyalty and intimacy.[1] We do not know whether or not younger children have some unverbalized recognition of loyalty and intimacy that they cannot express in an experimental setting, but from various studies, it does seem clear that adolescents are more consciously aware of the importance of these qualities in a relationship. Consequently, adolescents are more likely to choose and maintain friendships that offer them these qualities, and this tendency seems to increase with age and social development. Several empirical studies of adolescent peer affiliations have confirmed this developmental trend toward greater mutuality in friendships through loyalty and intimacy.[2]

What are the new insights that enable adolescents to develop a finer awareness of loyalty and intimacy, and of mutuality generally, in their friendships? In his large-scale interview study of children and adolescents, James Youniss analyzed the ways in which young adolescents develop these critical interpersonal notions.[3] Youniss asked his subjects to define friendship and to describe how two people initiate, maintain, and terminate a friendship. He also asked subjects how people become close friends, or best friends.

According to Youniss, there are two notions central to the emergence of adolescent friendship conceptions: *mutual understanding* (which subsumes *loyalty*) and *intimacy*. Mutual understanding means an appreciation of the reciprocal nature of friends' activities, abilities, and personalities. That is, it means understanding how different persons can interact in a mutually beneficial way with one another. An early version of this appreciation was present even during childhood, since it is implicit in all acts of cooperation, and children do cooperate in their sharing and helping activities. For this reason, Youniss argues, friendship at all ages is a fertile ground for the growth of mutual understanding in some form, however primitive. But earlier in childhood, the appreciation of reciprocal exchange between friends is still incomplete, and the promise of genuine mutuality between friends is still unfulfilled. This is because prior to adolescence, children do not fully understand one another as "persons."

Understanding another's "personhood" means knowing that others share some of one's own abilities, interests, and inner experiences, but also that the other has a distinct personality that differs from one's own in significant ways. A landmark of early adolescence is a fascination with the particular interests, life histories, and personalities of one's friends. In short, there is a wish to understand one's friends as individual persons, and an accompanying need to be understood by one's friends in a similar manner. People are considered special and unique. As a consequence, adolescents begin choosing their friends carefully, since they now understand the challenge of coordinating two differing personalities in order to maintain the friendship relation. They also realize

---

[1] Selman, 1976b; Bigelow & LaGaipa, 1975; Bigelow, 1977; Berndt, 1981.

[2] Douvan & Adelson, 1966; Douvan & Gold, 1966; Coleman, 1970, 1974.

[3] Youniss, 1980.

the potential advantages of two persons with different strengths and abilities pooling their efforts for each other's benefit. In this sense, adolescents gain new insights into the complementary nature of friendship.

Once adolescents realize that friends are unique persons who share a complementary relationship, writes Youniss, they have a firmer sense of commitment to the relationship. This is because they understand that in a friendship, two different persons extend themselves for each other's benefit: friends share experiences, are interested in one another, get to know one another, and offer each other help and consolation when necessary. Such a relationship by nature must be long-lasting. Adolescents therefore express a sense of commitment to their friendships. Related to this sense of commitment is the new loyalty to one's friends. For Youniss, this loyal commitment is simply another aspect of the mutual understanding that develops during the adolescent years.

Intimacy, the second notion critical to adolescent friendship development, is constructed in three interrelated ways, according to Youniss. First, adolescents see friendships as a forum for *self-revelation.* One can openly share one's innermost feelings and opinions with a friend. One adolescent put it this way:

> A friend is a person you can talk to, you know, show your feelings and he'll talk to you. You can talk more freely to a friend. Someone you can tell your problems to and she'll tell you her problems. They are open. You can tell a friend everything. A friend is a person you can really tell your feelings to; a person you can. . .confide in; tell them what you feel and you can be yourself with them.[4]

Hand in hand with self-revelation go the other two aspects of intimacy, *confidence* and *exclusivity*. Confidence is one's belief that one's self-revelations in a friendship will not be used against one. This belief enables one to "be oneself" with friends without suspicion. Exclusivity, a characteristic often noted in teenage peer relations, is the belief that one's intimacies should be limited to certain selected friendships. Consequently, one need not fear that one's secret inner experiences will be exposed to the world at large, but rather that they will be shared only with trusted friends. In the words of another adolescent:

> Friends can keep secrets together. They can trust that you won't tell anybody. You won't expect them to tell anybody else. You know she won't tell anybody anything. If you tell somebody something, they won't use it to get revenge on you when you get in a fight. You talk about things you wouldn't tell other people.[5]

In general, adolescents tend to piece together a number of new insights into the nature of persons and interpersonal relations, forging in the process a new conception of friendship. The central features of this new conception are mutual understanding and intimacy, which support one another in the adolescent's thinking. For example, the adolescent believes that one can reveal oneself intimately to a friend precisely because friends understand one another in a

---

[4] Ibid., p. 181. [5] Ibid.

special way. The greater empathy that flows from this shared understanding assures one that an intimate confidence will not be betrayed. In this sense, mutual understanding and intimacy feed into one another, and make possible further extensions of oneself in friendship. As one of Youniss's subjects put it:

> You can tell her everything. They understand you more than other people do. A friend is a person I trust in and have faith in; you can believe in friends.[6]

Similar trends in adolescent friendships are revealed in the upper levels of Robert Selman's developmental friendship sequence.[7] Like Youniss, Selman reports that adolescent friendships are marked by a conscious sense of mutuality, intimacy, and loyal commitment. Selman, however, describes two developmental levels of friendship during adolescence, the first emerging during the transition from childhood to adolescence and the second during the mid to late teen years. In Selman's sequence, these are levels 3 and 4, respectively, following from his three childhood levels (0, 1, and 2) described in Chapter 5 of this book.

Selman's level 3 sounds very much like Youniss's analysis of adolescent conceptions. Selman calls this the stage of "intimate and mutually shared relationships," and writes that at this level "friendships are seen as a basic means of developing mutual intimacy and mutual support; friends share personal problems."[8] This sense of mutual intimacy, writes Selman, enables the young teenager to place trust in the stability and continuity of the relationship. Even though one may experience conflicts with a friend, one can still maintain the friendship. Selman contrasts this belief with the "fair-weather" view of friendship prevalent at level 2. Adolescents, unlike children, see friendships enduring in spite of difficult and painful incidents that friends may encounter together. Friendship, therefore, becomes more than simply an exchange of favors or a shared intention to cooperate with one another on particular occasions. It becomes an ongoing relation that transcends particular events, however disagreeable. In fact, there is even the sense that conflicts and disagreements may in the long run strengthen a friendship.

Interestingly, in analyzing the adolescent's construction of this new friendship conception, Selman focuses on a notion that was also central in Youniss's analysis: the adolescent's awareness of the unique personalities of others. In Selman's analysis, however, this awareness plays a somewhat different role than in Youniss's account. Selman writes that, because the adolescent is aware that friends can differ from one another on deep personal grounds, adolescents recognize that some conflicts and disagreements inevitably will arise between even the closest friends. Such conflicts, it is now realized, reveal nothing negative about the quality of the friendship. In fact, conflicts and disagreements may be seen as a sign of a good friendship. They are an expression of open communication between people who are "being them-

[6] Ibid., p. 184.
[7] Selman, 1980.

[8] Ibid., p. 111.

selves" (as one should with friends), and who therefore will differ with one another on occasion, since all persons are to some extent different from all others. For both Selman and Youniss, therefore, knowing others "as persons" helps adolescents establish continuing, long-lasting friendships. Selman shows how this knowledge gives the adolescent a better perspective on conflict within a friendship. Youniss, on the other hand, emphasizes its role in the development of genuine mutual understanding between persons with complementary yet different interests, abilities, and personalities.

Selman's level 4, the stage of "autonomous interdependent friendships," builds on the strengths of level 3, but it extends the notion of friendship beyond the early adolescent peer groups. The notion of mutual intimacy is maintained, but it no longer implies exclusivity or limitation of friendships to a select few. Rather, writes Selman, friendships become "autonomous" in the sense that "each person accepts the other's need to establish relations with others and to grow through such experiences."[9] This means that lines of intimate communication are kept open to persons far beyond the tight-knit "cliques" of the early teen years. Yet the "interdependence" of friends is still recognized, in the sense that friends are seen as mutually supportive in a psychological way. Only now, this support is seen on a broader scale, extending to a variety of friendship relations of differing significance and intensity.

The Peer Social Life of the Adolescent

Observations from sociological studies of adolescent social life have confirmed both Youniss's and Selman's accounts of developmental trends in adolescent friendships. In a classic study of urban adolescent peer groups, Dexter Dunphy made extended field observations of three hundred adolescents ages thirteen to twenty-one during their everyday social encounters.[10] Dunphy followed his subjects to beaches, social clubs, parties, street corners, and inside their homes, recording the pattern of their social interaction. He also interviewed each of his subjects about their friendships and other peer associations. Dunphy observed some striking age differences in the peer-group formation of his teenage subjects. Dunphy's sociological analysis of these age differences reveals some important features of adolescent social development.

Dunphy, like other sociologists before him, noted the two types of group structure commonly found in adolescent peer society: *cliques* and *crowds*. According to the standard definition, a clique is a close-knit group of two or more persons who are "related to one another in an intimate fellowship that involves going places and doing things together, a mutual exchange of ideas, and the acceptance of each personality by the other."[11] A crowd is larger and less cohesive than a clique. It is also less exclusive, because crowd membership is more loosely defined than is membership in a clique. Unlike crowds, "exclusion of those who do not belong is the express purpose of the clique." The

[9] Ibid., p. 113.
[10] Dunphy, 1963.
[11] Hollingshead, 1949.

clique, therefore, is an intensely intimate but constraining form of adolescent peer interaction, whereas a crowd is a looser and more expansive system of peer contact.

Among his three hundred subjects, Dunphy found forty-four cliques ranging in size from three to nine members, with an average membership of six. In addition, Dunphy found twelve crowds among the same population of subjects. The crowds varied in size from fifteen to thirty, with an average of twenty members. As can be seen from these numbers, many subjects were members of both a clique and a crowd simultaneously. Dunphy's conclusion was that adolescent crowds are informal associations of two to four cliques. The within-clique social life of the adolescent allows for intimate relations with a few select friends, and the superordinate crowd to which the clique belongs allows for exposure to a more extended set of acquaintances. Clique membership is therefore a prerequisite for crowd membership. Adolescents who were isolated from cliques were also isolated from crowds: no single subject without a clique belonged to a crowd. The reverse, however, did not hold: there were a number of cliques that were not joined to crowds. The clique, therefore, is the basic unit of adolescent social life, with the crowd offering an extended offshoot in most cases.

We can conclude from Dunphy's findings that the within-clique social life of adolescents allows for intimate relations with a few select friends. In contrast, the crowd to which the adolescent's clique often belongs exposes the adolescent to a more extended but casual type of peer acquaintance. Dunphy likens the clique to a family and remarks that the size of cliques (three to nine members) is not accidental. This approximates the size of a typical family. It is therefore a size with which the adolescent feels "at home" in his first extrafamilial set of intimate relations. The clique's "similarity in size to the family possibly facilitates the transference of the individual's allegiance to them and allows them to provide an alternative center of security."[12] The crowd, on the other hand, offers breadth but not depth in social relationships. Accordingly, the predominate activity within cliques is talking, and most clique meetings take place during the normal school week. In contrast, the predominate activity of crowds is parties and other organized social functions, almost always taking place on weekends.

From a developmental point of view, Dunphy's most interesting finding concerned the changing relation between cliques and crowds as adolescents grow older. As can be seen in Figure 7-1, Dunphy found five age-related stages of group development in his adolescent population. Each of these stages represents a different structure of peer-group membership. At stage 1, teenagers belong to single-sex cliques that are isolated from other cliques. At stage 2, there is some minimal interaction between cliques. This introduces the teenager to a superficial form of heterosexual contact and is the first (and most primitive) version of the crowd. At stage 3, the "upper status" members of

[12] Dunphy, 1963, p. 245.

unisex cliques begin to form ancillary heterosexual cliques, while still maintaining their original unisex clique associations. This is a transitional stage, leading the way to the formation of new, sexually integrated cliques at stage 4. These heterosexual cliques are linked to one another in superordinate group membership. Finally, at stage 5, the adolescent crowds break up, and the cliques often reduce themselves to heterosexual couples who "go steady" or become engaged.

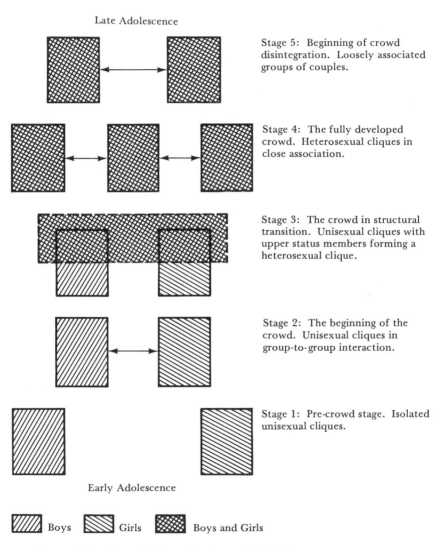

Late Adolescence

Stage 5: Beginning of crowd disintegration. Loosely associated groups of couples.

Stage 4: The fully developed crowd. Heterosexual cliques in close association.

Stage 3: The crowd in structural transition. Unisexual cliques with upper status members forming a heterosexual clique.

Stage 2: The beginning of the crowd. Unisexual cliques in group-to-group interaction.

Stage 1: Pre-crowd stage. Isolated unisexual cliques.

Early Adolescence

Boys   Girls   Boys and Girls

Figure 7-1. Stages of Group Development in Adolescence.

Source: D. Dunphy, The social structure of urban adolescent peer groups. *Sociometry*, 1963, *26*, 236. Reprinted with permission.

In Dunphy's developmental analysis, therefore, we see the adolescent moving from intimate single-sex friendships through a series of casual and intimate heterosexual contacts to a final phase of heterosexual intimacy. As one commentator has observed, Dunphy's research shows that "the real significance of the crowd is that it provides a means of transition from unisexual to heterosexual social relationships by facilitating interclique activities."[13] The adolescent's initial forays into intimacy are on the safe ground of single sex friendships within a family-size clique. The crowd offers opportunities for casual (and thus nonthreatening) acquaintances with the opposite sex. When the adolescent is ready, these acquaintances themselves become intimate, and the crowd structure is reorganized. Eventually, when it is no longer needed, the crowd is done away with, and the clique itself takes on a different, and even more intimate, meaning.

Sexual Relations

The adolescent's transition from unisexual cliques to heterosexual groupings opens the way for a special type of peer interaction: the sexual relationship. Sexuality adds several new dimensions to peer encounters. First, there are the intense physical sensations that often accompany sexual engagement. Second, there is the potential for new sorts of intimacy that sexuality alone engenders. Third, a sexual relationship often brings about a number of changes in the adolescent's role and position relative to other social groupings.

In American social life, the teenager's initial foray into sexual relations is called "dating." Large-scale sociological surveys of heterogenous populations of youth have shown that for teenagers, dating serves many diverse purposes:[14] *recreation*, including entertainment and sexual stimulation; *status seeking*, as a way of enhancing one's reputation and one's popularity; *independence assertion*, as a means of separating oneself from one's family; *social-skill seeking*, as a means of increasing one's interpersonal competence; *experimentation*, particularly with regard to previously unexperienced sexual activity; and *courtship*, as a means of more or less permanent mate selection.[15]

These different incentives are sometimes experienced in combination with one another, but more often vary systematically with the particular type of dating relationship that the adolescent has established. Casual relations are initiated and maintained with a different set of incentives and expectations than are more serious ones. Scholars have proposed that adolescent motivations for dating can be characterized as being along two independent continua: (1) expressive versus instrumental, and (2) emotional involvement versus uninvolvement.[16] On the first dimension, adolescents who consider dating to be a pleasurable end in itself are considered to be expressively oriented, whereas those who believe that it is a means to extrinsic goals (such as status or skill) are

[13] Coleman, 1980, p. 418.
[14] Smith, 1962; Grinder, 1966.
[15] McDaniel, 1969; Husbands, 1970; Rice, 1975.
[16] Skipper & Nass, 1966.

considered to be instrumentally oriented. On the second dimension, those who are intensely consumed by the dating relation are considered to be emotionally involved, whereas those who are relatively detached are considered to be uninvolved. Since each of these dimensions is a continuum, an adolescent's orientation to dating may fall anywhere on either dimension. But some patterns are particularly common and particularly significant. An instrumental orientation combined with emotional uninvolvement generally accompanies a casual relationship. Often such relations are short-lived and nonmonogamous. In contrast, a high instrumental orientation combined with emotional involvement generally accompanies mate-seeking relations, which tend to be relatively stable and monogamous. Expressive orientations combined with emotional involvement, on the other hand, accompany intense but often brief affairs.

Conflict and distress occur when the partners in a dating relationship do not share the same combination of orientations. For example, when one partner's incentives are expressive and emotional and the other partner's incentives are instrumental and unemotional, a conflictual state of disequilibrium is inevitable. Adolescent sexual relationships are frequently characterized by such states. This is particularly true in the mid-adolescent years, when teenagers begin dating in earnest. The transition to adulthood is marked by a greater concordance in the motivations and mutual expectations of dating partners. This results from a more conscious communication of intentions between the partners. But neither conflict nor instability in sexual relations are completely left behind in the adolescent years.

One systematic view of adolescent dating patterns has been presented by J. Delora in a structural analysis of dating ends (incentives), norms, and roles.[17] Delora analyzed typical patterns of sexual relations, such as the casual relation and "going steady." In each pattern, Delora found certain typical combinations of ends, norms, and roles. These ends, norms, and roles of predominant adolescent dating patterns are presented in Table 7-1. As can be seen from this scheme, each dating pattern has some internal coherence and regulating principles. Here again we see that problems occur when two partners differ in their view of which dating pattern they have established. Since during adolescence these patterns are being constructed for the first time, we might expect frequent discordancies and other errors of this type.

The wide variation of possible incentives and outcomes makes the sexual relationship among the most complex forms of peer interaction that the adolescent encounters. Not only must the adolescent make choices concerning the type of relationship to establish with a partner, but the adolescent also must coordinate these choices with the partner's expectations. For both partners, the heart of the challenge is to integrate the physical and social aspects of sexuality. This is no easy matter for the young teenager who only recently has become acquainted with sexual impulses and whose competence at establishing intimate relations with peers is only just forming. We might expect, therefore, that learning to express one's sexuality with another in a mutually satisfying

[17] Delora, 1963.

Table 7–1 Types of Dating Compared on Basis of Social Structure (Type of Dating)

Structural element	Casual	Steadily	Going steady	Engaged to be engaged	Engaged
Ends*	Getting acquainted	Entertainment Enjoyment	Companionship	Trial engagement	Getting ready for marriage
Norms	Impersonal Uninvolved Rational	Individualistic Free No commitment	Personalized Monogamous Intimate Emotional	Personalized Monogamous Intimate Emotional Oriented to future	Personalized Monogamous Intimate Emotional Oriented to future Rational plans
Status-role	Initiation of action by male Dominance of male authority	Initiation of action by male Dominance of male authority	Two-way initiation of action Equal authority	Two-way initiation of action Equal authority	Two-way initiation of action Equal authority Male-female assumption of specific responsibilities

*The *ends* of dating tended to be compounded as a couple moved from one type to the next.
Source: J. Delora, Social systems of dating on a college campus. *Marriage and Family Living*, 1963, *25*, 81–84. Reprinted with permission.

relationship would be a gradual and difficult process. This is an achievement that demands not only an understanding of one's own physical and social needs, but also the ability to communicate intimately with another about both parties' needs.

Despite mass-media accounts of widespread teenage sexuality, most adolescents are slow to develop sexual relations. Although many young teenagers experiment with brief sexual contact of one sort or another, sustained sexuality with another is normally a late occurrence.

> The public myths of the "appalling increase" of sexuality among high-school students may apply to some teen-agers, but it is not applicable to our group. The sexual feelings and impulses were recognized slowly and seemed to parallel, in a negative reciprocal way, the attachment that the adolescents felt to their mothers. In the beginning of the high-school years the majority of the students tended to deny the existence of strong sexual feelings. They coped with the energizing sexuality by becoming active in sports, studying, or "going out with boys." Toward the end of the high-school years the attitude changed. They were now interested in being with the opposite sex and wanted some experimentation in order to understand their own feelings and those of the girls. Did the fact that sexuality was essentially repressed during the first three years of high school harm the students? We have not found any evidence to support the theory that our students suffered either from arrested development or inhibited development; they are, however, developing slowly.[18]

Most research into teenage social life reveals the same pattern: a hesitant emergence of sexuality in the mid-adolescent years, beginning with casual experimentation and only gradually leading to sustained and intimate sexual relations.[19] The stable, intimate, and mutually satisfying heterosexual relation during adolescence is the exception rather than the rule. More commonly, teenage sexual partners do not share the same interpersonal goals and do not even communicate about the discrepancy. Often the two interact in an egocentric and almost "parallel" manner, with little interest in one another's expectations for the relationship.

Sometimes the adolescent failure to combine intimate communication with sexual engagement persists despite the establishment of formal arrangements such as marriage. In all-too-many cases, the teenage marriage is the result of extrinsic societal pressures, rather than an extension of a stable, close relationship in which the various goals of a sexual relationship have been integrated and shared by the two partners. One extreme instance of this was described by August Hollingshead in his classic study of middle-American adolescence, *Elmtown's Youth*.[20] Although few teenage marriages occur under such violent circumstances, the considerations that instigated this union are unfortunately paradigmatic for all-too-many such cases. The story begins when a young country girl, "mildly hysterical," walks seven miles through a rainstorm to the local prosecuting attorney's office:

---

[18] Offer, 1969, p. 214.

[19] Sorensen, 1973; Miller & Simon; 1980.

[20] Hollingshead, 1949.

That morning she had told her mother she was pregnant, and a family quarrel ensued among the girl, mother, and grandmother. When the father came home for lunch, he was told of the girl's condition. Another quarrel developed, this time between the father and the girl, with the grandmother and the mother doing what they could to keep the father from "horsewhipping" the girl. In his rage, the father told her to marry the boy before sunset. "When I come home, if you aren't married, I'll kill you both." The girl also reported that the father took his shot gun and a box of shells out to his truck and drove off to work. The girl's mother said, "You better go marry him; you know your father." The girl requested the prosecuting attorney to find the boy and make him marry her "right now." The attorney sent a sheriff's deputy and had the boy brought to the courthouse. The prospective groom drove a truck, which he parked in front of the courthouse while he came in with the deputy. The girl sat silent and wooden-faced in the attorney's office as the boy was brought in and confronted with her statement. He admitted he had been "with her a few times." The attorney asked, "Do you know what this means?"

"Sure I'll marry her, but I won't live with her. The kid isn't mine."

"When do you intend to marry Martha?"

"Now's as good a time as any. I gotta' deliver that load yet tonight; so let's get goin'."

The attorney turned to Martha and asked, "Do you want to get married now?"

"Yeh, the sooner the better; the old man means business."[21]

There is a widespread popular belief that teenage sexual relations have changed dramatically in the past twenty years, beginning with the "sexual revolution" of the 1960s. According to this common belief, teenagers have become sexually active at increasingly earlier ages, are more open and less constrained in their expressions of sexuality, and value promiscuity rather than stable monogamous relationships. Examinations of historical data, however, suggest that the notion of a recent "revolution" in teenage sexual practices and values is something of a myth. There have been some real, but gradual, changes in the ages at which adolescents initiate sexual activity. But these changes have been taking place since early in this century, with the greatest increase in early sexual activity occurring shortly after World War I, rather than in the 1960s.[22] Clinical evidence indicates that teenagers are as secretive and wary of sex as ever.[23]

As for sexual values, there is no evidence whatsoever that the vast majority of today's teenagers have revolted against earlier generations' mores by seeking promiscuity rather than stable relationships. There has always been a sex difference in teenage values, with boys more likely to seek "sexual adventure" with a number of partners, and girls more likely to seek a "romantic relationship" with one partner.[24] In addition, there has been a long-term trend, occurring over several decades, toward valuing premarital sexual intercourse with one's partner.[25] But the majority of adolescents still seek stability and commitment in their sexual relationships. They profess a desire eventually to

[21] Ibid., pp. 430–31.
[22] Rutter, 1980.
[23] Diament, 1970.

[24] Reiss, 1954.
[25] Reiss, 1976.

be married, and they expect fidelity from their mates.[26] Although a minority of adolescents do reject the idea of marriage in favor of sexual freedom, a far larger number hold traditional ideals of permanent relationships, monogamy, and family. For a surprisingly large number of contemporary adolescents (40 percent in one survey), consummate sexuality has been experienced only with the person one ultimately marries.[27]

In short, establishing mutually satisfying sexual relationships is as difficult and problematical for today's adolescents as for those in prior generations. The expression of sexuality in an interpersonal relation is a complex achievement that requires the coordination of many types of social and physical competencies, including communicative skills, empathy, and a firm sense of self. The British psychiatrist Michael Rutter writes:

> It is sometimes thought that sexual competence somehow "comes naturally" and that sexual experience is necessarily pleasurable by some innate mechanism, but it is evident that neither is the case. Sexual behavior includes many learned components and depending upon whether a person's first sexual experience is enjoyable or unpleasant he may not try again for many years or he may have intercourse again within a few days and continue to have sex regularly and frequently. . .Sexual intercourse tends to be most pleasurable within the context of a long relationship, emphasizing that sexuality and socialization are linked.[28]

Rutter and others have found that harmonious sexual relationships are rare in adolescence. Initial attempts to establish such relationships are normally unsuccessful because they are associated with tension and strife. Surveys of adolescent sexual attitudes typically find that most adolescents believe that they have sexual problems of one kind or another, and many report intense anxiety concerning sexual matters.[29] As we shall see again in the next chapter, sexual development is clearly one of the most challenging tasks in an individual's social development, presenting perhaps the greatest potential for interpersonal risks and rewards.

Family Relations during Adolescence

Because the adolescent spends a far greater proportion of time outside the home than the child or the infant, it seems natural to emphasize the significance of the adolescent's peer relations at the expense of the adolescent's family ties. Many social scientists have done just this, citing not only the obvious changes in how teenagers spend their time, but also some new attitudes and value orientations that teenagers frequently express. But it would be a mistake to underestimate the role of the family in the adolescent's social development. Parents continue to be of primary importance during the teenage years, in both direct and indirect ways. Directly, parents still communicate their knowledge and

---

[26] Sorenson, 1973; Yankelovich, 1974.
[27] Schofield, 1973.

[28] Rutter, 1980, p. 23.
[29] Schofield, 1973.

values to their teenagers; indirectly, parents serve as a crucial emotional support for their teenagers' broadening extra-familial social life. The popular notion that the family is ignored or abandoned during adolescence is wholly untrue in most cases.

One reason that the significance of adolescent family relations has been obscured in many social-scientific accounts is that methods for studying such relations are limited to surveys and interviews. The observational techniques that many researchers use to analyze parent-child relations are no longer appropriate when the child becomes an adolescent. Parents and adolescents are not normally together during prime daytime observational hours, and in most contemporary families do not even eat together with any regularity.[30] Further, the adolescent is more aware of an observer's presence than is a child, so that the observer risks recording interactions that are self-conscious, stilted, and therefore atypical. As a consequence, our knowledge of teenage family life is mostly indirect, deriving from questionnaires given to teenagers and their parents. Some questionnaire data have been informative, and we shall draw on them in this section. In such instances, interviews have been administered in sufficient depth to capture the quality of the adolescent's family interactions. Far too often, however, survey questions have avoided the central issues in adolescent family relations. Because of this and other methodological short-comings noted below, many such studies have come to misleading conclusions concerning adolescent social development. In examining the available evidence, therefore, we shall need to carefully evaluate the studies in this area in order to sift the accurate from the inaccurate accounts.

The Parental Role

Whatever the popular myths concerning "rebellious" or "alienated" adolescents, most empirical research has found that adolescents generally are attached to their home life in a strong and positive way. The large majority of adolescents find their family situations happy and harmonious.[31] Most adolescents say that they communicate well with their parents on all issues, including their most pressing problems and concerns.[32] Further, most adolescents share their parents' values and attitudes toward moral and political issues.[33] They frequently turn to their parents for guidance, particularly about their most important academic, career, and personal choices.[34] In general, the overall picture is that parents continue to be the primary source of advice and emotional support during the adolescent years. In large part, this is because they remain the most admired and trusted people in the adolescent's life.[35] It would be a mistake, therefore, to underestimate the parental role during adolescence.

The popular notion that adolescents reject parental influence in favor of peer influence has also been disproved by empirical research. In fact,

[30] Douvan & Adelson, 1966.
[31] Meissner, 1965; Offer, 1969.
[32] Meissner, 1965; Bengtson, 1970.
[33] Jennings & Niemi, 1968, 1975.
[34] Larson, 1972.
[35] Douvan & Adelson, 1966.

researchers find that parental and peer influences generally are concordant with one another; and in the occasional instance when they are in conflict, adolescents are as likely to follow parental guidance as peer guidance. In a series of studies on "parent-peer cross pressures," Clay Brittain posed parent-peer conflicts to groups of adolescents.[36] He found that adolescents were likely to choose the parent's course of action in situations having implications for career goals and future plans. Peer influence proved greater than parental influence only when issues of popularity and position in the adolescent's current peer society were at stake. Brittain concluded that adolescents respect the advice of both parents and peers, though in somewhat different areas of life. Other studies have confirmed this, reporting that parents are particularly heeded in educational and career matters.[37] On many central issues facing adolescents, such as marital, political, and economic choices, peer and parental influence are likely to be in the same direction, supporting rather than conflicting with each other.

Why do these frequently reported findings violate so many of our intuitive expectations about adolescent behavior and attitudes? There are a number of answers to this, each of which sheds some further light on the nature of adolescent development. One answer is that some adolescents are indeed disoriented and rebellious with parents, even though they may only be a small proportion of the total population. Yet many written accounts of this age period have focused exclusively on this small minority of troubled adolescents. This is certainly true of much literary work, like the American novelist J.D. Salinger's *Catcher in the Rye.* Many less troubled adolescents, of course, do identify with the heroes of such fictional work. But this does not mean that their lives are as tumultuous, or their futures as bleak, as the extremely troubled adolescents of much literary fiction.

Most clinical descriptions of adolescence also come out of unusual case data: psychotherapeutic sessions with disturbed teenage patients.[38] As one reviewer has written, "most of the clinical descriptions of stormy adolescence derive from studies of patient groups."[39] Such descriptions, of course, pertain mostly to those adolescents who are in sufficient stress to seek professional help. Yet these clinical descriptions often constitute our best-known psychological accounts of adolescence, and they are therefore taken as representative of this age period. Research with this population of adolescents often yields trends that are diametrically opposed to findings of research with normal adolescents. For example, one study found a strong tendency toward parent-child alienation and turmoil in adolescents with psychiatric disorders.[40] In light of the research cited above, it would clearly be a mistake to generalize this finding to normal adolescents.

Social science has contributed in yet another way to the popular underes-

---

[36] Brittain, 1963, 1968, 1969.
[37] Lesser & Kandel, 1969.
[38] Blos, 1962, 1970; Erikson, 1968.

[39] Rutter, 1980, p. 33.
[40] Rutter, Graham, Chadwick, & Yule, 1976.

timation of the parental role in adolescent development. Some of the major surveys of adolescent attitudes, because of their design, have provided data that lead to questionable conclusions concerning teenage perspectives on their relations with parents. The classic study of this kind was James Coleman's survey of seven thousand Chicago youth during the 1950s.[41] Coleman asked his subjects a number of questions that required them to compare their attitudes toward parents with their attitudes toward peers. Subjects' responses led Coleman to believe that there is a gulf between the adolescent peer culture and the adult world. Coleman wrote that today's teenagers live in an "adolescent society," with the peer culture being primary and sharply segregated from the adult culture. Coleman found that a surprising number of teenagers would rather incur a parent's disapproval than break up with a friend and would follow a friend's guidance on social life over that of a parent. Further, the personal qualities most valued by adolescents seemed to be peer-oriented rather than adult-oriented. In Coleman's sample, most teenagers preferred athletic accomplishment to academic achievement and prized popularity, humor, and leadership over moral or career-related personal virtues. Coleman's report bolstered the already-prevalent notion that contemporary adolescents have a culture of their own, separate and somewhat alien from the adult culture. This notion received further support from the media in the 1960s, when the phrase "generation gap" came to signify the alleged deterioration of relations between parents and adolescents. Coleman's conclusion set the stage for this bleak view:

> In our modern world of mass communication and rapid diffusion of ideas and knowledge, it is hard to realize that separate subcultures can exist right under the noses of adults—subcultures with languages all their own, with special symbols, and most importantly, with value systems that may differ from adults'. Any parent who has tried to talk to his adolescent son or daughter recently knows this. . . . To put it simply, these young people speak a different language. What is more relevant to the present point, the language they speak is becoming more and more different.[42]

But scholars have come to question Coleman's data as well as his interpretation of them. Some have pointed out that his procedure failed to elicit from subjects an in-depth view of their relations with parents.[43] Rather, the procedure forced children to contrast parental with peer influence, without obtaining information about the influence of parents in and of themselves. As a result, Coleman offered his subjects no opportunity to say that they may have been oriented *both* to parents and peers at the same time. In fact, many investigators believe that teenagers usually do hold this kind of dual orientation to parents and peers.[44] These investigators emphasize that an acceptance of peer values does not necessarily imply a rejection of parental values, and that

[41] Coleman, 1961.
[42] Ibid., p. 3.
[43] Offer, 1969.
[44] Rutter, 1980.

for most teenagers, the goal is to respect both and to coordinate them in a nonconflicting way.

Some researchers have concluded that coordinating the two sets of values is not such a difficult task for the teenager, since in many respects parental and peer values overlap. One researcher has reinterpreted Coleman's own data to show that "peer culture" defined by Coleman is largely a reflection of the adult culture, rather than a divergence from it.[45] For example, Coleman's finding that most teenagers value athletics over academics does not in itself mean that parental values were being rejected. The parents themselves may have communicated to their children a belief that athletics will make one more popular, and therefore happier, than academics during the school years. If so, there was really no discrepancy between the parental and peer value systems after all, at least insofar as they were communicated to the individual teenager. Unfortunately, Coleman did not gather enough data on parental influence apart from peer/parent contrasts to tell us how often such concordances between peer and parental values actually occur.

A final problem with Coleman's conclusions is that they were derived from data that were limited to one generation of adolescents who all shared similar historical experiences while growing up. Scholars who are sensitive to historical forces in human development are particularly disturbed by this limitation in Coleman's study, since it means that his data may be time-bound and relevant only to one specific cohort of youth. For example, one such scholar points out that the adolescents in Coleman's study were born in the early 1940s, and that an unusually high proportion of them therefore were deprived of their fathers' presence during their early years.[46] We know from other studies that father absence in the early years is often associated with family stress and conflict, particularly after the father returns. Children of this wartime birth cohort may have experienced unusual alienation from their parents throughout their development, but such alienation may be unique to this cohort (as well as to other occasional father-absent cohorts). If so, the peer orientation reported by Coleman would be an artifact of his time-bound study design. Although this conclusion is speculative, it makes us aware of how history can shape the lives of certain generations in special ways that do not touch other generations. The "life-course" approach to human development was established in order to take account of such special historical forces.[47]

Developmental Changes in Parent-Child Relations during Adolescence

The parental role in guiding and supporting the child continues to be essential during the teen years. Nevertheless, adolescence brings some important changes in the nature of the parent-child relation. These changes reflect the child's developing ability to make independent judgments about social issues, as well as both the parent's and the child's respect for this developing

[45] Offer, 1969.
[46] Elder, 1980.

[47] Ibid.

ability. The changes do not disturb the still indisputable leadership of the parent on most family matters, but they do restructure the family's views on this leadership, as well as the way in which the leadership is implemented.

What kinds of developmental transformations in the parent-child relation occur during adolescence? As we noted in Chapters 4 and 5, children establish very different types of relations with parents than with peers. The parent-child interaction is based on "complementarity," an indirect kind of reciprocity in which the child exchanges obedience for the parent's help and care. In this relation, the parent's authority is submitted to without choice or question. In contrast, the peer relation during childhood is based upon *direct* reciprocity. Peer interaction is on an equal footing, and children work toward finding mutually acceptable solutions in instances where they disagree. Because of this difference in the quality of the two relations, James Youniss hypothesized that the parent-child relation was the root of the child's knowledge and respect for the rules of the social order, whereas the child-child relation was the root of the child's concern for equality, fairness, and mutuality.

During adolescence the quality of both relations undergoes change. The developmental changes in adolescent peer relations have been described earlier in this chapter, in the section on friendship. As for the parent-child relation, it begins to take on some of the qualities that all along have characterized the peer relation. The complementarity of parent-child interactions is replaced by a more direct kind of reciprocity, as children and parents begin to see themselves as equals. The adolescent's obedience to the adult is still considered necessary, but now it is seen as a voluntary kind of obedience, subject to negotiation and compromise, rather than a forced and inflexible submission to authority. Adolescents still defer to their parents' knowledge and opinions, but they also believe that they have their own ideas of merit, distinct from those of their parents, and that these ideas can make a positive contribution to their families.

The result is a relation between parent and adolescent that contains a curious mixture of elements found in earlier child-child and child-adult relations. On the one hand, the authority of the adult is maintained, but on the other hand, the adolescent brings to this authority relation a peer-like orientation, based upon the parent's and adolescent's increasing respect for the adolescent's opinions. The following quotes from Youniss's teenage subjects demonstrate this new blend of self-respect combined with parental respect:

> Adults teach you what kindness is. When you're little, they say, this is what kindness is. You think your parents are perfect and hear what they say and do it. But you also meet other people's opinions like friends and their parents and they come to be your own opinions.
>
> It's easier for adults to be kind... They think in bigger terms, like helping the poor. Children think of little things, like sharing with friends.
>
> Basically their ideas are the same, but everybody thinks a little bit different. They may think it's kind not to associate with certain (peers), but you may think it's kind. (Where do you learn about it?) You pick it up from everybody here and there. When people do something to you, you do it back.
>
> Adults understand more and might know better. But sometimes you both

don't understand each other because everybody has a whole different mind. And they have different opinions. (What do you mean?) Like not being allowed to play with a friend because your parents have a bad impression of him. They misunderstand him; the way he is.[48]

Although the adolescent defers to the adult's greater knowledge and experience, the adolescent also recognizes that one has access to ideas and experience unknown to the adult. Further, the adolescent has confidence in the validity of these independent ideas and experiences. These conceptions result from the adolescent's earlier interpersonal insights formed in the course of peer interactions. The child initially discovers the possibilities of direct reciprocity and mutuality while sharing ideas with peers, and later he applies this discovery to relations with parents. The insights initially develop in the realm of peer relations because it is far easier to conduct directly reciprocal relations with an equal than with a superior. Combining an authority orientation with a determination to act as an equal is a more complex accomplishment. It borrows from insights acquired in both the peer and adult interactions of earlier days, and it integrates these insights into a new blend unique to adolescence.

The fascinating aspect of Youniss's analysis is that it reverses the usual common-sense notions about the relation betwen peer and adult learning. We normally expect that children learn social behavior from adults, and that they then apply what they have learned to their extra-familial friendships. Youniss believes that the social understanding process is played out in exactly the opposite direction. Children transform their relations with their parents during adolescence because of insights about equality and mutuality that they have acquired in earlier interactions with peers. Not only are the critical insights learned independently of adult instruction, but they also end up determining the nature of the adult's relational role in the child's life.

Life-Course Studies of the Adolescent's Family Life

Historians and other scholars working within the "life-course" approach have shown how particular historical forces can shape the nature and direction of adolescents' relations with their parents. For example, recent social-history research has documented several economic conditions of the past that have influenced parents' control over adolescents. In colonial New England, there was a major decline of parental control over adolescent boys in the space of a few generations.[49] This decline was the result of changes in economic opportunities for youth. During the first generation of settlers, fathers exercised firm and continuing control over their sons by holding onto land from their estates until relatively late in their children's lives. Since agriculture was the primary means of earning a living at that time, sons were forced to remain at home, under their father's authority, until well into maturity. By the third and fourth generations, however, the economic climate had changed. There was a rise in

[48] Youniss, 1980, pp. 266–67.   [49] Greven, 1970.

the population of cities and towns and an increasing scarcity of available land in the countryside. Because of this, there was a shift toward new occupations that one pursued outside the family. Sons would leave home, find jobs in the outside world, and marry early. Consequently, they would assume autonomous and equal relations with their parents while still teenagers. This was a move toward independence that would have been rare only a few generations earlier.

Other life-course studies have demonstrated similar historical influences on parenting during adolescence. In some cases societal changes have worked in the opposite direction of those in early New England, increasing rather than decreasing parental control over adolescents. The industrial revolution of the early nineteenth century stopped the increasingly early departure of teenagers from their families.[50] Rather than entering into jobs or apprenticeships, young adolescents now stayed in school in order to learn the advanced skills required by a more complex technological society. Secondary school education became the norm, rather than a privilege for the wealthy. Consequently, children remained at home throughout most of the teen years, under the continued support and authority of their parents. One historian has claimed that the decreased independence of adolescents resulting from this economic shift was "the most pronounced change in family roles caused by industrialization."[51]

In general, historians have found that parental control over adolescents is highly sensitive to economic and societal conditions. Forces that lead children out of their family homes at early ages decrease the degree and duration of parental control. Such forces include urbanization, wars, and depressions.[52] Forces that keep children at home—such as economic demands for prolonged schooling—increase parental control. Throughout history, boys have been most affected by family conditions related to economic opportunities, whereas girls have been most affected by family conditions related to marriage opportunities (and indirectly connected to the economic climate). This difference between the sexes, however, may be disappearing with the growing tendency of young women in technological societies to seek their own careers. In any case, the social-developmental implications of historically induced changes in family roles and teenage autonomy are clear. Such changes no doubt profoundly affect the development of interpersonal relations during adolescence, as well as the adolescent's search for a personal identity and a sense of self.

The Adolescent and Society: Moral and Political Development

As children grow into adolescence, they venture more and more beyond the confines of intimate family and friendship relations. These close relations are not replaced; family and friends continue to be of primary importance all

[50] Katz, 1975.
[51] Bloomberg, 1974.

[52] Elder, 1974; Modell, Furstenberg & Hershberg, 1976; Kett, 1977.

through adolescence. But added to the adolescent's continuing engagement in intimate social relations is a new awareness of social institutions and a new interest in the workings of society-at-large. The young adolescent either attains or anticipates a career, marriage, and full participant citizenship. As a consequence, he realizes that his social interactions may have an economic, legal, or political significance that goes beyond interpersonal meanings. In short, the transition to adolescence requires a perspective on collective social realities, a perspective that focuses on concerns broader than those contained within intimate interpersonal relations. The social system itself, with its laws, norms, procedures, and organizational features, becomes a matter of major attention during adolescence. This new orientation colors adolescent values and social conceptions of every kind.

Moral Development

In a very brief section of *The Moral Judgment of the Child,* Piaget tentatively describes a new moral awareness emerging in early adolescence. Piaget treats this new awareness as stage 4 or rule-following behavior, following developmentally from the first three childhood stages that we discussed in Chapter 4. Since the heart of Piaget's book was the transition from stage 2 to stage 3 (reflecting the child's shift from heteronomous to autonomous morality), Piaget gives only cursory treatment to stage 4. Yet, his brief descriptions reveal some central themes in the moral development of adolescents.

After Piaget documented the trend toward cooperation and mutual respect that he found in children moving from stage 2 to stage 3, he noted that the oldest children in his sample (ages eleven to thirteen) were doing something more than simply cooperating. Not only were these young teenagers participating as equals in the administering and following of game rules, but they were taking a special interest in the rules themselves. The interest was expressed by long discussions on the rationale behind certain rules and by efforts to construct new rules that would take care of previously unanticipated possibilities. The concerns of these young adolescents were in large part directed toward hypothetical situations. They seemed to take great pleasure in imagining complex situations that would require them to invent new rules or to qualify old ones. This fascination with rule making, according to Piaget, follows from the adolescents' acquisition of formal reasoning abilities enabling them first to anticipate all possible circumstances and then to invent new ways to deal with them. Piaget cites an example of this adolescent delight in the formal codification of behavior:

> We have described elsewhere the extraordinary behavior of boys. . .who, in order to throw snow-balls at each other, begin by wasting a good quarter-of-an-hour in electing a president, fixing the rules of voting, then in dividing themselves into two camps, in deciding upon the distances of the shots, and finally in foreseeing what would be the sanctions to be applied in cases of infringements of these laws.[53]

[53] Piaget, 1932, p. 91.

Piaget links this new interest in codification to the often-noted ideological concerns of adolescents. The teenager can now critically examine the laws and codes of society. Moral thought, therefore, operates on a plane of complex social and political reality, rather than simply on a plane of interpersonal relations. The result is an idealistic passion for reworking the social system from the group up, often expressed in political discussion and action.

By far the most extensive account of adolescent moral development has been provided by Lawrence Kohlberg's twenty-year research program.[54] Kohlberg's initial study was a set of in-depth interviews with seventy-two boys between the ages of ten and sixteen.[55] Subsequently, Kohlberg followed these boys through the next twenty years of their lives, reinterviewing them every three years. The result was an ambitious longitudinal investigation documenting the major moral transitions between late childhood and middle adulthood. Although Kohlberg's theory is intended to be a life-span account of moral development, we shall discuss it in this chapter for two reasons. First, most of the important developmental transitions described by the theory normally occur during adolescence. Second, the theory is most solid in its treatment of the major moral transitions between adolescence and adulthood. Childhood morality is better described by the accounts discussed in Chapter 4 than by Kohlberg's early stages.

Kohlberg's methodological approach was to embody the traditional issues of moral philosophy in a series of stories and dilemmas. The moral issues included the respective values of human life and property, the boundaries of one's personal responsibility for another's welfare, and the meaning of social rules and laws, the value of honesty, and the importance of one's contractual arrangements. Kohlberg's story-dilemmas present these abstract issues in a format that even fairly unsophisticated children and adolescents can grasp —although researchers have questioned whether such complex issues, even in story form, have much meaning for children younger than ten or so.[56] Kohlberg's most famous methodological embodiment of these moral issues is his "Heinz dilemma," which goes as follows:

In Europe, a woman was near death from a special kind of cancer. There was one drug that the doctors thought might save her. It was a form of radium that a druggist in the same town had recently discovered. The drug was expensive to make, but the druggist was charging ten times what the drug cost him to make. He paid $200 for the radium and charged $2,000 for a small dose of the drug. The sick woman's husband, Heinz, went to everyone he knew to borrow the money, but he could only get together about half of what it cost. He told the druggist that his wife was dying and asked him to sell it cheaper or let him pay later. But the druggist said:"No, I discovered the drug and I'm going to make money from it." So Heinz got desperate and broke into the man's store to steal the drug for his wife. Should the husband have done that?[57]

[54] Kohlberg, 1963, 1964, 1969, 1971, 1976; Kohlberg & Kramer, 1969.

[55] Kohlberg, 1963.

[56] Damon, 1977; Eisenberg-Berg & Neal, 1979.

[57] Kohlberg, 1963, p. 17.

After the subject's initial response, Kohlberg probed the subject's moral reasoning further with follow-up questions. In addition, Kohlberg presented subjects with other dilemmas focusing on similar moral crises. For example, Kohlberg's stories included hypothetical situations like the account of a doctor deciding whether to perform euthanasia on a long-suffering patient, an air-raid officer deciding whether his true obligation during an attack was to his family or to the citizenry at large, and a judge deciding on an appropriate punishment for a well-meant but illegal act.

Kohlberg's stories were more dramatic, more removed from everyday social experience, and more complex than the stories and questions used by Piaget and others who have focused more on childhood moral judgment. For example, Piaget's procedures focused on such mundane concerns as the rules of a marble game and the accidental breaking of tea cups. Damon's moral dilemmas focused on sharing rewards and respecting adult household demands. Naturally, these are more child-oriented problems than those introduced by Kohlberg, not only because they are more familiar and simpler to grasp, but also because they may be resolved by principles of interpersonal relationships. Kohlberg's dilemmas, in contrast, pull for principles that reflect a societal perspective, engaging issues like law and the broader political context. For this reason, we might expect Kohlberg's view of adolescent moral development to be sharper than that of other researchers. His descriptions of the childhood origins of morality, on the other hand, may be questionable, due to the inappropriateness of his methods for pre-adolescents.

On the basis of subjects' responses to his story-dilemmas, Kohlberg defined six stages of moral development (see Table 7-2). A Kohlberg moral stage defines a person's general orientation to a moral problem, including the considerations and justifications that a person takes into account during the process of moral deliberation. Thus, a stage of reasoning does not determine a subject's moral action. Rather, a wide variety of choices are available at each stage, many of which are in direct opposition to one another. Kohlberg's stage sequence, therefore, is intended to be a highly formal and "content-free" system of structural analysis. It is presented as a fixed sequence of universal principles that should apply everywhere, whatever the demands of a specific situation may be. Other developmental stage sequences reviewed in this book are less formal and universalistic, and more directly tied to particular choices and actions at each stage.

The general structural principle that Kohlberg bases his universal stage descriptions on is called the *level of sociomoral perspective*.[58] This is the point of view taken by the individual in both defining social reality and choosing moral values. According to Kohlberg, an individual's level of perspective on social and moral events is the core feature of the individual's moral judgment. It organizes all other moral beliefs, values, and principles around it. There is a particular level of sociomoral perspective associated with each of Kohlberg's

[58] Kohlberg, 1976.

six stages, defining the stage's essence. In order to convey the structural basis for Kohlberg's developmental sequence, we shall briefly discuss the stages in terms of their core levels of perspective.

At stage 1, Kohlberg identifies the sociomoral perspective as an *egocentric point of view* from which one does not separate the needs and interests of others from one's own.[59] One's own social perspective is also confused with the social perspectives of those in authority, so that one defers absolutely to social power. The result is the *punishment and obedience orientation* of stage 1: goodness or badness is determined by how well an action conforms to the dictates of authority. The possibility that someone may have a valid claim in conflict with the judgment of authority is not recognized, since all points of view are conflated by this egocentric level of perspective. This is a morality of the strong over the weak, maintaining the social order by favoring those in power over those without power. The worth of persons varies according to their status or possessions, and it is morally wrong to disobey those of greater worth than oneself. In this regard, Kohlberg's stage 1 is very similar to Piaget's heteronomous morality, described in Chapter 4. In Kohlberg's data, stage 1 statements are most frequent at age ten, and decrease rapidly after that.[60]

Stage 2 in Kohlberg's system is characterized by a *concrete individualistic perspective*. The subject becomes aware that all persons have their own interests to pursue and that sometimes these interests conflict with one another. Because the subject sees all people as essentially equal, each person's interests are seen as valid to some degree, even though they may differ from other people's interests. Justice is seen as an exchange system in which people work out a mutually satisfactory balance of interests through compromise or bargaining. The result is a primitive form of moral reciprocity leading to exchanges of favors ("You scratch my back and I'll scratch yours") or blows ("An eye for an eye, a tooth for a tooth"). Although other persons are viewed mainly as a means to the end of one's own gratification, it is understood that others have their own points of view that must be contended with. For this reason, others must be treated with respect, if only for the purpose of one's own self-interest. Thus, stage 2 blends the principle of *instrumental hedonism* (using others for one's own interests) with the principle of fair exchange. As an example of a stage 2 exchange, subjects at this stage often answer the Heinz dilemma by saying that one should steal the drug because "you may need him to do the same for you someday." Kohlberg reports that stage 2 moral judgments are also most frequent at age ten, although they decrease less rapidly during the later years than do stage 1 judgments.

Stage 3, writes Kohlberg, is based upon a *social-relational perspective* that values the mutual expectations deriving from interpersonal relations. Shared feelings and agreements take primacy over the individual's own self-interests. Because interpersonal relations are now the main context for moral behavior, being a good person and being oriented to the needs of others, particularly

---

[59] Ibid.   [60] Kohlberg, 1969.

Table 7-2 The Six Stages of Moral Judgment

Stage	Social perspective	Content of stage	Individual's moral considerations
PRECONVENTIONAL LEVEL			
Stage 1 Punishment and Obedience	Egocentric Point of View	Literal obedience of rules Avoiding punishment Obedience to authorities, who have superior power. Not doing physical harm to people or property.	A person at this stage doesn't consider the interests of others or recognize they differ from actor's, and doesn't relate two points of view. Actions are judged in terms of physical consequences rather than in terms of psychological interests of others. Authority's perspective is confused with one's own.
Stage 2 Individual Instrumental Purpose and Exchange	Concrete Individualistic Perspective	Following rules when it is to someone's immediate interest. Serving one's own or other's interests and needs. Making fair deals to serve both self and other.	A person at this stage separates own interests and points of view from those of authorities and others. He or she is aware everybody has individual interests to pursue and these conflict, so integrates or relates conflicting interests to one another through instrumental exchange of services, need for the other and the other's goodwill, or through fairly giving each person the same amount.
CONVENTIONAL LEVEL			
Stage 3 Mutual Interpersonal Expectations, Relationships, Conformity	Individual in Relationship to Other Individuals; Putting Self in Others' Position	Being motivated to follow rules and expectations. Needing to be good (nice) in order to live up to expectations of people close to one. Being concerned about other people and their feelings. Maintaining trust, loyalty, respect, gratitude.	A person at this stage is aware of shared feelings, agreements, and expectations, which take primacy over individual interests. The person relates points of view through the "concrete Golden Rule," putting oneself in the other person's shoes. He or she does not consider generalized "system" perspective.

Stage 4 Social System and Conscience Maintenance	Societal Point of View	Doing one's duty in society. Upholding the social order. Maintaining the welfare of society or the group. Obeying laws, except in extreme cases where they conflict with other fixed social duties and rights.	A person at this stage takes the viewpoint of the system, which defines roles and rules. He or she considers individual relations in terms of place in the system.
TRANSITIONAL LEVEL **Stage 4½** Transitional	Outside Society	Choice is personal and subjective, based on emotions. Conscience is relative.	The person at this stage considers himself as an individual making decisions without a generalized commitment or contract with society. One can pick and choose obligations, which are defined by particular societies, but one has no principles for such choice.
POSTCONVENTIONAL AND PRINCIPLED LEVEL **Stage 5** Prior Rights and Social Contract	Prior-to-Society Perspective	Asserting basic rights, values, and legal contracts of a society, even when they conflict with the concrete rules and laws of the group. group; but usually obey them because they are the social contract, which is for the good of all.	The person at this stage is aware of values and rights prior to social attachments and contracts. He or she integrates perspectives by formal mechanisms of agreement, contract, objective impartiality, and due process. He or she considers the moral point of view and the legal point of view, recognizes they conflict, and finds it difficult to integrate them.
Stage 6 Universal Ethical Principles	Moral Point of View	Commitment to universal principles of justice. When laws violate these principles, one acts in accord with the principle.	The person at this stage recognizes that social arrangements derive from or are grounded in the moral point of view. He recognizes the nature of morality and respects other persons as ends, not means.

Source: Based on L. Kohlberg, *The Philosophy of Moral Development*, Vol. I. San Francisco: Harper & Row, 1981, pp. 409–12.

others with whom one is closely associated, are of primary importance. This is the stage of the *Golden Rule*, in which generosity, forgiveness, and helpfulness toward others whom one knows are most highly valued. In one experimental study, subjects at stage 3 correctly interpreted the Golden Rule to mean that one should treat others *as if* they were the self, whereas subjects who had not yet reached stage 3 believed that the saying meant that one should treat others nicely *so that* they would reciprocate in kind.[61] Stage 3 therefore represents an *ideal* form of moral reciprocity, more advanced than the pragmatic tit-for-tat exchange advocated at stage 2. At stage 3 there is a genuine attempt to "put yourself in the other guy's shoes." There is also a concern for the other person's opinion: one's moral worth at this stage is largely determined by one's social reputation. For this reason, stage 3 is a "conventional" type of morality that works best in close, face-to-face social engagements. Kohlberg reports the highest incidence of stage 3 responses between the ages of thirteen and sixteen, although for many individuals, a stage 3 orientation continues throughout life.

Stage 4 reflects a *member-of-society perspective* in which the individual adopts the point of view of the social system itself. The social order, with its existing laws and rules, is considered primary. Moral behavior is defined in terms of what maintains the social order. This would include good citizenship, working hard, maintaining the law of the land, and other socially virtuous conduct. Individual interests and social relations are valued only if they contribute to the well-ordered functioning of the social system. Unlike at previous stages, they are not valued in themselves, and they are disregarded if they conflict with the existing rules of society. Justice is no longer a matter of pragmatic or ideal reciprocity between individuals, but rather a matter of carefully regulated relations between an individual and society-at-large. These relations are regulated by the particular rules of the individual's society; and even if these rules may seem unwise in some cases, they must be followed if the greater danger of social chaos is to be avoided. Kohlberg finds stage 4 morality becoming predominate during middle to late adolescence, and frequently continuing throughout life.

Whereas the essence of stage 4 is a societal perspective, stage 5 is based upon a *prior-to-society perspective*. This means that the individual values the idea of a social system and willingly participates in the social order but does not believe it necessary to maintain any given set of social rules or arrangements. In other words, the individual sees the importance of entering into a social contract with others, but always strives to improve upon the particular social-contractual arrangements of the existing social system. Kohlberg calls this a "law-creating" perspective, in contrast to the "law-maintaining" perspective of stage 4. At stage 5, the procedures and mechanisms for constructing just laws are considered primary. The individual at stage 5 values social contracts that ensure an equal distribution of power, as well as the protection of one's liberties and rights. Thus, it is the democratic process that is most important,

[61] Selman, 1971.

rather than the specific codes that are on the books at any one time. At stage 5, an individual can evaluate such specific codes in terms of general values such as equality and liberty, and attempts to revise the codes if they conflict with these values. For the first time, the individual asks of a law, "Is it moral as well as legal?" Kohlberg finds stage 5 moral judgments appearing with increasing frequency during late adolescence and throughout the college years in our society. Even among adults, however, stage 5 does not normally become the predominant mode of moral reasoning. Most persons, according to Kohlberg's data remain at stage 3 or stage 4, with the exception of only a small proportion of persons in Western industrial societies.

If stage 5, even among adults, is relatively rare, stage 6 is for all practical purposes nonexistent. After years of longitudinal studies, Kohlberg concluded that stage 6 was found so rarely among normal populations that he would drop it from his scoring system.[62] This decision changed the status of stage 6 into a theoretical construct that defines the hypothetical end point of Kohlberg's developmental sequence. We do not know whether this is an actual end point or not, because Kohlberg was not able to find normal individuals who had progressed that far. Most of Kohlberg's ideas for stage 6, as well as the examples of it that he has quoted over the years, come from a few interviews with philosophers and from his own introspections. In any case, Kohlberg believes that stage 6, if it exists, reflects a *rational moral perspective* that values certain abstract moral principles above all else. These principles are considered to be universal and absolutely binding, although they are quite flexible in their interpretation and application. One such principle, for example, is that people are ends in themselves and must be treated as such. The value of human life, therefore, is unimpeachable in a moral sense. When laws or social norms conflict with such principles, one must act in accordance with the principles, whatever the personal consequences. Kohlberg believes that this is the stage at which Ghandi, Thoreau, Martin Luther King, and other champions of civil disobedience acted when they followed the dictates of their conscience rather than the demands of society. There is, at stage 6, a continuing respect for the social order, except when the social order violates human rights or principles of justice. One hopes that such occasions rarely occur in a just society, but when they do occur, one is morally obliged to ignore the social order in favor of human rights and social justice. In other words, the social order is only valued as necessary means to a moral ends, but never as an end in itself. The sought-after end for stage 6 is a moral course of action that any rational person with an appreciation of universal moral principles and no self-interest in the present situation would consider fair.

As noted above, Kohlberg believes that his six stages are universal because of the general applicability of their underlying structural principles (the levels of sociomoral perspective). In addition to this universalist claim, Kohlberg believes that the sequential order of the six stages is invariant across all

[62] Kohlberg, 1978.

persons. In other words, people everywhere go through the stages in the same order, from 1 to 6, during the course of their moral development. No stages are ever skipped or reversed with one another. Of course, as Kohlberg's data show, not many individuals get past stage 4 in the sequence and practically no one reaches stage 6. However, as far as one goes in the sequence, one invariably proceeds in the sequential order. This is because, according to Kohlberg, each stage *requires* the stage prior to it. Without the perspective and knowledge acquired at the earlier stage, it would be impossible to acquire the later stage. This can be most easily understood in terms of the sociomoral perspectives upon which the stages are based. For example, it is easy to see how a prior-to-society perspective (stage 5) would follow from a member-of-society perspective (stage 4), because a focus on the processes of creating laws and social contracts requires appreciation of the existing social system, with its particular set of laws and arrangements. Similarly, the stage 4 member-of-society perspective presupposes the stage 3 social-relational perspective, because an orientation toward others on an interpersonal level is necessary for the development of respect for society as a whole. In this manner, the developmental links between any adjacent stages in Kohlberg's system can be identified, and the sequence as a whole can be seen to have a necessary logic deriving from the progression from one level of sociomoral perspective to the next.

Not all social scientists have accepted Kohlberg's claims about the universal and invariant nature of his moral stage sequence. Some believe that the sequence reflects values that are dominant in Western society, but that would be inappropriate elsewhere. For example, as many critics have noted, Kohlberg's higher stages incorporate the principles of a liberal, democratic society. Kohlberg's own cross-cultural studies within non-Western cultures like Turkey and Taiwan generally have found very few people attaining stages higher than stage 3.[63] Are societies with non-Western governing principles, and the people living in these societies, less advanced morally than Western societies and their inhabitants? Many reject this possibility, as well as all other aspects of Kohlberg's claim to universalism. As one author writes, "The definition of the stages and the assumptions underlying them, including the view that the scheme is universally applicable, are ethnocentric and culturally biased."[64]

Female moral development: Carol Gilligan's approach. Some people believe that even within our own culture, Kohlberg's theory may not apply equally well to all people. Kohlberg's stages were derived from a study of adolescent males. Are these stages valid for females as well? There are conflicting reports about this in the literature. Carol Gilligan cites evidence that suggests that females consistently score lower than males on Kohlberg's moral judgment interview.[65] Such a finding could be interpreted as an indication of

[63] Kohlberg, 1969.
[64] Simpson, 1974.

[65] Gilligan, 1982.

male moral superiority—a notion, incidentally that Freud and others have taken quite seriously.[66] But there is another possible interpretation of this finding, offered extensively by Gilligan. This is the possibility that Kohlberg's stages are sexually biased.

Gilligan argues that women score most often at stage 3 on a Kohlberg moral dilemma because women are interpersonally oriented. (Stage 3, as noted above, is the one moral position based exclusively on a social-relational perspective.) This places women lower than men on Kohlberg's scale, since men frequently score at stages 4 and 5. But Kohlberg's scale, claims Gilligan, may not do justice to women. Rather, argues Gilligan, women's morality should not be ordered on the same scale as men's morality, because women approach moral problems with an entirely different set of values and ideals than do men. These values and ideals spring from a uniquely feminine orientation to life, deeply rooted in childhood experience.

The essence of this feminine orientation is a sense of *connectedness with others* that girls acquire at an early age, and that distinguishes them from boys, who grow up more with a sense of their own separateness. This sex difference is engendered in infancy, when girls become aware that they are similar in gender to their mothers and boys become aware they are different. The difference pervades the moral orientations of the two sexes. Values like benevolence and caring come more naturally to women since they are oriented to the welfare of others. Men, on the other hand, assume their separateness from others, and they believe that formal social rules are necessary to reconcile the inevitable conflicts that will arise between themselves and others with different interests. Gilligan believes that the interpersonal benevolence of women is neither inferior nor superior to the formal rule-bound morality of men and that it is a mistake to score the former at a developmentally lower stage than the latter. Male and female moral orientations should be considered apart from one another, and development within each should be studied on its own terms.

To date, the weight of empirical research has not supported Gilligan's arguments. Recent literature reviews have found little evidence of women scoring lower than men on Kohlberg's system; and the little evidence of this that does exist virtually disappears when subjects' educational and occupational backgrounds are controlled.[67] As for Gilligan's claim that women have their own distinct stream of development, there is nothing in the psychological literature to guide us in identifying the characteristics of such a stream. Until Gilligan presents a model for analyzing female development on its own terms, it will be impossible to provide a fair test of her ideas.

Critiques of Kohlberg's highest stages.   A number of other controversies have arisen over Kohlberg's universalistic claims, particularly in relation to his two highest stages. Some believe that stages 5 and 6 should not be part of a developmental ordering at all because they represent individual differences in

---

[66] Freud, 1908, 1925.   [67] Rest, 1983, Walker, 1983.

personality and character structure.[68] According to this position, stage 5 reflects a personality oriented to social concerns and stage 6 a personality oriented to individualistic concerns. Since these are individual rather than developmental differences, neither is superior to the other in a moral sense. Other authors have agreed, though for different reasons, that Kohlberg's two highest stages do not capture true developmental differences in morality. Some have suggested reformulating these stages in terms of new structural principles.[69] Others have suggested keeping them but abandoning the notion that they are developmentally ordered.[70]

Kohlberg's own response to the criticisms of his highest two stages has been twofold. First, as noted earlier, he has dropped stage 6 for all practical purposes and has revised stage 5 to include some of the virtues once reserved for stage 6. Second, *within* each stage Kohlberg has defined different moral positions that parallel the societal and individualistic orientations posited by his critics.[71] That is, he has agreed that there are individual differences in moral judgment, and that these differences stem from personality characteristics, rather than developmental achievements. But Kohlberg believes that such differences are best understood within his developmental stage model since they cut across the stage distinctions captured by the model. To put it simply, one can be societally or individually oriented at any of Kohlberg's stages. Kohlberg believes that information about such orientations adds to, and need not compete with, information about developmental stages. Ideally, in order to understand an individual's moral views, we should be able to assess both; Kohlberg's most recent scoring manual provides a means of doing so.[72]

Kohlberg and his colleagues have also collected data that support his claims regarding the invariant nature of his stage sequence. In one series of studies, adolescents and young adults were presented with moral arguments above and below their own level of moral judgment.[73] Generally subjects understood and appreciated arguments one stage higher than their own stage, rejected arguments below their own stage, and could not comprehend arguments more than one stage higher than their own stage. Often, the presentation of one-stage-higher moral arguments encouraged subjects to adopt the higher-stage perspective in their own moral judgments. This was not true of arguments that were either lower or more than one stage higher. This means that, as Kohlberg's theory would predict, subjects were influenced mostly by moral reasoning at the next stage in the sequence, rather than by just any moral statements that they happened to hear. The overall picture from these studies is that of subjects advancing slowly along Kohlberg's developmental sequence in the order of the stages. Subjects did not tend to copy reasoning that they considered either inferior or too difficult to comprehend. Instead, they attempted to produce the best moral judgment that their developmental abilities

[68] Hogan, 1975a.
[69] Turiel, 1978a.
[70] Gibbs, 1977.
[71] Kohlberg, 1976.

[72] Colby, Gibbs, & Kohlberg, 1978.
[73] Rest, Turiel, & Kohlberg, 1969; Turiel, 1966, 1969; Rest, 1973.

allowed them to grasp. From whatever point subjects began along Kohlberg's sequence, this best judgment reflected that of the next highest moral stage.

These studies, as well as other empirical work presented by Kohlberg and his research group, have been widely criticized because of their unorthodox methods, as well as their often incomplete reporting of data.[74] Questions have been raised concerning the validity of Kohlberg's moral judgment interview.[75] What does it really tap—a person's actual mode of reaching moral decisions, or merely a person's intellectual way of rationalizing a choice on a hypothetical problem far removed from the person's life? Questions have also been raised concerning the reliability of Kohlberg's scoring procedures, which call for a large degree of subjective inference on the part of the scorer.[76] Other methodological concerns focus on whether proper statistics were used to analyze data in the experiments on the influence of higher- and lower-stage moral arguments, and whether these data were accurately interpreted in the final data reports.[77]

Some of these criticisms have been answered by Kohlberg's recent work. New scoring procedures have been designed to deal with problems of subjectivity and reliability.[78] A final longitudinal study using these procedures has resulted in findings that strongly support Kohlberg's theory.[79] In this study, subjects were followed from early adolescence through middle adulthood. According to the results of this study, subjects not only progress along Kohlberg's stages in order, but they also manage to maintain coherent, integrated moral positions throughout the course of this lifelong developmental process. These results are consistent with Kohlberg's claims that his stages are structured wholes at the same time as they are part of a dynamic developmental sequence. In other words, according to Kohlberg, an individual's moral judgment system has a good deal of internal consistency even as it is continually evolving to a more advanced state. Kohlberg's twenty-year longitudinal study seems to confirm this view.

Perhaps the most difficult challenge for Kohlberg's work is the question of what his moral judgment interview reveals about real-life morality. Are a subject's ruminations over Heinz an indication of how the subject will handle the moral dilemmas and events of everyday life? Or are they largely an intellectual exercise, unconnected to the subject's social behavior?

Unfortunately, this is an issue still obscured by a lack of data. As one review of the moral judgment literature has concluded, "the connection between story problem morality and conduct is still. . .mostly unknown."[80] Practically the only data that shed light on this came from a study of Berkeley college students who had participated in the Free Speech Movement during the mid-1960s.[81] During the course of this movement, some students chose to

[74] Kurtines & Greif, 1974; Hoffman, 1977.
[75] Baumrind, 1978.
[76] Kurtines & Greif, 1974.
[77] Hoffman, 1970; Kurtines & Grief, 1974.
[78] Colby, Gibbs & Kohlberg, 1978.

[79] Colby, Gibbs, Kohlberg, & Lieberman, 1983.
[80] Brown & Herrnstein, 1975, p. 326.
[81] Haan, Smith, & Block, 1968.

protest university policies concerning political activity on campus by occupying the central administration building. For those who participated, the consequence of "sitting in" was forcible eviction and arrest on charges of trespassing. Social psychologists administered Kohlberg's moral judgment interviews to two groups of students in the Free Speech Movement: those who chose to sit in despite the consequences, and those who chose not to. Comparisons were then made between the students' moral judgment scores and their action choices during the campus sit-in. In addition, students were interviewed directly about their decisions to sit in or not.

Results from this study showed the difficulty of making unambiguous predictions about moral action on the basis of Kohlberg's stages. Both activists (students who sat in) and non-activists were found at every Kohlberg stage. The main difference was that students at different moral judgment stages offered different reasons to justify their action choices. For example, stage 2 students who sat in explained their activism in terms of individual rights and liberty (a "do your own thing" type of moral explanation). Stage 3 activists justified their conduct on the grounds that the campus administrators had acted disreputably and thus had forsaken their legitimate authority. For stage 4 activists, the main issue was the administration's violation of legal contracts, in particular the Bill of Rights of the U.S. Constitution (which, the activists claimed, protects free speech everywhere in this country). Stage 5 students argued more in terms of the general principles underlying our formal legal system, especially principles of democratic governance and minority rights. The moral stage, therefore, did not determine an individual's action, but it did influence the individual's reasons and justifications for the action.

Nevertheless, even though both activism and non-activism existed at each of Kohlberg's stages, there was a greater likelihood that students at certain stages would be among the activists. In particular, students at stages 2 and 5 were most likely to sit in, and students at stages 3 and 4 were the least likely. This makes sense, since stage 2 represents an individualistic position that has not yet acquired respect for impersonal societal standards, and stage 5 represents a principled position that is sometimes critical of existing societal standards. Both of these positions, for different reasons, could likely lead to the rejection of societal imperatives like obeying a noxious set of codes. Stages 3 and 4, on the other hand, are representative of conventional moral positions that advocate acceptance of social standards, regardless of the nature of the standards. These moral positions could likely lead to conformity to social rules and authority, even during a time of political protest. Students' action choices did correlate with their moral judgment in a manner consistent with the logic of Kohlberg's stages, but this correlation was far from perfect. In other words, the students' stages of moral judgment guided their conduct in certain directions, but did not absolutely determine their choices. This is, in part, because any choice can be made and defended at any stage, even though some choices flow more naturally from certain stage-related modes of moral judgment than do others. A person who typically reasons at stage 5 will often act differently in moral situations than a person reasoning at stage 4, and we can make some good guesses about the overall nature of these differences.

In general, from the small bit of empirical data that we have, it seems that information about a person's moral judgment stage can help us make tentative predictions about the individual's social conduct, but these predictions and guesses will never approach certainty, because no moral stage leads unambiguously to a particular choice. Moral stages reflect general principles underlying decision making, but the decisions themselves are made in the context of specific moral problems. Because of this, decisions must be created in each situation, often on the spur of the moment.

Such decisions cannot be a rote, mechanical application of the structural principles of a moral judgment stage, but rather they must make use of these principles in a flexible, context-appropriate manner. In constructing moral decisions, individuals at every moral stage have a wide variety of choices available to them, and good decisions require evaluating these choices on their own merits. Often this must be done without the help of the stage's general moral principles because good and effective action cannot be derived from principles alone. They must work in the context of the real world. Boris Pasternak, describing a young idealistic revolutionary in *Doctor Zhivago*, expressed this same notion when he wrote: "And if he were really to do good, he would have needed, in addition to his principles, a heart capable of violating them—a heart which knows only of the particular, not of general cases, and which achieves greatness in little actions."

Social-Conventional Development

Kohlberg's stages are strictly stages of moral development, focusing on how individuals deal with concerns of justice at various periods in their lives. Justice is a primary means of regulating human social interactions, but it is only one of many such means. There are also social rules and conventions that have little to do with justice. For example, there are sex-role conventions of the type discussed in Chapter 5: If a boy wears a dress to school, there may be serious social consequences for him, but this is because he has violated a social convention rather than a principle of fairness or justice. Researchers studying adolescence believe that a critical challenge in adolescent social development is distinguishing moral principles from other types of social rules.[82] For various reasons that we shall discuss below, adolescents often confuse the two. Since each type of regulation is necessary for successful integration into society, the adolescent must sort out and recognize the special demands of each.

In terms of Kohlberg's stage system, it is during the transition from stage 4 to stage 5 that people untangle moral from social-conventional concerns. In those individuals who do make this transition, it normally occurs in late adolescence, and it is a period marked by internal conflict and disequilibrium

[82] Turiel, 1975, 1978a.

in one's personal values. (We shall see further manifestations of this when we take up the adolescent's "identity crisis" in the following chapter.) Turiel has analyzed the developmental transition from stage 4 to stage 5 in terms of the adolescent's struggle to separate principles that are truly moral from those that spring from convention or custom.[83] According to Turiel, moral principles are universal and binding, whereas conventional norms are matters of choice. This is because moral principles are necessary for social living everywhere (such as prohibitions against killing or stealing), whereas conventions are appropriate only in certain cultures or social contexts (such as prohibitions against going nude in public). Turiel performed a case-by-case analysis of seven adolescents who were in the process of moving from stage 4 to stage 5 in their moral judgments. A part of this process involved identifying principles that the adolescent could accept as binding in a moral sense, and distinguishing these from other guidelines for social behavior, particularly conventional guidelines that the adolescent could accept as somewhat voluntary and even arbitrary.

According to Turiel's analysis, there are a number of conceptual realizations that characterize the developmental transition from stage 4 to stage 5. First, the adolescent who moves beyond stage 4 begins questioning the sole authority of society and social laws over moral matters. The adolescent recognizes that society is comprised of various individuals, many of whom differ in their moral beliefs. The adolescent assumes that each of the differing views may have some validity. Thus, society is no longer seen as operating with a single authoritative voice, but with many conflicting voices, all of which should be valued. From these beliefs arises a "moral relativity": that is, a sense that all values are relative, and that everyone must decide for himself what is right and what is wrong. The only limits on this relativity are that one cannot harm others or society. In this manner, some of the stage 4 respect for the social order is maintained, but in the new context of a primary respect for individual freedom of moral choice. Turiel quotes one of his subjects:

> It is just that I really believe you can't go into someone else's mind and tell them what is right. I can't see the world through someone else's eyes. The world might be totally different through someone else's eyes and really justifies a morality that is totally different from that. I really can't say they are wrong for themselves. They might be wrong for society. And if they go out hurting other individuals, then I guess I would have to judge them and possibly punish them. . . If their vision of reality is very much different from the socially acceptable vision, then they are going to come to different conclusions as to morality. And I can't condemn a man simply because he has a different view of morality. It may be one that is not very efficient or does not work very well. It may be one that hurts other people, but I can't condemn them for having that view of reality.[84]

This type of thinking leads the adolescent to some new conclusions concerning the importance of various social norms. Whereas at stage 4 the adolescent valued all of society's rules on the grounds that obedience to the

---

[83] Turiel, 1974.   [84] Ibid., p. 21.

social order is the only way to avoid social chaos and injustice, the adolescent moving out of stage 4 now believes that specific social rules are arbitrary, and that their moral worth is relative to the beliefs of the individuals living under them. In other words, it is up to individuals to decide for themselves the importance of particular social rules, and *depriving individuals of this right is an abrogation of their freedom.* Freedom, therefore, becomes an overriding moral principle in its own right, more valued than any particular, "arbitrary" social rule. According to this belief, the worst thing an individual or a society can do is "impose" its values on someone. In this manner, the adolescent has taken the first step toward constructing a set of overriding moral principles that are more valued and more binding than other types of social rules. Some typical samples of adolescent reasoning along these lines follow:

> I don't think anyone can help but judge other people. I mean, the minute you meet someone, immediately you start judging them by your own system of values. I think it is impossible not to judge anybody else, to be totally objective about people —you can't do it. However, you shouldn't let your opinions of other people get in the way of their freedom.[85]

> In any given value judgment most people would tend to lean in one direction. Because of that, I guess society says that would be morally right. So for society, that is morally right. However, for the individual, in the end you have to live according to your own conscience. You have to compromise society to some extent. You have to live in society. But I think to everyone, it is vastly more important to follow their own conscience.[86]

Freedom is only the first of several moral principles that adolescents will eventually accept as universal once they consolidate their moral reasoning at stage 5. Others include the value of human life, the equal rights of individuals (including those in a social minority), and so on. During the transitional period from stage 4 to 5, the adolescent vacillates back and forth between accepting the idea that there is such a set of overriding principles and the idea that all rules in the end are arbitrary. This is a confusing time in an adolescent's moral development, marked by much inconsistency and contradiction. In Turiel's quotes, one can almost sense the internal moral turmoil that will ultimately lead to a progressive reorganization of the adolescent's moral thinking:

> Let me say this, if there is a blind code. If there is a God—the Jewish people, for example, have a God who says not only don't kill and don't commit adultery and don't steal, but wear fringes on your garments. You are supposed to do that. Wear fringes to signify the presence of God. The religion says God recognizes that one is more important than the other—in the original Ten Commandments. But if there is a God and he is telling you what is right, then he can prescribe all kinds of conduct. If it all comes from God, maybe it is just as important to wear fringes on your garments as to abstain from killing. But if society is just claiming to have or adhere to a divine or some kind of a priori or supernatural, or any kind of superhuman code, and I don't see any basis for it, it doesn't matter to me if the code prohibits killing or the code prohibits going nude.[87]

[85] Ibid., p. 22.
[86] Ibid., p. 21.

[87] Ibid., p. 25.

It is clear from the above quote and from Turiel's analysis, that the major confusion to be resolved between stages 4 and 5 is the confusion between moral and social-conventional codes. Once this is resolved, we see a movement to stage 5 in a moral sense. What about the adolescent's opinions concerning social conventions? Even though they may be less universal and less binding than moral principles, conventions in themselves are an important part of social living, bearing real and serious consequences for those who do not abide by them. True, we do not send people to jail for unconventional dress or manners. But in a lesser sense, such "eccentric" behavior can affect an individual's adaptation to society. How adverse the effect is (and in some conditions, there may not even be an adverse effect), depends on the specifics of individual cases. Conventions and customs themselves are a critical ingredient in the social order, and one fundamental aspect of social development is coming to terms with them. Consequently, Turiel has investigated social-conventional development in its own right, apart from its relation to moral development.

In order to study social-conventional development, Turiel interviewed hundreds of children and adolescents on societal rules that have nothing to do with justice or other moral issues.[88] For example, one of Turiel's stories deals with a boy who was accustomed to calling teachers by their first names. The boy's mode of address conflicts with an accepted convention at his new school, where teachers and principal demand to be called by their formal titles. Should the boy follow his old custom or the new convention? Another story concerns a lawyer who does not wish to wear a necktie to work; another, a boy who wishes to become a nurse. There are also questions about manners (like eating with a knife and fork instead of with one's hands), about culturally different patterns of living (fathers in some cultures who live apart from their families), and about conventional symbols (saluting the flag).

According to Turiel's findings, children and adolescents develop through seven successive levels in which they first accept, then reject, the validity of conventions (see Table 7-3). This vacillation continues throughout the entire developmental sequence presented by Turiel, from the beginning to the advanced levels. This affirmation-negation of conventions changes very much with each successive pair of levels.

At Turiel's level 1, children show a merely descriptive understanding of social conventions, founded on impressions of the way people act. This level is found in children approximately aged six or seven. At this level, there is a conception of what is socially normal, that is, of the regularities in people's daily behavior. But there is no sense that such regularities serve a social function. In other words, there is no sense of regulation as an intrinsic part of a social system, beyond an awareness of certain "empirical uniformities"—regularities without social significance—that may be commonly observed.

> These subjects stated that titles are necessarily associated with certain classes of people, and that occupations (nurse, doctor) are necessarily associated with the

[88] Turiel, 1978b, 1978c.

Table 7-3 Social-Conventional Development

Level	Age	Respect for conventions	Individual's conception	Social significance of conventions
Level 1	6–7 yrs.	Affirmed	Conventions are uniform, observable, and compulsory	None.
Level 2	8–9 yrs.	Negated	Conventions are uniform, observable, but not compulsory.	None.
Level 3	10–11 yrs.	Affirmed	Rules and "authoritative" social expectations are an important part of the social system.	Conformity to rules is necessary to maintain the social order.
Level 4	Early Adolescence	Negated	Conventions, unlike other social rules, are considered a matter of individual preference and without inherent validity.	Conventions are not considered an important violation of the social order.
Leve. 5	Mid-Adolescence	Affirmed	Social conventions must be respected so social system will not be weakened.	Conventions are recognized as a necessary part of the social system, which in turn is recognized as essential for civilized life.
Level 6	Mid-Adolescence	Negated	There is respect for the social order, but also the belief that the social system can function without social conventions.	Social conventions are not considered an important part of the social order.
Level 7	End of Adolescence	Affirmed	Specific rules are arbitrary, but potentially useful. Conventions are valued when they promote social harmony; they lose their value, and are abandoned in favor of alternate rules, when they do not.	Conventions can help groups of individuals live together harmoniously.

Source: Based on E. Turiel, Social regulations and domains of social concepts. In W. Damon (Ed.), *New Directions for Child Development: Social Cognition.* San Francisco, Jossey-Bass, 1978.

class of male and female. Thus, for these subjects, titles are not signs of role or status, nor are they seen as serving communicative functions. Rather, titles are descriptive of the person.[89]

In addition, children at this level associate—again in a merely descriptive way —certain observed sanctions with the violation of social conventions. For example, a child may state that if a boy becomes a nurse, he will be laughed at. As with the child's view of conventions in general, such sanctions are not seen as serving a social function, nor are they linked in any other way with the social system; rather, they are seen simply as part of a uniform chain of events, a continuation of the behavioral regularity that the child has observed in the social world.

At level 2, among children a year or two older (ages eight or nine), Turiel found a negation of social conventions that is based on a conception similar to that found at the first level. In other words, children still view conventions as nothing but "empirical uniformities" in behavior, but the mere fact of social regularity no longer implies the necessity of maintaining the regularity—that is, of deferring to conventions. For example, at this level, a child might say that he realizes that nurses are usually women, but that there is no compelling reason why this must be so. The child can construct examples in which a man might make a good nurse. Or the child might justify breaking the convention by citing an instance in which the convention has already been violated (a male nurse that the child may know about). Conventions at this level are assumed to be essentially arbitrary social regularities. Because of their arbitrariness, they are not seen as compulsory; the mere fact of observed regularity no longer carries the mandatory force that it did at the earlier level.

Levels 3 and 4 bear the same relation to one another as do levels 1 and 2. That is, level 3 represents an affirmation of conventions based upon a new social conception, whereas level 4 represents a negation of conventions based upon a rejection of the appropriateness and value of this conception. At level 3, the child's new social insight is that rules and "authoritative" social expectations are an important part of the social system. Children at level 3, approximately ten and eleven years old, assert that conformity to such rules is necessary because the social order must be maintained: "If there wasn't any rules, everybody would be doing things they wanted to do. . .like running in the corridor and knocking over people."[90]

Level 4, found in early adolescence, begins when subjects reject all rules but moral ones. Unlike moral rules, conventional rules are seen as meaningless, having no inherent validity. They are therefore thought of as merely arbitrary; they no longer retain a mandatory status because the rules in such cases are believed to be unjustly constraining. Unconventional acts are considered to be relatively unimportant violations of the social system, bearing none of the social or personal consequences of moral rule breaking. Deferral to a

[89] Turiel, 1978c, p. 63. [90] Ibid., p. 65.

convention is again seen as a question of individual preference, even though social rules in general are still considered important and obligatory. Only the possibility of sanctions encourages children at this level to respect conventions; otherwise, social conventions contain none of the inherent legitimacy of social law or moral regulation.

Levels 5 and 6, which emerge in mid-adolescence, derive from the adolescent's new insights concerning the importance of the social order. As we have seen elsewhere in this chapter, at this age, the adolescent recognizes the role of social structure and societal institutions in civilized life. Along with this recognition, there is also an understanding of the nature of social hierarchies, as well as an understanding of the realities of social power within the hierarchy. At level 5, conventions are seen as a necessary part of this social system. Conforming to conventions is affirmed, because, as one seventeen-year-old put it, one must "go along with the ways of other people in your society" as a means of demonstrating respect for the social system.[91] Without such respect, the system is weakened, and if the system is weakened, congenial social relations themselves are ultimately endangered.

At level 6, a similar respect for the social order is maintained, but conventions are no longer seen as an essential part of this order. Their value is once again negated, this time because the adolescent believes that the social system can function perfectly well without them.

Finally, at level 7 (emerging at the end of adolescence), conventions are again affirmed because they are seen as potentially useful, though not a necessary means of establishing shared norms that help groups of individuals live together harmoniously. The specific conventional rule in each case is viewed as arbitrary, and it is realized that alternative rules could be equally successful in gaining the same end of social harmony. But this end is seen as generally aided by maintaining conventions, whatever they may be. Conventions are therefore viewed in light of their potential to facilitate the operation of the social system. When a specific convention is seen to further this overall purpose, it is valued; when it is seen as not serving such a purpose, it loses its value, and alternate means may be sought. As one nineteen-year-old at this level states:

> Conventions make things move along smoothly and. . .are most consistently understandable communication. . .If you communicate with somebody about something, you probably have some conventional way of talking about the thing you want to communicate, and the person you are trying to communicate to is also familiar with the general way of communicating this convention. Therefore he is able to follow you more quickly because he automatically is familiar with the way you start to do something, if it is the conventional way of doing something. So he doesn't have to stop and think how is that working, how is this thing said, because he has already been familiar with it. It shortens the process in many cases.[92]

---

[91] Ibid., p. 69.   [92] Ibid., p. 70.

Political Socialization

For many adolescents, the teenage years awaken an interest in politics; increasingly, these adolescents engage in political action and develop some sort of political ideology. But this is by no means a universal occurrence. Many adolescents continue to be apolitical, and in some cases, remain so throughout life. Even among those who do become politically active, this action is often sporadic and nonideological in character. In short, there is widespread variation in the intensity and nature of political involvement during adolescence. In part, this variation can be explained by aspects of social development that we have already discussed, such as the individual's moral development. In addition, there are other social and personal conditions that have direct influence on the course of an adolescent's "political socialization."

Joseph Adelson and Robert O'Neil[93] posed the following problem to adolescents aged eleven through eighteen: A thousand men and women move to a small Pacific island and are free to set up whatever government and legal code they wish. What choices would they make and why? Adelson and O'Neil found many differences between the answers of their younger and older subjects. For one thing, the eleven-year-olds personalized government, focusing on the consequences to themselves of various governmental practices. Older adolescents were more likely to view the social order as a whole, understanding that the community extends beyond the individual and has its own claims to protection. At the same time, somewhat paradoxically, the older subjects were less authoritarian than the younger subjects, and they were more sensitive to the individual's right to liberty and personal freedom. The older subjects realized that certain political arrangements could ensure both community and individual rights, and that present political choices, therefore, have serious future consequences for everyone in society. In short, Adelson and O'Neil conclude that middle adolescence (ages fifteen to eighteen) is marked by "the birth of ideology." This implies "orderliness and internal consistency" in their reasoning, a coherent and well-articulated sense of government functioning, and an "inner concordance of political belief."[94] Adelson and O'Neil attribute this political development to cognitive capacities that emerge during adolescence. Alluding to Piaget's model of formal operations, Adelson and O'Neil mention "the adolescent's increasing ability to weigh the relative consequences of actions, the attainment of deductive reasoning. . .the escape (from the) compulsion toward the immediate, the tangible, the narrowly pragmatic. . . ."[95]

In a theoretical model of adolescent political development, Richard Merelman identified even more explicitly the developmental roots of political involvement during adolescence.[96] Merelman points first to moral-judgmental factors of the kind described by Kohlberg. For example, Merelman believes that the adolescent's development of a relativistic morality (beginning at

[93] Adelson & O'Neil, 1966.
[94] Ibid., p. 305.
[95] Ibid.
[96] Merelman, 1971.

Kohlberg's stage 2) leads to a questioning of the existing social order, which in turn may lead to direct political action. Further, the adolescent's respect for the importance of social organization (Kohlberg's stage 4) helps the adolescent realize that one source of personal unhappiness may lie in the social system itself, beyond any one individual's control. This, too, may lead the adolescent into political activity intended to change the social system.

Merelman's model also identifies developmental factors that are strictly cognitive rather than moral. One such cognitive factor is the growth of *causal understanding*. As a number of cognitive scientists have demonstrated, by early adolescence, one normally develops the capacity to connect chains of events in a logical manner true to verifiable physical or social laws.[97] In other words, the adolescent can explain causes and effects of events without resorting to supernatural forces or inconsistent, ad hoc reasons. Politically, this advance in causal understanding helps the adolescent realize that "the world of human events is contingent on the behavior of men and social forces, neither of which is entirely beyond human control."[98] Another cognitive spur to political action during adolescence is the development of *hypothetical thought*, another intellectual advance that has been widely documented by researchers studying adolescent psychology.[99] Through hypothetical thought, the adolescent can imagine a social world that is constructed differently than the existing one. This includes imagining what the world would be like under conditions that are radically different from the social reality that we have come to expect—a world, for example, without war or social inequality. Finally, according to Merelman, there are two other cognitive advances that encourage adolescents to become politically engaged. Through new *role-taking skills*, the adolescent identifies with an ever-increasing circle of humanity, thus becoming more concerned with contributing to others' welfare. Conversely, through a clearer understanding of *linkage*, the adolescent sees how imperfections in the social system can affect his or her own personal life.

The result of these advances in moral and cognitive judgment during adolescence is a new political consciousness, and for some, an initial attempt at political action. The adolescent now sees that the world can be different than it now is, and she understands that changes come about through a predictable sequence of cause-and-effect. The adolescent also realizes that the condition of society is of direct consequence to her own welfare, as well as to the welfare of others, and she has the capacity to sympathize with the plight of an ever-increasing range of others. Finally, the adolescent can question the moral underpinnings of the existing social order, imagining changes that would lead to moral and practical improvements. Whether the resulting awakening in political consciousness results in idle political discourse, voting, campaigning, or political protests, depends upon the individual adolescent, as well as the current political climate. But the intellectual seeds for political interest and

---

[97] Inhelder & Piaget, 1958; Flavell, 1977.
[98] Merelman, 1971, p. 1040.

[99] Inhelder & Piaget, 1958; Neimark, 1975; Keating, 1980.

involvement have been sown by the cognitive and moral changes common to most adolescents.

There have been three empirical confirmations of Merelman's model, one by Merelman himself and two by other developmental psychologists studying the societal views of youth.[100] In Merelman's own study, he surveyed the attitudes of forty middle-class eighth-grade and twelfth-grade students about poverty.[101] Merelman chose poverty as the focal issue of his interview, because it is an undeniable fact of social life everywhere, because it is a political problem with moral implications, because the causes of poverty are complex and multidimensional, and because the existence of poverty in society affects even the lives of middle-class persons, though in somewhat obscure ways. The issue of poverty, therefore, is a natural test of an individual's capacity for hypothetical, causal, and linkage thinking about a complex political problem of the current social order. For Merelman's middle-class subjects, it was also a test of their capacity to take the role of others in a less fortunate position than themselves.

Merelman found a number of striking differences in his subjects' attitudes about poverty and its political implications. Interestingly, some of these differences were age-related and others were not. The age-related differences (that is, those that distinguished the answers of the eighth-graders from the answers of the twelfth-graders) were the following: in their *moral thinking* about poverty, virtually all subjects believed that poverty was wrong and should be corrected, but for different reasons and in different ways. The younger adolescents believed poverty to be wrong for its adverse material effects on people (lack of food, clothes). They believed that poverty should be corrected by simply giving gifts to the poor. Older adolescents focused on moral principles like equality, social reciprocity, and equity, favoring long-range political solutions like assuring equal opportunity to all members of society. In addition, older subjects tended to believe that it was the collective responsibility of everyone in society to alleviate a person's poverty, whereas the younger subjects tended to limit the responsibility to those directly associated with the poverty victim. The final age difference was in relation to the linkage thinking of Merelman's subjects; in other words, in middle-class subjects' capacities to see for themselves the personal consequences of others' poverty. The younger adolescents could not see how societal poverty could affect the non-poor at all, except in the psychological sense of their feeling sorry and compassionate for those in need. The older adolescents, on the other hand, believed that poverty has direct consequences for everyone in society, including the economic effects of sharing responsibility for caring for the poor ("It costs us all money" and "You see part of your pay check go out to welfare") and the political effects of social conflict and potential turmoil.

In addition to these age differences, Merelman found other individual

---

[100] Connell, 1971; Merelman, 1971; Furth, 1980.   [101] Merelman, 1971.

differences that had nothing to do with the age of his adolescent subjects. For example, some adolescents understood that poverty is a "vicious circle" with multiple related causes. Poor housing and nutrition affect a child's educational opportunities and social contacts, which in turn affect the child's motivation and later career opportunities, which in turn affect how the next generation is raised, housed, and fed, and so on. Many adolescents, however, did not connect these adverse conditions to one another, relying on single causal explanations that seem to arise from nowhere. Similarly, some adolescents realized that poverty has multiple effects—both of a physical and psychological sort—on its victims, whereas others focused solely on the physical deprivations. Finally, some could imagine a world without poverty and could outline courses of political action that might produce such a world, whereas others could not imagine, even on a hypothetical level, significant changes in existing social conditions.

Because some of the differences that Merelman found were age-related and others were not, he speculates that cognitive and moral development during adolescence is a partial but incomplete explanation for political socialization. Other factors may include the values of the adolescent's family and peer group, the opportunities for political engagement in the adolescent's home community, and the various combinations of psychodynamic and personal factors that influence any individual's choices of conduct in the world.

Adolescent political development was also illustrated in a summary of the political knowledge of Australian youth in 1968.[102] Although many of the questions and answers in the study pertain to particular political personalities and problems of that time (Australian Prime Ministers Menzies, Holt, and Gorton; the Vietnam War), the conceptual understanding reflected in subjects' answers sheds light on the general awakening of political consciousness in the adolescent years. The subjects in this study ranged in age from five through eighteen. As might be expected, five-year-olds display at most a spotty and dim awareness of political reality. Because children at this age rarely experience events external to their friends and families, "details about real politics are mere scraps, variously woven together and filled in with themes and details from the child's own life and imagination." There is some sense that politicians perform certain actions, like making speeches or running for elections, but there is no understanding of politics as a distinct sphere of activity with its own social roles and functions.

In middle childhood, children develop the notion that those in public office occupy a special political role or position. This notion can be described as a "task pool" conception. In other words, children at this age know that politicians perform a coordinated set of tasks unlike those assigned to other members of society. These tasks might include making laws, working with the military or the police, appearing at public functions, or informing the public about important news. But at this age, there is still no knowledge of the political

[102] Connell, 1971.

order, because the child does not understand that society is organized in a hierarchical fashion, with some persons occupying positions of great political power relative to others.

It is during adolescence that the structure of the political order is first fully understood. Not only does this mean that adolescents recognize the existence of a political hierarchy in their society, but it also means that they realize the significance of this hierarchy to political choice and conflict. They understand that politicians vie for power and that citizens in society disagree about where and to whom political power should be allocated. This new awareness leads to an understanding of the role of political parties and other political-action groupings. It also makes the adolescent aware of potential avenues for political action within the social system: the adolescent now knows that one may make choices about whom to support and begins to learn about appropriate mechanisms (voting, campaigning) for making and implementing such choices. Again, we see how the awakening of political awareness makes possible political participation.

A recent study of English youth further confirmed the developmental trends in political development that we have been describing.[103] In this study, children were asked about societal institutions that are directly linked to the political order, such as the use and purpose of money. Similar to the results of the study discussed above, it was found that young children have only a sporadic awareness of money. They know what coins and bills are, but not what they represent in a societal sense. That is, these children understand money as an object of exchange, but have little idea about the rules or purpose of the exchange. It is almost as if money were being exchanged for playful reasons, much as children trade toys or objects of interest. Later in childhood, children develop a partial knowledge of money as an instrument for buying goods. They know that things must be paid for and that money works in this regard. But they do not understand where money comes from. They also have a dim understanding of rules of monetary transactions. For example, a child might believe that one pays money to a storekeeper for goods, and one then receives the goods and some "change" in addition. The child may then make the assumption that the change one receives is the source of one's future money, so that, according to this childhood belief, one actually gains one's money by buying goods and receiving change. By the end of childhood there is a more accurate realization that one gains money by earning it and that the change one receives from paying transactions cannot be the source of one's money because it is always a lesser amount than one had prior to the payment. In the adolescent years, there develops the additional understanding of the economic rationales for earning, buying, and selling. Institutions like the profit system are understood in terms of the social necessity of manufacturing, distributing, and exchanging goods. This, of course, makes evident the political implications

---

[103] Furth, 1980.

of both maintaining and changing current economic conditions, and it adds one further dimension to the adolescent's emerging political consciousness.

Aside from the developing political knowledge that prepares an adolescent for participation in the political part of citizenship, what else explains the extent and nature of an adolescent's actual engagement in political activities? As we know, there is enormous variation in the political life of individuals. True "ideologists" who are deeply committed to a particular doctrine and who dedicate large portions of their time and resources to political causes are rare: one survey found that only 2½ percent of the adolescent population could be characterized in this way. But to a lesser degree, many teenagers do become affiliated with political parties, causes, or candidates, either on the local or national level. These teenagers, like the adult population, differ greatly among themselves, not only in the seriousness of their commitment, but also in their political values and inclinations. What accounts for such differences?

Over the past twenty years, several studies in political socialization have attempted to answer this question. As with most attempts to explain human behavior, these studies have not yielded a clear-cut, single answer to this question. Nevertheless, the results from these studies have informed us about the relative strength of certain influences on adolescent political behavior. The most obvious influences, and the focus of many political socialization studies, are the political values and behavior of the adolescent's parents. Generally, researchers have found positive but modest correlations between parental politics and the politics of their adolescent offspring.[104] This research pertains both to the beliefs and to the actual political involvement of parents and their children. Typically, teenagers will accept many of their parents' general precepts and political orientation (pro- or anti-socialism, conservative or liberal), but often they disagree about specific contemporary issues (school integration, abortion, drinking laws). As noted earlier in this chapter, there is little actual evidence for a major "generation gap" between parents and children, but there are still widespread areas of variance and disagreement. For this reason, researchers are careful to disavow theoretical models which claim that parents directly transmit political values to their children. Another argument against such models is the finding that correlations between the political beliefs of siblings are also positive but low.[105] Similarity, where it exists, is again partial and irregular. It seems clear from such evidence that the familial influence on political socialization is indirect at best.

Other studies shed further light on the types of home environments likely to have the greatest influence on adolescent political behaviors.[106] In these studies, adolescents from homes that encouraged open discussion of political ideas were the ones most likely to engage in political action. In particular, adolescents living in "pluralistic" home environments in which there was

[104] Hyman, 1959; Hess & Torney, 1967; Jennings & Niemi, 1968; Connell, 1972.
[105] Hess & Torney, 1967.

[106] Stone & Chaffee, 1970; Chaffee, McLeod, & Wackman, 1973; Chaffee, 1977.

frequent debate and political argument were likely to be both highly informed and to accept civic responsibility as a natural part of life's duties. In contrast, adolescents living in homes that offered no opportunities for political discussion were less likely to become politically active. The adolescents who were least active and who had the lowest level of political knowledge were those living in "protective" families that not only discouraged political discussion but also stressed harmony and obedience to the prevailing social order.

The other obvious candidate for influencing adolescent political attitudes is the school environment, and several studies have attempted to identify the nature and strength of such influence. The most widely known of these studies concluded that schools do indeed have a large effect on the politics of their pupils.[107] This conclusion was based on the finding that the political values of young adolescents corresponded closely to those of their teachers. This and other findings led the authors of this study to speculate that schools have an even greater impact on political socialization than do parents: "The school apparently plays the largest part in teaching attitudes, conceptions, and beliefs about the operation of the political system."[108] But some researchers believe that this conclusion overstates the school's case. For one thing, the survey questions in this study were broadly based and did not pin down either students or teachers to specific political opinions. There is still, therefore, the possibility that considerable teacher-pupil disagreement may have been undisclosed by this study's methodology. One reviewer has written that this study reveals the school's indisputable influence on the adolescent's general political concepts and principles, but not on the adolescent's actual political leanings.[109] In other words, schools educate students about political institutions like constitutional government, and in the process, orient students to certain broad political considerations. The teacher may emphasize one or another feature of the political system, thus communicating a certain attitude that may influence the adolescent's perspective on political engagement. But within this broad sphere of influence, there is great individual leeway in the formation of the political attitudes that determine actual political choices and behaviors. Researchers have found that the role of the mass media (T.V., newspapers) can work in the same way, conveying political information that helps adolescents form concepts of the social system, but having relatively minor impact on everyday political conduct.[110]

A number of researchers have also attempted to identify the personality characteristics of political activists versus those of nonactivists, hoping to explain political involvement in terms of the individual's internal makeup, rather than in terms of external social influences like family and school. By and large, the results of these studies have been contradictory. Some studies have portrayed student activists in highly positive terms, as altruistic, bright, sin-

---

[107] Hess & Torney, 1967.
[108] Ibid., p. 218.
[109] Gallatin, 1980.

[110] Connell, 1971; Jennings & Niemi, 1975; Chaffee, 1977.

cerely motivated, and high academic achievers.[111] Others have taken a more negative view of activists, portraying them as alienated, uncommitted, psychologically imbalanced, and hedonistic.[112] Both views are probably true, because student activists no doubt become politically involved for a variety of reasons; the same political action may be conducted from two entirely different points of view, one reflecting a well-considered political belief and the other a personal grievance or disturbance. As noted above in the morality section of this chapter, the study of the Berkeley Free Speech Movement found that students with both low and high levels of moral judgment worked together for the same political cause and engaged in identical political actions. For a full understanding of an adolescent's political behavior, we must know the meaning to the adolescent of various courses of conduct. This is a matter closely related to the adolescent's development of self-identity, a matter to which we shall return in the following chapter.

Strategic Social Interactions and Their Role in Adolescent Development

Social interactions at all phases of life have some consequences for personality formation, as we have pointed out in earlier chapters of this book. During adolescence, the personality function of social interactions becomes more consciously directed than previously—that is, the adolescent "stages" social interactions that are directly intended to project his personality and to enhance his sense of self. Although he does not fully realize the psychological implications of such interactions in the sense that we are about to describe them, there is a new awareness of their potential use.

The adolescent demonstrates this awareness by a marked increase in self-consciousness during social interactions, as well as a new sense of "planfulness." Words and acts are often guided and guarded, usually with a view to their personal effects. Because the adolescent begins to consciously exploit social occasions for the enhancement of the self, his social behavior becomes imbued with strategy and caution. Social scientists have coined the phrase *strategic interactions* to capture this quality in the social behavior that emerges during adolescence.[113]

According to sociologist Erving Goffman's definition, a strategic interaction is a social engagement in which one or both of the parties attempts to convey, conceal, or acquire information indirectly.[114] In other words, it is an interaction with a "double message": the surface behavior and the information-directed intent underlying it. The prototype of a strategic interaction is a poker game. While going about the business of managing their dealt hands, poker players are busy bluffing their opponents, inferring their opponents'

Sociobiol.

[111] Fishman & Solomon, 1964; Keniston, 1968.

[112] Watts & Whittaker, 1966; Fishkin,

Keniston, & MacKinnon, 1973.

[113] Goffman, 1969; Elkind, 1980.

[114] Goffman, 1969.

positions, and presenting false signals about their own cards. A less combative example of a strategic interaction is a dinner between business associates who are seeking both an enjoyable evening and a closer business relationship.

Adopting Goffman's term for the purposes of developmental psychology, David Elkind has analyzed teenage "strategic interactions."[115] Adolescents are ripe for strategic interactions, believes Elkind, because of changes in their intellectual capacities as described by Piaget and others.[116] Specifically, adolescents are able to see several possible consequences of an action, and they are able to perform for an imaginary or hypothetical audience. Both of these abilities are essential in conducting a strategic interaction.

Elkind writes that, for the adolescent, the goal of strategic interactions is the enhancement of self-esteem. This is in contrast to the information-directed goals of the adult strategic interactions that Goffman describes. According to Elkind, teenagers typically engage in several types of strategic interactions, all of which share the common function of bolstering their still-shaky sense of self.

As we shall further explore in the next chapter, the personal side of adolescent social development largely revolves around the problem of establishing a coherent self-identity. Some theorists have called this a time of crisis in the search for identity, because of the intense uncertainty that the adolescent feels about the self during this period. In addition, as Elkind points out, the teenager is in between sources of emotional support. As he begins breaking away from the family, the old sources of parent-child support may be weakened, but he has not yet established adult sources of support like his own career and family. For all these reasons, self-esteem during adolescence is often on shaky ground. Strategic social interactions enable the teenager to bolster his sense of self, because they offer an opportunity to "enhance, maintain, and defend self-esteem in relation to an audience."[117]

Elkind notes several types of strategic social interactions in which American teenagers typically engage. The first is "phoning and being phoned." Teenagers, writes Elkind, prove their own popularity to themselves and others by receiving and making numerous phone calls. Other strategies for demonstrating popularity by way of the telephone include staying on the phone for long periods of time (and thus having potential callers receive frequent busy signals), or conversely, cutting short phone conversations because one "expects other calls."

A second type of teenage strategic interaction occurs in the context of friendship. Relations with friends, of course, serve the many essential psychological functions noted earlier in this chapter, such as companionship, intimacy, and self-disclosure. But in addition, writes Elkind, friendship interactions can be used strategically, to demonstrate one's self-worth. Acquiring many friends, belonging to selected cliques, and even rejecting some friendship overtures from certain "outsiders," all can be used to demonstrate

---

[115] Elkind, 1980.
[116] Inhelder & Piaget, 1958; Flavell, 1977.
[117] Elkind, 1980.

one's own attractiveness. Similarly, being recognized by others in public places and failing to recognize "low status" others (a tactic called "cutting") are convincing indicators of one's social worth.

The sexual side of teenage friendships, dating, provides adolescents with even higher-stake opportunities for strategic interactions. In every aspect of the dating process—from asking the other for a date to sexual engagement—there are multiple possible rewards and risks from a strategic point of view (Of course, as with nonsexual friendship, dating serves other real psychological needs, but here we are considering only its strategic self-enhancement function.) According to Elkind, every aspect of dating offers an opportunity to prove one's attractiveness to oneself and others. In fact, writes Elkind, teengers often seek dates more for the sake of their "audience" than for the sake of their own needs or pleasure. "Getting a date" can demonstrate one's attractiveness, as can refusing date offers from others. As for sexual activity itself, this too can be used strategically, aside from its intrinsic appeal. The direction of the strategic goal traditionally has differed between boys and girls: "The boy's strategy is to try and 'get' as much as he can with the girl's permission, or at least without violent protest. A usual strategy for the boy it to test the limits nonverbally with the aid of slowly moving arms and crawling fingers. The girl communicates equally nonverbally by either moving toward or away from the boy and by accepting or pushing away the troublesome hands."[118] For a boy, each advance in sexual contact is an achievement that can be shared with an audience, whereas girls typically have been more ambivalent about the self-esteem rewards of "giving in." This sex difference, however, may be on the wane in current times.

Elkind believes that most adolescents soon outgrow their need for using social interactions to enhance their self-esteem. Strategic interactions continue, and even increase in complexity and frequency, as adolescents begin to engage in career and other formal societal matters. The use of strategic interactions for the sake of one's self-esteem continues only for those whose "ego-gratification" needs remain at the adolescent level of maturity. As we shall see in the next chapter, the problem is closely entwined with how and when one resolves one's "identity crisis."

Summary

Peer relations during adolescence multiply and become transformed in nature and significance. Same-sex friendships become imbued with qualities of loyalty and intimacy. Adolescent friends understand one another as "persons." This means knowing that one's friend shares some of one's own abilities, interests, and inner experiences, but that the friend also has a distinct personality that differs from one's own. Consequently, there is a wish to understand

[118] Ibid., p. 439.

one's friends, as individuals, all with their own particular life histories and points of view, as well as a wish to be understood by others in this way. These wishes are the source of loyalty, because they provide a sense that only through a lasting commitment can two distinct individuals coordinate their personalities in a complementary, mutually beneficial manner. They are also the source of intimacy, because the wish to understand and be understood as oneself leads to a sharing of confidences and self-revelations in friendships.

Developmentalists have shown how these adolescent insights into friendship are amplified and elaborated throughout this age period. In interview studies, it has been found that early in adolescence, loyalty and intimacy are generally seen as features of exclusive, closed friendships. Later in adolescence, it is realized that these qualities can be attained through a variety of different types of friendships, none of which needs to be exclusive in character. This developmental analysis corresponds to sociological descriptions of friendship patterns during early and late adolescence. Young teenagers congregate in unisex cliques, often with no more than two or three members. Eventually, these cliques become larger and heterosexual in nature, and then they extend into large, looser-knit "crowds." The adolescent's initial forays into intimacy, therefore, are carried out on the relatively safe ground of the exclusive clique and only gradually extend to individuals from the more widely open teenage crowds.

Another new element of some peer relations during adolescence is sexuality. Teenage sexuality can serve several purposes, including recreation, status seeking, independence assertion, social-skill seeking, and courtship. Sexual relations can be casual or serious, short- or long-lived, monogamous or nonmonogamous. In a sexual relationship, the greatest conflict and stress occur when partners do not seek the same type of relation on any of these dimensions. Adolescent sexual relations are frequently characterized by such conflict and stress because adolescents often have not learned how to communicate effectively with sexual partners about their mutual goals. The difficulty in learning to do so arises from the complexity of physical and social consequences of a sexual relationship. Accordingly, stable and mutually satisfying sexual relationships during adolescence are rare. This is as true for today's youth as for youth of past generations. Sociological surveys have shed doubt on the actual extent of the widely heralded "sexual revolution" during modern times.

Although peer relations often receive the spotlight in accounts of adolescent social relations, the family also retains its critical importance during this period. Most adolescents are still attached to their homes in a positive way, and they depend upon the approval and emotional support of their parents. Most adolescents share their parents' attitudes toward moral and political issues, and they accept their parents' guidance on academic, career, and personal matters. In short, research has not confirmed popular notions about alienated youth or the generation gap. Although some research has found important differences between the adolescent's peer and family cultures, most investigators have concluded that this does not mean that the two necessarily conflict. The great majority of adolescents are positively oriented toward both their peers and their parents. They generally do not feel torn between the two, except on certain minor issues (dress styles, social habits) where adolescents may reject the attitudes of their parents in favor of the norms of their peers.

Although parental guidance and support continue during the adolescent years, there are some important changes in the nature of the parent-child relation. Gradually, adolescents see themselves more and more as equals to their parents. The relation turns from one of complementary exchange, an indirect reciprocity in which the child's obedience is exchanged for the parent's help and care, to one of direct reciprocity in which parents and teenagers negotiate family regulations together. In addition, teenagers begin to apply some lessons that they earlier have learned in peer interactions to their relations with their parents. Mutuality of respect and communication emerge, also enhancing the increasing sense of equality between parent and child.

Historians and other scholars working within the "life-course" tradition have shown how particular historical forces can shape the lives and social development of adolescents. For example, the extent of parental control over adolescents changes greatly during certain historical periods, often depending upon economic conditions in society-at-large. Other historical forces, such as urbanization, wars, and industrialization, also have been shown to play a part. Such forces can either remove adolescents from their homes at early ages or keep them at home, under their parents' continued control, for long periods of time. Either way, these kinds of historical influences can have major implications for teenage autonomy, identity, and sense of self.

As children grow into adolescence, they acquire a perspective on collective social realities that goes beyond their previous conceptions of family and peer relations. They now understand that one's social interactions may have economic, political, or legal significance, in addition to the interpersonal meanings of such interactions. The adolescent's attention turns to the social system itself, with its institutions, laws, procedures, and other organizational features. This new "societal" orientation colors adolescent values and social conceptions of every kind.

Many developmentalists have noted adolescents' awakening interest in ideology and in the process of codifying rules. Piaget's last stage in his moral judgment sequence was a description of this new *social systems thinking*, which emerged in early adolescence. Kohlberg's stage sequence elaborates on this trend toward thinking about moral concerns in terms of their social-order consequences. Kohlberg's higher stages describe the progressively more sophisticated manner in which adolescents rely on societal concerns in their moral reasoning. At stage 3, social expectations and conventions are respected; at stage 4, laws and the social system itself are respected; whereas by stage 5, it is moral principles (equality, liberty) underlying the social contract that are respected. This is because stage 3 is based on a "social-relational perspective," stage 4 on a "member-of-society" perspective, and stage 5 on a "prior-to-society" perspective. Kohlberg has also described a sixth moral stage, but he has not been able to furnish much evidence that it actually exists.

Controversies surround Kohlberg's claims that his moral stage sequence is universal. Some have claimed that his stages are culturally biased because higher-level reasoning is rarely found in non-Western societies. Others have claimed that the sequence is sexually biased because women sometimes score lower than men. This, one author claims, is due to the greater interpersonal sensitivity of women relative to men, a sensitivity that consigns women's moral judgments to stage 3 rather than to Kohlberg's higher-level stages that are based more on rules and principles than on interpersonal concerns. Kohlberg recently has presented some longitudinal data that strengthen his claims about the invariant and holistic properties of his stage sequence (and other areas of controversy), but these data were collected from an American male population. Further empirical studies are required to resolve potential problems of cultural and sexual bias.

Studies relating adolescent moral judgment to moral conduct are few and far between. One of the rare efforts in this area was a study of students who "sat in" during the Berkeley Free Speech Movement. Students who sat in did tend to come from some stages—particularly 2 and 5—more than from others, as would be predicted by the logic of the Kohlberg stages. But the stage-action correlation was far from perfect, indicating that stages of moral judgment may guide conduct in certain directions, but they do not absolutely determine any specific action choice. At best, knowing a person's predominate moral stage may help us predict the person's general action tendencies in moral situations. But these predictions will never reach certainty because no moral stage leads directly to a particular choice. Moral stages reflect general principles underlying decision making, but the decisions themselves must be made in the context of moral problems that are always to some degree new. A flexible use rather than a rote application of moral principles is called for, and therefore there will always be some variation in how decisions to act are made at each stage.

Moral development, though critical, is only one part of socialization during the adolescent years. Another key aspect is the development of respect for social conventions. This entails both understanding the importance of social conventions and distinguishing social-conventional rules from genuine moral rules. Turiel has described a seven-level sequence in the development of social-conventional reasoning. In addition, he has shown how, during adolescence, the confusion between morality and convention is resolved, paving the way for the emergence of principled morality (Kohlberg's stage 5). Resolving this confusion, according to Turiel's analysis, is a difficult and conflictual process that requires serious soul-searching and reflection on the part of the adolescent.

For many adolescents, the teenage years mark the beginnings of a political awakening. Frequently, people experience their first commitment to a political ideology and even engage in direct political action during adolescence. Social scientists attribute this interest in politics to the cognitive and moral advances that occur during the transition from childhood to adolescence. In particular, researchers have cited the development of formal operations, especially with regard to sophisticated forms of causal and hypothetical reasoning, as well as the development of higher-stage moral judgment. Such advances enable adolescents to understand the causes of social ills, to imagine a better society, and to see how their own activity could contribute to the construction of such a society. No doubt because of such advances, studies of political knowledge in children and adolescents have found that a sophisticated and realistic understanding of the political system develops some time in middle adolescence, at which point teenagers are ready to assume political responsibility as citizens in society. The exact nature of the adolescent's political choices depends upon many factors, including the particular family and school influences that the adolescent encounters. In addition, the adolescent's own personality characteristics determine, to a large degree, the nature and extent of the adolescent's dramatic increase in political awareness.

During adolescence, the personality function of social interaction becomes more consciously directed than during the childhood years. Psychologists and sociologists have shown how adolescents "stage" social interactions in order to enhance their sense of self. Elkind has described a number of these "strategic interactions" commonly found during the teenage years. In middle-class Western society, some typical strategic interactions include telephoning and being telephoned, attracting and rejecting friends, and broadcasting one's sexual appeal through acquiring dates and engaging in sexual activity. Elkind believes that by the end of adolescence, most individuals outgrow their need to use social interactions to enhance their self-esteem. During adolescence, however, such behavior is a valuable means of shoring up the self at a time when one must disengage from the family and construct one's own personal identity as an individual who is fundamentally alone in the world.

Chapter 8

Adolescent Identity
and the Consolidation of Self

In the opinion of many scholars, the major psychosocial task of adolescence is the formation of a coherent personal identity. In fact, most contemporary psychologists define the timing of adolescence according to this psychosocial task, rather than according to a particular age range or set biological event (such as puberty). Adolescence is the time in life that begins with an intense concern for defining one's individual nature, and it ends when one has established a consolidated sense of self-identity. By this standard, the age of adolescence can vary widely from individual to individual. In some cases, due to a prolonged identity crisis, it may last until well into middle age. Typically, however, adolescence, according to this psychosocial definition, ends in the years immediately following secondary school. Research has shown that, at least for middle-class Western youth, the challenge of identity formation normally is resolved between the ages of eighteen and twenty-two.[1]

Identity formation serves a dual function—psychological and social. On the one hand, constructing a personal identity is a psychological endeavor, instigated by one's own need to organize and understand one's experience of individuality. On the other hand, it is a social process, instigated by others'

[1] Stark & Traxler, 1974.

demands that one identify oneself in terms of chosen familial, occupational, and societal roles. The search for identity occurs in response to both internal and external forces, requiring a solution that meets the challenges of both. For the sake of one's own internal satisfaction, there is a need to establish an identity that is consistent, comprehensive, and without serious intrinsic contradictions. For the sake of one's relations with others, one must establish an identity that determines one's role in the various social networks to which one belongs, and that makes clear one's status and position in the general social order. Because psychosocial identity must serve these dual functions, the adolescent's task is doubly complex: not only must the adolescent weave an identity structure that is conceptually sound (meeting cognitive standards such as logical adequacy, coherence, systematicity), but at the same time this identity must be realistic and effective in one's transactions with society-at-large.

We shall consider identity formation as a task particularly associated with adolescence, and as the essential definitional feature of adolescence. But the process of identity construction does not begin in adolescence, nor does it end there, despite the seminal feat of identity consolidation that marks the culmination of the adolescent period. Rather, the search for identity has its roots in infancy and childhood, as we have witnessed in Chapters 3 and 6, and even after adolescence there continues to be a lifelong process of revising and reorganizing one's identity. What is special to the adolescent period is the intensity, and in many cases the sense of crisis, that accompanies the adolescent's initial attempt at constructing a coherent and socially responsive personal identity. Never before or again are the stakes of this search so high, or the possibilities so open.

The Need for Autonomy and Individuation in Adolescence

Why is adolescence a time of intense concern for individuality and self-identity? The multiplicity of changes in the adolescent's biological, personal, and social make-up encourages the adolescent to forge an increased sense of autonomy from others. In addition, these changes prepare the adolescent for a radically new understanding of self, an understanding that provides a sound basis for separating oneself from others while maintaining a belief that one is still connected, in important ways, to others in society. The changes that trigger these advances in autonomy and individuality reflect a coincidence of inner and outer influences that begin to be felt soon after childhood.

The major biological change for the adolescent is the onset of puberty, commonly defined as a series of rapid changes in the reproductive system occurring shortly after childhood.[2] No new components are added during puberty, but there is rapid maturation in already existing components of sexual functioning. This includes sudden growth in the genitalia, as well as in other

[2] Tanner, 1962, 1974a; Petersen & Taylor, 1980.

reproduction-related bodily organs (such as breasts in young women), and large increases in sex-related hormonal activity. Although these biological systems were all present at birth, during adolescence they cease being latent and become fully functional. This happens very quickly and without much bodily warning. In fact, at no other period of life, except during infancy (and before the development of highly conscious self-awareness), is there such a sudden and dramatic change in one's physiology. Little wonder that major psychological and social consequences accompany this change.

The most important of puberty's psychosocial consequences is the adolescent's detachment and separation from certain others, particularly parents and family. Psychoanalytic theory has described this process in great detail.[3] In Freudian terms, puberty reawakens sexual desires that have been latent since childhood. The initial objects of these sexual desires were the parents, as Freud documented in his writings on the Oedipal fantasies. When these long-latent desires reemerge during puberty, their immediate focus is again the parents. For the now self-conscious adolescent, however, the realization of this desire creates anxiety, and it results in a defensive reaction against the desire. Ultimately, this leads to the diminishing of emotional ties of all kinds toward the parents and to the "reinvestment of primary sexual and affectional needs outside the family."[4] Hence the adolescent's striving for emotional autonomy from those very persons with whom the closest of relationships had previously been shared. This not only represents a revolution in the individual's interpersonal orientation, but also a new conception of the relational characteristics of the self.

Aside from changes in the reproductive system, other psychologically significant biological changes also occur during the post-childhood years. Among these are physiological increases in brain cells that contribute to important advances in cognitive functioning.[5] The most noted such cognitive advance during adolescence is the emergence of formal-operational reasoning.[6] This includes the ability to think hypothetically, to imagine a range of possibilities and future events, and to think systematically about one's own thinking.

These new intellectual powers enable the adolescent to reason critically and skeptically about previously held beliefs. Both one's own intellectual positions and those of others are challenged and reconsidered with an eye toward creating one's own personal world view. This world view will form the cornerstone of the adolescent's sense of individual uniqueness. As we saw in the last chapter, for many adolescents a fundamental part of this world view is an ideological commitment, made possible by the adolescent's increasing ability to understand complex societal issues and to imagine hypothetical possibilities. In addition, the changes in moral judgment that were documented in the

---

[3] Blos, 1962; A. Freud, 1946, 1958; S. Freud, 1905.
[4] Petersen & Taylor, 1980.
[5] Tanner, 1969, 1972.
[6] Kuhn & Angelev, 1976; Moshman, 1977; Keating, 1980.

last chapter contribute to the adolescent's quest for an autonomous world view. The transition from conventional morality to principled morality spurs a critical reevaluation of both society's and one's own values. This provides an occasion for dissociating oneself from the moral views and moral influence of others. When a new system of moral belief is constructed out of the ashes of rejected values and rules, it is done with a sense of self-choice and independence. For this reason, most scholars consider principled morality to be the only truly autonomous mode of moral judgment.[7] In this, as in other spheres of life, the adolescent begins to realize what it means to determine one's own course of conduct and choice.

The Process of Individuation

Because of the strong strivings for independence experienced by many adolescents, psychologists have traditionally considered the adolescent period as a time of rebellion. Particularly within psychoanalytic theory, adolescence has been described as a period of personal "storm and stress."[8] Some psychoanalysts have emphasized, above all, the adolescent's rebellious relations with the parents, writing that this period is marked by a spirit of "detachment" because of the adolescent's wholehearted attempt to "stamp out" the parent's influence.[9] But as we saw in the previous chapter, most adolescents still rely heavily on their parents for emotional support and personal guidance. Rebellion may be an aspect of the parent-child relation during adolescence, but it is certainly not the whole story. For most teenagers, tension and disagreement between themselves and their parents take place within the context of a close, cooperative, and even somewhat dependent relationship.

The paradoxically rebellious yet close relationship between adolescents and parents reveals some central characteristics of the adolescent's growth toward personal independence and autonomy. Ruthellen Josselson believes it is similar, in formal features, to the infant's struggle for autonomy, experienced a decade prior to adolescence.[10] Josselson described adolescent personal development in terms of Mahler's model of infant individuation, summarized in Chapter 3 of this book, in order to capture the polar spirits of rebelliousness and conciliation that teenagers often feel in their parental relations.

According to Josselson, the process of individuation, whenever it occurs during life, consists of four distinct subphases. These subphases are similar in structure, whether they occur in infancy or in adolescence, despite the many obvious differences between the search for autonomy during these widely separate age periods. As noted in Chapter 3, the four subphases of individuation are (1) differentiation, (2) practice and experimentation, (3) rapprochement, and (4) consolidation. In terms of infant individuation, these four subphases describe the infant's progression through the following sequence:

---

[7] Keniston, 1970; Kohlberg, 1976; Kohlberg & Gilligan, 1971.
[8] A. Freud, 1946, 1958.
[9] Schafer, 1973.
[10] Josselson, 1980.

first, the initial discovery that mother and self are separate persons; second, the elaboration of this discovery through playful refusals to follow the mother's instructions; third, the infant's demands for the mother's acceptance of the infant's newfound autonomy; and fourth, the infant's development of a stable attachment to the mother on the basis of a consolidated sense of an independent self.

In adolescence, the battle for personal autonomy is fought around a different set of issues, but it unfolds in a sequence that parallels the general structure of individuation, whenever it occurs. In Josselson's analysis, young adolescents just leaving childhood are faced with the problem of removing themselves from the overwhelming influence of their parents. During childhood, the parents are the main source of many psychological necessities, from self-esteem to judgments and decisions about one's life course. Gradually, adolescents must find other sources for these needs, particularly sources within themselves. The first phase of this search requires the adolescent to question the parent's values and behavior, at least insofar as they serve as guides for the adolescent's own way of life. During this *differentiation phase*, the adolescent realizes that one's parents are different from oneself, in a psychological sense. They have their own personal attributes and predilections, many of which are not relevant to oneself or one's own life choices. This realization may cause the adolescent to reject parental advice: the childhood presumption of parental omniscience changes into an adolescent willingness to reject parental wisdom out of hand. At first, the need to adopt a rejecting attitude may be so pressing that the adolescent overreacts by throwing out reasonable advice along with inappropriate advice.

The initial realization of personal autonomy during the differentiation subphase is followed by a *practicing subphase* in which young adolescents delight in trying out the spirit of psychological independence from their parents. During this subphase, adolescents may often have feelings of omnipotence; they may often believe they can do no wrong, denying the need for caution or moderation in their behavior. Just as in a structurally parallel phase of infancy, when infants in the "terrible twos" delight in saying "no" whenever possible to the mother, adolescents at this time intentionally seek occasions for contradicting their parents. Irritating their elders is often a goal in itself and is pursued with great ingenuity and cleverness. At the same time, adolescents' increasing bonds with friends outside the home help provide them with the approval that they formerly received from adults. Puberty, with its accompanying desire to seek extra-familial sexual relations, provides adolescents with an additional push away from parents and toward the peer group.

But adolescents continue to need their parents' support, as we have noted elsewhere, and this need is expressed in the third phase of the individuation process, *rapprochement*. When the adolescent convincingly establishes a sense of separateness from the parent, there are often feelings of pain and fear that are associated with this achievement in autonomy. The adolescent worries that separation, whatever its personal benefits, will result in the loss of the parents' love. Josselson writes that "The most common complaint of middle adolescence is, 'my parents don't understand me.'"[11] During this phase, adolescents realize that even autonomous individuals need home bases to return to from time to time. This realization leads to more conciliatory behavior toward parents and to a reacceptance of parental directives. This reacceptance, however, is conditional and partial. The lessons of autonomy have not been forgotten, only integrated into the adolescent's rediscovery of the necessity for a continued bond with the parent. The reestablished bond, in fact, is stronger precisely because it now connects two autonomous individuals, and therefore it is a bond based upon freedom of choice and voluntary cooperation. As noted in Chapter 7, this new consensual spirit transforms the nature of virtually all interpersonal interactions between adolescents and adults.

The final subphase of adolescent individuality, the *consolidation of self*, will be the main topic for the remainder of this chapter. During this phase, the adolescent constructs a sense of identity that provides her with a conceptual and personal basis for asserting her independence and individuality. In constructing a personal identity, she borrows selectively from childhood identifications and parental guidance. The choices of what to accept and what to reject from her parents and her past are self-determined. Because the adolescent has by now experienced the press for both separation and rapprochement with her parents, she can approach the identity construction task with a sense of balance. That is, the adolescent knows that, as an autonomous individual, she makes her own choices concerning her destiny and her nature; and yet she also knows that she sometimes can be aided in those choices by listening to those with whom she shares a close attachment. She adopts an attitude of respectful selectivity in relation to her parents' guidance. This attitude contributes both to a continuing and viable relation with her parents and to an effective sense of self. Josselson quotes one of her later adolescent subjects, at the end of this fourth subphase, reflecting on the process of her own individuation:

> Up to a certain age, I believed everything my parents said. Then, in college, I saw all these new ideas and I said, "Okay, I'm not going to believe all that stuff you told me," and I rejected everything and said to myself, "Okay, now I'm going to make a new Debby which has nothing to do with mother and father. I'm going to start with a clean slate," and what I started to put on were all new ideas. These ideas were opposite to what my parents believed. But slowly, what's happening is that I'm adding on a lot of things which they told me and I'm taking them as my own and I'm coming more together with them.[12]

Adolescent Self-Understanding

In Chapters 3 and 6, we discussed the important developmental changes in self-understanding that take place during infancy and childhood. Self-

[11] Ibid., p. 195.   [12] Ibid., p. 192.

understanding continues to develop throughout adolescence. Not only are there major changes in the adolescent's self-definition, but there are also radical shifts in adolescents' perspectives on their aspirations, their futures, and on their own role in shaping their destinies. In this section, we shall continue the discussions of Chapters 3 and 6, chronologically documenting the course of self-understanding beyond childhood. In some cases, we shall be reporting the findings of the same researchers who provided our childhood accounts of self-understanding for the earlier chapters. The current discussion will focus on the advanced levels of these researchers' developmental models.

Developmental Levels

There is noteworthy convergence in findings from several independently conducted studies of adolescent self-understanding. Virtually all researchers have found that, with development, adolescent self-understanding shows an increasing use of psychological concepts, a stronger belief in the self's agency and volitional power, a clearer awareness of the social-relational nature of the self, and a tendency toward integration of the disparate aspects of self into an internally consistent construct system. In addition to these features, some researchers have also shown how other special features of adolescent thinking, such as self-reflection, have an impact on the adolescent's conception of self.

The developmental sequence of self-awareness decribed by Robert Selman continues into the adolescent years, with its final two levels emerging in early and late adolescence, respectively.[13] Selman's level 4 (his first in adolescence) is defined by the self's awareness of its own self-awareness. This implies that the young adolescent knows that she can consciously monitor her own self-experience. Not only does this new awareness explain the increased self consciousness of young adolescents, but it also accounts for adolescents' increased sense of personal agency. Because the adolescent now knows the possibility of self-reflection, she conceives of the mind as an active processor of experience, and ultimately as a potential manipulator of her experience. This establishes a new mode of self-control. Selman offers the following examples of fourth-level reasoning: in response to a question asking about one's reactions to the loss of the puppy in Selman's dilemma (see Chapter 6), a young adolescent might say, "I can fool myself into not wanting to see another puppy if I keep on saying to myself, 'I don't want a puppy; I don't ever want to see another puppy.'"[14]

Although the adolescent at Selman's level 4 generally believes that she has control over her thoughts and emotions, she is also aware that certain mental experience is beyond her volitional reach. For example, Selman quotes one young adolescent who said, "If I did something wrong, I really can't forget about it because of time. I really can't make myself forget; I will always

---

[13] Selman, 1980. [14] Ibid., p. 103.

remember it."[15] But this apparent incongruity with the above notion of self-control poses an unresolvable contradiction to the young adolescent, who simply segregates the two irreconcilable notions of self in disparate, unrelated statements. Only at level 5, according to Selman, does the older adolescent resolve this problem by constructing the notion of conscious and nonconscious levels of experience (or some parallel version of this notion). The level 5 solution is that there are mental experiences that can influence one's actions but that are not available for conscious inspection. For example, Selman quotes one level 5 response to the question "Why did Mike say he didn't want to ever see another puppy again?" The adolescent replies, "He may not want to admit to himself that another dog could take Pepper's place. He might feel at some level that would be unloyal to Pepper to just go out and replace the dog. He may feel guilty about it. He doesn't want to face these feelings, so he says, no dog." (Is he aware of this?) "Probably not."[16]

According to Selman, therefore, self-understanding in adolescence begins with a global notion of self as a self-reflective, active controller of one's experience, with some uncoordinated recognition that there are limits to this awareness and control. Later in adolescence develops the notion of two different levels of mental experience, one conscious and one nonconscious, both of which can influence one's thoughts and actions. In this manner, the adolescent conceptually constructs a unified self-system while still preserving the notion that self-awareness and conscious self-control have their boundaries.

Selman's self-understanding research is somewhat limited by his exclusive focus on self-awareness and by his consequent reliance on perspective taking as the "underlying" explanation for conceptual development in this area. John Broughton's research, more broadly based and more directly aimed at self-specific issues, reveals some further trends in adolescent self-understanding development, in addition to replicating the basic findings reported by Selman. Broughton, like Selman, proposes two levels of self-knowledge in adolescence (levels 3 and 4 in Broughton's scheme).[17] During early adolescence, an initial distinction is made between mental and physical reality. According to Broughton, this level 3 distinction has several important implications for young adolescents' self-conceptions. First, the mind, now seen as an entity in its own right, takes on volitional characteristics independent of the self's physical activity. For example, the mental self is seen as capable of evaluating the self's actions, as in this example from one of Broughton's teenage subjects: "With our minds we can make our own judgments and do what we feel is right."[18] Second, the young adolescent sees the self as a stable way of mentally processing information, as a characteristic mode of knowing the world. One of Broughton's subjects replied that the self is "the way your thoughts go."[19] Third, since the mental functions of self are recognized, the self

---

[15] Ibid.
[16] Ibid., p. 106.
[17] Broughton, 1978.

[18] Ibid., p. 87.
[19] Ibid., p. 88.

is seen as having complete and private access to its own inner processes. The self knows itself, and this knowledge is neither shared by anyone else nor extended to others. That is, the self is seen as totally self-aware in a way special to itself. As an example, one young adolescent told Broughton, "I know what I feel about things, and I don't know someone else."[20]

Although the young adolescent recognizes the distinction between mental and physical, and bases a new understanding of self on this recognition, there is still little appreciation of the mental self's unique qualities. Broughton believes that such an appreciation develops late in adolescence and is the defining aspect of his level 4. At this point, the adolescent has some understanding of the mental world's internal system of relations and regulations. This enables the adolescent to conceive of the mental self as a system of distinct elements, sometimes operating concordantly and sometimes "divided." For example, Broughton quotes one adolescent who speaks of two inner mental selves, one of which is "natural" and one of which "imitates" its ideal.[21] This, writes Broughton, is one typical version of this reasoning level, since it represents an attempt to understand both the complexity and the unity of the mental self. Other examples include adolescents who introspect about the logical mechanisms that characterize their thought processes, positing "real" and "phony" mental activities, "logical" and "irrational" ones, and so on. In later levels of his developmental sequence (levels 5 and 6), Broughton describes further changes in individuals' understanding of the mental self, but these changes occur during adulthood and are beyond the scope of this chapter.

Broughton's analysis of adolescent self-understanding converges with Selman's on the following points: First, both authors agree that the young adolescent views the self in primarily mental terms, as an active processor of experience. Both also agree that this conception is associated with the adolescent's new respect for the self's volitional powers, either in the sense of monitoring and manipulating its own thoughts and actions (Selman) or in the sense of evaluating itself (Broughton). The adolescent tendency toward self-reflection is thus connected by both authors to a new and stronger sense of personal agency. Finally, both authors agree that later in adolescence develops a more realistic and adequate view of mental processes. Selman and Broughton both believe that this change enables the adolescent to understand the uneven and sometimes divided workings of mental life, while at the same time maintaining a belief in the unity of the self-system. Selman stresses the adolescent's construction of conscious and nonconscious levels of mental experience, whereas Broughton stresses the adolescent's construction of such notions as the "real" mental self versus the "imitative" or "phony" mental self. But both authors portray the effects of the change as a move away from the notion of a global mental self with mysterious, unexplored workings, to a view of a

---

[20] Ibid. [21] Broughton, 1980.

systematic mental self consisting of distinct elements that operate according to definable laws and regularities.

Paul Secord and Barbara Peevers's study of self-understanding in children and adolescents found the same developmental patterns reported by Selman and Broughton.[22] They used a free-response method of questioning subjects and analyzed responses intuitively, rather than with the aid of a formal coding scheme. Their impressionistic account of their data not only dovetails nicely with Selman and Broughton's findings but also suggests some further features of adolescent self-understanding. The first developmental shift noted by Secord and Peevers occurs at the beginning of adolescence. At this age, the young adolescent describes the self in terms of abstractions and general evaluations, rather than in terms of specific acts and qualities, as during childhood. Also, Secord and Peevers report that young adolescents are likely to describe themselves in terms of their past and future selves, whereas younger children almost invariably describe themselves in terms of the immediate present.

The next shift noted by Secord and Peevers occurs in middle adolescence (as revealed by the authors' sample of eleventh-graders). Here we see many of the qualities reported by Selman and Broughton, though at a somewhat earlier age (during the *first* of the other two researchers' adolescent levels). This discrepancy could result from either differences in research populations or from the relative informality and open-endedness of Secord and Peevers's testing procedure when compared with the more intensively probed interviews of Selman and Broughton. In any event, Secord and Peevers found that their adolescent subjects developed notions of self-reflectivity, volition, and self-evaluation as critical components of their self-understanding. For example, a typical self-reflective statement by a subject was, "I saw myself back in high school—just like I could sit back and watch myself go to school."[23] As an example of the awakened sense of adolescent volition, another subject said, "If I don't like a subject, I won't do anything in the subject. . .and, on the other hand, the subjects I do like—my science and mathematics—I really work."[24] This, the authors write, demonstrates a recognition that inner processes like motivation determine the course of one's life events. Thus, the self is seen as active and self-generating: "There is a kind of projection of activities (at this age)—self as agent enacting various scenes, rather than as being with qualities."[25] Finally, in another manifestation of self-reflection and self-determinacy, the self is seen as its own evaluator. This, according to Secord and Peevers, takes place mostly on moral grounds, as in the following example: "But I still think that I consider popularity too important above other things more than I should. . .I don't like people who talk about other people behind their backs because it's—they wouldn't like it if they were talked about, and I don't think it's right."[26]

[22] Secord & Peevers, 1974.
[23] Ibid., p. 136.
[24] Ibid., p. 139.
[25] Ibid., p. 138.
[26] Ibid.

A study by Robert Bernstein elaborates some of the trends noted by Secord and Peevers, particularly the early adolescent trends not mentioned by Selman or Broughton.[27] Bernstein asked ten-, fifteen-, and twenty-year-olds three types of questions designed to reveal their conceptions of the "self-system." The first type of question was directed at differentiation in self-system conceptions; for example, "Everyone behaves differently in different situations with different people. List all the ways that you act." The second type of question, directed at abstractness in self-system conceptions, was of the following sort: "You have listed a number of different ways that you act. What does each of these tell you about yourself?" The third type of question was aimed at integration and asked the subject to "Put all of this together in a statement about yourself."

Bernstein expected that older subjects would demonstrate greater differentiation in their self-system conceptions than younger subjects by making statements from a larger number of self categories. This expectation was unconfirmed. But Bernstein did find an age-related difference in the types of categories that subjects used. At age ten, children were likely to refer to situational, behavioral, and emotional aspects of self (e.g., "I play at the playground"; "I hit my brother"; "I get mad at my mother"). Adolescents at ages fifteen and twenty were likely to refer to their social-personality characteristics, their beliefs, and their acceptance of social rules, as respectively, "I am really friendly, so I can make new friends easily"; "I think being a good sport is important, so if we lose a game, I am never a spoil-sport"; "My mother thinks that it is wrong to cheat, so I don't."

As for abstraction in self-system conceptions, Bernstein reports that his youngest subjects generally were quite concrete, linking the self to direct action in most of their statements (e.g., "I mow the lawn at home"). Subjects in mid-adolescence linked together a variety of self-actions according to one common theme, thus demonstrating an initial abstraction from self-system characteristics. An example might be, "Going to the drive-in with my friends is just something I do with them, like I also play basketball with them." In his oldest subjects, Bernstein found some abstracting on the basis of "an underlying dimension which provides internal consistency for behaviors which appear discrepant."[28] For example, a twenty-year-old might say, "I help my brother with his homework, but I don't help my sister with hers because my brother really needs help, while my sister is lazy. I mean it's fair to help him and not her."

Bernstein found a similar developmental trend in adolescent tendencies toward conceptual integration of the self-system. Integrating statements of ten-year-olds were generally confined to a simple reiteration of previous self-definitions, without recognition of possible contradiction in diverse definitions. By mid-adolescence, diversity of self-definition is recognized, but no coordinating principle between discrepant elements is yet constructed. For example, one

[27] Bernstein, 1980.   [28] Ibid., p. 237.

such response might be, "Well, when I am around my friends, I am really talkative and animated, but just around my family I sort of keep to myself. It's sort of like I am two different people; I don't know why." By the end of adolescence, according to Bernstein, integrating principles that recognize diversity yet maintain the coherence of the self-system are found. An example of an amended version of the above statement might be, "When I am around my friends, I am really talkative because I feel like they are treating me like a person who has something interesting and important to say. My family doesn't listen to what I say, so I just don't feel like talking to hear myself speak." The principle that coordinates here between the two contradictory self-statements (talkativeness and silence) is the self's desire to engage in meaningful communication when talking.

Like the research summarized above, Bernstein's work shows the adolescent transition from action-based conceptions of self to conceptions based upon psychological characteristics, such as beliefs. Bernstein's research also taps into the "divided self" of adolescence as portrayed by Broughton. Like Broughton and Selman, Bernstein shows how older adolescents resolve the contradictions of this division by constructing conceptual principles that coordinate the various features of self into a coherent system. Like Secord and Peevers, Bernstein also stresses the adolescent tendency toward abstraction around stable, unifying qualities of self. One such quality that emerges as primary in Bernstein's work is the social-personality aspect of self. Bernstein shows how the young adolescent moves from a definition of self in terms of transient actions and emotions to a definition of self in terms of stable personality traits with social implications. When, in later adolescence, the notion of stable personality becomes combined with the notion of characteristic belief systems, the adolescent is able to establish an understanding of self that is self-reflective, complex, and systematic.

Two studies that asked children and adolescents to make up free descriptions of themselves have uncovered many of the same age trends reported by Bernstein and others. The first, by Montemayor and Eisen[29] used Gordon's standardized self-concept coding system[30] to analyze the free self-descriptions of subjects between the ages of nine and eighteen. The researchers found that, with increasing age, adolescents more frequently used the following categories from Gordon's system in their self-descriptions: ideological beliefs, interpersonal style, psychic style, existential-individuating, sense of self-determination, and sense of unity. Although the nominal labels of these categories differ somewhat from the language other authors have used, the concordance of results becomes apparent when we translate "existential" into "self-reflective," "sense of self-determination" into "sense of volition" (or personal agency), "interpersonal style" into "social-personality characteristics," and "psychic style" into "manner of mentally processing experience." Also in

[29] Montemayor & Eisen, 1977.   [30] Gordon, 1968.

accord with other studies, Montemayor and Eisen found that with increasing age, adolescents use the following categories *less* frequently: territoriality-citizenship, possessions, and body image. The other free-response study of children's and adolescents' self-descriptions was a similar though less comprehensive effort by Livesly and Bromley.[31] Age trends for categories like "general personality attributes" and "beliefs, attitudes, and values" were compatible with Montemayor and Eisen's findings regarding similar categories.

Even studies primarily focusing on self-esteem have tapped essentially identical developmental patterns in adolescent self-understanding. Morris Rosenberg's broad-based series of studies on self-concept included three components relevant to the issue in this review.[32] Rosenberg asked subjects aged eight through eighteen questions on the following areas of concern: points of pride and shame in self ("Could you tell me what things are really best about you? Do you have any weak points, that is, any things not as good about you?"); sense of distinctiveness and commonality ("In what ways are you different from most other kids you know? In what ways are you the same?"); and ideal self ("What kind of person would you like to be when you grow up?"). Rosenberg found that, in response to these questions, children generally describe themselves in terms of physical and active qualities, whereas adolescents refer to psychological aspects of self. In addition, Rosenberg reports the rising importance of the self's social-personality characteristics during adolescence. When questioned about points of pride, 9 percent of the eight-year-olds' responses consisted of interpersonal traits (e.g., friendly, shy), while 17 percent of the fourteen-year-olds' and 28 percent of the sixteen-year-olds' responses were interpersonal traits. When asked about the person the subject would like to become, 36 percent of the eight-year-olds' responses were interpersonal traits, while 69 percent of the fourteen- to-sixteen-year-olds' responses were interpersonal traits. Finally, Rosenberg found that the self's ability to control itself becomes much more prominent during adolescence. When questioned about points of shame, only 14 percent of the eight-year-olds' responses were general traits reflecting self-control, while 32 percent of the fourteen- to-sixteen-year-olds' responses were these kinds of general traits.

In a second aspect of his study, Rosenberg investigated the locus of both "interior" and "exterior" self-knowledge, that is, who knows the self best. The exterior self was operationalized as attitudes about intelligence, morality, and aesthetics; for example, "If I asked you and your mother how smart you were, and you said one thing and she said another, who would be right—you, or your mother?" A corresponding question for the interior self probed emotions and feelings in the following way: "Now who knows best what kind of person you really are deep down inside—your mother, your father, yourself, or your best friend?"

Rosenberg found that locus of self-knowledge shifts with age from the

[31] Livesly & Bromley, 1973.   [32] Rosenberg, 1979.

other—especially the parent—to the self. Concerning the exterior self, Rosenberg reports, "Almost half of the older children, but less than one-sixth of the younger children, placed the locus of exterior self-knowledge within the self."[33] Locus of interior self-knowledge followed a similar trend: about half of the younger children thought the parent knew the child better than the child knew himself, while only 36 percent of the twelve- to fourteen-year-olds believed the parent knew him better than the child knew himself. These findings, of course, agree with Broughton's description of the consequences of the distinction between mental and physical. Once the mental is seen to be unique, according to Broughton, the self is seen to be a privileged and omniscient processor of the self's experience, leading to an awareness that no one can ever understand one's experience as fully as one can oneself.

A Developmental Model of Adolescent Self-Understanding

Research findings of self-understanding through the adolescent period reveal some widely observed developmental patterns. Most important are: (1) the shift from physicalistic to psychological self-conceptions, (2) the increasingly volitional and self-reflective nature of self-understanding, (3) the emergence of stable social-personality characterizations of self, and (4) the tendency toward the conceptual integration of diverse aspects of self into a unified self-system. Some of these trends are in line with changes in perception and general cognitive ability that have been documented for this age period. For example, Carl Barenboim has found that person perception in childhood and adolescence develops as follows: Children in the elementary school years understand persons by comparing people's overt behavior. In early adolescence, persons are understood through "psychological constructs" that posit stable personality characteristics of people. Finally, by mid-adolescence, persons are compared with one another on the basis of these psychological constructs.[34] Parallel trends also can be seen in self-understanding development. John Flavell and others have noted that person perception generally tends to develop in the direction of "surface-to-depth" in the childhood and adolescent years.[35] The physical-psychological shift in self-understanding can be seen as another example of this. Finally, the systematization of self can be seen as another example of the formalization of reasoning during adolescence.[36]

Nevertheless, it would be a mistake to reduce a developmental account of self-understanding to a list of changes along a few general cognitive dimensions. Such an account would fail to recognize the special features of self-understanding development. Neither the "physical to psychological" nor the more general "surface-to-depth" notions define the developmental sequence in a totally accurate way. This is because (1) there is much in early self-understanding that does not meet the criterion of "physicalistic," and (2) there

---

[33] Ibid., pp. 243–44.
[34] Barenboim, 1981.
[35] Flavell, 1977; Higgins, Ruble, & Hartup, 1983.
[36] Inhelder & Piaget, 1958; Keating, 1975.

is much in advanced self-understanding that does not meet the criterion of "psychological." For example, very young children express self-conceptions that are primarily active rather than physical; they sometimes also make self-statements that are social (e.g., group membership) and even psychological (e.g., emotional states). Moreover, the physical, social, and active self all remain important to most individuals throughout life, long after they are capable of predominantly psychological self-conceptions. In fact, psychologists have long noted that the physical self, after a period of relative neglect, once again becomes significant for a person's self-concept at the end of adolescence.[37]

William Damon and Daniel Hart have posited a developmental model specific to self-understanding in which it is shown that each aspect of the self continues to develop and interact with the others as the child grows older (Table 8-1).[38]

The logic of the model is as follows. The front face of the cube represents the self-as-object (James's *me*), divided into its four basic constituents (the physical, active, social, and psychological self). At all ages, children have some knowledge of each of these four constituent self schemes, however cursory and primitive this knowledge may be. At different ages, knowledge of the constituents of the *me* changes in character; these changes are represented along the vertical dimensions (the columns of the model's front face).

In addition to these "vertical" developmental trends within each of the four self schemes, there is another important developmental trend in children's understanding of the self-as-object. This is an age-related shift that favors, in turn, the physical, active, social, and then psychological aspects of self, depending on the child's age. This movement is represented along the outlined boxes that are along the diagonal of the model's front face. This movement has been the focus of previous uni-dimensional accounts of self-concept development. Although Damon and Hart believe that these previous accounts have erred in their too-exclusive focus on this one developmental movement, they still believe that it is a dominant dimension within a multidimensional developmental progression. Thus, they believe that with age, one is more and more likely to rely upon social and psychological aspects of self for the purpose of defining oneself than on physical and active notions.

The horizontal dimensions (the rows) show the knowledge at each age of the various constituents. The four aspects of self-knowledge are linked at each developmental level because they share characteristics deriving from the dominant conception of self at that level. Thus at each new level, a new aspect of self assumes dominance and lends its characteristics to parallel-level conceptions of other aspects of self. These characteristics become, in essence, the organizing principles of self-understanding at that level.

The four general developmental levels of self-understanding with respect to the *me* are organized as follows: At level 1, all self-understanding is to some

[37] S. Freud, 1922; Kohlberg & Gilligan, 1971.   [38] Damon & Hart, 1982.

Table 8-1 The development of self-understanding

The I dimensions (Continuity, Distinctness, Volition, Self-reflection):

	Continuity	Distinctness	Volition	Self-reflection
1. Infancy and Early Childhood	self-continuity is equivalent to unchanging physical body	distinctness dependent on bodily or normal attributes	body	
2. Middle and Late Childhood	self-continuity is attributed to the psychological and physical processes through which the nature of self continues to evolve	distinctness arises from the subjectivity and privacy of the self's experience	one body part "tells" another to do something	
3. Early Adolescence			active self-initiated modification of conscious experience	
4. Late Adolescence			awareness of body features, typical unconscious psychological activities, and action capabilities	recognition of conscious and unconscious psychological processes

The me dimensions:

Developmental Period	Physical self	Active self	Social self	Psychological self
4. Late Adolescence	physical attributes reflecting volitional choices, or personal and moral standards	active attributes that reflect choices, or personal and moral standards	moral or personal choices concerning social relations or social-personality characteristics	belief systems, personal philosophy, self's own thought processes
3. Early Adolescence	physical attributes that influence social appeal and social interactions	active attributes that influence social appeal and social interactions	social-personality characteristics	social sensitivity, communicative competence, and other psychologically related social skills
2. Middle and Late Childhood	activity-related physical attributes	capabilities relative to others	activities that are considered with reference to reactions (approval or disapproval) of others	knowledge, learned skills, motivation, or activity-related emotional states
1. Infancy and Early Childhood	bodily properties or material possessions	typical behavior	fact of membership in particular social relations or groups	momentary moods, feelings, preferences, and aversions

Source: W. Damon & D. Hart, The development of self-understanding from infancy through adolescence. *Child Development*, August 1982. Reprinted with permission.

extent physicalistic in the sense that it is chiefly descriptive of surface features. That is, even when concerned with the self's actions, social interactions, or emotions, it treats these only nominally and descriptively, as if they were physical objects. Similarly, at level 2 each of the four aspects are to some extent treated actively, at level 3 socially, at level 4 psychologically. The qualifier "to some extent" is necessary here because each of the four aspects still retains its unique substance at each level.

The side face of the model shows the understanding of self-as-subject (James's *I*), especially with regard to the understanding of continuity, distinctness from others, volition, and self-reflection. Development here is represented as a shift from one pole to the other along the four respective dimensions, rather than as a progression from level to level (as is the case with understanding the *me* aspect of the self). This is because there is nothing in the self-understanding literature to indicate that between childhood and adolescence there are a series of qualitatively distinct levels in the awareness of the *I*. Rather, the literature indicates that during this age range, there is a gradual emergence of some new notions in each of these four dimensions, which are briefly described along the side face of the table.

The cubical shape of the model indicates that, during the transition from childhood to adolescence and throughout the development of self-understanding, changes in understanding the *me* interact with changes in understanding the *I*. It is not possible to determine whether, for example, a more advanced understanding of volition transforms one's understanding of various *me* constituents, or whether, in contrast, a new mode of defining the *me* makes possible the understanding of *I* dimensions like volition. Probably the wisest guess is that throughout ontogenesis there is mutual influence between the two basic aspects of self-understanding. Although the *I* and the *me* are structured around distinct conceptual issues, developmental progress in either seems to inform and encourage developmental progress in the other.

Generally, this model has much in common with Erikson's genetic model of identity formation. Erikson's model, which we introduced in Chapter 2, also presents a developmental scheme that, at the same time, is both multidimensional and systematically related to central developmental patterns. In both models, the dominant developmental trends are shown along the horizontal, although there are also significant changes represented in each of the vertical dimensions. Relations within each developmental level are shown on the horizontal, signifying that there are important links between different aspects of psychological development within any particular age period. Erikson's scheme is, of course, broader than Damon and Hart's self-understanding scheme, since it encompasses all of ego development, rather than strictly the conceptual bases of self-conception. In the following section, we shall take up Erikson's model with renewed emphasis, especially because the model's greatest strength is in its analysis of identity formation during the adolescent years. Because we shall scrutinize Erikson's scheme with renewed care, it may be

Table 8-2 Erikson's Developmental Model

	1	2	3	4	5	6	7	8
VIII Mature Age								INTEGRITY vs. DESPAIR
VII Adulthood							GENERATIVITY vs. STAGNATION	
VI Young Adult						INTIMACY vs. ISOLATION		
V Adolescence	Temporal Perspective vs. Time Confusion	Self-Certainty vs. Self-Consciousness	Role Experimentation vs. Role Fixation	Apprenticeship vs. Work Paralysis	IDENTITY vs. IDENTITY CONFUSION	Sexual Polarization vs. Bisexual Confusion	Leadership and Fellowship vs. Authority Confusion	Ideological Commitment vs. Confusion of Values
IV School Age				INDUSTRY vs. INFERIORITY	Task Identification vs. Sense of Futility			
III Play Age			INITIATIVE vs. GUILT		Anticipation of Roles vs. Role Inhibition			
II Early Childhood		AUTONOMY vs. SHAME, DOUBT			Will to Be Oneself vs. Self-Doubt			
I Infancy	TRUST vs. MISTRUST				Mutual Recognition vs. Autistic Isolation			

Source: E. H. Erikson, *Identity: Youth and Crisis*. New York: W. W. Norton, 1968, p. 94. Reprinted with permission.

useful at this point to reproduce it once again, for the sake of convenient reference (see Table 8-2).

Establishing Personal Identity

The centerpiece of Erikson's life span developmental model is crisis of *identity versus identity diffusion*, which takes place during the adolescent years. In fact, as noted at the beginning of this chapter, the search for identity is so associated with the adolescent period that many contemporary psychologists define adolescence itself as the time of this search. The end of adolescence, according to this psychosocial definition, comes when the individual has established a consolidated personal identity.

What is a personal identity? In Erikson's terms, it is the individual's way of organizing all the past and present identifications, attributes, desires, and orientations that the individual believes best represent the self. Cognitively it is similar to the individual's self-understanding, as discussed in the previous section. But identity in the Eriksonian sense has other, noncognitive components as well. For one thing, it includes many affective components, such as one's positive and negative feelings toward oneself, one's will to grow in a certain direction, and one's emotional orientations toward the people and events in one's life.

In addition, unlike the general knowledge of self discussed in cognitive-developmental analyses of self-understanding, personal identity is particularized and content-bound. As we saw, an individual's self-understanding can be analyzed according to its developmental level and compared with the self-understanding of other individuals at the same level. This is because self-understanding has formal cognitive properties that may be abstracted and developmentally ordered by scientists seeking general similarities and differences between people's self-conceptions. Identity, too, has certain formal properties that may be abstracted for scientific purposes. But abstracting these properties does not tell us very much about the nature of an individual's identity. This is because the function of one's personal identity includes, but goes beyond, the cognitive function of understanding the nature of one's individuality. The individual's sense of identity guides the individual cognitively, affectively, and behaviorally through all of life's choices that have some bearing upon what one is like. As such, identity must be composed of specifics. It is not only a way of conceptualizing the self (as is self-understanding, as we analyzed it). Identity is a particular set of statements, beliefs, and feelings about the self and the self's behavior. Accordingly, in each individual case, it is a unique totality. It defies abstraction and generalization between individuals because, in essence, it must be particularized if it is to serve its function properly: namely, the function of establishing one's individuality and one's individual direction in life.

Perhaps the best definition of identity from an Eriksonian perspective has been provided by James Marcia, who writes:

Identity has been called a "sense," an "attitude," a "resolution," and so on. I would like to propose another way of construing identity: as a self-structure—an internal, self-constructed, dynamic organization of drives, abilities, beliefs, and individual history. The better developed this structure is, the more aware individuals appear to be of their own uniqueness and similarity to others and of their own strengths and weaknesses in making their way in the world. The less developed this structure is, the more confused individuals seem to be about their own distinctiveness from others and the more they have to rely on external sources to evaluate themselves.[39]

Self-understanding is one important component among many in an individual's personal identity. An individual's awareness of "uniqueness and similarity to others" is certainly aided by a sophisticated understanding of self, since such an understanding enables the individual to distinguish between the self and others on grounds that are rational, systematic, stable, and internally derived. The more advanced one's level of self-understanding, the more this is so, since the higher developmental levels provide the surest means of making cognitively effective and genuinely self-constructed distinctions. But however much a well-developed mode of self-understanding contributes to one's identity structure, it is not the whole story. Determining one's particular "strengths and weaknesses," deciding how one should "make one's way in the world," even defining one's own special nature, requires an affective orientation and a particularized set of attitudes toward oneself that go beyond the general features of how one construes one's distinctness and similarity to others. Although an advanced developmental level of self-understanding is a necessary condition for the successful construction of a coherent personal identity, there are also other necessary prerequisites in the identity construction task.

The Identity Crisis in Adolescence

In Erikson's developmental model, the identity crisis begins after the crisis of industry versus inferiority is resolved. As discussed in Chapter 6, this previous crisis focuses on the child's sense of competence, particularly in relation to school and occupational skills. If a positive sense of industry is achieved, the child will come away with a set of *task identifications*—that is, a set of beliefs in one's own ability to accomplish things and "make things work." This legacy of confidence in one's task-related competence is the direct precursor to the identity search of the adolescent years. This is because one's occupational choice is at the heart of one's personal identity. Thus, a successful resolution of the adolescent identity crisis owes its most direct debt to the task identification forged at the end of childhood.

The process of identity formation entails an evaluation of all of one's past and present attributes, as well as a judgment about the kind of person one would like to become in the future. It means constructing a new totality out of all of one's earlier childhood identifications. For the sake of this totality, some

[39] Marcia, 1980, p. 159.

identifications must be subordinated to others, and some may even be repudi-
ated entirely. The identity that emerges is a wholistic configuration that is
dominant over any particular identification or personal attribute. Erikson calls
it "a new, unique Gestalt that is greater that the sum of any of its parts." Once
constructed, it has a life and meaning of its own. Because a personal identity
establishes one's social role and one's personal nature, it guides future choices
and makes possible future engagements with society and with other individuals. An identity, therefore, is more than just a static label. It is a dynamic force
in one's life, bearing implications for future directions in one's career, one's
interpersonal relationships, and one's activities as a citizen in society.

Erikson has called the identity search a "crisis" which can be an all-
consuming preoccupation for many adolescents. But for most, it is a prolonged
trial, resolved by a piecemeal process that often takes years to complete. The
adolescent gradually "tries out" new opinions and behaviors, much as one
would try on suits of clothes. There is always the possibility that a suit will not
fit at all, and that it must be rejected. Or if a suit does fit, it may need to be
tailored to conform to the individual. Similarly, the adolescent slowly makes a
wide variety of tentative choices, always reflecting on the appropriateness of
these choices for her sense of self.

The identity structure is consolidated only when the adolescent can
anticipate the appropriateness of a particular decision for her chosen sense of
self before the decision is actually made. This requires considerable experimentation with alternative courses of conduct and various possible ideological
stances. Most importantly, it requires rejecting those avenues of conduct and
opinion that do not suit one's sense of self. Such rejections are necessary for
definitive acceptance of the choices that do accord with one's self-identity. This
process of experimentation, rejection, and final acceptance eventually enables
the individual to gain foresight, so that the individual can anticipate those
choices that will be identity-appropriate and those that will not be, without
needing to go through them. This is what is meant by a "consolidated" identity.
Weaving such an identity takes time, as well as concentrated effort, inner
conflict, and some inevitable personal anguish.

The signs of a consolidated identity are both conscious and nonconscious.
This is another distinction between personal identity and self-understanding,
which consists only of one's consciously realized, cognitive sense of self. Identity, in contrast, includes a general acceptance of oneself, and feelings of
comfort and appropriateness with one's self-image. As Erikson writes:

> An optimal sense of identity. . . .is experienced merely as a sense of psycho-social
> well-being. Its most obvious concomitants are a feeling of being at home in one's
> body, a sense of "knowing where one is going," and an inner assuredness of
> anticipated recognition from those who count.[40]

In Erikson's "I am" phraseology, a successful identity resolution results

[40] Erikson, 1968, p. 134.

in a sense that "I am what I am," or final acceptance of one's total individuality. As we shall see at the end of this chapter, this sets the stage for the
individual's productive engagement with others, first in the post-adolescent
phase of intimacy and then in the middle-adult phase of generativity. In fact,
the identity consolidation at the end of adolescence marks the last point at
which Erikson uses the "I am" formulations at all. This is because he believes
that once one has established a firm sense of personal identity, one is ready to
"lose oneself" in other human beings. The "I am" statements then become
"We are" statements. For example, the formulation for the upcoming intimacy
struggle is, "We are what we love." One's identity thus becomes intermingled
with another's identity and destiny to the ultimate enhancement of both
persons' lives. Before such a productive union is possible, however, one must
establish one's own definitive sense of direction through a consolidated sense of
self-identity. We shall now examine some of the pitfalls of failing to do so in the
adolescent years.

Identity Confusion during Adolescence

All adolescents find the identity crisis difficult, but some react pathologi-
cally, or close to it. Erikson writes that identity-related psychopathology is the
most common clinical disturbance in the first two decades of life. Even much
later in adulthood, many individuals experience conflicts that can be traced
back to contradictions or insufficiencies in their identity resolutions. In fact,
writes Erikson, the challenge of the identity crisis is so problematical that
almost all persons experience some of the psychopathological symptoms of
identity confusion at some time in their lives. Although in most cases this does
not signal an abnormal clinical condition, it does lead many to believe that they
"share the condition," in Erikson's words.[41] Because of this, Erikson believes
identity confusion to be a developmental disorder, experienced briefly and
partially by many persons in the normal course of development. A relatively
few experience the whole ensemble of symptoms together, becoming severely
and permanently impaired in their everyday functioning.

Identity confusion can manifest itself in a number of ways. In Table 8-2,
the horizontal dimension of the identity line spells out some of the negative
consequences of identity confusion. Of these, the most severe is the first, a
diffusion of one's perspective on time. This can result in a state of catatonic
immobility, as the adolescent loses a sense that time and activity may bring
change in his life. The patient first slows down, writes Erikson, "as if he were
moving in molasses." Then efforts of all kinds may stop altogether:

> It is hard for him to go to bed and face the transition into a state of sleep, and it is
> equally hard for him to get up and face the necessary restitution of wakefulness; it
> is hard to come to the therapeutic appointment, and hard to leave it. Such
> complaints as "I don't know," "I give up," and "I quit," are by no means mere

---

[41] Ibid., p. 187.

habitual statements reflecting a mild depression; they are often expressions of the kind of despair. . .on the part of the ego "to let itself die."[42]

This is an identity-related problem that is frequently associated with suicide, and that was present in Erikson's most "malignantly regressed" young patients.[43] The severity of the time diffusion problem stems from its special link to a failure in basic trust. This can be seen in Table 8-2: the genetic precursor to a normal temporal perspective during adolescence is basic trust in infancy. In the same scheme, mistrust is shown as an antecedent of time confusion. This means that the diffusion of a time perspective, which appears as a potentially life-threatening psychological disorder in adolescence, is presently connected to the adolescent's identity crisis and developmentally connected to basic trust problems leading back to the infant years. Indeed, Erikson writes that adolescents experiencing a diffusion in time are suffering even then from a "mistrust of time as such." Like infants, they often cannot tolerate momentary delays of gratification, having no confidence that time will bring a remedy: "every delay appears to be a deceit, every wait an experience of impotence, every hope a danger, every plan a catastrophe, every possible provider a potential traitor."[44] Normally, this intolerance of delay is worked out in infancy, as the infant learns that postponing satisfaction does not lead to continued frustration. But when such basic trust is not established, the individual may be plagued for years to come with uncertainties about the world. In adolescence, this uncertainty can reemerge in a particularly dangerous form: a failure to trust in time and all that time brings, including one's own future.

The next two symptoms of identity confusion shown in Table 8-2—self-consciousness and role fixation—are genetically linked to the earlier crises of autonomy and initiative, respectively. A failure to establish autonomy at the end of infancy results in a legacy of shame in one's public self and doubt in how others will receive this self. This legacy can adversely affect the adolescent's struggle for an autonomous identity, since the adolescent's assertions of self can be hampered by lingering feelings of shamefulness. Another adverse possibility is that the adolescent will overcompensate for such feelings with a sense of blatant shamelessness and aggrandizing narcissism in the face of legitimate critical advice. The guilt that is associated with a failure to resolve the childhood crisis of initiative can also show up during adolescence in a pathological questioning of the self's worth. In the case of initiative-related guilt, the symptoms consist of a fixation on self-defeating roles. For example, adolescents may choose delinquent roles or roles without social usefulness (such as that of the "lazy student"), out of a sense that they are not worthy of anything better. This not only can impair their efforts to establish viable personal identities, but it can also lead to real conflict between themselves and society.

The fourth symptom of identity confusion is work paralysis. This is also the last of the symptoms springing from developmental failures prior to the

---

[42] Ibid., p. 151.

[43] Ibid., p. 152.

[44] Ibid.

identity crisis. Work paralysis results from a sense of inadequacy concerning one's task-related competence. It traces back to a "sense of futility" born in the childhood struggle with industry versus inferiority. As with other psychopathological conditions, work paralysis can manifest itself in a number of disparate ways. For some adolescents, it is an inability to concentrate on any required task. For others, it is an obsessive and one-sided focus on a single activity out of all proportion to its value, as in the case of one patient who practically "read himself blind," while ignoring all other essential obligations. In some cases, adolescents afflicted by work paralysis do not perceive it as a sign of their own inadequacy. Rather, they believe in their own competence to an unrealistic degree, harboring grandiose expectations for their task performances. When these expectations inevitably are disappointed, these adolescents often give up their efforts entirely. They may then frantically switch from new activity to new activity, forever in search of a task that will show their true worth. Rarely are these new tasks completed, because no completion could match in quality their exaggerated belief in their own abilities. This leaves these adolescents with little opportunity to develop true expertise in any area, and it seriously hinders their search for an occupational component in their identities.

The last three boxes along the identity row of Table 8-2 indicate symptoms of identity confusion that presage more severe problems later in life. Although these symptoms may be somewhat disturbing during adolescence, their import is in their genetic connections to problems in resolving future life crises. For example, bisexual confusion sometimes occurs in adolescents who find a commitment to their stereotype gender roles oppressive. These adolescents are hesitant "clearly to be a member of one sex or another," a hesitancy that can certainly leave them feeling uncomfortable in their interpersonal interactions.[45] But the real crisis for these adolescents will come in the next developmental phase, the crisis of intimacy versus isolation. According to Erikson, the challenge of establishing sexual intimacy with another person "fully reveals the latent weakness of identity" in those persons who have not satisfactorily resolved the identity crisis. This is because one must have a firm sense of self in order to "lose oneself" in another person. One's sexual identity is a critical part of one's overall sense of self, and it is particularly important in establishing sexual intimacy. For those who have left adolescence with a continuing sense of bisexual confusion, the demands of sexual intimacy will be particularly difficult:

> During lovemaking or in sexual fantasies a loosening of sexual identity threatens; it even becomes unclear whether sexual excitement is experienced by the individual or by his partner, and this applies in either heterosexual or homosexual encounters. The ego thus loses its flexible capacity for abandoning itself to sexual and affectional sensations in a fusion with another individual who is both partner to the sensation and guarantor of one's continuing identity: fusion with another becomes identity's loss. A sudden collapse of all capacity for mutuality threatens, and a desperate wish ensues to start all over again, with a (quasi-deliberate)

---

[45] Ibid., p. 155.

regression to a stage of basic bewilderment and rage such as only the very small child experiences.[46]

Because bisexual confusion during adolescence may lead to far more serious problems during the post-adolescent crisis of intimacy, it is often easier for the observer to recognize a weakness in an individual's sexual identity at this later crisis period than during adolescence, when the identity crisis is itself confronted. Similarly, the two remaining adolescent symptoms of identity confusion—authority confusion and confusion of values—are more easily detected during the adult years than during adolescence, when they first appear. These two symptoms revolve around, respectively, the adolescent's need to establish positions of leadership and followership vis-à-vis others in society, and to develop a commitment to an ideology and a way of life. These needs will not emerge in full bloom until the adult's capacity for citizenship in society is put to its full test. At that point, it is essential for the individual to assume a responsible role in the social hierarchy, and to give this role meaning through dedication to a system of political and personal beliefs. Although during adulthood the specific ideals of youth may be transcended, the process of self-reflective commitment begun in adolescence provides a necessary foundation for making adult choices that one can believe in and defend.

Empirical Research on Identity Formation

Perhaps because of the metaphoric quality in Erikson's theorizing, the construct of psychosocial identity has proven elusive to empirical study. Recently, however, there has been an upsurge in efforts to collect data on this most central issue in adolescent personality development. Some new methodological devices have made possible the use of Erikson's theoretical notions for scientific investigations.[47] Conceptually, the main advance has been the definition of four categories of "identity status."[48] Individuals may be classified within one of these categories according to their progress in consolidating their identities. Classification of individuals by these categories has proven reliable to a scientifically acceptable degree.[49] The four categories are as follows:

Foreclosure. Individuals in a state of foreclosure have never experienced an identity crisis. Rather, they have prematurely established an identity on the basis of their parents' choices rather than on their own. They have made occupational and ideological commitments, but these commitments reflect more an assessment of what one's parents or authority figures could do rather than an autonomous process of self-assessment. This is a kind of "pseudo-identity" that generally is too fixed and rigid to serve as a foundation for meeting life's future crises.

Identity Diffusion. Individuals experiencing identity diffusion have found

[46] Ibid., pp. 158–59.
[47] Constantinople, 1969; Simmons, 1970; Bourne, 1978; Rosenthal, Gurney, & Moore, 1982.
[48] Marcia, 1980.
[49] Marcia, 1976.

neither an occupational direction nor an ideological commitment of any kind, and they have made little progress toward these ends. They may have experienced an identity crisis, but if so they were unable to resolve it.

Moratorium: This category is reserved for those who have begun to experiment with occupational and ideological choices, but who have not yet made definitive commitments to either. These individuals are directly in the midst of an identity crisis and are currently examining alternate life choices.

Identity Achievement: This signifies a state of identity consolidation in which the individual has made his or her own conscious, clear-cut decisions concerning occupation and ideology. The individual is convinced that these decisions were autonomously and freely made, and that they reflect the individual's true nature and deep inner commitments.

Research has found that individuals with different identity statuses vary in their emotional outlook, as well as in their self-esteem. Highest in anxiety are those in the midst of identity crisis (the "moratoriums" according to the above classification system).[50] Lowest in anxiety are those who are in a state of foreclosure, who are thus temporarily avoiding the issues of identity altogether.[51] Highest in self-esteem are those who have achieved identity, followed by those in the moratorium state.[52] Lowest in self-esteem are those in states of foreclosure or identity diffusion.[53] The latter two classes of individuals were also those with the most unstable self-esteem, who changed their evaluations of themselves quickly when receiving external positive or negative feedback.[54] The combination of these findings indicates that persons who have prematurely established a pseudo-identity (those in foreclosure) are temporarily non-anxious but are negative and unstable in their opinions of themselves. Those who are wrestling with the task of identity formation (classified as being in moratorium) are anxious but self-valuing. Those who have achieved identity are stable and positive in their self-esteem, and they experience anxiety to a normal and moderate degree.

In terms of values and attitudinal orientations, those in a state of foreclosure have been shown to be highly authoritarian, espousing and practicing obedience to authority above all else.[55] They are also lower on autonomy and self-directedness than other individuals, relying heavily on their families for their life decisions.[56] As for moral reasoning, individuals who are in moratorium, and those who have achieved identity, score at the postconventional level (level 5) of Kohlberg's sequence, whereas those who are in states of foreclosure

[50] Marcia, 1967; Oshman & Manosevitz, 1974.
[51] Podd, Marcia, & Rubin, 1970.
[52] Breuer, 1973.
[53] Bunt, 1968.

[54] Gruen, 1960; Marcia, 1967.
[55] Marcia & Friedman, 1970.
[56] Waterman & Waterman, 1971; Orlofsky, 1978.

and identity diffusion rarely score above the conventional levels (levels 3 and 4). In addition, research has found that those who have achieved identity tend to be more ethically oriented than those who have not.[57]

Developmental studies have reported that individuals generally change in their identity status between the ages of eighteen and twenty-two.[58] During this age period, individuals generally shift from states of foreclosure or identity diffusion to the state of identity achievement. In our society, these are the college years. Alan Waterman writes that: "It is during the college years that the greatest gains in identity formation appear to occur" because "college environments provide a diversity of experiences that can serve both to trigger considerations of identity issues and to suggest alternative resolutions for identity concerns."[59] In addition, he notes, college helps individuals specify occupational plans, introduces individuals to a range of ideological choices, and often forces individuals to question traditional religious beliefs. Waterman concludes that "the results of numerous studies confirm that, in general, senior men and women have a stronger sense of personal identity than do their freshman counterparts and that the identity commitments held as seniors are more likely to have been arrived at through the successful resolution of identity crises."[60]

Other developmental studies have generally confirmed the psychosocial connections proposed by Erikson in his theoretical model. For example, a number of studies have found a strong correlation between feelings of task-related competence, occupational commitment, and the achievement of identity.[61] Other studies have linked together identity-related dimensions like basic trust, autonomy, sexual identity, and intimacy.[62] Although there is still a paucity of true longitudinal research that could trace the relation between how one resolves psychosocial crises early in life and strengths and weaknesses in identity later in life, the correlational data that do exist support Erikson's theoretical assertions almost without fail.[63]

Further, there are by now a number of case studies in the literature that provide a different kind of empirical confirmation for Erikson's model.[64] Though less respectable in a scientifically conventional sense, data from such case studies are nevertheless often richer and more informative than statistical reports. Erikson himself has argued, along with other distinguished personality theorists, that such data are the most appropriate empirical base for the study of human lives.[65] We shall consider one such case study later in this chapter.

With respect to most aspects of identity development, males and females

[57] Hogan, 1973.
[58] Offer, Marcus, & Offer, 1970; Stark & Traxler, 1974.
[59] Waterman, 1982, p. 346.
[60] Ibid.
[61] Waterman & Waterman, 1972; Waterman, Geary, & Waterman, 1974; Water-

man & Goldman, 1976.
[62] Dignan, 1965; Constantinople, 1969; Orlofsky, Marcia, & Lesser, 1973.
[63] Bourne, 1978.
[64] Gothals, 1971; Paranjpe, 1976.
[65] Murray, 1938; Erikson, 1964; White, 1972.

show few differences. Waterman writes that "males and females are more similar than different in their use of developmental processes."[66] On most measures, male and female adolescents are equally represented among the four identity statuses, indicating that they develop at a similar pace in much the same manner. Studies that have reported sex differences in developmental patterns are in the minority, and they are often contradicted by evidence from other studies.

Research, however, has left one open question regarding sex differences in identity formation. A number of studies have suggested that the four identity statuses may have different psychological significance for males than for females.[67] Although both sexes are equally well adjusted to identity achievement, and neither copes well with identity diffusion, females in contrast to males often seem relatively well adjusted to foreclosure. This finding could be interpreted in a number of ways. It may be an artifact of different questions asked of male and female subjects. In many studies, females have been asked a greater proportion of questions about sexual commitments than have males, and such questions may especially elicit forclosure-type answers. Or it could be, as one author suggests, that women have greater culture support for a foreclosure status than do men, and that some women's easier adjustment to this status may be a reflection of this.[68] In any case, this difference concerns only the small proportion of men and women who remain in foreclosure beyond the adolescent years. For the great majority of others, as Waterman concludes, "males and females undergo similar patterns of identity development."[69]

Developmental Relations between Identity and Intimacy

Theory and research stemming from Erikson's model of psychosocial development assumes that identity formation is a prerequisite to intimacy, a prior step in the genetic sequence. But there is another point of view on the developmental relation between identity and intimacy, explicated in the "interpersonal psychiatric" theory of Harry Stack Sullivan.[70] Sullivan believed that adolescence begins not with a search for identity but with a need for intimacy, and that the construction of self-identity is made possible by one's participation in intimate interpersonal relations, rather than the other way around.

According to Sullivan, a powerful longing for intimacy arises at the end of childhood. This longing is expressed in feelings of loneliness and isolation. The parent-child relation cannot cure this loneliness because parents and children do not communicate or cooperate with one another in the fullest possible sense. This means that young adolescents must look to peers for satisfying their new intimacy needs.

---

[66] Waterman, 1982, p. 351.
[67] Marcia, 1980; Waterman, 1982.
[68] Marcia, 1980.

[69] Waterman, 1982, p. 351.
[70] Sullivan, 1953.

Initially, at the end of childhood when the new intimacy needs are first felt, they can be met in the context of unisex relations. The late childhood "chumships" that Sullivan described (discussed in Chapter 5) are a common example of such unisexual intimate relations. But not long into adolescence, a new longing arises. This is what Sullivan calls the "lust dynamism" associated with puberty, and which is not normally satisfied by the unisexual relation. The introduction of this new interpersonal need forces young adolescents to radically revise their approach to intimacy. In the words of George Gothals:

> One must at the risk of one's own personal security transfer the intimacy need from members of the same sex to members of the opposite sex; one must integrate the intimacy need itself with the powerful motive of lust; and finally, one must not let this new and powerful motive drive one to reject or avoid the possibility of intimacy.[71]

For Sullivan, accomplishing this difficult task is possible only through establishing a "collaborative," that is, mutual and cooperative relation with members of the opposite sex. (This process is similar to that described in the last chapter under the topic of adolescent sexuality.) The unique element in Sullivan's theory is his view on the developmental significance of accomplishing such heterosexual intimacy. In Sullivan's opinion, one discovers the self only through participating in intimate relations, first of a unisexual kind and then of a heterosexual kind. One knows oneself by knowing others, one feels secure in one's self-worth by becoming close with others, and one accepts one's total personal identity by showing to others all one's strengths and limitations. This is a reversal of Erikson's position, since for Erikson one must know and accept oneself before one risks intimacy with another.

Sullivan's theory leads us to question the functional values of identities formed without adequate experience in intimacy. These persons may be the ones with special problems after the adolescent identity crisis is resolved. Perhaps their subsequent struggles with the post-adolescent intimacy crisis are not a normal phase of psychological development, as Eriksonian theory implies, but rather the sign of a weak sense of self. Erikson himself admits that failure to establish intimacy may be the surest revelation of a nonconsolidated identity, although Erikson's point is that identity therefore must be considered essential to intimacy rather than the other way around. The available empirical evidence could be read in either way: a legitimate case can be made for either being the prerequisite for the other.

At this point in our knowledge of adolescent social development, it is wisest simply to conclude that identity and intimacy go hand-in-hand in the course of development, with both being ultimately necessary for well-adjusted psychosocial functioning. There are ways in which both processes—constructing identity and establishing interpersonal intimacy—contribute to one another. Several questions, however, must be answered before we decide if a fully

[71] Gothals, 1971.

consolidated identity is necessary for real intimacy, or vice versa. First, we must better define intimacy, both theoretically and operationally. Are the dating relations of early adolescence qualitatively the same as the post-adolescent heterosexual intimacy of which Erikson writes? What about the chumships of late childhood? Clearly there are important differences between these types of intimacies, but we do not yet have a good sense of how such differences matter developmentally. That is, we do not know exactly what kind of intimacy aids the development of identity, or possibly is necessary for identity. Nor do we know, conversely, what kind of intimacy is made possible by a consolidated sense of self-identity. These are questions that can only be answered by scientific research. Until such research is accomplished, the exact developmental relations between identity and intimacy will remain unknown.

Case Studies of Identity Formation

Real-life accounts of adolescent identity crises are not hard to come by. For one thing, adolescence is a recent enough period for most adults to remember the psychological struggles of that time, and the identity search is usually adolescence's central psychological struggle. For another thing, identity is a dynamic structure that has lifelong implications for one's personality and behavioral choices. The nature of one's initial identity consolidation at the end of adolescence is therefore of continuing concern to the individual. As a consequence, personal histories and autobiographies are rife with statements bearing on the process of identity formation.

One recent example of this is the widely acclaimed autobiography of the late Anwar el-Sadat.[72] In his autobiography, significantly called *In Search of Identity*, Sadat cites a critical moment when as a young man he "comes to know that 'self' of mine."[73] Sadat's self-discovery was made during a time of youth when he was participating in various attempts to overthrow the British-imposed government of Egypt. Sadat and his revolutionary compatriots were jailed several times over the space of a few years. During his last and longest jail term, just prior to the final liberation of Egypt, for the first time Sadat had the opportunity fully to come to terms with himself. He writes, "Two places in this world make it impossible for a man to escape from himself: a battlefield and a prison cell."[74]

Sadat spent the long prison hours reviewing his past, present, and future plans in light of his deepest values. On the basis of these self-reflections, he made major changes in his life. For example, he reassessed his premature marriage to a relative (a practice in rural Egypt). Believing that he understood himself for the first time, he decided that he and his wife had little in common, and he became determined to seek a divorce. Besides instigating such important

[72] El-Sadat, 1977.
[73] Ibid., p. 66.

[74] Ibid., p. 58.

decisions, Sadat's realization of self-identity generally gave him a sense of assurance and confidence in his future. Sadat's description of this positive psychological state is reminiscent of the sense of psychosocial well-being that, according to Erikson, accompanies identity consolidation:

> Nothing is more important than self-knowledge. Once I had come to know what I wanted, and got rid of what I didn't, I was reconciled to my "self" and learned to live at peace with it. To return to my village became a beautiful dream, and to work in any field enchanting. In short, the future—both foreseeable and unforeseeable —was a joy to contemplate.[75]

Such autobiographical statements provide valuable supporting material for theories of social development. They are all the more convincing because they are made by persons who have no particular stake in proving or disproving a particular theory. Further, such statements spring from a total account of an individual's life in all of its complexity and particularity. For such reasons, some within social science believe that the study of social and personality development should be centered on individual life histories. Henry Murray wrote that the whole individual life must be a unit of study, and that "the history of the organism *is* the organism."[76] Murray's approach (which he called "personology") influenced scores of followers to cull empirical evidence for psychological theories from single case histories. Today, this is called the *ideographic* approach to psychological research, standing in contrast to the *nomothetic* focus on general comparisons between groups of individuals.[77]

The systematic use of individual case histories to provide empirical support for social-developmental theories has contributed greatly to our understanding of adolescent personality formation. The case-study approach has flourished more with adolescent subjects than with younger subjects because it relies heavily on the subject's own introspections and self-reflections. Preadolescents are unprepared for such psychological collaboration. The few case studies of infants and children are generally based on observations and lack the detailed richness of the best adolescent case histories. For this reason, we found Jean-Paul Sartre's autobiographical recollections (discussed in Chapter 6) to be more illuminating than any case study of childhood individuality currently in the social science literature. But for our current discussion of adolescence, we need not look beyond the domain of psychological investigation.

A. C. Paranjpe, working in India and Canada, conducted an especially revealing set of case studies on identity formation.[78] Paranjpe's research focuses mostly on Indian youth. This gives Paranjpe an opportunity to test the universal validity of Erikson's theory, since Erikson himself developed his theory mainly from his observations of Western youth. Further, Paranjpe includes both young men and young women in his sample, offering us a chance to compare the identity searches of the two sexes in a culture in transition from traditional to contemporary male-female roles. Finally, Paranjpe adds to his

---

[75] Ibid., p. 72.
[76] Murray, 1938.

[77] Allport, 1961; Mischel & Mischel, 1977.
[78] Paranjpe, 1976.

report the case history of one Westerner, a Canadian youth of similar age to the youth in Paranjpe's Indian sample. This addition helps highlight the parallels in personality development between two very different cultures.

For our present purposes, we shall discuss four of Paranjpe's case histories: one male Indian, two female Indians, and the young man from Canada. Of course, as with any individual case study, we must be hesitant about taking any of these single life histories as completely representative of any whole group of individuals. Other female Indians, for example, will differ in many particulars from the two that we have chosen to discuss, and these particulars do matter with regard to the course of their identity formation. Although individual histories may help us understand general processes, and indeed may provide in-depth insights unavailable through any other research technique, the individual always remains, to some extent, unique. Inevitably, there will be idiosyncrasies in any individual life that will defy generalization and that make the individual absolutely unrepresentative of anyone else. Both the strength and the challenge of a good case study are that it is committed to exploring such idiosyncrasies, as well as to analyzing them in a way that proves relevant to human life in general.

The first of Paranjpe's cases that we shall consider is that of a young man named Vinu, born into an upwardly mobile family. Though raised in adverse circumstances, Vinu's father managed to obtain an advanced diploma and to become a high-school teacher. Personally, the father was dominating and ambitious. The mother was less educated and less demanding, and Vinu makes little mention of her in his self-reflections. Vinu's case history is based entirely on personal diaries that the young man wrote between the ages of seventeen and twenty-seven.

Vinu's diary begins with his first year at college, a difficult year in which he experienced migraine headaches, stomach pains, and other physical discomforts. Paranjpe takes these as psychosomatic signs of adolescent "storm and stress," stemming from Vinu's uncertainty concerning his future direction. During this period, Vinu expected to become a businessman and took commerce courses in college. But he was dissatisfied with his choice, performed without distinction on his exams, and wrote in his diary, "Never in my life have I thought so intensely about the purpose of my life." His emotional state reflected the uncertainty of his life course: "I am oscillating between moods of joy and sorrow, enthusiasm and apathy. It is all right once in a while, but I should not let my mind be tossed like an object on big waves."[79]

Vinu's dissatisfaction with his life grew into an intense state of boredom and work paralysis. He lost interest in his studies and became entirely unable to prepare for his exams. His self-questioning reflects this immobilized state, as well as his deepest doubts about life's very meaning:

> After all, do these studies mean everything? That is really the question. What is life? What type of life should I live?

[79] Ibid., p. 97.

What should be the goal of life?
What is my goal?
Where do I have to go?
Shall I get an answer?
Is the goal of becoming a business executive a proper goal for me? (If I am competent enough even to become one!) But if I become an executive I will lose my freedom. I will certainly lose all my freedom if I get married.
Life itself is a big mirage. Moreover, there are all sorts of complications in it. A man is bound to be caught into it as into a whirlpool.[80]

Complaining of further stomach pains and a general inability to function, Vinu dropped out of college. He attempted to enter an *Ashram* (an Indian monastery) but was turned down. This was certainly the low point of his young life. He writes, "I find darkness everywhere."[81] In Eriksonian terms, Vinu was in a state of identity confusion, simultaneously suffering many of the disturbing symptoms of this condition. Among these symptoms were Vinu's work paralysis, his loss of basic confidence in life itself ("Life is a mirage. . .I find darkness everywhere"), and his extreme self-consciousness (reflected in his elaborate diary entries). In addition, Vinu experienced the sexual confusion that is often associated with this condition. As is common with many adolescents in a state of identity crisis, Vinu dealt with the unbearable tensions of sexuality by rejecting the idea of sex altogether. During this period in his life, he became an advocate of celibacy, renouncing sensuality and "useless" pleasures of the flesh.[82]

Vinu spent the next few years, until the age of twenty-two, drifting in and out of college, constantly searching for something to inspire him. He read Marx and Gandhi, found and followed a number of "gurus," and experimented with various ideological commitments. All this time, he searched for a direction that would satisfy him for more than a brief period of time. He decided that this search must begin within himself, in order to determine his true nature:

> Now, while thinking about the "self," I should not forget that my goal is to attain knowledge, or, in other words, "Know thyself." This goal is obviously very difficult to reach. However, I must try to reach this goal in whatever way possible, intellectually, physically, or through mysticism. . .To me the most valuable thing in life is knowledge of the self.[83]

Vinu then entered a long period of self-testing. He tried and rejected a series of religious commitments, finally weaving his own personalized version of an Indian doctrine. He also tried a number of occupational commitments, including that of teacher and journalist. The latter suited his abilities and interests. His academic performance improved greatly, and he passed his M.A. examination with honors. His diary entries of this period reflected his new-found joy in commitment and success:

[80] Ibid., p. 111.
[81] Ibid., p. 114.
[82] Ibid., p. 121.
[83] Ibid., p. 122.

> The feeling of achievement is something. . .Most important of all, I have regained the confidence which was lost during the past few years. I feel confident in all fields. The feeling of restlessness is gone, and I have a feeling that, "Yes! I can do that also." I will be able to stabilize in the professional field very soon. Now onward march in every field![84]

Vinu's inner sense of confidence is matched with an outer sense of recognition: "Most people look at me from a changed point of view. I have earned status and recognition."[85] Thus, Vinu experiences the internal and external satisfaction of psychosocial identity. His views on sexual intimacy change concomitantly with the emergence of this new self-acceptance: "I have learned from experience during the past year that there is no use trying to suppress the tensions arising from sex."[86] Within the next few years, Vinu decides that he is ready to marry. Subsequently, he accepts a young woman that, in Indian tradition, his parents have selected for him to marry. Once married, Vinu's diary accounts of his life cease. Apparently, Vinu's intimate relation with his new wife replaces his need for solitary self-reflection.

Vinu's story is a classic case of identity crisis and resolution as described by Eriksonian theory. After a severe bout with identity confusion, during which time he exhibited physical as well as psychological symptoms, Vinu consciously sought to define himself and the meaning of his life. He went through a period of "role experimentation," trying out ideologies and occupations until finally settling on beliefs and career goals that he was comfortable with. This helped him better define himself. Once he knew and accepted himself, his emotional and physical state improved rapidly. He experienced the state of psychosocial well-being described by Erikson, and his attitudes toward work and sex relaxed considerably. Vinu's turbulent adolescence demonstrates Erikson's admonition that identity confusion should be considered a developmental disorder, rather than a psychopathological condition. Even in cases like that of Vinu, where several of the identity confusion symptoms converge to create a serious loss of functioning, normal processes of personality development eventually can lead the adolescent out of the condition spontaneously. For this reason, the identity crisis must be considered a transient life phase rather than an attack of mental illness.

The cases of Meera and Sheela, the young women in Paranjpe's study, were investigated through interviews and projective tests conducted over a three-year period. During the first three years at college, Meera and Sheela were interviewed every four to six months. Some of the interviews were open-ended, consisting of general questions about life and their goals and aspirations. Other sessions included: taking a self-description test in which they were asked to write twenty sentences describing themselves in the third person; another a "prospective autobiography" questionnaire in which each woman was asked to imagine it was the year 2000 and write an autobiography of

[84] Ibid., p. 124.
[85] Ibid., p. 126.
[86] Ibid.

herself; and having a value and ideology interview in which Meera and Sheela were asked to express their views on contemporary social problems and various ideological positions.

In many respects, the identity searches of Meera and Sheela were similar to one another, and to the general pattern of late adolescent identity formation as described by Erikson. Both women experienced uncertainties about their futures, experimented with various career choices, and finally settled on paths of their own choosing (and, for both women, in opposition to their father's advice). In these respects, neither case was remarkable, and we shall not dwell on them here. But both cases had some noteworthy aspects that illuminate the special identity challenges faced by women in a traditional society. With respect to this issue, the two women were somewhat different from one another, though each illustrates, in her own way, a feminine identity struggle in Indian culture.

Meera, despite her career aspirations, was most strongly oriented toward obtaining a husband and establishing a family. Because of this, she refused to take a stand on many issues that usually are part of an individual's identity formation. For example, she consciously refrained from adopting a personal ideology because she believed that her future husband should determine this for her. "Being a girl I have my own limit," she said during one interview. Paranjpe describes the gist of Meera's beliefs on this matter:

> She said that her choice of ideology would depend on the kind of partner she married. She gave examples of girls who had firm and strong political opinions that were opposed to those of their husbands. She had observed some cases of clash between husband and wife on matters of political attitudes where the girls ultimately had to convert to the man's opinions. She thought it was better not to develop strong attitudes in political matters rather than be forced to change them later.[87]

Paranjpe concludes that Meera chose to be in a state of identity foreclosure with respect to her ideological commitment. "She thought that as a woman her first loyalty must be to her home," writes Paranjpe.[88] For this reason, she forsook social and political activity, even though she had genuine interests in politics. As Erikson himself has noted, this is a typical way for women to keep their identities "open for the peculiarities of the man to be joined."[89] For Meera, as for so many women in traditional cultures, the keystone of identity was her role as a wife and mother. In order to prepare themselves for this role, many women believe that they must keep other aspects of their identity in foreclosure. As the research cited in the previous section indicates, this is also true of many American women, even in our contemporary "liberated" society.

Sheela was quite unusual in this regard, especially for a woman in traditional Indian society. Against her parents' strongest objections, she purposively rejected all the insignia of a woman's role. As soon as she reached

[87] Ibid., p. 214.
[88] Ibid., p. 217.
[89] Erikson, 1968, p. 141.

college, she stopped wearing the bangles and other ornaments that typically adorn Indian women. She chose to wear working clothes, rather than *saris* or other traditional women's dress. She avoided household work even in the face of her parents' warnings that this would impair her chances of securing a husband. In all these ways, she was even different from other well-educated, professional women like Meera. Even more important for Sheela's identity search, she adamantly insisted on developing her own ideological point of view, whatever the consequences to her future marriage prospects. Further, she was aware of the societal implications of her decision. During one interview, late in her adolescent years, Sheela said:

> The contrast between the traditional type of woman and the modern type is increasing. Formerly, a woman had to tolerate whatever the husband did. She had to think of husband as God. No value was given to her opinions. Now this is the era of equal rights. Formerly the man of the house had the final say in every matter. Now women can assert their opinions emphatically.[90]

As she herself realizes, Sheela represents a type of woman that is becoming increasingly common in modern times. She sees marriage and family as an important part of her life, but she refuses to submerge other aspects of her personal identity to them. About husband-wife relations, she says, "If there is friction, they should be separated."[91] Sheela clearly had a way of achieving identity that is closer to the typical male way than to the traditional female way.

Does this mean that Sheela adjusted better psychosocially than Meera? We would certainly say that she was more liberated from social conventions. But as for psychosocial adjustment, this is determined not only by the cohesiveness of the individual's inner identity structure, but also by the manner in which it is adapted to society-at-large. Psychosocial well-being, the reward of a successful identity consolidation, is a by-product of social recognition as well as of psychological self-acceptance. From this perspective, Paranjpe believes that Meera may be better adjusted to her society as it was at the time of the study (though, of course, if the society is truly in transition it may "catch up" to Sheela in time for Sheela to receive the social recognition she deserves). Paranjpe writes that, with respect to the essential Indian task of finding a husband:

> Meera seemed better prepared than Sheela was. She not only specified the qualities of the right kind of man, but also chose a particular young man to be friendly with. . .she was extremely well prepared in managing the household. . .In all these respects, and to the extent to which she seemed confident in facing challenges at home and outside. . .Meera was fairly advanced in her identity formation.[92]

It is not our intention here to debate the psychosocial merits of traditional versus contemporary sex roles. Certainly there could be hazards in choosing

---

[90] Paranjpe, 1976, p. 270.
[91] Ibid., p. 276.

[92] Ibid., p. 281.

either, particularly in societies that are in transition from one role stereotype to the other. During periods of rapid social change, there are always individuals who suffer personally because they are a bit ahead of changes in the mainstream, just as there are individuals who feel outpaced and outmoded by the swirl of events around them. The present point is that there are a number of ways to establish a functional psychosocial identity. For women in today's world, there seem to be at least two major choices: an identity can be constructed around interpersonal relations and impending marriage, with other aspects subordinated to the prospects of one's role as wife and mother; or identity can be constructed around occupational and ideological commitments, much as it is for the majority of males. Because contemporary society is in flux, and therefore is heterogeneous with respect to accepted sex roles, both paths of feminine identity formation have their advantages and risks. Many young women like Meera and Sheela are conscious of these advantages and make their choices with full self-awareness. In such cases, whatever the choice, we may be confident that the identities are being constructed on sure ground.

Paranjpe uses his Canadian subject, a young man named Ian, to demonstrate the cross-cultural validity of Erikson's theory. Ian's case history was culled mostly from diaries that he kept between grade ten and his last year of college. These diaries were in the form of letters to a fictitious friend. Ian's case is striking in its similarity to many of Paranjpe's male Indian cases. For example, Ian reports in his early diaries that his worries about the future were confusing and immobilizing him:

> Lately I've been in a daze, and I can't think straight. Maybe because some of my brain cells are dying and I'm just about sixteen. My whole world is changing. Before I used to have a regular routine and all I was concerned with was school. But now I'm thinking of my future.[93]

Ian reports the same kind of work paralysis that we observed in Vinu: "Lately I have become frustrated and confused. I'm losing interest in school and I hardly do any homework any more."[94] He even questions the value of sexual enjoyment, as did Vinu in his adolescence: "despite all the advancements man has made, no one yet has found a way to control his urge of sex. Of course sex is necessary, but it isn't in my opinion, something to perk one up. Sex is a sacred act and should be treated that way."[95] All of these doubts converge to disturb Ian's confidence in the future and in life itself: "I am afraid of what the future holds for me. . .What is life? Can you, or for that matter anyone, define that word?"[96]

Ian resolves his identity crisis in much the same manner as most adolescents, including Paranjpe's Indian subjects. He commits himself to a profession (that of schoolteacher), and adopts his own personal blend of religious, philosophical, and political beliefs. This comes after a period of experimentation

[93] Ibid., p. 338.
[94] Ibid., p. 341.
[95] Ibid., p. 340.
[96] Ibid., p. 344.

and reflection about the meaning of life, God, mystical experience, careers, and his own inner self. Ian ends up a dedicated teacher, a proud Canadian, a political conservative, and an advocate of marriage and family. Paranjpe concludes that, despite the fact of individual variation, the process of identity formation in adolescence is the same across cultures:

> . . .the specific tasks that the particular adolescent must accomplish may vary from individual to individual. . .(But) there is remarkable similarity between the symptoms of identity confusion described by Erikson on the basis of his observations in the modern U.S.A. and our case histories from contemporary India and Canada. If we speculate on the applicability of the identity crisis concept to a broad range of variation in cultural patterns on the basis of our cross-cultural observations, there seems to be no particular reason to doubt its universality.[97]

Summary

The major psychosocial task of adolescence is forming a coherent personal identity. In fact, many social scientists define the end of adolescence not by chronological age but by the consolidation of one's sense of self-identity. For the adolescent, this means weaving an identity structure that is both personally satisfying and socially effective.

Because of a number of biological and cognitive changes that occur around the time of puberty, the adolescent experiences a need to become autonomous from the home and family. Adolescents turn increasingly to peers and other sources outside the family for communication and for support of their self-esteem. At the same time, they continue to need the support and guidance of their parents. The adolescent's search for autonomy goes through a series of phases similar in form to those found in infancy: initially there is a sharp differentiation from the parents, then a phase of practicing one's independence, and finally a rapprochement with the parents based on a new sense of the autonomous self. This all occurs early in adolescence, just prior to the main challenge of the period, the formation and consolidation of self-identity.

The cognitive aspect of identity formation is the development of self-understanding. As in the childhood years, self-understanding continues to be elaborated and reconceptualized throughout the adolescent years. During adolescence, conceptions of self become increasingly psychological, centering on one's physical or active self. In addition, adolescents see themselves as more volitional than previously, believing that they have effective control over their own destinies. There also emerges a sense that one has distinct and stable social-personality characteristics. Finally, adolescents are able, for the first time, to integrate all the diverse aspects of themselves into a systematic, well-organized self-conception. This resolves many of the contradictions and irregularities in children's earlier representations of self.

[97] Ibid., p. 374.

Identity includes self-understanding but goes beyond it in important ways. For one thing, identity consists of affective as well as cognitive components. Affective elements of identity include one's positive and negative feelings toward oneself, one's will to grow in a certain direction, and one's emotional orientation toward the people and events in one's life. In addition, one's identity is particularized and content-bound. Unlike self-understanding, it is not an abstraction of general categories that apply to the self. It is composed of a particular set of statements, beliefs, and feelings about the self and the self's behavior. Identity is a unique totality of specific characteristics that establish one's individuality and one's direction in life. A general understanding of the nature of self contributes greatly to this totality, but it is still only one part of the picture.

The process of identity formation entails an evaluation of all one's past and present attributes, as well as a judgment about the kind of person one would like to become in the future. It means constructing a new totality out of all one's earlier childhood identifications. Erikson has called the identity search a "crisis" which can be an all-consuming preoccupation for many adolescents. For most adolescents, however, it is a prolonged trial, resolved by a piecemeal and gradual process of experimentation with countless life options. The adolescent must reject those that do not fit, as well as accepting those that do. The identity structure is consolidated only when the adolescent can anticipate the appropriateness of a particular decision for his sense of self before the decision is actually made.

The signs of a consolidated identity are both conscious and nonconscious. The main ones are: an acceptance of oneself and one's actions, a feeling of comfort and appropriateness associated with one's self-image, and a general sense of psychosocial well-being. Then the adolescent can say with satisfaction, "I am what I am."

For adolescents who have not yet resolved the identity crisis, the experience can be psychologically discomforting. Cases of prolonged identity confusion often result in temporary pathological symptoms. These include a diffusion of time, an acute self-consciousness, role fixation, work paralysis, and bisexual confusion. Erikson is careful to note that these psychological states are developmental disorders, rather than true clinical disturbances. This is because most persons with symptoms of identity confusion eventually grow out of them through normal developmental processes, and do not require special psychotherapeutic treatment.

Empirical research on identity formation has found that one's success in resolving the identity crisis is related to one's emotional outlook, one's self-esteem, one's values, and one's sense of direction in life. Most persons in our culture succeed in consolidating their identities between the ages of eighteen and twenty-two. Research has shown that women in our society follow essentially the same path to identity as man, despite traditional differences between women's and men's social roles. Consequently, such differences may be gradu-

middle-class?

ally disappearing in contemporary social life, and with them the divergence between men's and women's paths.

Identity and intimacy go hand in hand at the end of adolescence. There is some dispute in the literature as to which of the two is the developmental prerequisite for the other. Some believe that a firm sense of self is necessary if one is to take on the risks of commitment to another. Others believe that it is impossible to "find oneself" without first experiencing intimate relations with others. Identity and intimacy may be achieved concomitantly with one another, by virtue of each other's assistance. In any case, the two represent the final accomplishment of the adolescent years, paving the way for successful work and love relationships in adulthood.

References

Adelson, J., & O'Neil, R. Growth of political ideas in adolescence: The sense of community. *Journal of Personality and Social Psychology*, 1966, *4*, 295–306.

Ainsworth, M. *Infancy in Uganda: Infant Care and the Growth of Love.* Baltimore: Johns Hopkins University Press, 1967.

Ainsworth, M. D. S. The development of infant-mother attachment. In B. M. Caldwell & H. N. Ricciuti (Eds.), *Review of Child Development Research* (Vol. 3). Chicago: University of Chicago Press, 1973.

Ainsworth, M. Infant-mother attachment. In M. Richards (Ed.), *The Child's Integration into the Social World.* New York: Cambridge University Press, 1978.

Ainsworth, M. D. S., & Bell, S. M. Attachment, exploration, and separation: Illustrated by the behavior of one-year-olds in a strange situation. *Child Development*, 1970, *41*, 49–67.

Ainsworth, M. D., Blehar, M. C., Waters, E., & Wall, S. *Patterns of Attachment.* Hillsdale, N.J.: Erlbaum, 1978.

Allport, G. W. *Pattern and Growth in Personality.* New York: Holt, Rinehart & Winston, 1961.

Amsterdam, B. K. Mirror self-esteem reactions before age two. *Developmental Psychology*, 1972, *5*, 297–305.

Ariès, P. *Centuries of Childhood.* New York: Vintage Books, 1965.

Aristotle. *The Nichomachaean Ethics* (Book 1). W. D. Ross (Tr.). New York: Oxford University Press, 1980.

Aronson, E., & Carlsmith, J. M. The effect of the severity of threat on the devaluation of forbidden behavior. *Journal of Abnormal and Social Psychology*, 1963, *66*, 584–88.

Asher, S., Oden, S., & Gottman, J. Children's friendships in school settings. In L. Katz (Ed.), *Current Topics in Early Childhood Education* (Vol. 1). Norwood, N.J.: Ablex, 1977.

Bachman, J. G. *Youth in Transition: The Impact of Family Background and Intelligence on Tenth-Grade Boys* (Vol. 2). Ann Arbor, Mich.: Survey Research Center Institute for Social Research, 1970.

Bakeman, R., & Brownlee, J. The strategic use of parallel play: A sequential analysis. *Child Development*, 1980, *51*, 873–78.

Baldwin, A. Socialization and the parent-child relationship. *Child Development*, 1948, *19*, 127–36.

Baldwin, A. *Behavior and Development in Childhood*. New York: Dryden Press, 1955.

Baldwin, J. M. *Social and Ethical Interpretations in Mental Development* (3rd ed.). New York: Macmillan, 1902.

Ball, S., & Bogatz, G. A. Summative research on Sesame Street: Implications for the study of preschool children. In A. D. Pick (Ed.), *Minnesota Symposium on Child Psychology* (Vol. 6). Minneapolis: University of Minnesota Press, 1972.

Baltes, P., Reese, W., & Lipsitt, L. Life-span developmental psychology. *Annual Review of Psychology*, 1980, *31*.

Bandura, A. *Social Learning Theory*. Englewood Cliffs, N.J.: Prentice-Hall, 1977.

Bandura, A., & McDonald, F. J. Influence of social reinforcement and the behavior of models in shaping children's moral judgments. *Journal of Abnormal and Social Psychology*, 1963, *67*, 274–81.

Bandura, A., Ross, D., & Ross, S. Transmission of aggression through imitation of aggressive models. *Journal of Abnormal and Social Psychology*, 1961, *63*, 375–82.

Bandura, A., Ross, D., & Ross, S. Imitation of film-mediated aggressive models. *Journal of Abnormal and Social Psychology*, 1963, *66*, 3–11.

Bandura, A., & Walters, R. H. *Social Learning and Personality Development*. New York: Holt, Rinehart & Winston, 1963.

Barenboim, C. The development of person perception in childhood and adolescence: From behavioral comparisons to psychological comparisons. *Child Development*, 1981, *52*, 129–44.

Barnes, K. Preschool play norms: A replication. *Developmental Psychology*, 1971, *5*, 99–103.

Barrett, D. E. A naturalistic study of sex differences in children's aggression. *Merrill-Palmer Quarterly*, 1979, *25*, 191–203.

Bates, J. The concept of difficult temperament. *Merrill-Palmer Quarterly*, 1980, *26*, 299–319.

Bates, J., Olson, S., Pettit, G., & Bayles, K. Dimensions of individuality in the mother-child relationship at six months of age. *Child Development*, 1982, *53*, 446–61.

Battle, E., & Casey, B. A context for hyperactivity in children over time. *Child Development*, 1972, *43*, 757–73.

Baumrind, D. Child care practices anteceding three patterns of preschool behavior. *Genetic Psychology Monographs*, 1967, *75*, 43–88.

Baumrind, D. Note: Harmonious parents and their preschool children. *Developmental Psychology*, 1971, *4*, 99–102.

Baumrind, D. The development of instrumental competence through socialization. In A. D. Pick (Ed.), *Minnesota Symposium on Child Psychology* (Vol. 7). Minneapolis: University of Minnesota Press, 1973.

Baumrind, D. Socialization determinants of personal agency. Paper presented at the biennial meetings of the Society for Research in Child Development, New Orleans, 1977.

Baumrind, D. A dialectical materialist's perspective on knowing social reality. In W. Damon (Ed.), *Moral Development* (New Directions for Child Development, No. 2). San Francisco: Jossey-Bass, 1978.

Beck, A. T. *Depression: Clinical, Experimental, and Theoretical Aspects.* New York: Hoeber, 1967.

Bee, H. L. Parent-child interaction and distractability in nine-year-old children. *Merrill-Palmer Quarterly,* 1967, *13,* 175–90.

Bell, R. Q. A reinterpretation of the direction of effect in studies of socialization. *Psychological Review,* 1968, *75,* 81–95.

Bell, R. Q. Contributions of human infants to caregiving and social interaction. In M. Lewis & L. A. Rosenblum (Eds.), *The Effect of the Infant on Its Caregiver* (Vol. 1). New York: Wiley, 1974.

Bell, S. M. The development of the concept of object as related to infant-mother attachment. *Child Development,* 1970, *41,* 291–311.

Belsky, J. Mother-father-infant interaction: A naturalistic observational study. *Developmental Psychology,* 1979, *15,* 601–9.

Bengtson, V. L. The generation gap: A review and typology of social-psychological perspectives. *Youth and Society,* 1970, *2,* 7–32.

Berndt, T. J. Relations between social cognition, nonsocial cognition, and social behavior: The case of friendship. In J. H. Flavell & L. D. Ross (Eds.), *Social Cognitive Development.* New York: Cambridge University Press, 1981.

Bernstein, B. A Sociolinguistic approach to socialization: With some reference to educability. In F. Williams (Ed.), *Language and Poverty: Perspectives on a Theme.* Chicago: Markham, 1970.

Bernstein, R. M. The development of the self-system during adolescence. *Journal of Genetic Psychology,* 1980, *136,* 231–45.

Bigelow, B. J. Children's friendship expectations: A cognitive-developmental study. *Child Development,* 1977, *48,* 246–53.

Bigelow, B. J., & LaGaipa, J. J. Children's written descriptions of friendship: A multidimensional analysis. *Developmental Psychology,* 1975, *11,* 857–58.

Bigelow, B. J., & LaGaipa, J. J. The development of friendship values and choice. In H. McGurk (Ed.), *Issues in Childhood Social Development.* London: Methuen, 1979.

Bijou, S., & Baer, D. M. *Child Development* (Vol. 1). New York: Appleton-Century-Crofts, 1961.

Birch, H. G. Health and the education of socially disadvantaged children. *Developmental Medicine and Child Neurology,* 1968, *10.*

Blehar, M., Lieberman, A., & Ainsworth, M. Early face-to-face interaction and its relation to later infant-mother attachment. *Child Development,* 1977, *48,* 182–94.

Block, J. H. *Lives through Time.* Berkeley, Calif.: Bancroft Books, 1971.

Block, J. H., & Block, J. The role of ego-control and ego-resiliency in the organization of behavior. In W. A. Collins (Ed.), *Development of Cognition, Affect, and Social*

Relations (Minnesota Symposium on Child Psychology, Vol. 13). Hillsdale, N.J.: Erlbaum, 1980.

Bloomberg, S. H. The household and the family: The effects of industrialization on skilled workers in Newark, 1840–1860. Paper presented at the Organization of American Historians, Denver, 1974.

Blos, P. *On Adolescence: A Psychoanalytic Interpretation.* Glencoe, Ill.: Free Press, 1962.

Blos, P. *The Young Adolescent: Clinical Studies.* New York: Free Press, 1970.

Blurton-Jones, N. G. An ethological study of some aspects of social behaviour in children in nursery school. In D. Morris (Ed.), *Primate Ethology.* London: Weidenfeld & Nicolson, 1967.

Borke, H. Chandler and Greenspan's "Ersatz egocentrism": A rejoinder. *Developmental Psychology,* 1972, *7,* 107–9.

Borke, H. Piaget's mountains revisited: Changes in the egocentric landscape. *Developmental Psychology,* 1975, *11,* 240–43.

Bourne, E. The state of research on ego identity: A review and appraisal. *Journal of Youth and Adolescence,* 1978, *7,* 223–51 (Part 1), and 371–92 (Part 2).

Bower, T. G. R. *A Primer of Infant Development.* San Francisco: W. H. Freeman, 1977.

Bowlby, J. *Maternal Care and Mental Health.* Geneva: World Health Organization, 1951.

Bowlby, J. Separation anxiety. *International Journal of Psychoanalysis,* 1960, *41,* 89–113.

Bowlby, J. *Attachment and Loss* (Vols. 1 and 2). New York: Basic Books, 1969.

Brazelton, T. B. Psychophysiologic reactions in the neonate: I. The value of observation of the neonate. *The Journal of Pediatrics,* 1961, *58,* 508–12.

Brazelton, T. *Neonatal Bahavioral Assessment Scale.* Philadelphia: J. P. Lippincott, 1973.

Brazelton, T. B. Early parent-infant reciprocity. In V. C. Vaughan & T. B. Brazelton (Eds.), *The Family: Can It Be Saved?* Chicago: Yearbook Medical Publishers, 1976.

Brazelton, T. B., & Collier, G. A. Infant development in the Zinncanteco Indians of Southern Mexico. *Pediatrics,* 1969, *44,* 274.

Brazelton, T. B., Koslowski, B., & Main, M. The origin of reciprocity in the mother-infant interaction. In M. Lewis & L. Rosenblum (Eds.), *The Effect of the Infant on Its Caregiver.* New York: Wiley, 1974.

Brenner, J., & Mueller, N. Shared meaning in boy toddlers' peer relations. *Child Development,* 1982, *53,* 380–91.

Bretherton, I., & Bates, E. The emergence of intentional communication. In I. C. Izgiris (Ed.), *Social Interaction and Communication during Infancy.* San Francisco: Jossey-Bass, 1979.

Breuer, H. Ego identity status in late-adolescent college males, as measured by a group-administered incomplete sentences blank and related to inferred stance toward authority. Unpublished doctoral dissertation, New York University, 1973.

Bridges, K. M. B. A study of social development in early infancy. *Child Development,* 1933, *4,* 36–49.

Brim, O. G. Life span development of the theory of oneself: Implications for child development. In H. W. Reese (Ed.), *Advances in Child Development and Behavior* (Vol. 2). New York: Academic Press, 1976.

Brittain, C. Adolescent choices and parent-peer cross-pressure. *American Sociological Review*, 1963, *28*, 385–91.

Brittain, C. An exploration of peer compliance and parent compliance in adolescence. *Adolescence*, 1968, *2*, 445–58.

Brittain, C. A comparison of rural and urban adolescents with respect to peer versus parent compliance. *Adolescence*, 1969, *13*, 59–68.

Bronfenbrenner, U. *Two Worlds of Childhood*. New York: Russell Sage, 1970.

Bronson, W. Peer-peer interactions in the second year of life. In M. Lewis & L. A. Rosenblum (Eds.), *Friendship and Peer Relations*. New York: Wiley, 1975.

Bronson, W. *Toddlers' Behavior with Agemates: Issues of Interaction, Cognition, and Affect*. Norwood, N.J.: Ablex Publishing, 1981.

Broughton, J. Development of concepts of self, mind, reality, and knowledge. *New Directions for Child Development*, 1978, *1*, 75–100.

Broughton, J. The divided self in adolescence. *Human Development*, 1980, *24*, 13–32.

Brown, J. V., & Bateman, R. Relationships of human mothers with their infants during the first year of life: Effects of prematurity. In R. W. Bell & W. P. Smotherman (Eds.), *Maternal Influences and Early Behavior*. Holliswood, N.Y.: Spectrum, 1978.

Brown, R., & Herrnstein, R. *Psychology*. Boston: Little Brown, 1975.

Bruner, J. S. The organization of early skilled action. *Child Development*, 1973, *44*, 1–11.

Bruner, J., Jolly, A., & Sylva, K. (Eds.). *Play: Its Role in Development and Evolution*. Introduction. New York: Basic Books, 1976.

Bruner, J. S., Postman, L., & Rodrigues, J. Expectation and the perception of color. *American Journal of Psychology*, 1951, *64*, 216–27.

Bruner, J., & Sherwood, V. Peek-a-boo and the learning of rule structures. In J. Bruner, A. Jolly, & K. Sylva (Eds.), *Play: Its Role in Development and Evolution*. New York: Basic Books, 1976.

Buhler, C. The social behavior of children. In C. A. Murchison (Ed.), *A Handbook of Child Psychology*. Worcester, Mass.: Clark University Press, 1933.

Buhler, C. *From Birth to Maturity*. London: Lund, Humphries, 1935.

Bunt, M. Ego identity: Its relationship to the discrepancy between how an adolescent views himself and how he perceives that others view him. *Psychology*, 1968, *5*(3), 14–25.

Buss, D., Block, J. H., & Block, J. Preschool activity level: Personality correlates and developmental implications. *Child Development*, 1980, *51*, 401–8.

Cairns, R. Attachment and dependency: A psychobiological and social-learning synthesis. In J. Gewirtz (Ed.), *Attachment and Dependency*. Washington, D.C.: Winston, 1972.

Carlsson, S. G., Fagersburg, G., Hwang, C. P., Larsson, K., Rodholm, M., Schaller, J., Daniellson, B., & Gundewall, C. Effects of various amounts of contact between mother and child on the mother's nursing behavior: A follow-up study. *Infant Behavior and Development*, 1979, *2*, 209–14.

Cattell, R. B. *Personality and Motivation: Structure and Measurement*. New York: Harcourt Brace Jovanovich, 1957.

Chaffee, S. H. Mass communication in political socialization. In S. A. Renshon (Ed.), *Handbook of Political Socialization: Theory and Research*. New York: Free Press, 1977.

Chaffee, S. H., McLeod, J. M., & Wackman, D. B. Family communication patterns and adolescent political participation. In J. Dennis (Ed.), *Socialization to Politics*. New York: Wiley, 1973.

Chapman, M., & Zahn-Waxler, C. Young children's compliance and noncompliance to parental discipline in a natural setting. *International Journal of Behavioral Development*, 1982, *5*, 81–94.

Chomsky, N. *Reflections on Language*. New York: Pantheon, 1975.

Clarke-Stewart, K. A. And daddy makes three: The mother-father-infant interaction. *Child Development*, 1978, *49*, 466–78.

Clarke-Stewart, K. A. The father's contribution to children's cognitive and social development in early childhood. In F. A. Pederson (Ed.), *The Father-Infant Relationship*. New York, Praeger, 1980.

Colby, A., Gibbs, J., & Kohlberg, L. *The Assessment of Moral Judgment: Standard Form Moral Judgment Scoring Manual*. Cambridge, Mass.: Moral Education Research Foundation, 1978.

Colby, A., Gibbs, J., Kohlberg, L., & Lieberman, M. A longitudinal study of moral development. *Monographs of the Society for Research in Child Development*. Chicago: University of Chicago Press, 1983.

Coleman, J. C. *The Adolescent Society*. Glencoe, Ill.: Free Press, 1961.

Coleman, J. C. Study of adolescent development using a sentence-completion method. *British Journal of Educational Psychology*, 1970, *40*, 27–34.

Coleman, J. C. *Relationships in Adolescence*. Boston & London: Routledge & Kegan Paul, 1974.

Coleman, J. C. Friendship and the peer group in adolescence. In J. Adelson (Ed.), *Handbook of Adolescent Psychology*. New York: Wiley, 1980.

Coles, R. *Children of Crisis: A Study of Courage and Fear*. Boston: Little, Brown, 1967.

Coles, R. *Children of Crisis* (Vol. 4). Boston: Little, Brown, 1975.

Collins, W. A. Learning of media content: A developmental study. *Child Development*, 1970, *41*, 1133–42.

Collins, W. A. Social antecedents, cognitive processing, and comprehension of social portrayals on television. In E. T. Higgins, D. N. Ruble, & W. W. Hartup (Eds.), *Social Cognition and Social Behavior: Developmental Perspectives*. New York: Cambridge University Press, 1983.

Collins, W. A., Wellman, H., Keniston, A., & Westby, S. Age-related aspects of comprehension of televised social content. *Child Development*, 1978, *49*, 389–99.

Condon, W. S., & Sandor, L. Neonate movement is synchronized with adult speech: Interactional participation and language acquisition. *Science*, 1974, *183*, 99–101.

Connell, R. W. *The Child's Construction of Politics*. Carlton, Victoria: Melbourne University Press, 1971.

Connell, R. W. Political socialization in the American family: The evidence re-examined. *Public Opinion Quarterly*, 1972, *36*, 323–33.

Conner, J. M., & Serbin, L. A. Behaviorally based masculine and feminine activity preference scales for preschoolers: Correlates with other classroom behaviors and cognitive tests. *Child Development*, 1977, *48*, 1411–16.

Constantinople, A. An Eriksonian measure of personal development in college students. *Developmental Psychology,* 1969, *1,* 357–72.

Cooley, C. H. *Human Nature and the Social Order.* New York: Scribner's, 1912.

Coopersmith, S. *The Antecedents of Self-Esteem.* San Francisco: W. H. Freeman, 1967.

Crain, W. *Theories of Development: Concepts and Applications.* Englewood Cliffs, N.J.: Prentice-Hall, 1980.

Crandall, R. The measurement of self-esteem and related constructs. In J. P. Robinson & P. R. Shaver (Eds.), *Measures of Social Psychological Attitudes* (rev. ed.). Ann Arbor, Mich.: Institute for Social Research, 1973.

Damon, W. Early conceptions of positive justice as related to the development of logical operations. *Child Development,* 1975, *46,* 301–12.

Damon, W. *The Social World of the Child.* San Francisco: Jossey-Bass, 1977.

Damon, W. Why study social-cognitive development? *Human Development,* 1979, *22,* 206–11.

Damon, W. Patterns of change in children's social reasoning: A two-year longitudinal study. *Child Development,* 1980, *51,* 1010–17.

Damon, W., & Hart, D. The development of self-understanding from infancy through adolescence. *Child Development,* 1982, *53,* 831–57.

Decarie, T. G. *Intelligence and Affectivity in Early Childhood.* New York: International University Press, 1965.

DeChateau, P., & Wilberg, B. Long-term effect on mother-infant behavior of extra contact duration at 36 hours. *Acta Paediatrica Scandanavia,* 1977, *66,* 137–43.

Delora, J. Social systems of dating on a college campus. *Marriage and Family Living,* 1963, *25,* 81–84.

de Mause, L. *The History of Childhood.* New York: The Psychohistory Press, 1974.

Deutsch, C. P. Social class and child development. In B. M. Caldwell & H. N. Ricciuti (Eds.), *Review of Child Development* (Vol. 3). Chicago: University of Chicago Press, 1973.

Deutsch, M., Katz, I., & Jensen, A. R. (Eds.). *Social Class, Race, and Psychological Development.* New York: Holt, Rinehart & Winston, 1968.

Diament, L. Premarital sexual behavior, attitudes, and emotional adjustment. *Journal of Social Psychology,* 1970, *82,* 75–80.

Dignan, M. H. Ego identity and maternal identification. *Journal of Personality and Social Psychology,* 1965, *1,* 476–83.

DiPietro, J. Rough and tumble play: A function of gender. Unpublished manuscript, Psychology Department, Stanford University, 1979.

Douvan, E., & Adelson, J. *The Adolescent Experience.* New York: Wiley, 1966.

Douvan, E., & Gold, H. Modal patterns in American adolescence. In M. L. Hoffman & L. W. Hoffman (Eds.), *Review of Child Development Research* (Vol. 2). New York: Russell Sage, 1966.

Dreeban, R. The contribution of schooling to the learning of norms. *Harvard Educational Review,* 1967, *37,* 211–37.

Dunphy, D. C. The social structure of urban adolescent peer groups. *Sociometry,* 1963, *26,* 230–46.

Dweck, C. S., & Bush, E. S. Sex differences in learned helplessness: I. Differential debilitation with peer and adult evaluators. *Developmental Psychology,* 1976, *12,* 147–56.

Dweck, C. S., Davidson, W., Nelson, S., & Enna, B. Sex differences in learned helplessness: II. The contingencies of evaluative feedback in the classroom. III. An experimental analysis. *Developmental Psychology,* 1978, *14,* 268–76.

Eckerman, C. O., & Whatley, J. L. Toys and social interaction between infant peers. *Child Development,* 1977, *48,* 1645–56.

Eckerman, C. O., Whatley, J., & Kutz, S. Growth of social play with peers during the second year of life. *Developmental Psychology,* 1975, *11,* 42–49.

Edwards, C. P., & Whiting, B. Sex differences in children's social interaction. Unpublished report to the Ford Foundation, 1977.

Edwards, C. P., & Whiting, B. B. Differential socialization of girls and boys in light of cross-cultural research. In C. M. Super & S. Harkness (Eds.), *Anthropological Perspectives on Child Development* (New Directions for Child Development, No. 8). San Francisco: Jossey-Bass, 1980.

Eiduson, B. Child rearing patterns in alternate family life styles. *Ethos,* 1979, *8,* 38–45.

Eisenberg-Berg, N., & Neal, C. Children's moral reasoning about their own spontaneous prosocial behavior. *Developmental Psychology,* 1979, *15,* 228–29.

Elder, G. H., Jr. *Children of the Great Depression.* Chicago: University of Chicago Press, 1974.

Elder, G. H., Jr. Adolescence in historical perspective. In J. Adelson (Ed.), *Handbook of Adolescent Psychology.* New York: Wiley, 1980.

Elkind, D. Strategic interactions in early adolescence. In J. Adelson (Ed.), *Handbook of Adolescent Psychology.* New York: Wiley, 1980.

El-Sadat, A. *In Search of Identity.* New York: Macmillan, 1977.

Emde, R. Levels of meaning for infant emotions. In F. Horowitz, M. Hetherington, S. Scarr-Salapatek, & G. Siegel (Eds.), *Review of Child Development Research* (Vol. 4). Chicago: University of Chicago Press, 1975.

Emde, R. N. Levels of meaning for infant emotions: A biosocial view. In W. A. Collins (Ed.), *Development of Cognition, Affect, and Social Relations* (Minnesota Symposium on Child Psychology, Vol. 13). Hillsdale, N.J.: Erlbaum, 1980.

Emler, N. P., & Rushton, J. P. Cognitive-developmental factors in children's generosity. *British Journal of Social and Clinical Psychology,* 1974, *13,* 277–81.

Emmerich, W. Structure and development of personal-social behaviors in economically disadvantaged preschool children. *Genetic Psychology Monographs,* 1977, *95,* 191–245.

Enright, R. D., Manheim, L. A., & Franklin, C. C. Children's distributive justice reasoning: A standardized and objective scale. *Developmental Psychology,* 1980, *18,* 193–202.

Enright, R. D., & Sutterfield, S. J. An ecological validation of social cognitive development. *Child Development,* 1980, *51,* 156–61.

Erikson, E. H. *Young Man Luther.* New York: W. W. Norton, 1958.

Erikson, E. H. *Insight and Responsibility.* New York: W. W. Norton, 1964.

Erikson, E. H. *Identity: Youth and Crisis.* New York: W. W. Norton, 1968.

Erikson, E. H. *Gandhi's Truth: On the Origins of Militant Nonviolence.* New York: W. W. Norton, 1969.

Erikson, E. H. *Identity and the Life Cycle.* New York: W. W. Norton, 1980.

Escalona, S. Basic modes of social interaction: Their emergence and patterning during the first two years of life. *Merrill-Palmer Quarterly,* 1973, *19,* 205–32.

Escalona, S. K., & Corman, H. H. Early life experience and the development of competence. *International Review of Psychoanalysis,* 1974, 151–68.

Fafouti-Milenkovic, M., & Uzgiris, I. C. The mother-infant communication system. In I. C. Uzgiris (Ed.), *Social Interaction and Communication during Infancy* (New Directions for Child Development, No. 4). San Francisco: Jossey-Bass, 1979.

Farson, R. *Birthrights.* New York: Vintage, 1974.

Feffer, M., & Gourevitch, V. Cognitive aspects of role-taking in children. *Journal of Personality,* 1960, *28,* 383–96.

Fein, G. Echoes from the nursery: Piaget, Vygotsky and the relationship between language and play. In H. Gardner & E. Winner (Eds.), *Fact, Fiction and Fantasy in Early Childhood* (New Directions for Child Development, No. 6). San Francisco: Jossey-Bass, 1979.

Feshbach, N. D. The relationship of child-rearing factors to children's aggression, empathy, and related positive and negative behaviors. In J. de Wit and W. W. Hartup (Eds.), *Determinants and Origins of Aggressive Behavior.* The Hague: Mouton Press, 1974.

Feshbach, N. D. Studies on the empathic behavior in children. In B. A. Maher (Ed.), *Progress in Experimental Personality Research* (Vol. 8). New York: Academic Press, 1977.

Feshbach, N. D., & Feshbach, S. The relationship between empathy and aggression in two age groups. *Developmental Psychology,* 1969, *1,* 102–7.

Feshbach, S., & Singer, R. *Television and Aggression.* San Francisco: Jossey-Bass, 1971.

Fishkin, J., Keniston, K., & MacKinnon, C. Moral reasoning and political ideology. *Journal of Personality and Social Psychology,* 1973, *27,* 109–19.

Fishman, J. R., & Solomon, F. Youth and social action: An introduction. *Journal of Social Issues,* 1964, *20,* 1–27.

Flavell, J. H. *Cognitive Development.* New York: Prentice-Hall, 1977.

Flavell, J. H. et al. *The Development of Role-Taking and Communication Skills in Children.* New York: Wiley, 1968.

Flavell, J. H., & Ross, L. (Eds.), *Social Cognitive Development: Frontiers and Possible Futures.* Cambridge, Eng.: Cambridge University Press, 1981.

Fraiberg, S. Blind infants and their mothers. In M. Lewis & L. A. Rosenblum (Eds.), *The Effect of the Infant on Its Caregiver* (Vol. 1). New York: Wiley, 1974.

Fraiberg, S. *Insights from the Blind.* New York: Basic Books, 1977.

Freud, A. *The Ego and the Mechanisms of Defense.* New York: International Universities Press, 1946.

Freud, A. Adolescence. In R. S. Eissler et al. (Eds.), *Psychoanalytic Study of the Child* (Vol. 13). New York: International Universities Press, 1958.

Freud, A., & Dann, S. An experiment in group upbringing. *Psychoanalytic Study of the Child,* 1951, *6,* 127–68.

Freud, S. The transformation of puberty. In J. Strachey (Tr. and Ed.), *The Complete Psychological Works* (Vol. 17). New York: W. W. Norton, 1976. (Orig. published 1905.)

Freud, S. Character and anal erotism. In J. Strachey (Tr. and Ed.), *The Complete Psychological Works* (Vol. 9). New York: W. W. Norton, 1976. (Orig. published 1908.)

Freud, S. *Beyond the Pleasure Principle.* J. Strachey (Tr. and Ed.). New York: W. W. Norton, 1975. (Orig. published 1920.)

Freud, S. *Group Psychology and the Analysis of the Ego.* J. Strachey (Tr. and Ed.). New York: W. W. Norton, 1975. (Orig. published 1922.)

Freud, S. Some psychical consequences of the anatomical distinction between the sexes. In J. Strachey (Tr. and Ed.), *The Complete Psychological Works* (Vol. 19). New York: W. W. Norton, 1976. (Orig. published 1925.)

Freud, S. *Civilization and Its Discontents.* J. Strachey (Tr. and Ed.). New York: W. W. Norton, 1962. (Orig. published 1930.)

Freud, S. *New Introductory Lectures on Psychoanalysis.* J. Strachey (Tr. and Ed.). New York: W. W. Norton, 1965. (Orig. published 1933.)

Frodi, A. M., & Lamb, M. Sex differences in responsiveness to infants: A developmental study of psychophysiological and behavioral responses. *Child Development,* 1978, *49,* 1182–88.

Frodi, A. M., MacCaulay, J., & Thome, P. R. Are women always less aggressive than men? A review of the experimental literature. *Psychological Bulletin,* 1977, *84,* 634–60.

Furth, H. *The World of Adults.* New York: Elsevier Press, 1980.

Gallatin, J. Political thinking in adolescence. In J. Adelson (Ed.), *Handbook of Adolescent Psychology.* New York: Wiley, 1980.

Gardner, H. Developmental psychology after Piaget: An approach in terms of symbolization. *Human Development,* 1979, *22,* 73–88.

Garvey, C. Some properties in social play. *Merrill-Palmer Quarterly,* 1974, *20,* 163–80.

Garvey, C. *Play* (The Developing Child Series). Cambridge, Mass.: Harvard University Press, 1977.

Garvey, C., & Hogan, R. Social speech and social interaction: Egocentrism revisited. *Child Development,* 1973, *44,* 562–68.

Gelman, R., & Gallistel, R. *The Child's Concept of Number.* Cambridge, Mass.: Harvard University Press, 1977.

Gerson, R. R., & Damon, W. Moral understanding and children's conduct. In W. Damon (Ed.), *Moral Development* (New Directions for Child Development, No. 2). San Francisco: Jossey-Bass, 1978.

Gewirtz, J. Attachment, dependence and a distinction in terms of stimulus control. In J. Gewirtz (Ed.), *Attachment and Dependency.* Washington, D.C.: Winston, 1972. (a)

Gewirtz, J. On the selection and use of attachment and dependency indices. In J. Gewitz (Ed.), *Attachment and Dependency.* Washington, D.C.: Winston, 1972. (b)

Gibbs, J. Kohlberg's stages of moral development: A constructive critique. *Harvard Educational Review,* 1977, *47,* 43–61.

Gilligan, C. *In a Different Voice: Psychological Theory and Women's Development.* Cambridge, Mass.: Harvard University Press, 1982.

Gilligan, C. et al. Moral reasoning about sexual dilemmas: The development of an interview and scoring system. Technical report of the U.S. Commission on Obscenity and Pornography (Vol. 1). Washington, D.C.: U.S. Government Printing Office, 1971.

Ginsburg, H. *The Myth of the Deprived Child: Poor Children's Intellect and Education.* Englewood Cliffs, N.J.: Prentice-Hall, 1972.

Glucksberg, S., Kraus, R. M., & Higgens, T. The development of referential communication skills. In F. D. Horowitz (Ed.), *Review of Child Development Research* (Vol. 4). Chicago: University of Chicago Press, 1975.

Goffman, E. *Strategic Interaction.* Philadelphia: University of Pennsylvania Press, 1969.

Gordon, C. Self-conceptions: Configurations of content. In C. Gordon & K. J. Gergen (Eds.), *The Self in Social Interaction* (Vol. 1). New York: Wiley, 1968.

Goslin, D. *The School in Contemporary Society.* Glenview, Ill.: Scott Foresman, 1965.

Gothals, G. *Experiencing Youth.* New York: Collier, 1971.

Gottman, J., Gonso, J., & Rasmussen, B. Social interaction, social competence, and friendship in children. *Child Development,* 1975, *46,* 709–18.

Gottman, J., & Parkhurst, J. A developmental theory of friendship and acquaintance processes. In W. A. Collins (Ed.), *Development of Cognition, Affect, and Social Relations* (Minnesota Symposium on Child Psychology, Vol. 13). Hillsdale, N.J.: Erlbaum, 1980.

Gough, H. G. *Manual for the California Psychological Inventory* (rev. ed.). Palo Alto, Calif.: California Consulting Psychologists Press, 1969.

Green, F. P., & Schneider, F. W. Age differences in the behavior of boys on three measures of altruism. *Child Development,* 1974, *45,* 248–51.

Green, J., Gustafson, G., & West, M. Effects on infant development of mother-infant interactions. *Child Development,* 1980, *51,* 199–207.

Greven, P. J., Jr. *Four Generations: Population, Land, and Family in Colonial Andover, Massachusetts.* Ithaca, N.Y.: Cornell University Press, 1970.

Grinder, R. E. Relations of social dating attractions to academic orientation and peer relations. *Journal of Educational Psychology,* 1966, *57,* 27–34.

Gruen, W. Rejection of false information about oneself as an indication of ego identity. *Journal of Consulting Psychology,* 1960, *24,* 231–33.

Grusec, J., & Kuczynski, L. Direction of effect in socialization: A comparison of the parent's versus the child's behavior as determinants of disciplinary technique. *Developmental Psychology,* 1980, *16,* 1–9.

Guardo, C. J., & Bohan, J. B. Development of a sense of self-identity in children. *Child Development,* 1971, *42,* 1909–21.

Haan, N., Smith, B., & Block, J. Moral reasoning of young adults. *Journal of Personality and Social Psychology,* 1968, *10,* 183–201.

Halverson, C. F. J., & Waldrop, M. F. The relation of mechanically recorded play activity level to varieties of preschool play behavior. *Child Development,* 1973, *44,* 678–81.

Hanlon, B. J., & Gross, P. The development of sharing behavior. *Journal of Abnormal and Social Psychology,* 1959, *59,* 425–28.

Harlow, H. Love in infant monkeys. *Scientific American,* 1959, *200,* 68–74.

Harlow, H., & Harlow, M. K. Social deprivation in monkeys. *Scientific American,* 1962, *207,* 136–44.

Harris, M. B. Models, norms and sharing. *Psychological Reports,* 1971, *29,* 147–53.

Harter, S. A model of intrinsic mastery motivation in children: Individual differences and developmental change. In W. A. Collins (Ed.), *Minnesota Symposium on Child Psychology* (Vol. 14). Hillsdale, N.J.: Erlbaum, 1980.

Hartup, W. The social worlds of childhood. *American Psychologist,* 1979, *34,* 944–50.

Heider, E. R. Style and effectiveness of children's verbal communications within and between social classes. Doctoral dissertation, Harvard University, 1968.

Herron, R. E., & Sutton-Smith (Eds.). *Child's Play.* New York: Wiley, 1971.

Hess, E. Ethology and developmental psychology. In P. H. Mussen (Ed.), *Carmichael's Manual of Child Psychology* (Vol. 1) (3rd ed.). New York: Wiley, 1970.

Hess, R. D., & Shipman, V. C. Early experience and the socialization of cognitive modes in children. *Child Development,* 1965, *36,* 869–86.

Hess, R. D., & Torney, J. V. *The Development of Political Attitudes in Children.* New York: Anchor, 1967.

Hetherington, E. M. The effects of familial variables on sex-typing, on parent-child similarity, and on imitation in children. In J. P. Hill (Ed.), *Minnesota Symposium on Child Psychology* (Vol. 1). Minneapolis: University of Minnesota Press, 1967.

Hetherington, E. M., Cox, M., & Cox, R. Beyond father absence: Conceptualization effects of divorce. In E. M. Hetherington & R. D. Parke (Eds.), *Contemporary Readings in Child Psychology.* New York: McGraw-Hill, 1977.

Hetherington, E. M., & Deur, J. The effects of father absence on child development. *Young Children,* 1971, *26,* 233–48.

Higgins, E. T. Role-taking and social judgment: Alternative developmental perspectives and processes. In J. H. Flavell & L. Ross (Eds.), *New Directions in the Study of Social-Cognitive Development.* Cambridge, Mass.: Cambridge University Press, 1980.

Higgins, E. T., Ruble, D., & Hartup, W. W. (Eds.), *Social Cognition and Cognitive Behavior: Developmental Perspectives.* New York: Cambridge University Press, 1983.

Hinde, R. A. On describing relationships. *Journal of Child Psychology and Psychiatry,* 1976, *17,* 1–19.

Hoffman, M. L. Moral internalization, parental power, and the nature of the parent-child interaction. *Developmental Psychology,* 1967, *5,* 45–57.

Hoffman, M. L. Moral development. In P. H. Mussen (Ed.), *Carmichael's Manual of Child Psychology* (Vol. 2) (3rd ed.). New York: Wiley, 1970.

Hoffman, M. Identification and conscience development. *Child Development,* 1971, *42,* 1071–82.

Hoffman, M. L. Developmental synthesis of affect and cognition and its implications for altruistic motivation. *Developmental Psychology,* 1975, *11,* 607–22.

Hoffman, M. Empathy, role-taking, guilt, and development of altruistic motives. In T. Lickona (Ed.), *Moral Development and Behavior.* New York: Holt, Rinehart & Winston, 1976.

Hoffman, M. Moral internalization. In L. Berkowitz (Ed.), *Advances in Experimental Social Psychology* (Vol. 10). New York: Academic Press, 1977. (a)

Hoffman, M. L. Personality and social development. *Annual Review of Psychology,* 1977, *28,* 259–331. (b)

Hoffman, M. Affective and cognitive processes in moral internalization. In E. T. Higgins, D. N. Ruble, & W. W. Hartup (Eds.), *Social Cognition and Social Behavior: Developmental Perspectives.* New York: Cambridge University Press, 1983.

Hoffman, M. L., & Saltzstein, II. D. Parent discipline and the child's moral development. *Journal of Personality and Social Psychology*, 1967, *5*, 45–47.

Hogan, R. Moral conduct and moral character: A psychological perspective. *Psychological Bulletin*, 1973, *79*, 217–32.

Hogan, R. Moral development and personality. In D. J. DePalma & J. M. Foley (Eds.), *Moral Development: Current Theory and Research*. Hillsdale, N.J.: Erlbaum, 1975. (a)

Hogan, R. The terror of solitude (Review of *Attachment and Loss* by J. Bowlby). *Merrill-Palmer Quarterly*, 1975, *21*, 67–74. (b)

Hollingshead, A. B. *Elmtown's Youth*. New York: McGraw-Hill, 1949.

Holmberg, M. C. The development of social interchange patterns from 12–42 months: Cross-sectional and short-term longitudinal analyses. *Child Development*, 1981, *52*, 112–19.

Hubley, P., & Trevarthen, C. Sharing a task in infancy. In I. C. Izgiris (Ed.), *Social Interaction and Communication during Infancy*. San Francisco: Jossey-Bass, 1979.

Husbands, C. T. Some social and psychological consequences of the American dating system. *Adolescence*, 1970, *5*, 451–62.

Huttenlocher, J., & Higgins, E. T. Issues in the study of symbolic development. In W. A. Collins (Ed.), *Minnesota Symposium on Child Psychology* (Vol. 11). Hillsdale, N.J.: Erlbaum, 1978.

Hyman, H. *Political Socialization: A Study in the Psychology of Political Behavior*. Glencoe, Ill.: Free Press, 1959.

Inhelder, B., & Piaget, J. *The Growth of Logical Thinking from Childhood to Adolescence*. A. Parsons & S. Milgram (Trs.). New York: Basic Books, 1958.

Jacklin, C. N., & Maccoby, E. E. Social behavior at 33 months in same-same and mixed-sex dyads. *Child Development*, 1978, *49*, 557–69.

Jackson, E., Campos, J., & Fisher, K. The question of decalage between object permanence and person permanence. *Developmental Psychology*, 1975, *11*, 607–22.

Jahoda, M. *Current Concepts of Positive Mental Health*. New York: Basic Books, 1958.

James, W. *The Principles of Psychology: The Briefer Course*. New York: Henry Holt, 1892.

James, W. *Psychology*. New York: Harper Torch Books, 1961.

Jennings, M., & Niemi, R. The transmission of political values from parent to child. *American Political Science Review*, 1968, *62*, 169–84.

Jennings, M., & Niemi, R. Continuity and change in political orientations: A longitudinal study of two generations. *American Political Science Review*, 1975, *69*, 1316–75.

Jones, E. E., & Nisbett, R. E. *The Actor and the Observer: Divergent Perceptions of the Causes of Behavior*. Morristown, N.J.: General Learning Press, 1971.

Josselson, R. Ego development in adolescence. In J. Adelson (Ed.), *Handbook of Adolescent Psychology*. New York: Wiley, 1980.

Kagan, J. The concept of identification. *Psychological Review*, 1958, *65*, 296–305.

Kagan, J. *Change and Continuity in Infancy*. New York: Wiley, 1971.

Kagan, J. Resilience and continuity in psychological development. In A. M. Clarke &

A. D. B. Clarke (Eds.), *Early Experience: Myth and Evidence.* London: Open Books, 1976.

Kagan, J., & Brim, O. *Change and Continuity in Development.* New York: Basic Books, 1981.

Kant, I. *The Fundamental Principles of the Metaphysics of Morals* (Vol. 4). London: George Allen & Unwin, 1951.

Kaplan, H. B., & Pokorny, A. D. Self-derogation and psycho-social adjustment. *Journal of Nervous and Mental Disease,* 1969, *149,* 421–34.

Katz, M. B. *The People of Hamilton, Canada West: Family and Class in a Mid-Nineteenth-Century City.* Cambridge, Mass.: Harvard University Press, 1975.

Keating, D. P. Precocious cognitive development at the level of formal operations. *Child Development,* 1975, *46,* 276–80.

Keating, D. Thinking processes in adolescence. In J. Adelson (Ed.), *Handbook of Adolescent Psychology.* New York: Wiley, 1980.

Keller, A., Ford, L. H., Jr., & Meachum, J. A. Dimensions of self-concept in preschool children. *Developmental Psychology,* 1978, *14,* 483–89.

Kelman, H. C. Compliance, identification, and internalization: Three processes of opinion change. *Journal of Conflict Resolution,* 1958, *2,* 51–60.

Keniston, K. *Young Radicals: Notes on Committed Youth.* New York: Harcourt Brace Jovanovich, 1968.

Keniston, K. Student activism, moral development and morality. *American Journal of Orthopsychiatry,* 1970, *40,* 577–92.

Kett, J. F. *Rites of Passage.* New York: Basic Books, 1977.

Kimble, G. A., & Garmezy, N. *Principles of General Psychology.* New York: Ronald, 1968.

Klaus, M. H., & Kennel, J. H. *Maternal Infant Bonding.* St. Louis: C V Mosby Co., 1976.

Klein, M., & Riveria, J. *Love, Hate and Reparation.* New York: W. W. Norton, 1964.

Kohlberg, L. The development of children's orientations toward a moral order: I. Sequence in the development of human thought. *Vita Humana,* 1963, *6,* 11–33.

Kohlberg, L. Development of moral character and moral ideology. In M. L. Hoffman & L. W. Hoffman (Eds.), *Review of Child Development Research* (Vol. 1). New York: Russell Sage, 1964.

Kohlberg, L. A cognitive-developmental analysis of children's sex-role concepts and attitudes. In E. Maccoby (Ed.), *The Development of Sex Differences.* Stanford, Calif.: Stanford University Press, 1966.

Kohlberg, L. Stage and sequence: The cognitive-developmental approach to socialization. In D. A. Goslin (Ed.), *Handbook of Socialization Theory and Research.* Chicago: Rand McNally, 1969.

Kohlberg, L. From is to ought: How to commit the naturalistic fallacy and get away with it in the study of moral development. In T. Mischel (Ed.), *Cognitive Development and Epistemology.* New York: Academic Press, 1971.

Kohlberg, L. Moral stages and moralization: The cognitive-developmental approach. In T. Lickona (Ed.), *Moral Development and Behavior.* New York: Holt, Rinehart & Winston, 1976.

Kohlberg, L. Revisions in the theory and practice of moral development. In W. Damon

(Ed.), *Moral Development* (New Directions for Child Development, No. 2). San Francisco: Jossey-Bass, 1978.

Kohlberg, L. *The Philosophy of Moral Development* (Vol. 1). San Francisco: Harper & Row, 1981.

Kohlberg, L., & Gilligan, C. The adolescent as a philosopher: The discovery of the self in a postconventional world. *Daedalus,* 1971, *100,* 1051-86.

Kohlberg, L., & Kramer, R. B. Continuities and discontinuities in childhood and adult moral development. *Human Development,* 1969, *12,* 93-120.

Konner, M. Relations among infants and juveniles in comparative perspective. In M. Lewis & L. A. Rosenblum (Eds.), *Friendship and Peer Relations.* New York: Wiley, 1975.

Korner, A. F. Individual differences at birth: Implications for early experience and later development. *American Journal of Orthopsychiatry,* 1971, *41,* 608-19.

Korner, A. F. Sex differences in newborns. *Journal of Child Psychology and Psychiatry,* 1973, *14,* 19-29.

Korner, A. F. The effect of the infant's state, level of arousal, sex, and ontogenetic stage on the caregiver. In M. Lewis & L. A. Rosenblum (Eds.), *The Effect of the Infant on Its Caregiver* (Vol. 1). New York: Wiley, 1974.

Krauss, R. M., & Rotter, G. S. Communication abilities of children as a function of status and age. *Merrill-Palmer Quarterly,* 1968, *14,* 161-73.

Kuhn, D., & Angelev, J. An experimental study of the development of formal operational thought. *Child Development,* 1976, *47,* 697-706.

Kuiper, N., & Rogers, T. Encoding of personal information: Self-other differences. *Journal of Personality and Social Psychology,* 1979, *37,* 499-514.

Kurdek, L. Perspective taking as the cognitive basis of children's moral development: A review of the literature. *Merrill-Palmer Quarterly,* 1978, *24,* 3-28.

Kurtines, W., & Greif, E. The development of moral thought: Review and evaluation of Kohlberg's approach. *Psychological Bulletin,* 1974, *81,* 453-70.

Kutnick, P. The inception of school authority: The socialization of the primary school child. *Genetic Psychology Monographs,* 1980, *101,* 35-70.

Labov, W. D. *The Language of Elementary School Children.* Champaign, Ill.: National Council of Teachers of English, 1963.

Labov, W. The logic of nonstandard English. In V. Lee (Ed.), *Language Development.* New York: Wiley, 1979.

Lamb, M. E. The development of mother-infant and father-infant attachments in the second year of life. *Developmental Psychology,* 1977, *13,* 637-48. (a)

Lamb, M. E. Father-infant and mother-infant interaction in the first year of life. *Child Development,* 1977, *48,* 167-81. (b)

Lamb, M. E. (Ed.). *Social and Personality Development.* New York: Holt, Rinehart & Winston, 1978.

Lamb, M. E. The development of parent-infant attachments in the first two years of life. In F. A. Pederson (Ed.), *The Father-Infant Relationship.* New York: Praeger, 1980.

Lamb, M. E. Correlations between sociability and cognitive performance among eight-month-olds. *Child Development,* 1981, *52,* 711-13.

Lamb, M. E. Individual differences in infant sociability: Their origins and implications for cognitive development. In H. W. Reese & L. P. Lipsitt (Eds.), *Advances in Child Development and Behavior* (Vol. 6). New York: Academic Press, 1982.

Langer, J. *Theories of Development.* New York: Holt, Rinehart & Winston, 1969.

Larson, L. E. Influence of parents and peers during adolescence: The situation hypothesis revisited. *Journal of Marriage and the Family,* 1972, *34,* 67–74.

Larson, S., & Kurdek, L. Intratask and intertask consistency of moral judgment indices in first-, third-, and fifth-grade children. *Developmental Psychology,* 1979, *15,* 461–63.

Lenssen, B. G. Infants' reactions to peer strangers. Paper presented at the biennial meetings of the Society for Research in Child Development, Denver, March 1975.

Lepper, M. R. Dissonance, self-perception, and honesty in children. *Journal of Personality and Social Psychology,* 1973, *25,* 65–74.

Lepper, M. R. Social control processes, attributions of motivation, and the internalization of social values. In E. T. Higgins, D. N. Ruble, & W. W. Hartup (Eds.), *Social Cognition and Social Behavior: Developmental Perspectives.* New York: Cambridge University Press, 1983.

Lepper, M. R., & Greene, D. Turning play into work: Effects of surveillance and extrinsic reward on children's intrinsic motivation. *Journal of Personality and Social Psychology,* 1975, *31,* 479–86.

Lepper, M. R., Greene, D., & Nisbett, R. E. Undermining children's intrinsic interest with extrinsic rewards: A test of the over-justification hypothesis. *Journal of Personality and Social Psychology,* 1973, *28,* 129–37.

Lesser, G., & Kandel, D. Parental and peer influence on educational plans of adolescents. *American Sociological Review,* 1969, *34,* 213–23.

Levine, I. Distributive justice and sharing behavior in a Tel Aviv community. Unpublished manuscript, Tel Aviv University, 1980.

LeVine, R. A. Child rearing as cultural adaptation. In P. H. Leiderman, S. R. Tulkin, & A. Rosenfeld (Eds.), *Culture and Infancy.* New York: Academic Press, 1977.

LeVine, R. A. Anthropology and child development. *New Directions for Child Development,* 1980, *8,* 71–86.

Lewin, K., Lippett, R., & White, R. Patterns of aggressive behavior in experimentally created "social climates." *Journal of Social Psychology,* 1939, *10,* 271–99.

Lewis, M. State as an infant-environment interaction: An analysis of mother-infant interactions as a function of sex. *Merrill-Palmer Quarterly,* 1972, *18,* 95–121.

Lewis, M., & Brooks-Gunn, J. *Social Cognition and the Acquisition of Self.* New York: Plenum Press, 1979.

Lewis, M., & Rosenblum, L. A. Introduction. In M. Lewis & L. A. Rosenblum (Eds.), *The Effect of the Infant on Its Caregiver* (Vol. 1). New York: Wiley, 1974.

Lewis, M., Young, G., Brooks, J., & Michalson, L. The beginning of friendship. In M. Lewis & L. A. Rosenblum (Eds.), *Friendship and Peer Relations.* New York: Wiley, 1975.

Lieberman, A. F. Preschoolers' competence with a peer: Relationship with attachment and peer experience. *Child Development,* 1977, *48,* 1277–87.

Liebert, R. M., Neale, J. M., & Davidson, E. S. *The Early Window: Effects of Television on Children and Youth.* New York: Pergamon, 1973.

Livesly, W. J., & Bromley, D. B. *Person Perception in Childhood and Adolescence.* London: Wiley, 1973.

Lizd, T. *The Person: His Development through the Life Cycle.* New York: Basic Books, 1968.

Loeb, R. Content-concomitants of boys' locus of control examined in parent-child interactions. *Developmental Psychology,* 1975, *11,* 353–59.

Lorenz, K. *Studies in Animal and Human Behavior.* Cambridge, Mass.: Harvard University Press, 1970.

Lowe, M. Trends in the development of representational play in infants from one to three years: An observational study. *Journal of Child Psychology and Psychiatry and Allied Disciplines,* 1975, *16,* 33–47.

Luck, P. W., & Heiss, J. Social determinants of self-esteem in adult males. *Sociology and Social Research,* 1972, *57,* 69–84.

Lyle, J., & Hoffman, H. R. Children's use of television and other media. In E. A. Rubenstein (Ed.), *Televison and Social Behavior* (Vol. 4). Washington, D.C.: U.S. Government Printing Office, 1972.

Maccoby, E. *Social Development: Psychological Growth and the Parent-Child Relationship.* New York: Harcourt Brace Jovanovich, 1980.

Maccoby, E. E., & Jacklin, C. N. *The Psychology of Sex Differences.* Stanford, Calif.: Stanford University Press, 1974.

Maccoby, E., & Masters, J. Attachment and dependency. In P. H. Mussen (Ed.), *Carmichael's Manual of Child Psychology* (Vol. 2) (3rd ed.). New York: Wiley, 1970.

McDaniel, C. O. Dating roles and reasons for dating. *Journal of Marriage and the Family,* 1969, *31,* 97–107.

MacMurray, J. *Persons in Relation.* London: Faber & Faber, 1961.

Madsen, M. C. Developmental and cross-cultural differences in the cooperative and competitive behavior of young children. *Journal of Cross-Cultural Psychology,* 1971, *2,* 365–71.

Mahler, M. S. *On Human Symbiosis and the Vicissitudes of Individuation: Infantile Psychosis* (Vol. 1). New York: International Universities Press, 1968.

Mahler, M. *The Psychological Birth of the Infant.* New York: Basic Books, 1977.

Main, M. Exploration, play, and level of cognitive functioning as related to child-mother attachment. Doctoral dissertation, Johns Hopkins University, 1973.

Main, M., & Londerville, S. B. Compliance and aggression in toddlerhood: Precursors and correlates. Unpublished manuscript, University of California, 1978.

Marcia, J. E. Ego identity status: Relationship to change in self-esteem, "general maladjustment," and authoritarianism. *Journal of Personality,* 1967, *35*(11), 119–33.

Marcia, J. E. Studies in ego identity. Unpublished research monograph, Simon Fraser University, 1976.

Marcia, J. E. Identity in adolescence. In J. Adelson (Ed.), *Handbook of Adolescent Psychology.* New York: Wiley, 1980.

Marcia, J. E., & Friedman, M. L. Ego identity status in college women. *Journal of Personality,* 1970, *38*(2), 249–63.

Masangkay, Z. S., McCluskey, K. A., McIntyre, C. W., Sims-Knight, J., Vaugh, B. E., & Flavell, J. H. The early development of inferences about the visual percepts of others. *Child Development,* 1974, *45,* 357–66.

Matas, L., Arend, R. A., & Sroufe, L. A. Continuity of adaptation in the second year:

The relationship between quality of attachment and later competence. *Child Development,* 1978, *49,* 547–56.

Maudry, M., & Nekula, M. Social relations between children of the same age during the first two years of life. *Journal of Genetic Psychology,* 1939, *54,* 193–215.

Mead, G. H. *Mind, Self, and Society.* Chicago: University of Chicago Press, 1934.

Meissner, W. W. Parental interaction of the adolescent boy. *Journal of Genetic Psychology,* 1965, *107,* 225–33.

Merelman, R. The development of policy thinking in adolescents. *American Political Science Review,* 1971, *65,* 1033–47.

Milgram, S. *Obedience to Authority.* New York: Harper & Row, 1974.

Miller, P. Y., & Simon, W. The development of sexuality in adolescence. In J. Adelson (Ed.), *Handbook of Adolescent Psychology.* New York: Wiley, 1980.

Miller, S. *The Psychology of Play.* Middlesex, Eng.: Penguin, 1968.

Mischel, W., & Mischel, H. N. *Essentials of Psychology.* New York: Random House, 1977.

Modell, J., Furstenberg, F. F., Jr., & Hershberg, T. Social change and the transition to adulthood in historical perspective. *Journal of Family History,* 1976, *1,* 7–32.

Montemayor, R., & Eisen, M. The development of self-conceptions from childhood to adolescence. *Developmental Psychology,* 1977, *13,* 314–19.

Moshman, D. Consolidation and stage formation in the emergence of formal operations. *Developmental Psychology,* 1977, *13*(2), 95–100.

Much, N., & Shweder, R. Speaking of rules: The analysis of culture in breach. *New Directions for Child Development,* 1978, *2,* 19–39.

Mueller, E., & Brenner, J. The growth of social interaction in a toddler playgroup: The role of peer experience. *Child Development,* 1977, *48,* 854–61.

Mueller, E., & Lucas, T. A developmental analysis of peer interaction among toddlers. In M. Lewis & L. A. Rosenblum (Eds.), *Friendship and Peer Relations.* New York: Wiley, 1975.

Mueller, E., & Rich, A. Clustering and socially-directed behaviors in a playgroup of 1-year-old boys. *Journal of Child Psychology and Psychiatry,* 1976, *17,* 315–22.

Mueller, E., & Vandell, D. Infant-infant interaction. In J. Ososfsky (Ed.), *Handbook of Infancy.* New York: Wiley, 1978.

Munroe, R., Munroe, K., & Whiting, B. B. (Eds.), *Handbook of Cross-Cultural Human Development.* Introduction. New York: Garland, 1980.

Murphy, L. *Social Behavior and Child Personality.* New York: Columbia University Press, 1937.

Murray, H. A. *Explorations in Personality.* New York: Oxford University Press, 1938.

Mussen, P., & Eisenberg-Berg, N. *Roots of Caring, Sharing and Helping.* San Francisco: W. H. Freeman, 1977.

Mussen, P., Langer, J., & Covington, M. (Eds.), *Trends and Issues in Developmental Psychology.* New York: Holt, Rinehart & Winston, 1969.

Neimark, E. D. Intellectual development during adolescence. In F. D. Horowitz (Ed.), *Review of Child Development Research* (Vol. 4). Chicago: University of Chicago Press, 1975.

Newson, J. Towards a theory of infant understanding. *Bulletin of the British Psychological Society,* 1974, *27,* 251–57.

Offer, D. *The Psychological World of the Teenager: A Study of Normal Adolescent Boys.* New York: Basic Books, 1969.

Offer, D., Marcus, D., & Offer, J. L. A longitudinal study of normal adolescent boys. *American Journal of Psychiatry,* 1970, *126,* 917–24.

Olson, D. R. (Eds.), *The Social Foundations of Language and Thought.* New York: W. W. Norton, 1980.

Orlofsky, J. L. Identity formation: Achievements and fear of success in college men and women. *Journal of Youth and Adolescence,* 1978, *7,* 49–62.

Orlofsky, J. L., Marcia, J. E., & Lesser, I. M. Ego identity status and the intimacy vs. isolation crisis of young adulthood. *Journal of Personality and Social Psychology,* 1973, *27*(2), 211–19.

Oshman, H. P., & Manosevitz, M. The impact of the identity crisis on the adjustment of late-adolescent males. *Journal of Youth and Adolescence,* 1974, *3,* 207–16.

Paranjpe, A. C. *In Search of Identity.* New York: Wiley, 1976.

Parten, M. Social participation among pre-school children. *Journal of Abnormal Psychology,* 1932, *27,* 243–68.

Parten, M. Social play among preschool children. *Journal of Abnormal and Social Psychology,* 1933, *28,* 136–47.

Patterson, G. R. The aggressive child: Victim and architect of a coercive system. In L. A. Hamerlynck, L. C. Handy, & E. J. Mash (Eds.), *Behavior Modification and Families: I. Theory and Research.* New York: Brunner-Mazell, 1976.

Pawlby, S. J. Imitative interaction. In H. R. Shaffer (Ed.), *Studies in Mother-Infant Interaction.* New York: Academic Press, 1977.

Peller, L. E. Libidinal phases, ego development and play. *Psychoanalytic Study of the Child,* 1954, *9,* 178–98.

Peller, L. E. Libidinal phases, ego development and play. *Psychoanalysis,* 1955, *3*(3), 3–12.

Petersen, A. C., & Taylor, B. The biological approach to adolescence: Biological change and psychological adaptation. In J. Adelson (Ed.), *Handbook of Adolescent Psychology.* New York: Wiley, 1980.

Piaget, J. *The Moral Judgment of the Child.* New York: Free Press, 1965. (Orig. published 1932.)

Piaget, J. *The Child's Conception of Space.* New York: W. W. Norton, 1952.

Piaget, J. *The Construction of Reality in the Child.* New York: Basic Books, 1954.

Piaget, J. *The Language and Thought of the Child.* Cleveland: World Publishing, 1955.

Piaget, J. *Play, Dreams, and Imitation in Childhood.* New York: W. W. Norton, 1962.

Piaget, J. *The Origins of Intelligence.* New York: W. W. Norton, 1963.

Piaget, J. *The Child's Conception of Number.* New York: W. W. Norton, 1965.

Piaget, J. *Biology and Knowledge.* Chicago: University of Chicago Press, 1971. (Orig. published in 1966.)

Piaget, J., & Inhelder, B. *The Early Growth of Logic in the Child.* New York: W. W. Norton, 1969. (a)

Piaget, J., & Inhelder, B. *The Psychology of the Child.* New York: Basic Books, 1969. (b)

Podd, M. H., Marcia, J. E., & Rubin, B. M. The effects of ego identity and partner perception on a prisoner's dilemma game. *Journal of Social Psychology*, 1970, *82*, 117–26.

Putallaz, M., & Gottman, J. Social skills and group acceptance. In S. Asher & J. Gottman (Eds.), *The Development of Friendship: Description and Intervention*. New York: Cambridge University Press, 1981.

Rawls, J. *A Theory of Justice*. Cambridge, Mass.: Harvard University Press, 1971.

Redl, F., & Wineman, D. *Children Who Hate*. Glencoe, Ill.: The Free Press, 1951.

Reese, H. W., & Overton, W. F. Models of development and theories of development. In L. R. Goulet & P. B. Baltes (Eds.), *Life-Span Developmental Psychology: Research and Theory*. New York: Academic Press, 1970.

Reiss, I. L. The double standard in premarital intercourse: A neglected concept. *Social Forces*, 1954, *23*, 224–30.

Reiss, I. L. *Family Systems in America* (2nd ed). Hinsdale, Ill.: Dorsey Press, 1976.

Rest, J. Patterns of preference and comprehension in moral judgment. *Journal of Personality*, 1973, *41*, 86–109.

Rest, J. Morality. In J. H. Flavell & E. Markman (Eds.), *Carmichael's Manual of Child Psychology* (4th ed.). New York: Wiley, 1983.

Rest, J., Turiel, E., & Kohlberg, L. Relations between level of moral judgment and preference and comprehension of the moral judgment of others. *Journal of Personality*, 1969, *37*, 225–52.

Rheingold, H., & Eckerman, C. Fear of the stranger: A critical examination. In H. Reese (Ed.), *Advances in Child Development and Behavior* (Vol. 8). New York: Academic Press, 1973.

Rice, F. P. *The Adolescent: Development, Relationships and Culture*. Boston: Allyn and Bacon, 1975.

Robertson, J. *A Two-Year-Old Goes to the Hospital*. New York: New York University Film Library, 1952 (Film).

Robertson, J. Some responses of young children to loss of maternal care. *Nurse Times*, 1953, *49*, 382–86.

Robertson, J., & Robertson, J. Young children in brief separations: A fresh look. *Psychoanalytic Study of the Child*, 1971, *26*, 264–315.

Roff, M., Sells, S., & Golden, M. *Social Adjustment and Personality Development in Children*. Minneapolis: University of Minnesota Press, 1972.

Rosenberg, M. *Society and the Adolescent Self-Image*. Princeton: Princeton University Press, 1965.

Rosenberg, M. *Conceiving the Self*. New York: Basic Books, 1979.

Rosenthal, D., Gurney, R., & Moore, S. From trust to intimacy: A new inventory for examining Erikson's stages of psychological development. *Journal of Youth and Adolescence*, 1982, *11*, 411–19.

Rosenthal, M. Attachment and mother-infant interaction: Some research impasses and suggested change in orientation. *Journal of Child Psychology and Psychiatry*, 1973, *14*, 201–7.

Rotenberg, K. Self-conceptions in children ages four to twelve. Unpublished manuscript, University of Windsor, 1978.

Rotter, J. B. *Social Learning and Clinical Psychology*. New York: Prentice-Hall, 1954.

Rotter, J. B. Generalized expectancies for internal versus external control of reinforcement. *Psychological Monographs*, 1966, *80*.

Rousseau, J. J. *Emile or An Education*. London· Dent, 1974. (Orig. published 1763.)

Rubenstein, J., & Howeds, C. The effects of peers on toddler interaction with mother and toys. *Child Development*, 1976, *47*, 597–605.

Rubin, K. H. Egocentrism in childhood: A unitary construct? *Child Development*, 1973, *44*, 102–10.

Rubin, K. (Ed.). *Children's Play* (New Directions for Child Development, No. 9). San Francisco: Jossey-Bass, 1980.

Rubin, K. H., & Maioni, T. L. Play preference and its relationship to egocentrism, popularity, and classification skills in preschoolers. *Merrill-Palmer Quarterly*, 1975, *21*, 171–78.

Rubin, K. H., & Pepler, D. J. The relationship of child's play to social-cognitive growth and development. In H. Foot, J. Smith, & T. Chapman (Eds.), *Friendship and Childhood Relationships*. London: Wiley, 1980.

Ruble, D. The development of social comparison processes and their role in achievement-related self-socialization. In E. T. Higgins, D. N. Ruble, & W. W. Hartup (Eds.), *Social Cognition and Social Behavior: Developmental Perspectives*. New York: Cambridge University Press, 1983.

Ruble, D. N., Balaban, T., & Cooper, J. Development of responsiveness to sex-stereotyped information in children: A television study. Unpublished paper, Department of Psychology, Princeton University, 1979.

Ruble, D. N., Boggiano, A. K., Feldman, N. S., & Loebl, J. H. A developmental analysis of the role of social comparison in self-evaluation. *Developmental Psychology*, 1980, *16*, 105–15.

Rushton, J. P., & Weiner, J. Altruism and cognitive development in children. *British Journal of Social and Clinical Psychology*, 1975, *14*, 341–49.

Rutter, M. *Maternal Deprivation Reassessed*. Middlesex, Eng.: Penguin, 1972.

Rutter, M. Family, area, and school influences in the genesis of disorders. In L. Hersov, M. Berger, & D. Shaffer (Eds.), *Aggression and Antisocial Behaviour in Childhood and Adolescence* (Journal of Child Psychology and Psychiatry Book Series, No. 1). Oxford: Pergamon, 1978.

Rutter, M. Maternal deprivation 1972–1978: New findings, new concepts, new approaches. *Child Development*, 1979, *50*, 283–305.

Rutter, M. *Changing Youth in a Changing Society: Patterns of Adolescent Development and Disorder*. Cambridge, Mass.: Harvard University Press, 1980.

Rutter, M., Graham, P., Chadwick, O. F. D., & Yule, W. Adolescent turmoil: Fact or fiction? *Journal of Child Psychology and Psychiatry*, 1976, *17*, 35–56.

Rutter, M., Korn, S., & Birch, H. G. Genetic and environmental factors in the development of primary reaction patterns. *British Journal of Clinical Social Psychology*, 1963, *2*, 161.

Sagi, A., & Hoffman, M. L. Empathic distress in the newborn. *Developmental Psychology*, 1976, *12*, 175–76.

Sameroff, A. Organization and stability of newborn behavior: A commentary on the Brazelton Neonatal Behavioral Assessment Scale. *Monographs for the Society for Research in Child Development*, 1978, *43*(5–6, Serial No. 177).

Sameroff, A., & Chandler, M. Reproductive risks and the continuum of caretaking causality. In F. Horowitz, M. Hetherington, S. Scarr-Salapatek, & G. Siegel (Eds.), *Review of Child Development Research* (Vol. 4). Chicago: University of Chicago Press, 1975.

Sarbin, T. R. A preface to the psychological analysis of the self. *Psychological Review*, 1962, *59*, 11–22.

Sartre, J. P. *The Words*. New York: Vintage Books, 1964.

Scarlett, H. H., Press, A. N., & Crockett, W. H. Children's descriptions of peers: A Wernerian developmental analysis. *Child Development*, 1971, *42*, 439–53.

Schafer, R. Concepts of self and identity and the experience of separation-individuation in adolescence. *Psychoanalytic Quarterly*, 1973, *42*, 42–59.

Schaffer, H. R. Some issues for research in the study of attachment behavior. In B. M. Foss (Ed.), *Determinants of Infant Behavior* (Vol. 2). New York: Wiley, 1963.

Schaffer, H. R. (Ed.). *Studies in Mother-Infant Interaction*. New York: Academic Press, 1977.

Schaffer, H. R., & Emerson, P. E. The development of social attachments in infancy. *Monographs of the Society for Research in Child Development*, 1964, *29*, (3, Serial No. 94). (a)

Schaffer, H. R., & Emerson, P. E. Patterns of response to physical contact in early human development. *Journal of Child Psychology and Psychiatry*, 1964, *5*, 1–13. (b)

Schlosberg, H. The concept of play. *Psychological Review*, 1947, *54*, 229–31.

Schofield, M. *The Sexual Behavior of Young Adults*. London: Allen Lane, 1973.

Sears, R. R., Maccoby, E. E., & Levin, H. *Patterns of Child Rearing*. Evanston, Ill.: Row Peterson, 1957.

Sears, R. R., Rau, L., & Alpert, R. *Identification and Child Rearing*. Stanford, Calif.: Stanford University Press, 1965.

Secord, P., & Peevers, B. H. The development and attribution of person concepts. In T. Mischel (Ed.), *Understanding Other Persons*. Totowa, N.J.: Rowman & Littlefield, 1974.

Seligman, M. E. P. Depression and learned helplessness. In R. J. Friedman & M. M. Katz (Eds.), *The Psychology of Depression: Contemporary Theory and Research*. Washington, D.C.: Winston-Wiley, 1974.

Seligman, M. E. P. *Helplessness*. San Francisco: W. H. Freeman, 1975.

Selman, R. L. The relation of role-taking to the development of moral judgment in children. *Child Development*, 1971, *42*, 79–92.

Selman, R. Social-cognitive understanding. In T. Lickona (Ed.), *Moral Development and Behavior: Theory, Research, and Social Issues*. New York: Holt, Rinehart & Winston, 1976. (a)

Selman, R. L. Toward a structural analysis of developing interpersonal relations concepts: Research with normal and disturbed preadolescent boys. In A. D. Pick (Ed.), *Minnesota Symposium on Child Development* (Vol. 10). Minneapolis: University of Minnesota Press, 1976. (b)

Selman, R. L. *The Growth of Interpersonal Understanding*. New York: Academic Press, 1980.

Selman, R. L., & Byrne, D. F. A structural developmental analysis of levels of role-taking in middle childhood. *Child Development*, 1974, *45*, 803–6.

Selman, R. L., & Jaquette, D. Stability and oscillation in interpersonal awareness: A clinical-developmental approach. In C. B. Keasey (Ed.), *Nebraska Symposium on Motivation: Social Cognitive Development* (Vol. 25). Lincoln, Nebr.: University of Nebraska Press, 1978.

Serbin, L. A., Tonick, I. J., & Sternglanz, S. Shaping cooperative cross-sex play. *Child Development*, 1977, *48*, 924–29.

Shantz, C. U. The development of social cognition. In E. M. Hetherington (Ed.), *Review of Child Development Research* (Vol. 5). Chicago: University of Chicago Press, 1975.

Shantz, C. Social-cognitive development. In J. Flavell & E. Markman (Eds.), *Carmichael's Manual of Child Psychology* (Vol. 2) (4th ed.). New York: Wiley, 1983.

Shapiro, A., & Madsen, M. C. Between- and within-group cooperation and competition among kibbutz and nonkibbutz children. *Developmental Psychology*, 1971, *10*, 140–45.

Shatz, M., & Gelman, R. The development of communication skills: Modification in the speech of young children as a function of listener. *Monographs of the Society for Research in Child Development*, 1973, *38*, 1–38.

Shrauger, J., & Patterson, M. Self-evaluation and the selection of dimensions for evaluating others. *Journal of Personality*, 1974, *42*, 569–82.

Sigelman, E., Block, J., Block, J. H., & Van der Lippe, A. Antecedents of optimal psychological adjustment. *Journal of Consulting and Clinical Psychology*, 1970, *35*, 283–89.

Simmons, D. D. Development of an objective measure of identity achievement status. *Journal of Projective Techniques and Personality Assessment*, 1970, *34*, 241–44.

Simner, M. L. Newborn's response to the cry of another infant. *Developmental Psychology*, 1971, *5*, 136–50.

Simons, R., & Klaassen, M. Children's conceptions and use of rules of distributive justice. *International Journal of Behavioral Development*, 1979, *2*, 253–67.

Simpson, E. L. Moral development research: A case of scientific cultural bias. *Human Development*, 1974, *17*, 81–106.

Skinner, B. F. *The Behavior of Organisms: An Experimental Analysis*. New York: Appleton-Century-Crofts, 1938.

Skipper, J. K., & Nass, G. Dating behavior: A framework for analysis and an illustration. *Journal of Marriage and the Family*, 1966, *28*, 412–20.

Slaby, R. G., & Frey, K. S. Development of gender constancy and selective attention to same-sex models. *Child Development*, 1975, *46*, 849–56.

Smith, E. A. *American Youth Culture: Group Life in Teenage Society*. New York: The Free Press of Glencoe, 1962.

Smith, P., & Connolly, K. Patterns of play and social interaction in pre-school children. In N. B. Jones (Ed.), *Ethological Studies of Child Behavior*. Cambridge, Eng.: Cambridge University Press, 1972.

Smith, P. K., & Daglish, L. Sex differences in parent and infant behavior in the home. *Child Development*, 1977, *48*, 1250–54.

Sorenson, R. C. *Adolescent Sexuality in Contemporary America: Personal Values and Sexual Behavior Ages 13 to 19*. New York: World, 1973.

Spitz, R. A. Anxiety in infancy: A study of its manifestations in the first year of life. *International Journal of Psychoanalysis*, 1950, *31*, 138–43.

Spitz, R. A. *The First Year of Life*. New York: International University Press, 1965.

Spock, B. *Baby and Child Care*. New York: Random House, 1947.

Spock, B. *Baby and Child Care*. New York: Random House, 1982.

Sroufe, L. A. Wariness of strangers and the study of infant development. *Child Development*, 1977, *48*, 731–46.

Sroufe, L. A. Infant-caregiver and patterns of adaptation in preschool: The roots of maladaptation and competence. In M. Perlmutter (Ed.), *Minnesota Symposium in Child Psychology* (Vol. 16), in press.

Sroufe, L. A., & Waters, E. Attachment as an organizational construct. *Child Development*, 1977, *48*, 1185–99.

Sroufe, L. A., Waters, E., & Matas, L. Contextual determinants of infant affective response. In M. Lewis & L. Rosenblum (Eds.), *The Origins of Fear*. New York: Wiley, 1974.

Stark, P. A., & Traxler, A. J. Empirical validation of Erikson's theory of identity crises in late adolescence. *The Journal of Psychology*, 1974, *86*, 25–33.

Staub, E. *The Development of Prosocial Behavior* (Vol. 1). New York: Academic Press, 1979.

Stayton, D. J., Hogan, R., & Ainsworth, M. Infant obedience and maternal behavior: The origins of socialization reconsidered. *Child Development*, 1971, *42*, 1057–70.

Stein, A. H., & Friedrich, L. K. Impact of television on children and youth. In E. M. Hetherington (Ed.), *Review of Child Development Research* (Vol. 5). Chicago: University of Chicago Press, 1975.

Stern, D. *The First Relationship: Mother and Infant*. Cambridge, Mass.: Harvard University Press, 1977.

Stevenson, M. B., & Lamb, M. E. Effects of infant sociability and the caretaking environment on infant cognitive performance. *Child Development*, 1979, *50*, 340–49.

Stone, L. J., & Church, J. *Childhood and Adolescence: A Psychology of the Growing Person*. New York: Random House, 1957.

Stone, V., & Chaffee, S. H. Family communication patterns and source-message orientation. *Journalism Quarterly*, 1970, *47*, 239–46.

Sullivan, H. S. *The Interpersonal Theory of Psychiatry*. New York: W. W. Norton, 1953.

Svejda, M. J., Campos, J. J., & Emde, R. N. Mother-infant "bonding": Failure to generalize. *Child Development*, 1980, *51*, 775–79.

Tanner, J. M. *Growth at Adolescence*. Springfield, Ill.: Thomas, 1962.

Tanner, J. M. Growth and endocrinology of the adolescent. In L. I. Gardner (Ed.), *Endocrine and Genetic Diseases of Childhood*. Philadelphia: Saunders, 1969.

Tanner, J. M. Sequence, tempo, and individual variation in growth and development of boys and girls aged twelve to sixteen. In J. Kagan & R. Coles (Eds.), *Twelve to Sixteen: Early Adolescence*. New York: W. W. Norton, 1972.

Tanner, J. M. Sequence and tempo in the somatic changes in puberty. In M. M. Grumbach, G. D. Grave, & F. E. Mayer (Eds.), *Control of the Onset of Puberty*. New York: Wiley, 1974. (a)

Tanner, J. M. Variability of growth and maturity in newborn infants. In M. Lewis & L. A. Rosenblum (Eds.), *The Effect of the Infant on Its Caregiver* (Vol. 1). New York: Wiley, 1974. (b)

Taylor, S., & Fiske, S. Point of view and perception of causality. *Journal of Personality and Social Psychology*, 1975, *32*, 434–95.

Thomas, A., & Chess, S. *Temperament and Development*. New York: Brunner-Mazel, 1977.

Thomas, A., Chess, S., & Birch, H. G. *Temperament and Behavior Disorders in Children*. New York: New York University Press, 1968.

Thomas, A., Chess, S., & Birch, H. The origin of personality. *Scientific American*, 1970, *223*, 102–9.

Thompson, S. K. Gender labels and early sex-role development. *Child Development*, 1975, *46*, 339–47.

Tizard, B., & Hodges, J. The effect of early institutional rearing on the development of eight-year-old children. *Journal of Child Psychology and Psychiatry*, 1978, *19*, 99–118.

Tizard, B., & Joseph, A. Cognitive development of young children in residential care: A study of children aged 24 months. *Journal of Child Psychology and Psychiatry*, 1970, *11*, 177–86.

Tizard, B., & Rees, J. A comparison of the effects of adoption, restoration to the natural mother and continued institutionalization. *Child Development*, 1974, *45*, 92–99.

Tizard, B., & Rees, J. The effect of early institutional rearing on the behavioral problems and affectional relationships of four-year-old children. *Journal of Child Psychology and Psychiatry*, 1975, *16*, 61–74.

Torgerson, A. M. Temperamental differences in infants: Their cause as shown through twin studies. Doctoral dissertation, University of Oslo, Norway, 1973.

Trevarthen, C. Conversations with a two-month-old. *New Scientist*, 1974, *62*, 230–35.

Trevarthen, C. Descriptive analyses of infant communicative behavior. In H. R. Schaffer (Ed.), *Studies in Mother-Infant Interaction*. New York: Academic Press, 1977.

Turiel, E. An experimental test of the sequentiality of developmental stages in the child's moral judgments. *Journal of Personality and Social Psychology*, 1966, *3*, 611–18.

Turiel, E. Developmental processes in the child's moral thinking. In P. Mussen, J. Langer, & M. Covington (Eds.), *Trends and Issues in Developmental Psychology*. New York: Holt, Rinehart & Winston, 1969.

Turiel, E. Conflict and transition in adolescent moral development. *Child Development*, 1974, *45*, 14–29.

Turiel, E. The development of social concepts: Mores, customs, and conventions. In D. J. DePalma & J. M. Foley (Eds.), *Moral Development: Current Theory and Research*. Hillsdale, N.J.: Erlbaum, 1975.

Turiel, E. The development of concepts of social structure: Social convention. In J. Glick & K. A. Clarke-Stewart (Eds.), *The Development of Social Understanding*. New York: Gardner Press, 1978. (a)

Turiel, E. Social convention and morality. Two distinct conceptual and developmental systems. In C. B. Keasey (Ed.), *Nebraska Symposium on Motivation: Social Cognitive Development* (Vol. 25). Lincoln, Nebr.: University of Nebraska Press, 1978. (b)

Turiel, E. Social regulations and domains of social concepts. In W. Damon (Ed.), *Social Cognition* (New Directions for Child Development, No. 1). San Francisco: Jossey-Bass, 1978. (c)

Turiel, E. Domains and categories in social-cognitive development. In W. Overton (Ed.), *The Relationship between Social and Cognitive-Development*. Hillsdale, N.J.: Erlbaum, 1983.

Ugurel-Semin, R. Moral behavior and moral judgment of children. *Journal of Abnormal and Social Psychology*, 1952, *47*, 463–74.

Vandell, D. L. Toddler sons' social interaction with mothers, fathers, and peers. Unpublished doctoral dissertation, Boston University, 1976.

Vandell, D., Wilson, K., & Buchanan, N. Peer interaction in the first year of life: An examination of its structure, content, and sensitivity to toys. *Child Development*, 1980, *51*, 481–88.

Veroff, J. Social comparison and the development of achievement motivation. In C. P. Smith (Ed.), *Achievement Related Motives in Children*. New York: Russell Sage, 1969.

Vincze, M. The social contacts of infants and young children reared together. *Early Child Development and Care*, 1971, *1*, 99–109.

Vygotsky, L. S. Play and its role in the mental development of the child. *Soviet Psychology*, 1933, *3*, and in J. Bruner, A. Jolly, & K. Sylva (Eds.), *Play: Its Role in Development and Evolution*. New York: Basic Books, 1976.

Vygotsky, L. *Thought and Language*. Cambridge, Mass.: MIT Press, 1962.

Wald, M. Children's rights: A framework for analysis. *UCD Law Review*, 1979, *12*, 255–82.

Waldrop, M. F. Relations between preschool activity and aspects of intellectual and social behavior at age 7½. *Developmental Psychology*, 1976, *12*, 107–12.

Walker, L. Sex differences in the development of moral reasoning: A critical review. *Child Development*, 1983, *54*, 1103–41.

Waterman, A. S. Identity development from adolescence to adulthood: An extension of theory and a review of research. *Developmental Psychology*, 1982, *18*, 341–58.

Waterman, A. S., Geary, P. S., & Waterman, C. K. A longitudinal study of changes in ego identity status from the freshman to the senior year at college. *Developmental Psychology*, 1974, *10*, 387–92.

Waterman, A. S., & Goldman, J. A. A longitudinal study of ego identity development at a liberal arts college. *Journal of Youth and Adolescence*, 1976, *5*, 361–69.

Waterman, A. S., & Waterman, C. K. A longitudinal study of changes in ego identity status during the freshman year at college. *Developmental Psychology*, 1971, *5*, 167–73.

Waterman, A. S., & Waterman, C. K. The relationship between freshman ego identity status and subsequent academic behavior: A test of the predictive validity of Marcia's categorization system for identity status. *Developmental Psychology*, 1972, *6*, 179.

Waters, E. The reliability and stability of individual differences in infant-mother attachment. *Child Development*, 1978, *49*, 483–94.

Waters, E., Wippman, J., & Sroufe, L. A. Attachment, positive affect, and competence in the peer group: Two studies in construct validation. *Child Development*, 1979, *50*, 821–29.

Watson, J. B. *Psychology from the Standpoint of a Behaviorist*. Philadelphia: J. P. Lippincott, 1919.

Watts, W. A., & Whittaker, D. N. E. Free speech advocates at Berkeley. *Journal of Applied Behavior Science*, 1966, *2*, 41–62.

Weinraub, M., Brooks, J., & Lewis, M. The social network: A reconsideration of the concept of attachment. *Human Development*, 1977, *20*, 31–47.

Werner, E. E. *Cross-Cultural Child Development*. Monterey, Calif.: Brooks-Cole, 1979.

White, R. W. *The Enterprise of Living: Growth and Organization in Personality*. New York: Holt, Rinehart & Winston, 1972.

Whiting, B. (Ed.), *Six Cultures Series*. New York: Wiley, 1966.

Whiting, B. B., & Whiting, J. W. M. Altruistic and egoistic behavior in six cultures. In L. Nader & T. W. Maretzki (Eds.), *Cultural Illness and Health: Essays in Human Adaptation*. Washington, D.C.: American Anthropological Association, 1973.

Whiting, B. B., & Whiting, J. W. M. *Children of Six Cultures: A Psychocultural Analysis*. Cambridge, Mass.: Harvard University Press, 1975.

Whiting, J. W. M. Resource mediation and learning by identification. In I. Iscoe & H. W. Stevenson (Eds.), *Personality Development in Children*. Austin, Tex.: University of Texas Press, 1960.

Whiting, J. W. M., & Child, I. *Child Training and Personality: A Cross-Cultural Study*. New Haven: Yale University Press, 1953.

Winnicott, D. W. The theory of the parent-infant relationship. *International Journal of Psychoanalysis*, 1960, *41*, 585–95.

Winnicott, D. W. *The Child, The Family and the Outside World*. London: Pelican Books, 1974.

Witkin, H. *Cognitive Styles in Personal and Cultural Adaptation*. Heinz Werner Lecture Series (Vol. 11). Worcester, Mass.: Clark University Press, 1978.

Witkin, H. A., Dyk, R. B., Faterson, H. D., Goodenough, D. R., & Karp, S. A. *Psychological Differentiation*. New York: Wiley, 1962.

Witkin, H. A., Goodenough, D. R., & Karp, S. A. Stability of cognitive style from childhood to young adulthood. *Journal of Personality and Social Psychology*, 1967, *7*, 291–300.

Witkin, H., Price-Williams, D., Bertini, M., Christiansen, B., Ramirez, P., & Van Meel, S. Social conformity and psychological differentiation. *International Journal of Psychology*, 1974, *9*, 11–29.

Wylie, R. C. *The Self Concept* (Vol. 2). Lincoln, Nebr.: University of Nebraska Press, 1961.

Wyss, D. *Psychoanalytic Schools*. New York: J. Aronson, 1973.

Yankelovich, D. *The New Morality: A Profile of American Youth in the 70's*. New York: McGraw-Hill, 1974.

Yarrow, M. R., & Waxler, C. Z. Dimensions and correlates of prosocial behavior in young children. *Child Development*, 1976, *47*, 118–25.

Youniss, J. *Parents and Peers in Social Development: A Sullivan-Piaget Perspective*. Chicago: University of Chicago Press, 1980.

Youniss, J., & Volpe, J. A relationship analysis of children's friendship. In W. Damon (Ed.), *Social Cognition* (New Directions for Child Development, No. 1). San Francisco: Jossey-Bass, 1978.

Zahn-Waxler, C., Radke-Yarrow, M., & King, R. A. Child-rearing and children's pro-social initiations toward victims of distress. *Child Development*, 1979, *50*, 319–30.

Acknowledgments

Figures

Figure 1-1.   Reproduced, with permission, from the *Annual Review of Psychology*, Vol. 31. ©
1980 by Annual Reviews Inc.

Figure 2-4.   Reprinted by permission of the publisher from Ainsworth, M., Blehar, M., Waters,
E., and Wall, S., *Patterns of Attachment*. Hillsdale, N.J.: Lawrence Erlbaum Associates,
Inc., 1978.

Figure 3-1.   Reprinted by permission of the publisher from Lewis, M., and Brooks-Gunn, J.,
Social Cognition and the Acquisition of Self. New York: Plenum Publishing Corporation,
1979.

Figure 5-1.   From Baldwin, A., Socialization and the parent-child relationship, *Child Development*, 1948, *19*, pp. 130, 132. © The Society for Research in Child Development, Inc.
Reprinted by permission.

Figure 5-3.   From Albert Bandura, *Social Learning Theory*, p. 23.   © 1977. Reprinted by
permission of Prentice-Hall, Inc., Englewood Cliffs, N.J.

Figure 5-4.   Reprinted from Kohlberg, L., A cognitive-developmental analysis of children's sex-
role concepts and attitudes, in *The Development of Sex Differences*, edited by Eleanor E.
Maccoby, with the permission of the publishers, Stanford University Press. © 1966 by the
Board of Trustees of the Leland Stanford Junior University.

Figure 5-5.   From "A Model for the Understanding of School as a Socializing Agent" by Hilde
Himmelweit and Betty Swift in *Trends and Issues in Developmental Psychology*, edited by
Paul H. Mussen et al. Copyright © 1969 by Holt, Rinehart & Winston, Inc. Reprinted by
permission of Holt, Rinehart & Winston, CBS College Publishing.

Figure 7-1.   From Dunphy, D., The social structure of urban adolescent peer groups, *Sociometry*, Vol. 26, 1963, p. 236. Reprinted by permission of the American Sociological Association.

Tables

Table 2-1. Adapted from Sroufe, L. A., Infant-caregiver and patterns of adaptation in preschool: The roots of maladaptation and competence. Presented at the Minnesota Symposium, October 22, 1981. To appear in Perlmutter, M. (ed.), *Minnesota Symposium in Child Psychology*, Vol. 16, in press. Adapted by permission of Lawrence Erlbaum Associates, Inc.

Table 2-2. Adapted from Rutter, M., Maternal deprivation 1972–1978: New findings, new concepts, new approaches, *Child Development*, 1979, *50*, 283–305. © The Society for Research in Child Development, Inc. Used by permission of the University of Chicago Press.

Table 3-1. From *The Origin of Personality* by A. Thomas, S. Chess and H. Birch. Copyright © 1970 by Scientific American, Inc. All rights reserved.

Table 3-2. Reproduced from *Identity: Youth and Crisis* by Erik H. Erikson, by permission of W. W. Norton & Company, Inc. and Faber and Faber Ltd. Copyright © 1968 by W. W. Norton & Company, Inc.

Table 3-3. From Lewis, M., and Brooks-Gunn, J., *Social Cognition and the Acquisition of Self*. New York: Plenum Publishing Corporation, 1979. Used by permission of the publisher.

Table 4-1. From Peller, L. E., Libidinal phases, ego development, and play, *Psychoanalysis*, 1955, *3* (3), 3–12.

Table 4-2. From "Social-Cognitive Understanding" by Robert L. Selman in *Moral Development and Behavior*, edited by Thomas Lickona. Copyright © 1976 by Holt, Rinehart & Winston. Reprinted by permission of Holt, Rinehart & Winston, CBS College Publishing.

Tables 4-3 and 5-3. From Damon, W., Patterns of change in children's social reasoning: A two-year longitudinal study, *Child Development*, 1980, *51*, 1011. © The Society for Research in Child Development, Inc. Reprinted by permission of the University of Chicago Press.

Table 6-1. Adapted from *Identity: Youth and Crisis* by Erik H. Erikson, by permission of W. W. Norton & Company, Inc. and Faber and Faber Ltd. Copyright © 1968 by W. W. Norton & Company, Inc.

Table 7-1. From Delora, J., Social systems of dating on a college campus, *Marriage and Family Living*, 1963, Vol. 25, No. 1, pp. 81–84. Copyright © 1963 by the National Council on Family Relations. Reprinted by permission.

Table 7-2. Data (for table) from "The Six Stages of Moral Judgment," Appendix to *Essays on Moral Development, Vol. I: The Philosophy of Moral Development* by Lawrence Kohlberg. Copyright © 1981 by Lawrence Kohlberg. Reprinted by permission of Harper & Row, Publishers, Inc.

Table 8-1. From Damon, W., and Hart, D., The development of self-understanding from infancy through adolescence, *Child Development*, August 1982. © The Society for Research in Child Development, Inc. Used by permission of the University of Chicago Press.

Table 8-2. Reproduced from *Identity: Youth and Crisis* by Erik H. Erikson, by permission of W. W. Norton & Company, Inc. and Faber and Faber Ltd. Copyright © 1968 by W. W. Norton & Company, Inc.

Excerpts

Pages 102–3. From Garvey, C., *Play* (The Developing Child Series). Cambridge, Mass.: Harvard University Press, 1977. Reprinted by permission of Harvard University Press and Fontana Paperbacks, London.

Page 120. From Piaget, J., *The Language and Thought of the Child*, 1955. Reprinted by permission of Humanities Press, Inc., Atlantic Highlands, N.J. 07716, and Routledge & Kegan Paul Ltd.

Page 140. From Berndt, T. J., Relations between social cognition, nonsocial cognition and social behavior: The case of friendship. In Flavell, J. H., and Ross, L. D. (eds.), *Social Cognitive Development*. New York: Cambridge University Press, 1981. Reprinted by permission of the publisher.

Page 142. From Gottman, J., and Parkhurst, J., A developmental theory of friendship and acquaintance processes. In Collins, W. A. (ed.), *Development of Cognition, Affect and Social*

Relations. Hillsdale, N.J.: Lawrence Erlbaum Associates, Inc., 1980. Reprinted by permission of the publisher.

Pages 149–50. From Much, N., and Shweder, R., Speaking of rules: The analysis of culture in breach. *New Directions for Child Development*, 1978, *2*, 19–39. Reprinted by permission of Jossey-Bass Publishers.

Pages 193–95. From Labov, W., The logic of nonstandard English. In Lee, V. (ed.), *Language Development*. Reprinted by permission of the publisher, Croom Helm Ltd.

Pages 242–46. From Sartre, J. P., *The Words* (translated by Tony White). Reprinted by permission of Georges Borchardt, Inc. and the British publishers, Hamish Hamilton Ltd.

Pages 254–55. From Youniss, J., *Parents and Peers in Child Development*. © The Society for Research in Child Development, Inc. Reprinted by permission of the University of Chicago Press.

Page 263. From Hollingshead, A. B., *Elmtown's Youth*. New York: John Wiley & Sons, Inc., 1949. Reprinted by permission of the publisher.

Pages 269–70. From Youniss, J., *Parents and Peers in Child Development*. © The Society for Research in Child Development, Inc. Reprinted by permission of the University of Chicago Press.

Pages 286–87. From Turiel, E., Conflict and transition in adolescent moral development, *Child Development*, Vol. 45, 1974, pp. 21, 22, 25. © The Society for Research in Child Development, Inc. Reprinted by permission of the University of Chicago Press.

Pages 288–91. From Turiel, E., Social regulations and domains of social concepts. In Damon, W. (ed.), *New Directions for Child Development: Social Cognition*. San Francisco: Jossey Bass, 1978. Reprinted by permission of the publisher.

Page 312. From Josselson, R., Ego development in adolescence. In Adelson, J. (ed.), *Handbook of Adolescent Psychology*. New York: John Wiley & Sons, Inc., 1980. Reprinted by permission of the publisher.

Pages 338–44. From Paranjpe, A. C., *In Search of Identity*, 1976. Reprinted by permission of Macmillan India Limited.

Photographs

Page 16. Photograph by Suzanne Szasz.

Figure 2-1. Reproduced from "The Foundations of Intersubjectivity: Development of Interpersonal and Cooperative Understanding in Infants" by Colwyn Trevarthen in *The Social Foundations of Language and Thought*, edited by David R. Olson, with the permission of W. W. Norton & Company, Inc. Copyright © 1980 by David R. Olson.

Figure 2-2. With permission from *Studies in Infant-Mother Interaction*: Schaffer. Copyright © Dr. C. Trevarthen, 1977. Used by permission of Academic Press Inc. (London) Limited and Dr. C. Trevarthen, Department of Psychology, University of Edinburgh, Edinburgh, Scotland.

Figures 2-3 and 2-5. Photographs by Jennifer Wishart. Originally published in T. G. R. Bower, *A Primer of Infant Development*. San Francisco: W. H. Freeman, 1977.

Page 68. Photograph by Suzanne Szasz.

Page 100. Photograph by Suzanne Szasz.

Page 146. Photograph by Suzanne Szasz.

Figure 5-2. From Bandura, A., Ross, D., and Ross, S. A., "Imitation of film-mediated aggressive models," *Journal of Abnormal and Social Psychology*, 1963, *66*, p. 8. Photographs courtesy A. Bandura.

Page 204. Photograph by Suzanne Szasz.

Page 250. Photograph by Jim Caster; courtesy Black Star.

Page 306. Photograph by Suzanne Szasz.

Name Index

Subject Index

activity level, 72–76, 207–9, 239–40
adolescence:
  cognitive development in, 309–10
  dating in, 259–64
  defined, 307–8
  detachment and separation in, 309
  developmental levels and, 313–20
  family relations in, 264–71
  formal-operational reasoning in, 309–10
  identity confusion in, 328–31
  identity crisis in, 307, 326–28, 331–32
  and identity formation, 307–46
  need for individuation in, 308–10
  parental vs. peer influences in, 265–66
  peer social life in, 256–59
  and self-understanding, 312–25
  sexual values in, 263–64
  strategic interactions in, 299–301
  see also adolescent family relations; adolescent identity formation; adolescent peer relations; adolescent self-understanding; adolescent societal relations; puberty

adolescent family relations, 251, 264–71
  developmental changes in, 268–70
  difficulties in study of, 265
  economic conditions and, 270–71
  life-course studies of, 270–71
  parental role and, 265–68
  peer influence and, 265–68
  reciprocity in, 269
  self-esteem and, 269–70
  societal changes and, 271
adolescent identity formation, 307–46
  anxiety level and, 332
  authoritarian behavior and, 332
  bisexual confusion in, 330–31
  case studies of, 336–44
  developmental studies on, 333
  diffusion of time perspective in, 328–29
  empirical research on, 331–34
  as essential feature of adolescence, 308
  experimentation during, 327
  foreclosure in, 331
  identity achievement in, 332
  identity diffusion in, 331–32
  identity status in, 331–34